NORTH SEATTLE CHI
12351 8TH ⁄
SEATTLE, W⁄

MW01077996

Math 54

An Incremental Development

Second Edition

Math 54

An Incremental Development

Second Edition

Stephen Hake

John Saxon

Saxon Publishers, Inc.

Math 54: An Incremental Development

Second Edition

Teacher's Eddition

Copyright © 1995 by Stephen Hake and John Saxon

All rights reserved.

No part of this publication may be reproduced,
stored in a retrieval system, or transmitted
in any form or by any means, electronic,
mechanical, photocopying, recording, or
otherwise, without the prior written permission
of the publisher.

Printed in the United States of America.

ISBN: 1-56577-034-X

Production Supervisor: David Pond

Production Coordinator: Joan Coleman

Graphic Artists: Matthew Arrington,
                John Chitwood, Roger Hall, and
                Timothy Maltz

Fourth printing: June 1997

Printed on recycled paper.

> **Reaching us via the Internet**
>
> **WWW:** http://www.saxonpub.com
>
> **E-mail:** helpdesk@saxonpub.com

Saxon Publishers, Inc.
1320 W. Lindsey
Norman, OK 73069

Contents

viii   Contents

X   **Contents**

Preface

To The Teacher

This book grew out of a decade of intense classroom interaction with students in which the goal was for students to learn and **remember** the foundational skills of mathematics. The term "foundational" is appropriate because mathematics, perhaps more than any other subject, is a cognitive structure that builds upon prior learning. The ultimate height and stability of the mathematical structure within each individual are determined by the strength of the foundation. This book, as well as each book that precedes or follows it, provides the student with the time and opportunities necessary to build a rock-solid foundation in beginning mathematics. **For this to occur it is essential that all practice problems and all problem sets be completed by the student.**

How To Use This Book

This book presents a series of daily lessons, each of which is followed by a set of problems. Rather than providing practice in only the new topics, the problem sets review everything that has been taught previously. The sequence of the lessons and the content of the problem sets have been carefully planned. Do not skip lessons or problem sets. The teacher should briefly present the lesson, using the examples to lead the students through guided practice. The students should do the "Practice" at the end of each lesson as guided or independent practice before going on to the problem set. All work should be shown and all errors should be corrected. Consistent, honest effort will produce genuine learning with a high level of retention.

A test master containing two forms of tests for every five lessons is available. Students will make excellent progress if they are able to score 80 percent or better on the tests. Students who fall below the 80 percent level should be given remedial attention immediately. For remediation, the appendix contains additional practice problems for selected lessons. These practice sets may be used as a supplement to, not as a replacement of, the regular problem sets.

At the beginning of each lesson is a boxed set of activities that includes "Facts Practice," "Mental Math," and "Patterns" or "Problem Solving" exercises. The "Facts Practice" masters are located in the *Math 54 Test Masters*. These brief drills improve recall, increase problem-solving speed, and automate frequently needed skills. Opening class with these exercises in a competitive setting where students press to improve their time and accuracy produces focused concentration and often enthusiasm.

Mental math and pattern or problem-solving exercises are also suggested at the beginning of each lesson. These activities should be conducted orally with teacher direction. We do not intend for these exercises to be graded. Mental calculation improves with practice. Have students who successfully respond describe their problem-solving techniques to help other students. Students should be allowed to view the mental math exercises as they are read. As students become more adept, some may choose to challenge themselves by removing the visual cue, relying on the oral presentation only. Mental calculations should be performed without resorting to pencil and paper.

The pattern and problem-solving exercises are intended for open discussion. Non-routine problems may offer a sense of enjoyment for those who can unravel an involved problem and a sense of intimidation for those who cannot find a place to begin. It is more important for the teacher to keep the problem-solving task positive than to lead the search for a solution. Pencil and paper, calculators, manipulatives, and other mathematical tools should be available to students during the problem-solving exercises.

Acknowledgments

We thank Shirley McQuade Davis for her ideas on teaching word problem thinking patterns.

Stephen Hake   *John Saxon*
Temple City, California   *Norman, Oklahoma*

Review of Addition • Missing Addends, Part 1

a. 30
b. 44
c. 63
d. 15
e. 35
f. 18
Patterns:
  Final digits:
    0, 2, 4, 6, 8
  Not final digits:
    1, 3, 5, 7, 9

Facts Practice: 100 Addition Facts (Test A in Test Masters)[†]

Mental Math: Add ten to a number.

a.	20	**b.**	34	**c.**	10
	+ 10		+ 10		+ 53

d. $5 + 10$
e. $25 + 10$
f. $10 + 8$

Patterns: Have the class count by twos from 2 through 40 while the teacher or a student lists the numbers in a column on the board. Study the list. Which digits appear as final digits? Which digits do not appear as final digits?

Review of addition   When we count the dots on the top faces of a pair of number cubes (dice), we are adding. Addition is combining two groups into one group.

$$4 \quad + \quad 3 \quad = \quad 7$$

The numbers that are added are called **addends.** The answer is called the **sum.** The expression $4 + 3 = 7$ is a **number sentence.** A number sentence is a complete sentence that uses numbers and symbols instead of words. Here we show two ways to add 4 and 3.

4	addend		3	addend
+ 3	addend		+ 4	addend
7	sum		7	sum

Notice that if the order of the addends is changed, the sum remains the same. This is true for any two numbers. **When we add two numbers, either number may be first.**

$$4 + 3 = 7 \qquad 3 + 4 = 7$$

[†]For instructions on how to use the boxed activities, please consult the preface.

When adding three numbers, the numbers may be added in any order. Here we show six ways to add 4, 3, and 5. Each way the answer is 12.

$$
\begin{array}{cccccc}
4 & 4 & 3 & 3 & 5 & 5 \\
3 & 5 & 4 & 5 & 4 & 3 \\
+\,5 & +\,3 & +\,5 & +\,4 & +\,3 & +\,4 \\
\hline
12 & 12 & 12 & 12 & 12 & 12
\end{array}
$$

When we add zero to a number, the number is not changed.

$$4 + 0 = 4 \qquad 9 + 0 = 9 \qquad 0 + 7 = 7$$

Missing addends, part 1   If we know the sum and one addend, we can figure out the missing addend. Can you figure out the missing addend in this number sentence?

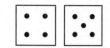

$$
\begin{array}{ccccc}
2 & + & ? & = & 7
\end{array}
$$

Since we know that $2 + 5 = 7$, the missing addend is 5. Some of the problems in this book will have an addend missing. We will use a letter to represent the missing number. When an addend is missing and the sum is given, the problem is to find the missing addend.

Example   (a) $\quad \begin{array}{r} 4 \\ +\,N \\ \hline 7 \end{array}$ (b) $B + 6 = 10$

(c) Write a number sentence for this picture.

Solution   (a) The letter N stands for a missing addend. Since $4 + 3 = 7$, the letter N stands for the number **3.**

(b) This time the letter B is used to stand for the missing addend. Since $4 + 6 = 10$, the letter B stands for the number **4.**

(c) A number sentence for the picture is **$4 + 5 = 9$.** The number sentence **$5 + 4 = 9$** is also correct.

Practice Add:

a. 5 + 6   11   b. 6 + 5   11   c. 8 + 0   8

d. 4 + 8 + 6   18   e. 4 + 5 + 6   15

Find the missing addend:

f. $7 + N = 10$ 3   g. $A + 8 = 12$ 4

Problem set 1 Find either the sum or the missing addend:

1. $\begin{array}{r} 5 \\ + 7 \\ \hline 12 \end{array}$ 2. $\begin{array}{r} 6 \\ + 3 \\ \hline 9 \end{array}$ 3. $\begin{array}{r} 9 \\ + 4 \\ \hline 13 \end{array}$ 4. $\begin{array}{r} 8 \\ + 2 \\ \hline 10 \end{array}$

5. $\begin{array}{r} 4 \\ + N \\ \hline 11 \end{array}$ 7   6. $\begin{array}{r} W \\ + 5 \\ \hline 8 \end{array}$ 3   7. $\begin{array}{r} 6 \\ + P \\ \hline 15 \end{array}$ 9   8. $\begin{array}{r} Q \\ + 8 \\ \hline 8 \end{array}$ 0

9. 3 + 4 + 5   12   10. 4 + 4 + 4   12

11. $6 + R = 10$ 4   12. $X + 5 = 6$ 1

13. $\begin{array}{r} 5 \\ 5 \\ + 5 \\ \hline 15 \end{array}$ 14. $\begin{array}{r} 8 \\ 0 \\ + 7 \\ \hline 15 \end{array}$ 15. $\begin{array}{r} 6 \\ 5 \\ + 4 \\ \hline 15 \end{array}$ 16. $\begin{array}{r} 9 \\ 9 \\ + 9 \\ \hline 27 \end{array}$

17. $\begin{array}{r} M \\ + 9 \\ \hline 10 \end{array}$ 1   18. $\begin{array}{r} 9 \\ + F \\ \hline 12 \end{array}$ 3   19. $\begin{array}{r} Z \\ + 5 \\ \hline 12 \end{array}$ 7   20. $\begin{array}{r} 0 \\ + N \\ \hline 3 \end{array}$ 3

21. 3 + 2 + 5 + 4 + 6   20

22. 2 + 2 + 2 + 2 + 2 + 2 + 2   14

Write a number sentence for each picture:

23.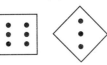

6 + 3 = 9

24.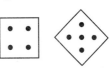

4 + 5 + 2 = 11

25. Show six ways to add 2, 3, and 4.   2 + 3 + 4 = 9;
2 + 4 + 3 = 9; 3 + 2 + 4 = 9; 3 + 4 + 2 = 9;
4 + 3 + 2 = 9; 4 + 2 + 3 = 9

LESSON 2

Missing Addends, Part 2

a. 50
b. 36
c. 49
d. 17
e. 19
f. 73
Patterns:
  Final digits:
    0 and 5
  Numbers in both lists:
    10, 20, 30, 40, 50, 60, 70, 80, 90, 100

Facts Practice: 100 Addition Facts (Test A in Test Masters)

Mental Math: Add ten to a number.

  a. 40 + 10   **b.** 26 + 10   **c.** 39 + 10
  d. 7 + 10   **e.** 10 + 9   **f.** 10 + 63

Patterns: Have the class count by fives from 5 to 100 while the teacher or a student lists the numbers on the board. Which digits appear as final digits? Which numbers in the list are numbers we say when we count by twos from 2 to 100?

Derek rolled a number cube three times. This picture shows the top face of the cube after the first two rolls.

The total number of dots on all three rolls was 12. Can you draw a picture of Derek's third roll?

We will write a number sentence for this problem. The first two numbers are 5 and 3. We do not know the number of the third roll, so we will use a letter. We know that the total is 12.

$$5 + 3 + T = 12$$

To find the missing addend, we first add 5 and 3, which is 8. Then we think, "Eight plus what number equals twelve?" Since 8 plus 4 equals 12, the third roll was ⬚.

Example   Find the missing number:

(a)   6
          N
     + 5
     ‾‾‾‾
     17

(b) $4 + 3 + 2 + B + 6 = 20$

Solution   (a) We add 6 and 5, which makes 11. We think, "Eleven plus what number equals seventeen?" Since 11 plus 6 equals 17, the missing number is **6**.

(b) First we add 4, 3, 2, and 6, which equals 15. Since 15 plus 5 is 20, the missing number is **5.**

Practice Find the missing number:

a. $8 + A + 2 = 17$ 7   **b.** $B + 6 + 5 = 12$ 1

c. $4 + C + 2 + 3 + 5 = 20$ 6

Problem set 2 Find either the sum or the missing addend:

†1.
(1)
$$\begin{array}{r} 5 \\ + 6 \\ \hline 11 \end{array}$$

2.
(1)
$$\begin{array}{r} 4 \\ + 7 \\ \hline 11 \end{array}$$

3.
(1)
$$\begin{array}{r} 9 \\ + N \\ \hline 13 \end{array}$$ 4

4.
(1)
$$\begin{array}{r} 7 \\ + 8 \\ \hline 15 \end{array}$$

5.
(1)
$$\begin{array}{r} P \\ + 6 \\ \hline 13 \end{array}$$ 7

6.
(2)
$$\begin{array}{r} 5 \\ 2 \\ + W \\ \hline 12 \end{array}$$ 5

7.
(1)
$$\begin{array}{r} 4 \\ 8 \\ + 5 \\ \hline 17 \end{array}$$

8.
(1)
$$\begin{array}{r} 9 \\ 3 \\ + 7 \\ \hline 19 \end{array}$$

9.
(2)
$$\begin{array}{r} 8 \\ B \\ + 3 \\ \hline 16 \end{array}$$ 5

10.
(1)
$$\begin{array}{r} 9 \\ 7 \\ + 3 \\ \hline 19 \end{array}$$

11.
(1)
$$\begin{array}{r} 2 \\ 9 \\ + 6 \\ \hline 17 \end{array}$$

12.
(1)
$$\begin{array}{r} 3 \\ 8 \\ + 2 \\ \hline 13 \end{array}$$

13.
(1)
$$\begin{array}{r} 9 \\ 5 \\ + 3 \\ \hline 17 \end{array}$$

14.
(2)
$$\begin{array}{r} 2 \\ M \\ + 4 \\ \hline 9 \end{array}$$ 3

15.
(2)
$$\begin{array}{r} 5 \\ 3 \\ + Q \\ \hline 9 \end{array}$$ 1

16.
(2)
$$\begin{array}{r} 2 \\ 3 \\ + R \\ \hline 7 \end{array}$$ 2

17.
(2)
$$\begin{array}{r} 5 \\ 3 \\ + T \\ \hline 10 \end{array}$$ 2

18.
(1)
$$\begin{array}{r} 8 \\ 4 \\ + 6 \\ \hline 18 \end{array}$$

19.
(2)
$$\begin{array}{r} 2 \\ X \\ + 7 \\ \hline 11 \end{array}$$ 2

20.
(1)
$$\begin{array}{r} 5 \\ 2 \\ + 6 \\ \hline 13 \end{array}$$

21. $5 + 8 + 2 + 7 + X + 3 = 30$ 5
(2)

22. $9 + 3 + 11 + 2 + 1 + N + 4 = 38$ 8
(2)

---

†The italicized numbers within parentheses underneath each problem number are called *lesson reference numbers*. These numbers refer to the lesson(s) in which the major concept of that particular problem is introduced. If additional assistance is needed, reference should be made to the discussion, examples, practice, or problem set of that lesson.

Write a number sentence for each picture:

23.
(1)
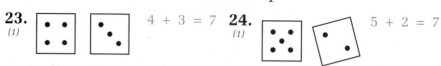
4 + 3 = 7

24.
(1)
5 + 2 = 7

25.
(1)
4 + 1 + 5 = 10

LESSON 3

Sequences

a. 40
b. 43
c. 53
d. 54
e. 80
f. 75
g. 35; 42; 64
Vocabulary:

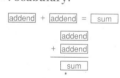

Facts Practice: 100 Addition Facts (Test A in Test Masters)

Mental Math: Add ten, twenty, or thirty to a number.

a.	20	b.	23	c.	43	d.	24	e.	50	f.	10
	+ 20		+ 20		+ 10		+ 30		+ 30		+ 65

g. One less than 24 is 23. What number is one less than 36? one less than 43? one less than 65?

Vocabulary: Copy these two patterns on a piece of paper. In each of the six boxes write either "addend" or "sum."

Counting is a math skill we learn early in life. Counting by ones, we say "One, two, three, four, five, ..."

1, 2, 3, 4, 5, ...

These numbers are called **counting numbers.** The counting numbers continue without end. We often count by a number other than one.

Counting by twos: 2, 4, 6, 8, 10, ...

Counting by fives: 5, 10, 15, 20, 25, ...

These are examples of counting patterns. A counting pattern is a **sequence.** The three dots mean that the sequence continues without end. A counting sequence may count up or count down. We may study a sequence to discover a rule for the sequence. Then we can find more numbers in the sequence.

Example 1   Find the next three numbers in this sequence:

10, 20, 30, 40, _____, _____, _____, ...

Solution   The pattern is "Count up by tens." Counting this way, we find that the next three numbers are **50, 60,** and **70.**

Example 2   Find the missing number in this sequence:

30, 27, 24, 21, _____, 15, ...

Solution   It looks like the rule is "Count down by threes." If we count down three from 21, we find that the next number in the sequence is **18.** We see that 15 is three less than 18, so 18 fits the pattern.

Practice   Write the next three numbers in each sequence:

   a. 10, 9, 8, 7, __6__ , __5__ , __4__ , ...

   b. 3, 6, 9, 12, __15__ , __18__ , __21__ , ...

Find the missing number in each sequence:

   c. 80, 70, __60__ , 50, ...   **d.** 8, __12__ , 16, 20, 24, ...

Problem set 3   Find either the sum or the missing addend:

1.
(1)
$$\begin{array}{r} 9 \\ 5 \\ 3 \\ +\ 9 \\ \hline 26 \end{array}$$

2.
(1)
$$\begin{array}{r} 4 \\ 2 \\ 4 \\ +\ 5 \\ \hline 15 \end{array}$$

3.
(1)
$$\begin{array}{r} 9 \\ 1 \\ 2 \\ +\ 7 \\ \hline 19 \end{array}$$

4.
(2)
$$\begin{array}{r} 8 \\ 3 \\ +\ N \quad 4 \\ \hline 15 \end{array}$$

5.
(2)
$$\begin{array}{r} 5 \\ M \quad 3 \\ +\ 4 \\ \hline 12 \end{array}$$

6.
(2)
$$\begin{array}{r} 8 \\ 2 \\ +\ W \quad 6 \\ \hline 16 \end{array}$$

Write the next number in each sequence:

7. 10, 20, 30, __40__ , ...
(3)

8. 22, 21, 20, __19__ , ...
(3)

9. 40, 35, 30, 25, __20__ , ...
(3)

10. 70, 80, 90, __100__ , ...
(3)

Write the next three numbers in each sequence:

11. 6, 12, 18, __24__ , __30__ , __36__ , ...
(3)

12. 3, 6, 9, __12__ , __15__ , __18__ , ...
(3)

13. 4, 8, 12, __16__ , __20__ , __24__ , ...
(3)

14. 45, 36, 27, __18__ , __9__ , __0__ , ...
(3)

Find the missing number in each sequence:

15. 8, 12, __16__ , 20, ...
(3)

16. 12, 18, __24__ , 30, ...
(3)

17. 30, 25, __20__ , 15, ...
(3)

18. 6, 9, __12__ , 15, ...
(3)

19. How many small rectangles are shown? Count by twos.
(3)

16 rectangles

20. How many X's are shown? Count by fours. 24 X's
(3)

XX XX XX
XX XX XX

XX XX XX
XX XX XX

21. Write a number sentence for this picture.
(1)

3 + 6 + 4 = 13

22.
(1)

    4
    8
    7
    5
  + 2

   26

23.
(1)

    9
    5
    7
    8
  + 3

   32

24.
(1)

    8
    4
    7
    2
  + 3

   24

25.
(1)

    2
    9
    7
    5
  + 4

   27

LESSON
4

a. 76
b. 49
c. 86
d. 68
e. 26
f. 70
g. 75; 48; 67

Problem Solving:

Number of Coins

Left	Right
0	10
1	9
2	8
3	7
4	6
5	5
6	4
7	3
8	2
9	1
10	0

Facts Practice: 100 Addition Facts (Test A in Test Masters)

Mental Math: Add ten, twenty, or thirty to a number.

a. 66 + 10 **b.** 29 + 20 **c.** 10 + 76
d. 38 + 30 **e.** 20 + 6 **f.** 40 + 30
g. What number is one less than 76? than 49? than 68?

Problem Solving: Tom has a total of ten coins in his left and right pockets. Copy and complete this table listing the possible number of coins in each pocket. Your table should have eleven rows.

Number of coins	
Left	Right
0	10
1	
2	

To write numbers we use digits. **Digits are the numerals 0, 1, 2, 3, 4, 5, 6, 7, 8, and 9.** The number 356 has three digits, and the last digit is 6. The number 67,896,094 has eight digits, and the last digit is 4.

Example 1 The number 64,000 has how many digits?

Solution The number 64,000 has **five digits.**

Example 2 What is the last digit of 2001?

Solution The last digit of 2001 is **1.**

Practice How many digits are in each number?

a. 18   2   **b.** 5280   4   **c.** 8,403,227,189
                                    10

What is the last digit in each number?

d. 19   9   **e.** 5281   1   **f.** 8,403,190   0

Problem set 4

Write the next three numbers in each sequence:

1. 5, 10, 15, 20, __25__, __30__, __35__, ...
(3)

2. 7, 14, 21, 28, __35__, __42__, __49__, ...
(3)

3. 8, 16, 24, 32, __40__, __48__, __56__, ...
(3)

4. 4, 8, 12, 16, __20__, __24__, __28__, ...
(3)

Find the missing number in each sequence:

5. 90, __80__, 70, 60, ...
(3)

6. 10, 8, __6__, 4, ...
(3)

7. 6, __9__, 12, 15, ...
(3)

8. 50, 45, __40__, 35, ...
(3)

9. 45, 54, __63__, 72, ...
(3)

10. 16, __24__, 32, 40, ...
(3)

11. How many digits are in each number?
(4)
    (a) 593   3   (b) 180   3   (c) 186,527,394
                                                            9

12. What is the last digit in each number?
(4)
    (a) 3427   7   (b) 460   0   (c) 437,269   9

Find either the sum or the missing addend:

13. 4   **14.** 9   **15.** 7   **16.** 8   **17.** 9
(1)   3   (1)   3   (2)   N 2 (2)   A 4 (2)   8
       + 5   + 8   + 6   + 7   + D 2
       ————   ————   ————   ————   ————
        12   20   15   19   19

18. Write a number sentence for this
(1)   picture.   6 + 6 = 12

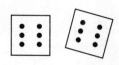

19. How many cents are in 4 nickels?
(3)   Count by fives.   20 cents

5¢   5¢

5¢   5¢

20. How many X's are in this pattern? Count by threes.
(3)   30 X's

X X X X X X X X X X

X X X X X X X X X X

X X X X X X X X X X

21. *(1)*	**22.** *(1)*	**23.** *(1)*	**24.** *(1)*
2	5	9	8
7	2	8	7
3	3	7	2
5	8	4	5
+ 4	+ 2	+ 3	+ 7
21	20	31	29

25. $5 + 4 + 3 + 2 + 1 + N = 20$ 5
(2)

LESSON
5

Place Value

a. 84
b. 46
c. 92
d. 63
e. 90
f. 27; 86; 53
Patterns:

Facts Practice: 100 Addition Facts (Test A in Test Masters)

Mental Math: Add a number ending in zero to another number.

a.	**b.**	**c.**	**d.**	**e.**
24	36	50	33	40
+ 60	+ 10	+ 42	+ 30	+ 50

f. What number is one less than 28? 87? 54?

Patterns: Copy this design of ten circles on your paper. In each circle, write a counting number from 1 to 10 that continues the pattern (1, skip, skip, 2, skip, skip, 3, ...).

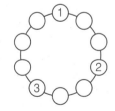

To help us with the idea of place value, we will use pictures to show different amounts of money. We will use $100 bills, $10 bills, and $1 bills.

Example 1   How much money is shown by this diagram?

Solution   Since there are 2 hundreds, 4 tens, and 3 ones, the amount of money shown is **$243.**

Example 2   Use play money or draw a diagram to show how to make $324 using $100 bills, $10 bills, and $1 bills.

Solution   To show $324, we draw 3 hundreds, 2 tens, and 4 ones.

    3 hundreds   2 tens   4 ones

Places are named by the value of the place. Three-digit numbers like 324 occupy three different places.

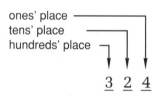

ones' place
tens' place
hundreds' place

$$\underline{3} \ \underline{2} \ \underline{4}$$

Example 3   The digit 7 is in what place in 753?

Solution   The 7 is in the third place from the right, which shows the number of hundreds. So the 7 is in the **hundreds' place.**

Practice   **a.** Use play money or draw a diagram to show $231 using $100 bills, $10 bills, and $1 bills.

     | 100 | | 10 | | 1 |
     2 hundreds   3 tens   1 one

   b. The digit 6 is in what place in each of these numbers?

      (1) 16 ones'   (2) 65 tens'   (3) 623 hundreds'

   c. Use three digits to write a number equal to 5 hundreds, 2 tens, and 3 ones.   523

Problem set 5 Find either the sum or the missing addend:

1.
(1)
$\begin{array}{r} 4 \\ + N \\ \hline 12 \end{array}$ 8

2.
(1)
$\begin{array}{r} 4 \\ 5 \\ + 3 \\ \hline 12 \end{array}$

3.
(1)
$\begin{array}{r} 13 \\ + Y \\ \hline 19 \end{array}$ 6

4.
(1)
$\begin{array}{r} 7 \\ + S \\ \hline 14 \end{array}$ 7

5.
(2)
$\begin{array}{r} 3 \\ N \\ + 2 \\ \hline 11 \end{array}$ 6

6.
(2)
$\begin{array}{r} 1 \\ M \\ + 5 \\ \hline 10 \end{array}$ 4

7.
(2)
$\begin{array}{r} D \\ 2 \\ + 7 \\ \hline 18 \end{array}$ 9

8.
(2)
$\begin{array}{r} 3 \\ N \\ + 2 \\ \hline 9 \end{array}$ 4

9. $4 + N + 5 = 12$ 3
(2)

10. $N + 2 + 3 = 8$ 3
(2)

Write the next three numbers in each sequence:

11. 9, 12, 15, __18__, __21__, __24__, ...
(3)

12. 30, 24, 18, __12__, __6__, __0__, ...
(3)

13. 12, 16, 20, __24__, __28__, __32__, ...
(3)

14. 35, 28, 21, __14__, __7__, __0__, ...
(3)

15. How many digits are in each number?
(4)
  (a) 37,432 5   (b) 5,934,286 7 (c) 453,000 6

16. What is the last digit in each number?
(4)
  (a) 734 4   (b) 347 7   (c) 473 3

17. Draw a picture to show $342.
(5)

3 hundreds 4 tens 2 ones

18. How much money is shown by this picture? $434
(5)

Find the missing number in each sequence:

19. 24, __30__, 36, 42, ...
(3)

20. 36, 32, __28__, 24, ...
(3)

21. How many ears are on 10 rabbits? Count by twos.
(3)   20 ears

22. The digit 6 is in what place in 365?   tens'
(5)

23. Write a number sentence for this
(1)   picture.   5 + 6 = 11

Find the missing addend:

24. 2 + 5 + 3 + 2 + 3 + 1 + N = 20   4
(2)

25. 4 + B + 3 + 2 + 5 + 4 + 1 = 25   6
(2)

LESSON 6

Ordinal Numbers • Months of the Year

a. 43
b. 42
c. 56
d. 55
e. 75
f. 74

Problem Solving:

Number of Coins

Left	Right
2	8
3	7
4	6
5	5
6	4
7	3
8	2

Facts Practice: 100 Addition Facts (Test A in Test Masters)

Mental Math: Nine is one less than ten. When adding 9 to a number, we may mentally add 10 and then think of the number that is one less than that number. For 23 + 9 we may think: 23 + 10 is 33, and one less than 33 is 32.

a.	33	**b.**	33	**c.**	46	**d.**	46	**e.**	65	**f.**	65
	+ 10		+ 9		+ 10		+ 9		+ 10		+ 9

Problem Solving: Tom has a total of ten coins in his left and right pockets. He has **some coins** (at least two) in each pocket. Make a table that lists the possible number of coins in each pocket.

Ordinal numbers   If we count the number of children in a line, we say, "One, two, three, four, ..." These numbers tell us how many children we have counted. To tell our place in a line, we use words like *first*, *second*, *third*, and *fourth*. Numbers that tell position or order are called **ordinal numbers.**

Example 1   There are ten children in the lunch line. John is fourth in line. How many children are in front of John? How many children are behind him?

Solution   A diagram may help us understand the problem. We begin by drawing a diagram and labeling the information given to us.

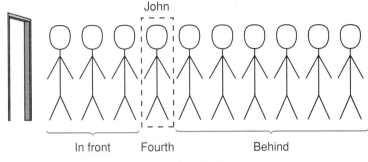

Lunch line

Since John is fourth in line, we see that there are **three children in front of him.** The rest of the children are behind John. From the diagram, we see that there are **six children behind him.**

   Many times ordinal numbers are abbreviated. The abbreviation consists of a counting number and the letters *st, nd, rd,* or *th.* Here we show some abbreviations.

first	1st	sixth	6th	eleventh	11th
second	2nd	seventh	7th	twelfth	12th
third	3rd	eighth	8th	thirteenth	13th
fourth	4th	ninth	9th	twentieth	20th
fifth	5th	tenth	10th	twenty-first	21st

Example 2   Andy is 13th in line. Carl is 3rd in line. How many students are between Carl and Andy?

Solution   Begin by drawing a diagram.

From the diagram we see that there are **nine students between Carl and Andy.**

Months of the year   We use ordinal numbers to name the months of the year and the days of each month. This table lists the twelve months of the year in order. A common year is 365 days long. A leap year is 366 days long. The extra day in a leap year is added to February.

ORDER	MONTH	DAYS
First	January	31
Second	February	28 or 29
Third	March	31
Fourth	April	30
Fifth	May	31
Sixth	June	30
Seventh	July	31
Eighth	August	31
Ninth	September	30
Tenth	October	31
Eleventh	November	30
Twelfth	December	31

Robert was born on the second day of June in 1988. Robert writes his birth date in month/day/year form this way.

6/2/1988

The "6" stands for the sixth month, which is June.

Example 3   Jenny wrote her birth date as 7/8/89. (a) In what month was Jenny born? (b) In what year was she born?

Solution   (a) In the United States we usually write the number of the month first. The first number Jenny wrote was 7. She was born in the seventh month, which is **July.**

(b) Years are often abbreviated using only the last two digits of the year, when confusion is unlikely. We assume that Jenny was born in **1989.**

Practice   a. John was third in line and Tom was eighth. How many people were between them?   4 people

b. Write your birth date in month/day/year form.
answer varies

Problem set   Find the missing addend:

6

1. (2)
```
    2
    6
+ X   7
―――
   15
```

2. (2)
```
    1
    Y   6
+   7
―――
   14
```

3. (2)
```
    3
    Z   4
+   5
―――
   12
```

4. (2)
```
    1
    N   6
+   6
―――
   13
```

5. (2)
```
    2
    5
+ W   3
―――
   10
```

6. (1)
```
    2
+ A   5
―――
    7
```

7. (1)
```
    R   6
+   5
―――
   11
```

8. (1)
```
    3
+ T   2
―――
    5
```

9. 2 + N + 3 + 7 = 16   4
(2)

10. What month is the eighth month of the year?   August
(6)

Write the next three numbers in each sequence:

11. 12, 15, 18, __21__, __24__, __27__, ...
(3)

12. 16, 20, 24, __28__, __32__, __36__, ...
(3)

13. 28, 35, 42, __49__, __56__, __63__, ...
(3)

Find the missing number in each sequence:

14. 30, __36__, 42, 48
(3)

15. 30, __35__, 40, 45
(3)

16. Draw a picture to show $432.
(5)
4 hundreds   3 tens   2 ones

17. Write a number sentence for this picture.
(1)   5 + 5 + 5 = 15

18. The digit 8 is in what place in 845?   hundreds'
(5)

19. Use three digits to write the number that equals 2
(5)   hundreds plus 3 tens plus 5 ones.   235

20. If the pattern is continued, what will be the next
(3)   number circled?   12

1, 2, ③, 4, 5, ⑥, 7, 8, ⑨, 10, ...

21. Seven boys have how many elbows? Count by twos.
(3)   14 elbows

22. (1)	**23.** (1)	**24.** (1)	**25.** (1)
5	5	9	8
8	7	7	7
4	3	6	3
7	8	5	5
4	4	4	4
+ 3	+ 2	+ 2	+ 9
31	29	33	36

LESSON 7

Review of Subtraction • Fact Families

a. 37
b. 53
c. 96
d. 83
e. 96
f. 68
Patterns:
  After January:
    February
  Month born:
    April

Facts Practice: 100 Addition Facts (Test A in Test Masters)

Mental Math: Add one less than ten to a number.

  a. 28 + 9   **b.** 44 + 9   **c.** 87 + 9

Review:

  d. 63 + 20   **e.** 46 + 50   **f.** 38 + 30

Patterns: The months of the year repeat. Twelve months after January is January of the next year. Twenty-four months after January is January again. What month is twenty-five months after January? On Valentine's Day, Nathan's sister was 22 months old. In what month was Nathan's sister born?

Review of subtraction

We remember that when we add, we combine two groups into one group.

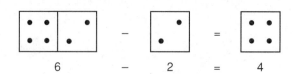

4   +   2   =   6

When we subtract, we separate a group into two groups. To take away two from six, we subtract.

6   −   2   =   4

When we subtract one number from another number, the answer is called the **difference.** If we subtract two from six, the difference is four.

$$
\begin{array}{r}
6 \\
-\ 2 \\
\hline
4
\end{array}\ \ \text{difference}
$$

We can check a subtraction problem by adding the two bottom numbers. **The sum of the two bottom numbers must equal the top number.** A good habit to develop is to "subtract down" to find the answer; then "add up" to check the answer.

SUBTRACT DOWN:			ADD UP:
Six minus two equals four.	↓	$\begin{array}{r} 6 \\ -\ 2 \\ \hline 4 \end{array}$ ↑	Four plus two equals six.

In the practice and problem sets for the rest of the book, all subtraction problems should be checked by adding.

Fact families The three numbers 2, 4, and 6 form an addition and subtraction fact family. A *fact family* is a group of three numbers that may be arranged to form four facts.

$$
\begin{array}{cccc}
2 & 4 & 6 & 6 \\
+\ 4 & +\ 2 & -\ 2 & -\ 4 \\
\hline
6 & 6 & 4 & 2
\end{array}
$$

Recognizing addition and subtraction fact families can help us learn the facts.

Example The numbers 3, 5, and 8 are an addition and subtraction fact family. Write two addition facts and two subtraction facts using these three numbers.

Solution
$$
\begin{array}{cccc}
3 & 5 & 8 & 8 \\
+\ 5 & +\ 3 & -\ 3 & -\ 5 \\
\hline
8 & 8 & 5 & 3
\end{array}
$$

Practice Subtract. Check by "adding up."

a.	**b.**	**c.**	**d.**	**e.**
$\begin{array}{r} 14 \\ -\ 8 \\ \hline 6 \end{array}$	$\begin{array}{r} 9 \\ -\ 3 \\ \hline 6 \end{array}$	$\begin{array}{r} 15 \\ -\ 7 \\ \hline 8 \end{array}$	$\begin{array}{r} 11 \\ -\ 4 \\ \hline 7 \end{array}$	$\begin{array}{r} 12 \\ -\ 5 \\ \hline 7 \end{array}$

f. The numbers 5, 6, and 11 form a fact family. Write two addition facts and two subtraction facts using these three numbers.

$5 + 6 = 11, 6 + 5 = 11, 11 - 6 = 5, 11 - 5 = 6$

Problem set 7

1. (7)
$$\begin{array}{r} 14 \\ -\ 5 \\ \hline 9 \end{array}$$

2. (7)
$$\begin{array}{r} 15 \\ -\ 8 \\ \hline 7 \end{array}$$

3. (7)
$$\begin{array}{r} 9 \\ -\ 4 \\ \hline 5 \end{array}$$

4. (7)
$$\begin{array}{r} 11 \\ -\ 7 \\ \hline 4 \end{array}$$

5. (7)
$$\begin{array}{r} 12 \\ -\ 8 \\ \hline 4 \end{array}$$

6. (7)
$$\begin{array}{r} 11 \\ -\ 6 \\ \hline 5 \end{array}$$

7. (7)
$$\begin{array}{r} 15 \\ -\ 7 \\ \hline 8 \end{array}$$

8. (7)
$$\begin{array}{r} 9 \\ -\ 6 \\ \hline 3 \end{array}$$

9. (7)
$$\begin{array}{r} 13 \\ -\ 5 \\ \hline 8 \end{array}$$

10. (7)
$$\begin{array}{r} 12 \\ -\ 6 \\ \hline 6 \end{array}$$

11. (1)
$$\begin{array}{r} 8 \\ +\ N \\ \hline 17 \end{array} \quad 9$$

12. (1)
$$\begin{array}{r} A \\ +\ 8 \\ \hline 14 \end{array} \quad 6$$

13. (1) $3 + W = 11$ 8

14. (2) $1 + 4 + M = 13$ 8

15. (7) The numbers 4, 6, and 10 are a fact family. Write two addition facts and two subtraction facts using these three numbers.

$4 + 6 = 10, 6 + 4 = 10, 10 - 4 = 6, 10 - 6 = 4$

Write the next three numbers in each sequence:

16. (3) 16, 18, 20, __22__, __24__, __26__, ...

17. (3) 21, 28, 35, __42__, __49__, __56__, ...

18. (3) 20, 24, 28, __32__, __36__, __40__, ...

19. (6) How many days are in the tenth month of the year?   31 days

20. (5) Draw a picture to show $326.   3 hundreds 2 tens 6 ones

21. (5) The digit 6 is in what place in 456?   ones'

Find the missing addend:

22. (2) $2 + N + 4 = 13$ 7

23. (2) $A + 3 + 5 = 16$ 8

24. (2) $4 + 7 + 8 + 6 + 4 + W = 30$ 1

25. (2) $1 + 2 + 3 + M + 5 + 6 = 20$ 3

**LESSON
8**

Writing Numbers Through 999

a. 65
b. 72
c. 57
d. 94
e. 90
f. 89
Problem Solving:

Number of Coins

Left	Right
2	8
3	7
4	6

Facts Practice: 100 Subtraction Facts (Test B in Test Masters)

Mental Math: Add one less than ten to a number.

    a. 56 + 9   **b.** 63 + 9   **c.** 48 + 9

Review:

    d. 74 + 20   **e.** 60 + 30   **f.** 49 + 40

Problem Solving: Tom has a total of ten coins in his left and right pockets. He has some coins in each pocket. He has more coins in his right pocket than in his left pocket. Make a table that lists the possible number of coins in each pocket.

Whole numbers are the counting numbers and zero.

$$0, 1, 2, 3, 4, 5, \ldots$$

To write the names of whole numbers through 999 (nine hundred ninety-nine), we need to know the following words and how to put them together:

0	zero	10	ten	20	twenty~
1	one	11	eleven	30	thirty
2	two	12	twelve	40	forty
3	three	13	thirteen	50	fifty
4	four	14	fourteen	60	sixty
5	five	15	fifteen	70	seventy
6	six	16	sixteen	80	eighty
7	seven	17	seventeen	90	ninety
8	eight	18	eighteen	100	one hundred
9	nine	19	nineteen		

You may look at this chart when you are asked to write the names of numbers in the problem sets.

The names of two-digit numbers greater than 20 that do not end with zero are written with a hyphen.

Example 1   Use words to write the number 44.

Solution   We use a hyphen and write **"Forty-four."** Notice that "forty" is spelled without a "u."

To write three-digit numbers, we first write the number of hundreds and then we write the rest of the number. **We do not use the word "and" when writing whole numbers.**

Example 2   Use words to write the number 313.

Solution   First we write the number of hundreds. Then we write the rest of the number: **three hundred thirteen.** (*Note*: We do **not** write three hundred *and* thirteen.)

Example 3   Use words to write the number 705.

Solution   First we write the number of hundreds. Then we write the rest of the number: **seven hundred five.**

Example 4   Use digits to write the number six hundred eight.

Solution   Six hundred eight means six hundreds and eight ones. There are no tens, so we write a zero in the tens' place: **608.**

Practice   Use words to write each number:

a. 0   zero

b. 81   eighty-one

c. 99   ninety-nine

d. 515   five hundred fifteen

e. 444
four hundred forty-four

f. 909   nine hundred nine

Use digits to write each number:

g. Nineteen   19

h. Ninety-one   91

i. Five hundred twenty-four   524

j. Eight hundred sixty   860

Problem set 8

Find the missing addend:

1.   2
(2)   3
    + N   8
    ——
    13

2.   3
(2)   N   5
    + 6
    ——
    14

3.   5
(2)   N   4
    + 2
    ——
    11

4.   2
(2)   6
    + N   7
    ——
    15

Subtract. Check by adding.

5.   13
(7)   − 5
    ——
    8

6.   16
(7)   − 8
    ——
    8

7.   13
(7)   − 7
    ——
    6

8.   12
(7)   − 8
    ——
    4

Use digits to write each number:

9. Two hundred fourteen
(8)   214

10. Five hundred thirty-two
(8)   532

Use words to write each number:

11. 301
(8)   three hundred one

12. 320
(8)   three hundred twenty

13. 312   three hundred twelve
(8)

14. Write a number sentence for this
(1)   picture.   3 + 5 = 8

Write the next three numbers in each sequence:

15. 12, 18, 24, __30__, __36__, __42__, ...
(3)

16. 15, 18, 21, __24__, __27__, __30__, ...
(3)

Find the missing number in each sequence:

17. 35, 42, __49__, 56, ...
(3)

18. 40, __48__, 56, 64, ...
(3)

19. How much money is shown by this picture? $303
(5)

20. The numbers 7, 8, and 15 are a fact family. Write two
(7) addition facts and two subtraction facts using these
three numbers.
7 + 8 = 15, 8 + 7 = 15, 15 − 7 = 8, 15 − 8 = 7

21. Brad was twelfth in line. His sister was sixth in line.
(6) How many people were between Brad and his sister?
5 people

22. Six nickels is equal to how many cents? Count by
(3) fives.   30 cents

23. 4 + 7 + 8 + 5 + 4   **24.** 2 + 3 + 5 + 8 + 5
(1)   28   (1)   23

25. 5 + 8 + 6 + 4 + 3 + 7 + 2   35
(1)

LESSON 9

Adding Money

a. 56
b. 55
c. 67
d. 66
e. 44
f. 43

Patterns:
Ten days after
Saturday:
  Tuesday
Ten days before
Saturday:
  Wednesday
Seventy days after
Saturday:
  Saturday

Facts Practice: 100 Subtraction Facts (Test B in Test Masters)

Mental Math: Nineteen is one less than 20. When adding 19
to a number, we may think of adding one less
than 20 to the number.

a.	36	**b.**	36	**c.**	47	**d.**	47	**e.**	24	**f.**	24
	+ 20		+ 19		+ 20		+ 19		+ 20		+ 19

Patterns: The days of the week repeat. Seven days before
Saturday was Saturday, and seven days after
Saturday is Saturday again. What day is ten days
after Saturday? What day was ten days before
Saturday? What day is seventy days after Saturday?

---

*Donna had $24. On her birthday she was given
$15. Then how much money did Donna have?*

We use $10 bills and $1 bills to add $15 to $24. The total is 3 tens and 9 ones, which is $39.

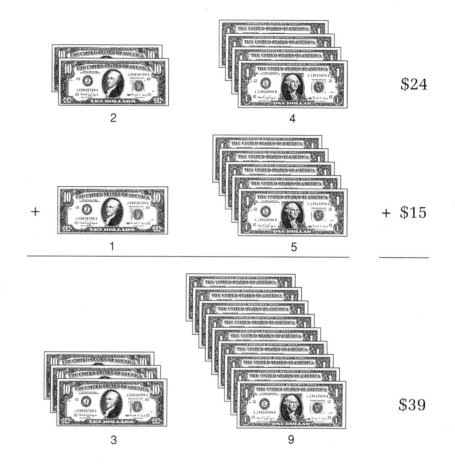

We may add $24 and $15 by acting out the addition with money, by mental math, or with pencil and paper. Using pencil and paper, we add the digits in the ones' place, and then the digits in the tens' place. Remember to include the dollar sign in the answer.

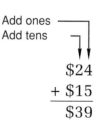

Practice

a. $53 + $26
$79

b. $14 + $75
$89

c. $36 + $42
$78

d. $27 + $51
$78

e. $15 + $21
$36

f. $32 + $23
$55

Problem set 9   Use digits to write each number:

1. Three hundred forty-three   343
(8)

2. Three hundred seven   307
(8)

3. Use words to write 592.   five hundred ninety-two
(8)

4.
(2)
$$\begin{array}{r} 2 \\ 4 \\ + N \quad 6 \\ \hline 12 \end{array}$$

5.
(2)
$$\begin{array}{r} 1 \\ R \quad 3 \\ + 6 \\ \hline 10 \end{array}$$

6.
(2)
$$\begin{array}{r} 1 \\ T \quad 6 \\ + 7 \\ \hline 14 \end{array}$$

7.
(2)
$$\begin{array}{r} 2 \\ 6 \\ + N \quad 5 \\ \hline 13 \end{array}$$

8.
(9)
$$\begin{array}{r} \$25 \\ + \$14 \\ \hline \$39 \end{array}$$

9.
(9)
$$\begin{array}{r} \$85 \\ + \$14 \\ \hline \$99 \end{array}$$

10.
(9)
$$\begin{array}{r} \$22 \\ + \$16 \\ \hline \$38 \end{array}$$

11.
(9)
$$\begin{array}{r} \$40 \\ + \$38 \\ \hline \$78 \end{array}$$

12.
(7)
$$\begin{array}{r} 13 \\ - 9 \\ \hline 4 \end{array}$$

13.
(7)
$$\begin{array}{r} 17 \\ - 5 \\ \hline 12 \end{array}$$

14.
(7)
$$\begin{array}{r} 17 \\ - 8 \\ \hline 9 \end{array}$$

15.
(7)
$$\begin{array}{r} 14 \\ - 6 \\ \hline 8 \end{array}$$

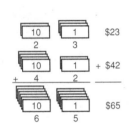

16. Draw a picture to show the addition of $23 and $42.
(9)

17. How many days are in four weeks? Count by sevens.
(3)   28 days

18. Sarah was born on the fifth day of August in 1987.
(6)   Write her birth date in month/day/year form.   8/5/87

Write the next three numbers in each sequence:

19. 12, 15, 18, __21__, __24__, __27__, ...
(3)

20. 28, 35, 42, __49__, __56__, __63__, ...
(3)

21.
(1)
$$\begin{array}{r} 5 \\ 8 \\ 7 \\ 6 \\ 4 \\ + 3 \\ \hline 33 \end{array}$$

22.
(1)
$$\begin{array}{r} 9 \\ 7 \\ 6 \\ 4 \\ 8 \\ + 7 \\ \hline 41 \end{array}$$

23.
(1)
$$\begin{array}{r} 2 \\ 5 \\ 7 \\ 3 \\ 5 \\ + 4 \\ \hline 26 \end{array}$$

24.
(1)
$$\begin{array}{r} 9 \\ 3 \\ 8 \\ 4 \\ 7 \\ + 6 \\ \hline 37 \end{array}$$

25.
(1)
$$\begin{array}{r} 4 \\ 8 \\ 7 \\ 4 \\ 5 \\ + 6 \\ \hline 34 \end{array}$$

**LESSON
10**

Adding with Regrouping

a. 37
b. 55
c. 52
d. 44
e. 65
f. 64

Problem Solving:

Tom has 7 coins in his right pocket and 3 coins in his left pocket.

Facts Practice: 100 Addition Facts (Test A in Test Masters)

Mental Math: Add 9 or 19 to a number.

   a. 28 + 9   **b.** 36 + 19   **c.** 43 + 9
   d. 25 + 19   **e.** 56 + 9   **f.** 45 + 19

Problem Solving: Tom has a total of ten coins in his left and right pockets. He has four more coins in his right pocket than in his left pocket. How many coins does Tom have in each pocket?

After her birthday, Donna had $39. Later she earned $14 more. Then how much money did Donna have?

We use $10 bills and $1 bills to add $14 to $39. The total is 4 tens and 13 ones, which is $53.

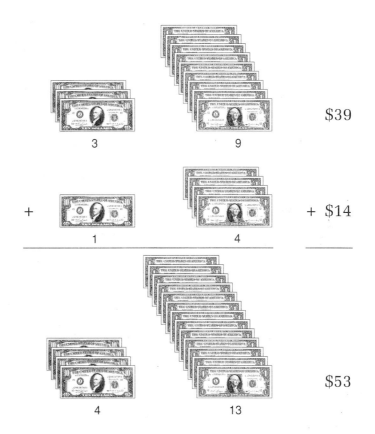

We can see the total easily if we exchange 10 of the ones for another $10 bill.

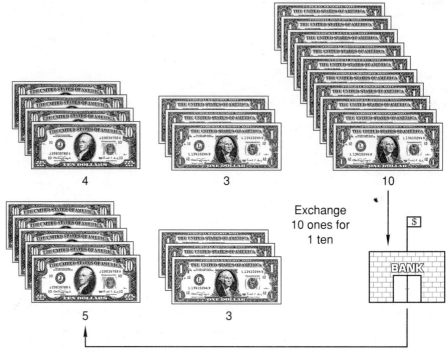

Now we see 5 tens and 3 ones, which is $53.

Using pencil and paper to add $14 to $39, we add the ones and get $13.

Add ones ⌐

$$\begin{array}{r} \$3 \quad 9 \\ + \$1 \quad 4 \\ \hline ⑬ \end{array}$$ ◄— 1 ten and 3 ones

Since 13 ones is the same as 1 ten and 3 ones, we write just the 3 in the ones' place. We will add the 1 ten to the other tens. We show this by writing a 1 either above the column of tens or below the column of tens. Then we add the tens.

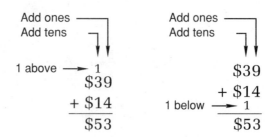

Practice   a. $36   b.   47   c. $57
              + $29   + 8   + $13
              ‾‾‾‾   ‾‾‾‾   ‾‾‾‾
               $65   55 $70

d. 68 + 24   92   e. $59 + $8 $67   f. 46 + 25   71

Problem set   Use digits to write each number:
10

1. Six hundred thirteen   **2.** Nine hundred one
(8)   613   *(8)*   901

3. Use words to write 941.   nine hundred forty-one
(8)

4.   2   **5.**   5   **6.**   H   4   **7.**   2
(2)   4   *(2)*   G   6   *(2)*   4   *(2)*   7
        + F   5   + 2   + 7   + N   7
        ‾‾‾‾   ‾‾‾‾   ‾‾‾‾   ‾‾‾‾
         11   13   15   16

8.   33   **9.** $47   **10.**   27   **11.** $49
(10)   + 8   *(10)*   + $18   *(10)*   + 69   *(10)*   + $25
        ‾‾‾‾   ‾‾‾‾   ‾‾‾‾   ‾‾‾‾
         41                  $65   96 $74

12.   17   **13.**   12   **14.**   9   **15.**   13
(7)   − 8   *(7)*   − 6   *(7)*   − 7   *(7)*   − 6
        ‾‾‾‾   ‾‾‾‾   ‾‾‾‾   ‾‾‾‾
          9   6   2   7

16. What is the name for the answer when we add?   sum
(1)

17. What is the name for the answer when we subtract?
(7)   difference

18. Which month is two months after the twelfth month?
(6)   February

Write the next three numbers in each sequence:

19. 30, 36, 42, __48__ , __54__ , __60__ , ...
(3)

20. 28, 35, 42, __49__ , __56__ , __63__ , ...
(3)

21. What digit is in the hundreds' place in 843?   8
(5)

22. 28 + 6   34   **23.** $47 + $28   **24.** 35 + 27   62
(10)   *(10)* $75   *(10)*

25. 4 + 5 + 7 + 8 + 4 + 6 + 3   37
(1)

LESSON 11

Even Numbers • Odd Numbers

a. 80
b. 84
c. 75
d. 75
e. 87
f. 53
Problem Solving:
Final digits:
 1, 3, 5, 7, 9
Sequence:
 21, 23, 25, 27,
 29, 31, 33, 35,
 37, 39

Facts Practice: 100 Subtraction Facts (Test B in Test Masters)

Mental Math: Review.

a. 20 + 60	**b.** 75 + 9	**c.** 45 + 30
d. 56 + 19	**e.** 47 + 40	**f.** 34 + 19

Problem Solving: Have each student write the counting numbers from 1 through 20 on a sheet of paper while the numbers are also written on the board. Then draw a line through every number on the list that we say when we count by twos from 2 to 20: 1, 2̸, 3, 4̸, 5, 6̸, 7, ... Say the numbers that remain. What are the final digits? Continue this sequence of numbers from 21 to 39.

Even numbers   The numbers we say when we count by twos are **even numbers.** Notice that every even number ends with either 2, 4, 6, 8, or 0.

$$2, 4, 6, 8, 10, 12, 14, 16, 18, 20, 22, 24, 26, \ldots$$

The list of even numbers goes on and on. We do not begin with zero when we count by twos. However, the number 0 is an even number.

Example 1   Which one of these numbers is an even number?

$$463 \qquad 285 \qquad 456$$

Solution   We can tell if a number is even by looking at the last digit. **A number is an even number if the last digit is even.** The last digits of these numbers are 3, 5, and 6. Of these, the only even digit is 6, so the even number is **456.**

Odd numbers   If a whole number is not an even number, then it is an **odd number.** We can make a list of odd numbers by beginning with the number 1. Then we add two to get the next odd number, add two more to get the next odd number, and so on. The sequence of odd numbers is

$$1, 3, 5, 7, 9, 11, \ldots$$

An even number of objects can be separated into two equal groups. Six is an even number. Here we show six dots separated into two equal groups.

If we try to separate an odd number of objects into two equal groups, there will be one extra object. Five is an odd number. Five dots will not separate into two equal groups because one dot is left over.

Example 2 There were the same number of boys and girls in the classroom. Which of these numbers could be the number of children in the classroom?

A. 25   B. 26   C. 27

Solution An even number of children can be divided into two equal groups. Since there are an equal number of boys and girls, there must be an even number of children in the classroom. The only even number among the choices is **B. 26.**

Example 3 List the five odd three-digit numbers that have a 7 in the hundreds' place and a 5 in the tens' place.

Solution The first two digits are 7 and 5.

$$\underline{7}\quad\underline{5}\quad\underline{\ }$$

The last digit can be either 1, 3, 5, 7, or 9. So the five numbers are

751, 753, 755, 757, and **759**

Practice   Write "even" or "odd" for each number:

a. 563   odd

b. 328   even

c. 99   odd

d. 0   even

e. List the five even three-digit numbers that have a 6 in the hundreds' place and a 3 in the tens' place.
630, 632, 634, 636, 638

Problem set 11

1. Use digits to write five hundred forty-two.   542
(8)

2. Use digits to write six hundred nineteen.   619
(8)

3. The numbers 4, 7, and 11 are a fact family. Write two
(7) addition facts and two subtraction facts using these three numbers.
4 + 7 = 11, 7 + 4 = 11, 11 − 4 = 7, 11 − 7 = 4

Use words to write each number:

4. 903   nine hundred three
(8)

5. 746
(8)   seven hundred forty-six

6. List the five odd three-digit numbers that have a 5 in
(11) the hundreds' place and a 0 in the tens' place.
501, 503, 505, 507, 509

7.
(2)
$$\begin{array}{r} 4 \\ N \quad 7 \\ + \ 3 \\ \hline 14 \end{array}$$

8.
(2)
$$\begin{array}{r} P \quad 7 \\ 4 \\ + \ 2 \\ \hline 13 \end{array}$$

9.
(2)
$$\begin{array}{r} 5 \\ Q \quad 2 \\ + \ 7 \\ \hline 14 \end{array}$$

10.
(2)
$$\begin{array}{r} R \quad 6 \\ 3 \\ + \ 2 \\ \hline 11 \end{array}$$

11.
(7)
$$\begin{array}{r} 15 \\ - \ 7 \\ \hline 8 \end{array}$$

12.
(7)
$$\begin{array}{r} 14 \\ - \ 7 \\ \hline 7 \end{array}$$

13.
(7)
$$\begin{array}{r} 17 \\ - \ 8 \\ \hline 9 \end{array}$$

14.
(7)
$$\begin{array}{r} 11 \\ - \ 6 \\ \hline 5 \end{array}$$

15.
(10)
$$\begin{array}{r} \$25 \\ + \ \$38 \\ \hline \$63 \end{array}$$

16.
(10)
$$\begin{array}{r} \$19 \\ + \ \$34 \\ \hline \$53 \end{array}$$

17.
(10)
$$\begin{array}{r} 42 \\ + \ 8 \\ \hline 50 \end{array}$$

18.
(10)
$$\begin{array}{r} 17 \\ + \ 49 \\ \hline 66 \end{array}$$

Write the next three numbers in each sequence:

19. 18, 21, 24, __27__, __30__, __33__, ...
(3)

20. 18, 24, 30, __36__, __42__, __48__, ...
(3)

21. Write a number sentence for this
(1) picture.   5 + 6 = 11

22. (1)	**23.** (1)	**24.** (1)	**25.** (1)
2	9	9	4
3	4	2	7
5	7	4	4
7	8	8	6
8	6	7	5
4	5	6	2
+ 5	+ 3	+ 2	+ 3
34	42	38	31

LESSON 12

"Some and Some More" Problems, Part 1

a. 58
b. 57
c. 87
d. 86
e. 96
f. 95

Patterns:
There were the same number of books in each pile.

Facts Practice: 100 Addition Facts (Test A in Test Masters)

Mental Math: Add a number ending in 9 to another number.

a. 28	**b.** 28	**c.** 37	**d.** 37	**e.** 56	**f.** 56
+ 30	+ 29	+ 50	+ 49	+ 40	+ 39

Patterns: The math books were stacked neatly on the shelf in two piles. Marla glanced at the shelf and knew instantly that there were an even number of books. How did she know?

Many word problems tell a story. Some stories are about **putting things together.** Look at this story.

John had 5 marbles. He bought 7 more marbles. Now John has 12 marbles.

There is a pattern to this story. John had **some** marbles. Then he bought **some more** marbles. When he put the marbles together, he found out the **total** number of marbles. We will call these problems **"some and some more"** problems. In this book we will often use the letters SSM to stand for "some and some more."

PATTERN	PROBLEM
Some	5 marbles
+ Some more	+ 7 marbles
Total	12 marbles ← Largest number

The "some and some more" pattern is an addition pattern. **We remember that the bottom number in an addition pattern is the largest number.** A "some and some more" pattern is shown in the box below. There are six lines and a plus sign. Three of the lines are for numbers. Three of the lines are for words. All the words are the same.

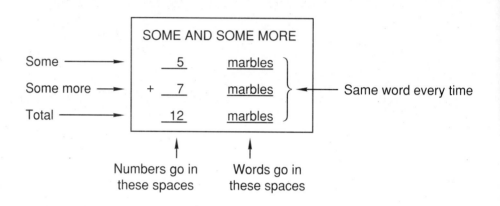

Example 1   Mickey saw 15 rabbits. Then he saw 7 more rabbits. How many rabbits did he see in all?

Solution   This problem has the idea of some and some more. To practice the pattern, we draw six lines and a plus sign.

Some   _____   _____

Some more   + _____   _____

Total   _____   _____

Next, we write "rabbits" in the three spaces on the right.

Some   _____   rabbits

Some more   + _____   rabbits

Total   _____   rabbits

Now we put in the numbers. In the beginning there were 15 rabbits. Then Mickey saw 7 more rabbits.

Some   15   rabbits

Some more   + 7   rabbits

Total N rabbits

Now we must find the missing number. We add 15 and 7 to find the total number.

Some		15	rabbits
Some more	+	7	rabbits
Total		22	rabbits

Mickey saw **22 rabbits** in all.

Example 2   Joan found 5 beans on the floor, 3 beans behind the stove, and 6 beans in the cupboard. How many beans did she find in all?

Solution   This problem puts beans together. There are 5 beans, 3 beans, and 6 beans to put together. This is a "some, and some more, and some more" problem.

Some		5	beans
Some more		3	beans
Some more	+	6	beans
Total		N	beans

If we add 5 beans and 3 beans and 6 beans, we find the total is 14 beans. She found **14 beans** in all.

Practice   Draw the lines and a plus sign to make the "some and some more" pattern for each problem. Then work the problem.

$$\begin{array}{r} 5 \text{ laps} \\ + \ 8 \text{ laps} \\ \hline N \text{ laps} \end{array}$$

a. Diane ran 5 laps in the morning. She ran 8 laps in the afternoon. How many laps did she run in all?   13 laps

$$\begin{array}{r} 3 \text{ pencils} \\ 5 \text{ pencils} \\ + \ 11 \text{ pencils} \\ \hline N \text{ pencils} \end{array}$$

b. Nathan found 3 pencils on the table, 5 pencils behind his desk, and 11 pencils under his bed. Altogether, how many pencils did Nathan find?   19 pencils

Problem set 12

$$\begin{array}{r} 17 \text{ balls} \\ + \ 8 \text{ balls} \\ \hline N \text{ balls} \end{array}$$

1. James had 17 balls. Then his brother gave him 8 more balls. How many balls does James have now? Draw a "some and some more" pattern.   25 balls
(12)

$$\begin{array}{r} 5 \text{ rabbits} \\ 3 \text{ rabbits} \\ + \ 4 \text{ rabbits} \\ \hline N \text{ rabbits} \end{array}$$

2. Samantha saw rabbits in the field. She saw 5 rabbits in the east field. She saw 3 rabbits in the west field. She saw 4 rabbits in the north field. How many rabbits did Samantha see in all? Draw a SSM pattern.   12 rabbits
(12)

3. Use digits to write seven hundred fourteen.   714
(8)

4. Use digits to write three hundred forty-seven.   347
(8)

Use words to write each number:

5. 706   seven hundred six   **6.** 532
(8)   (8)   five hundred thirty-two

7. List five even three-digit numbers that have a 5 in the
(11) tens' place and a 7 in the hundreds' place.
750, 752, 754, 756, 758

8.   4   **9.** B 5   **10.**   9   **11.**   5
(2) N 5   (2)   7   (2) N 0   (2)   2
       $+ 6$ $+ 4$ $+ 3$ $+ C$ 6
       $\overline{15}$ $\overline{16}$ $\overline{12}$ $\overline{13}$

12.   14   **13.**   18   **14.**   17   **15.**   12
(7) $- 7$ (7) $- 9$ (7) $- 5$ (7) $- 6$
        $\overline{7}$ $\overline{9}$ $\overline{12}$ $\overline{6}$

16. $27   **17.** $35   **18.**   28   **19.**   15
(10) $+ \$16$ (10) $+ \$38$ (10) $+ 9$ (10) $+ 8$
        $\overline{\$43}$ $\overline{\$73}$ $\overline{37}$ $\overline{23}$

20. Name the month that is just before the seventh month.
(6)   June

Write the next three numbers in each sequence:

21. 14, 21, 28, __35__ , __42__ , __49__ , ...
(3)

22. 24, 32, 40, __48__ , __56__ , __64__ , ...
(3)

23. 4 + 3 + 7 + 8 + 5 + 6 + 4   37
(1)

24. 2 + 5 + 8 + 7 + 4 + 8 + 2   36
(1)

25. 9 + 3 + 2 + 4 + 6 + 5 + 7   36
(1)

LESSON 13

Number Lines

a. 81
b. 72
c. 53
d. 75
e. 76
f. 91

Patterns:

1	2	3	4	5	6	7	8	9	10
11	12	13	14	15	16	17	18	19	20
21	22	23	24	25	26	27	28	29	30
31	32	33	34	35	36	37	38	39	40
41	42	43	44	45	46	47	48	49	50
51	52	53	54	55	56	57	58	59	60
61	62	63	64	65	66	67	68	69	70
71	72	73	74	75	76	77	78	79	80
81	82	83	84	85	86	87	88	89	90
91	92	93	94	95	96	97	98	99	100

Facts Practice: 100 Addition Facts (Test A in Test Masters)

Mental Math: Add a number ending in 9 to another number.

a. 52 + 29   **b.** 63 + 9   **c.** 14 + 39
d. 26 + 49   **e.** 57 + 19   **f.** 32 + 59

Patterns: This "hundred number chart" lists the whole numbers from 1 to 100. We have shaded the squares on this chart that contain even numbers. On another chart, shade the squares that contain the numbers we say when we count by threes from 3 to 99.

1	2	3	4	5	6	7	8	9	10
11	12	13	14	15	16	17	18	19	20
21	22	23	24	25	26	27	28	29	30
31	32	33	34	35	36	37	38	39	40
41	42	43	44	45	46	47	48	49	50
51	52	53	54	55	56	57	58	59	60
61	62	63	64	65	66	67	68	69	70
71	72	73	74	75	76	77	78	79	80
81	82	83	84	85	86	87	88	89	90
91	92	93	94	95	96	97	98	99	100

(Hundreds chart is available in Test Masters.)

A line continues without end. When we "draw a line" with a pencil, we are actually drawing a **line segment.** A line segment is part of a line.

Line segment

To illustrate a line, we draw an arrowhead at each end of the line segment. The arrowheads show that the line continues.

Line

To make a number line, we begin by drawing a line. Next, we put tick marks on the line, keeping the distance between the marks the same.

Then we label the marks with numbers. On some number lines, every mark is numbered. On other number lines, only some of the marks are numbered. A number on a number line tells us how far the mark is from zero.

Example 1   The arrow is pointing to what number on this number line?

Solution   If we count by ones from zero, our count matches the numbers given on the number line. So we know that the distance from one tick mark to the next tick mark is one.

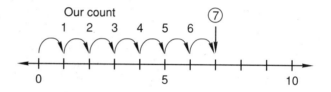

We find that the arrow is pointing to **7**.

On some number lines, the distance from one tick mark to the next is not one. We may need to count by twos or by fives or by tens or by some other number to find the distance between tick marks.

Example 2   The arrow is pointing to what number on this number line?

Solution   If we count by ones from tick mark to tick mark, our count does not match the numbers given on the number line. We try counting by twos and find that our count does match the number line. So the distance from one tick mark to the next tick mark on this number line is two. The arrow is pointing to a mark on the number line that is one mark after 4 and one mark before 8. The number that is two more than 4 and two less than 8 is **6**.

Example 3   The arrow is pointing to what number on this number line?

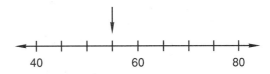

Solution   Zero is not shown on this number line, so we will start our count at 40. Counting by ones from tick mark to tick mark does not fit the pattern. Neither does counting by twos. Counting by fives does fit the pattern. The arrow is pointing to **55.**

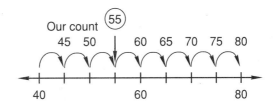

Practice   The arrow is pointing to what number on each number line below?

a.   25

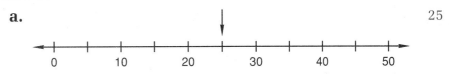

b.   16

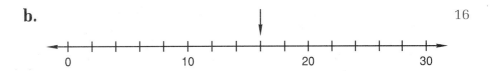

c.   40

d.   85

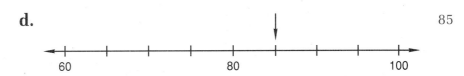

Problem set   **1.** Sandra saw 4 horses at the fair. Then she saw 13
13   (12)   horses on a farm. How many horses did Sandra see in
all? Draw a SSM pattern.   17 horses;   4 horses
                                        + 13 horses
                                          N horses

2. Mickey saw 14 gnomes in the forest and 23 gnomes in
(12)   the valley. How many gnomes did Mickey see in all?
Draw a SSM pattern.   37 gnomes;   14 gnomes
                                   + 23 gnomes
                                     N gnomes

3. Use digits to write six hundred forty-two.   642
(8)

4. Use digits to write three hundred twelve.   312
(8)

5. Use words to write 713.   seven hundred thirteen
(8)

6. List the five odd three-digit numbers that have a 5 in
(11)   the hundreds' place and a 7 in the tens' place.
571, 573, 575, 577, 579

7. To what number is the arrow pointing?   15
(13)

8. All the books were put into two equal stacks. Was the
(11)   number of books an odd number or an even number?
even number

9. (2)	**10.** (2)	**11.** (2)	**12.** (2)
5	N 7	7	M 4
B 6	5	A 1	2
+ 7	+ 3	+ 4	+ 8
18	15	12	14

13. (7)	**14.** (7)	**15.** (7)	**16.** (7)
12	14	12	13
− 3	− 7	− 8	− 6
9	7	4	7

17. (10)	**18.** (10)	**19.** (10)	**20.** (10)
74	93	28	28
+ 18	+ 39	+ 45	+ 47
92	132	73	75

Write the next three numbers in each sequence:

21. 12, 15, 18, __21__ , __24__ , __27__ , ...
(3)

22. 30, 36, 42, __48__ , __54__ , __60__ , ...
(3)

23. The numbers 5, 9, and 14 are a fact family. Write two
(7) addition facts and two subtraction facts using these
three numbers.
5 + 9 = 14, 9 + 5 = 14, 14 − 5 = 9, 14 − 9 = 5

24.   4   **25.**   4
(1)   3   (1)   3
             5   6
             8   7
             7   8
             6   4
          + 2   + 3
          ——   ——
            35   35

**LESSON
14**

Missing Numbers in Subtraction

a. 90
b. 93
c. 55
d. 92
e. 92
f. 55
Problem Solving:
  24 books

Facts Practice: 100 Addition Facts (Test A in Test Masters)

Mental Math: Review.
  a. 30 + 60   b. 74 + 19   c. 46 + 9
  d. 63 + 29   e. 42 + 50   f. 16 + 39

Problem Solving: There were more than 20 math books on the
shelf but fewer than 30. Todd arranged the
books into two equal piles, and then he
rearranged the books into three equal piles.
Use these clues to figure out how many
math books were on the shelf.

Since Lesson 1 we have practiced finding missing
numbers in addition problems. In this lesson we will
practice finding missing numbers in subtraction problems.

Remember that we "subtract down" to find the bottom number and "add up" to find the top number.

SUBTRACT DOWN:				**ADD UP:**
Nine minus six equals three.	↓	$\begin{array}{r} 9 \\ -6 \\ \hline 3 \end{array}$	↑	Three plus six equals nine.

We may use either "subtracting down" or "adding up" to find a missing number in a subtraction problem.

Example 1   Find the missing number:
$$\begin{array}{r} 14 \\ -\ N \\ \hline 6 \end{array}$$

Solution   We may either "subtract down" or "add up." Which way seems easier?

SUBTRACT DOWN:				**ADD UP:**
Fourteen minus what number equals six?	↓	$\begin{array}{r} 14 \\ -\ N \\ \hline 6 \end{array}$	↑	Six plus what number equals fourteen?

Often it is easier to find a missing number in a subtraction problem by "adding up." If we add 8 to 6, we get 14. So the missing number is **8.** We can check our answer by subtracting.

$$\begin{array}{r} 14 \\ -\ 8 \\ \hline 6 \end{array} \quad \text{check}$$

Since 14 − 8 = 6, we know our answer is correct.

Example 2   Find the missing number:
$$\begin{array}{r} B \\ -\ 5 \\ \hline 7 \end{array}$$

Solution   Try both "subtracting down" and "adding up."

SUBTRACT DOWN:				**ADD UP:**
What number minus five equals seven?	↓	$\begin{array}{r} B \\ -\ 5 \\ \hline 7 \end{array}$	↑	Seven plus five equals what number?

Since 7 plus 5 is 12, the missing number must be 12. We rewrite the original problem using 12 to check the answer.

$$
\begin{array}{r}
12 \\
-\ 5 \\
\hline
7 \quad \text{check}
\end{array}
$$

The answer checks. The missing number is **12.**

Practice Find each missing digit. Check your answer.

a.
$$
\begin{array}{r}
14 \\
-\ N \quad 8 \\
\hline
6
\end{array}
$$

b.
$$
\begin{array}{r}
N \quad 7 \\
-\ 5 \\
\hline
2
\end{array}
$$

c.
$$
\begin{array}{r}
9 \\
-\ N \quad 7 \\
\hline
2
\end{array}
$$

d.
$$
\begin{array}{r}
N \quad 12 \\
-\ 7 \\
\hline
5
\end{array}
$$

Problem set 14

42 acorns
+ 37 acorns
N acorns

1. Jimmy found forty-two acorns in the forest. Then he
(12) found thirty-seven acorns in his backyard. How many acorns did he find in all? Draw a SSM pattern.
79 acorns

2. At first thirty-five fairies were flying about. Later,
(12) twenty-seven more fairies began to fly about. In all, how many fairies were flying about? Draw a SSM pattern.   62 fairies; $\dfrac{35 \text{ fairies}}{+\ 27 \text{ fairies}}$
N fairies

3. Use digits to write the number seven hundred fifteen.
(8)   715

4. Use words to write 603.   six hundred three
(8)

5. Nathan was born on the seventh day of June in 1990.
(6)   Write his birth date in month/day/year form.   6/7/90

6. Write the largest three-digit number that has a 6 in the
(5)   ones' place and a 4 in the tens' place.   946

7. To what number is the arrow pointing?   70
(13)

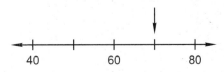

8.   5
(2)
      N   4
   + 6
   ─────
     15

9.   A   8
(2)
      2
   + 5
   ─────
     15

10.   7
(2)
       2
   + N   6
   ─────
     15

11.   4
(2)
      A   9
   + 2
   ─────
     15

12.   N   14
(14)
   − 6
   ─────
      8

13.   16
(7)
   − 8
   ─────
      8

14.   14
(7)
   − 7
   ─────
      7

15.   12
(14)
   − A   5
   ─────
      7

16.   B   12
(14)
   − 6
   ─────
      6

17.   13
(14)
   − C   5
   ─────
      8

18. $48
(10)
   + $16
   ─────
     $64

19. $37
(10)
   + $14
   ─────
     $51

Write the next three numbers in each sequence:

20. 28, 35, 42, __49__ , __56__ , __63__ , ...
(3)

21. 18, 21, 24, __27__ , __30__ , __33__ , ...
(3)

22. How many cents is nine nickels? Count by fives.
(3)   45 cents

23.   2
(1)
      3
      5
      7
      4
      8
   + 2
   ─────
     31

24.   2
(1)
      5
      7
      3
      5
      8
   + 4
   ─────
     34

25.   7
(1)
      3
      8
      5
      4
      3
   + 2
   ─────
     32

LESSON 15

Comparing Numbers

Patterns:

a. 700
b. 900
c. 550
d. 92
e. 73
f. 77

Patterns:

1	2	3	4	5	6	7	8	9	10
11	12	13	14	15	16	17	18	19	20
21	22	23	24	25	26	27	28	29	30
31	32	33	34	35	36	37	38	39	40
41	42	43	44	45	46	47	48	49	50
51	52	53	54	55	56	57	58	59	60
61	62	63	64	65	66	67	68	69	70
71	72	73	74	75	76	77	78	79	80
81	82	83	84	85	86	87	88	89	90
91	92	93	94	95	96	97	98	99	100

All shaded squares contain even numbers.

Facts Practice: 100 Addition Facts (Test A in Test Masters)

Mental Math: Add a number ending in two zeros to another number.

  a. 300 + 400   **b.** 600 + 300   **c.** 250 + 300

Review:

  d. 63 + 29   **e.** 54 + 19   **f.** 28 + 49

Patterns: Shade the squares on a hundred number chart that contain the numbers we say when we count by fours from 4 to 100. Which of the shaded squares also contain even numbers?

When we compare two numbers, we decide whether one number is greater than, equal to, or less than another number.

> Three **is equal to** three.
>
> Three **is less than** four.
>
> Four **is greater than** three.

The three sentences above compare two numbers. We may use digits and symbols to write the same sentences. We use the **equal sign** to show that two numbers are equal.

> 3 = 3   is read   "Three is equal to three."

We use the **greater than/less than** symbol to show the comparison for two numbers that are not equal.

> \>   <

The pointed end points to the smaller number. We read from left to right. If the pointed end comes first, we say "less than."

> 3 < 4   is read   "Three is less than four."

If the open end comes first, we say "greater than."

> 4 > 3   is read   "Four is greater than three."

Example 1   Use digits and a comparison symbol to write "Five is greater than four."

Solution   The pointed end must point to the smaller number.

$$5 > 4$$

Example 2   Compare the following numbers by replacing the circle with the proper comparison symbol:

$$12 \bigcirc 21$$

Solution   We use the greater than/less than symbol. Since 12 is less than 21, we let the pointed end point to 12.

$$12 < 21$$

We read this by saying "Twelve is less than twenty-one."

Example 3   Which of these numbers is the greatest?

$$123 \qquad 231 \qquad 213$$

Solution   All of these numbers have the same digits, but their values are different because the place values are different. The greatest (largest) of these three numbers is **231.**

Example 4   Arrange these numbers in order from the least to the greatest:

$$640 \qquad 406 \qquad 460$$

Solution   The least (smallest) is 406. The greatest is 640. Arranging the numbers in order, we write:

$$406 \qquad 460 \qquad 640$$

Practice   Write each statement using digits and a comparison symbol:

    a. Thirteen is less than thirty.   13 < 30

    b. Forty is greater than fourteen.   40 > 14

Replace each circle with the proper symbol:

c. 432 $\gtrless$ 324   **d.** 212 $\lessgtr$ 221   **e.** 316 $\eqcirc$ 316

f. Arrange the numbers 132, 123, and 213 in order from the least to the greatest.   123, 132, 213

Problem set 15

1. Forty-two students had red hair. Thirty-seven students did not have red hair. How many students were there in all? Draw a SSM pattern.   79 students;
(12)

$$\begin{array}{r} 42 \text{ students} \\ + 37 \text{ students} \\ \hline N \text{ students} \end{array}$$

$$\begin{array}{r} 17 \text{ students} \\ + 47 \text{ students} \\ \hline N \text{ students} \end{array}$$

2. Seventeen brave students rode the loop-o-plane at the fair. Forty-seven others just watched. How many students were there altogether? Draw a SSM pattern.
(12)
64 students

3. Use digits to write the number six hundred forty-two.
(8)
642

4. Use words to write the number 502.   five hundred two
(8)

5. Use digits and a comparison symbol to write "Fourteen is greater than seven."
(15)
14 > 7

6. Compare: 16 $\gtrless$ 12
(15)

7. To what number is the arrow pointing?   30
(13)

8. $\begin{array}{r} 4 \\ N \\ + 5 \\ \hline 13 \end{array}$ 4
(2)

9. $\begin{array}{r} N \\ 6 \\ + 2 \\ \hline 9 \end{array}$ 1
(2)

10. $\begin{array}{r} 5 \\ 2 \\ + P \\ \hline 14 \end{array}$ 7
(2)

11. $\begin{array}{r} 3 \\ 5 \\ + K \\ \hline 16 \end{array}$ 8
(2)

12. $\begin{array}{r} C \\ - 5 \\ \hline 7 \end{array}$ 12
(14)

13. $\begin{array}{r} 17 \\ - 9 \\ \hline 8 \end{array}$
(7)

14. $\begin{array}{r} 12 \\ - 6 \\ \hline 6 \end{array}$
(7)

15. $\begin{array}{r} 9 \\ - A \\ \hline 4 \end{array}$ 5
(14)

16. $\begin{array}{r} 37 \\ + 28 \\ \hline 65 \end{array}$
(10)

17. $\begin{array}{r} 36 \\ + 40 \\ \hline 76 \end{array}$
(9)

18. $\begin{array}{r} \$68 \\ + \$27 \\ \hline \$95 \end{array}$
(10)

19. $\begin{array}{r} \$49 \\ + \$24 \\ \hline \$73 \end{array}$
(10)

Write the next three numbers in each sequence:

20. 18, 27, 36, __45__ , __54__ , __63__ , ...
(3)

21. 32, 40, 48, __56__ , __64__ , __72__ , ...
(3)

22. 20, 24, 28, __32__ , __36__ , __40__ , ...
(3)

23. Todd wrote his birth date as 9/10/85. Rewrite Todd's
(6) birth date naming the month he was born and writing
the full year.   September 10, 1985

24. The numbers 7, 8, and 15 are a fact family. Write two
(7) addition facts and two subtraction facts using these
three numbers.
7 + 8 = 15, 8 + 7 = 15, 15 − 7 = 8, 15 − 8 = 7

25. 2 + 5 + 7 + 6 + 5 + 4   29
(1)

LESSON 16

Adding Three-Digit Numbers

a. 900
b. 920
c. 354
d. 93
e. 64
f. 46
Patterns:

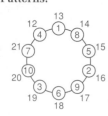

Facts Practice: 100 Addition Facts (Test A in Test Masters)

Mental Math: Add a number ending in two zeros to another
number.

   a. 400 + 500   **b.** 600 + 320   **c.** 254 + 100

Review:

   d. 64 + 29   **e.** 39 + 25   **f.** 19 + 27

Patterns: Copy this design of ten circles on
your paper, following the same
pattern as in Lesson 5. Then,
outside each circle, write the sum of
the numbers in that circle and in
the two circles next to that circle.
For example, the number outside of
circle 1 should be 13.

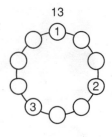

---

*Andrea had $675. When Denise landed on
Andrea's property, Denise paid Andrea $175 rent.
Then how much money did Andrea have?*

We will use bills to add $175 to $675. The sum is 7 hundreds, 14 tens, and 10 ones.

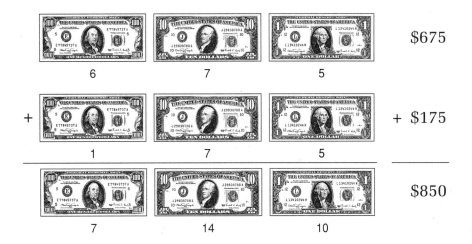

If we exchange 10 ones for 1 ten and 10 tens for 1 hundred, we will have 8 hundreds, 5 tens, and no ones, which is $850.

Using pencil and paper, we add the ones and regroup, add the tens and regroup, and then add the hundreds.

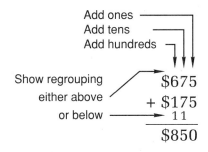

Example   Add: 456
             + 374

Solution   We begin by adding the digits in the ones' column. Then we move one column at a time to the left, writing the first digit of two-digit answers either above or below the next place column. The sum is **830.**

$$\begin{array}{r} 11 \\ 456 \\ + 374 \\ \hline 830 \end{array}$$

Practice

a.
$$\begin{array}{r} \$579 \\ + \$186 \\ \hline \$765 \end{array}$$

b.
$$\begin{array}{r} 408 \\ + 243 \\ \hline 651 \end{array}$$

c.
$$\begin{array}{r} \$498 \\ + \ \$89 \\ \hline \$587 \end{array}$$

d. $458 + 336$ 794 **e.** $56 + 569$ 625

Problem set 16

77 students
+ 19 students
N students

1. Seventy-seven students ran in circles and waved their
(12) arms. Nineteen students watched in amazement. How
many students were there in all? Draw a SSM
pattern.   96 students

75 birds
+ 38 birds
N birds

2. The king counted seventy-five birds on the way to the
(12) fair. The queen counted thirty-eight birds on the way
home. How many birds did the king and queen count
in all? Draw a SSM pattern.   113 birds

3. Use words to write the number 913.
(8) nine hundred thirteen

4. Use digits to write the number seven hundred forty-
(8) three.   743

5. Use digits and a comparison symbol to write
(15) "Seventy-five is less than ninety-eight."   75 < 98

6. Compare: 413 $\bigcirc{>}$ 314
(15)

7. The numbers 7, 9, and 16 are a fact family. Write two
(7) addition facts and two subtraction facts using these
three numbers.
7 + 9 = 16, 9 + 7 = 16, 16 − 7 = 9, 16 − 9 = 7

8. To what number is the arrow pointing?   84
(13)

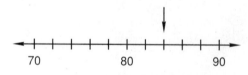

9.
(16)
$$\begin{array}{r} \$475 \\ + \$332 \\ \hline \$807 \end{array}$$

10.
(16)
$$\begin{array}{r} \$714 \\ + \$226 \\ \hline \$940 \end{array}$$

11.
(16)
$$\begin{array}{r} 743 \\ + 187 \\ \hline 930 \end{array}$$

12.
(16)
$$\begin{array}{r} 576 \\ + 228 \\ \hline 804 \end{array}$$

13.
(2)
$$\begin{array}{r} 8 \\ 5 \\ + K \quad 4 \\ \hline 17 \end{array}$$

14.
(2)
$$\begin{array}{r} 4 \\ N \quad 5 \\ + 6 \\ \hline 15 \end{array}$$

15.
(2)
$$\begin{array}{r} 9 \\ A \quad 2 \\ + 6 \\ \hline 17 \end{array}$$

16.
(2)
$$\begin{array}{r} N \quad 6 \\ 3 \\ + 7 \\ \hline 16 \end{array}$$

17. (14)
$$\begin{array}{r} 8 \\ - N \quad 6 \\ \hline 2 \end{array}$$

18. (7)
$$\begin{array}{r} 17 \\ - 8 \\ \hline 9 \end{array}$$

19. (7)
$$\begin{array}{r} 13 \\ - 7 \\ \hline 6 \end{array}$$

20. (14)
$$\begin{array}{r} N \quad 15 \\ - 8 \\ \hline 7 \end{array}$$

21. (14)
$$\begin{array}{r} 14 \\ - N \quad 8 \\ \hline 6 \end{array}$$

22. (14)
$$\begin{array}{r} 16 \\ - A \quad 7 \\ \hline 9 \end{array}$$

23. (14)
$$\begin{array}{r} N \quad 16 \\ - 9 \\ \hline 7 \end{array}$$

24. (10)
$$\begin{array}{r} \$49 \\ + \$76 \\ \hline \$125 \end{array}$$

25. (3) Write the next three numbers in this sequence:

28, 35, 42, __49__, __56__, __63__, ...

LESSON
17

"Some and Some More" Problems, Part 2

a. 90
b. 900
c. 9
d. 55
e. 66
f. 73

Patterns:

1	2	3	4	5	6	7	8	9	10
11	12	13	14	15	16	17	18	19	20
21	22	23	24	25	26	27	28	29	30
31	32	33	34	35	36	37	38	39	40
41	42	43	44	45	46	47	48	49	50
51	52	53	54	55	56	57	58	59	60
61	62	63	64	65	66	67	68	69	70
71	72	73	74	75	76	77	78	79	80
81	82	83	84	85	86	87	88	89	90
91	92	93	94	95	96	97	98	99	100

10, 20, 30, 40, 50, 60, 70, 80, 90, 100

Facts Practice: 100 Subtraction Facts (Test B in Test Masters)

Mental Math: Add three numbers.
  a. 30 + 40 + 20   **b.** 300 + 400 + 200   **c.** 3 + 4 + 2

Review:
  d. 36 + 19   **e.** 39 + 27   **f.** 44 + 29

Patterns: The multiples of 5 are 5, 10, 15, 20, and so on. Shade the squares on a hundred number chart that contain a multiple of 5. Which of the shaded squares also contain even numbers?

We have been working problems that have a "some and some more" thinking pattern. In the problems we have worked so far, both the "some" number and the "some more" number were given. We add these numbers to find the total. If we have 5 marbles and get 7 more marbles, we will have 12 marbles in all.

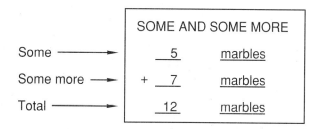

To review, we look at this thinking pattern carefully. The largest number is the total number. The largest number is at the bottom of the pattern.

Sometimes a "some and some more" problem gives us the total number and one other number. Then we must find the missing number. These problems are just like addition problems that have a missing addend.

Example 1   Walter had 8 marbles. Then Sam gave him some more marbles. He has 17 marbles now. How many marbles did Sam give him?

Solution   **If we can recognize the pattern, we can solve the problem.** Walter had some marbles. Then he received some more marbles. This problem has a "some and some more" pattern. We know the "some" number. We know the total number. We put these numbers in the pattern. In a "some and some more" pattern, the bottom number is the largest number. **The sum of the two addends must equal the bottom number.**

Some	8	marbles
Some more	+ N	marbles
Total	17	marbles

We see that this time one of the addends is missing. One way to find the missing number is to ask an addition question.

"Eight plus what number equals seventeen?"

$$\begin{array}{r} 8 \\ + N \\ \hline 17 \end{array}$$

Another way is to ask a subtraction question.

"Seventeen minus eight equals what number?"

$$\begin{array}{r} 17 \\ - 8 \\ \hline N \end{array}$$

Both answers are **9 marbles.**

The key to the problem is recognizing the pattern. Then finding the answer is easy!

Example 2 Jamie had some pies. Then Frank gave her 5 more pies. Now she has 12 pies. How many pies did Jamie have at first?

Solution This is a "some and some more" story problem. We fill in the pattern.

Some	N	pies
Some more	+ 5	pies
Total	12	pies

Finding the answer is easy now. We can find the missing number by asking an addition question or by asking a subtraction question.

"Five added to what number equals twelve?"   (7)

"Twelve minus five equals what number?"   (7)

At first Jamie had **7 pies.**

Practice Draw the lines to make a "some and some more" pattern for each problem. Then work the problem.

4 marigolds
+ *N* marigolds
17 marigolds

a. Lucille had 4 marigolds. Jim gave her some more marigolds. Now she has 17 marigolds. How many marigolds did Jim give Lucille?   13 marigolds

N agates
+ 8 agates
15 agates

b. Sid had some agates. Then he found 8 more agates. Now he has 15 agates. How many agates did he have at first?   7 agates

Problem set 17

11 towheads
+ 32 towheads
N towheads

1. There were 11 towheads in the hall. There were 32 towheads in the room. How many towheads were there in all? Draw a SSM pattern.   43 towheads
(12)

8 birds
+ *N* birds
17 birds

2. Christy saw 8 birds in the backyard. Then she saw some more birds in the front yard. She saw 17 birds in all. How many birds did she see in the front yard? Draw a SSM pattern.   9 birds
(17)

3. Think of any even number and think of any odd number. Then add the numbers. Is the sum even or odd? Try another even number and another odd number. Is the sum even or odd?   odd; odd
(11)

4. Use words to write the number 904.   nine hundred four
(8)

5. Use digits to write five hundred eleven.   511
(8)

6. Compare: 906 ⊙ 609
(15)

7. 6 + 5 + N + 3 + 2 + 1 = 20   3
(2)

8. To what number is the arrow pointing?   170
(13)

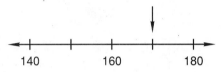

9. $693   **10.** $108   **11.**   524   **12.**   416
(16) + $148   (16)   + $699   (16)   + 219   (16)   + 328
      ———   ———   ———   ———
      $841 $807   743   744

13.   N   7   **14.**   4   **15.**   7   **16.**   5
(14)   − 2   (1)   + A   4   (1)   + P   6   (14)   − K   4
        ———   ———   ———   ———
         5   8   13   1

17.   12   **18.**   15   **19.**   4   **20.**   C   3
(14)   − P   5   (14)   − X   6   (2)   N   5   (2)   5
        ———   ———   + 6   + 7
         7   9   ———   ———
                                                  15   15

21. How many sides are on seven triangles? Count by
(3)   threes.   21 sides

22. Write a number sentence for this picture.
(1)   3 + 4 + 5 = 12

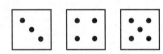

23. What month is two months after the eleventh month?
(6)   January

24. The numbers 6, 7, and 13 are a fact family. Write two
(7)   addition facts and two subtraction facts using these
      three numbers.
      6 + 7 = 13, 7 + 6 = 13, 13 − 6 = 7, 13 − 7 = 6

25. Write the next three numbers in this sequence:
(3)

    42, 35, 28, __21__ , __14__ , __7__ , ...

LESSON 18

Subtracting Without Regrouping • Missing Two-Digit Addends

a. 900 b. 540 c. 65
d. 84 e. 95 f. 73
Patterns:

The pattern is 1, skip, skip, 2, etc. Outside each circle is the sum of the numbers in that circle and the two circles next to that circle.

Facts Practice: 100 Subtraction Facts (Test B in Test Masters)

Mental Math: Add three numbers.

   a. 200 + 300 + 400 **b.** 240 + 200 + 100 **c.** 36 + 20 + 9

Review:

   d. 45 + 10 + 29   **e.** 56 + 20 + 19   **f.** 24 + 39 + 10

Patterns: Design a pattern of numbered circles like those in Lessons 5 and 16 using seven circles instead of ten. Describe the pattern to a classmate or write a description.

Subtracting without regrouping

By carefully looking at the numbers in a subtraction problem, we can see if regrouping is necessary. Regrouping is necessary if the ones' digit of the bottom number is greater than the ones' digit of the top number. Which of these two subtractions can be done without regrouping?

$$\begin{array}{r} \$54 \\ -\ \$23 \\ \hline \end{array} \qquad \begin{array}{r} \$53 \\ -\ \$24 \\ \hline \end{array}$$

The subtraction in the left-hand example can be done without regrouping because the bottom ones' digit, 3, is less than the top ones' digit, 4. However, to subtract the numbers in the right-hand example, regrouping is necessary because the 4 is greater than the 3.

$$\begin{array}{r} \$54 \\ -\ \$23 \\ \hline \$31 \end{array} \qquad \begin{array}{r} \$53 \\ -\ \$24 \\ \hline ? \end{array}$$

In this lesson, we will practice subtracting when regrouping is not necessary.

Example 1 Subtract 123 from 365.

Solution Order matters when we subtract. We begin with 365 and subtract 123. When we subtract three-digit numbers with pencil and paper, we subtract the ones first. Then we subtract the tens. Then we subtract the hundreds.

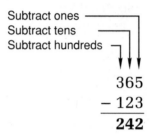

Example 2 Subtract thirty-two from eighty-five.

Solution We write the numbers using digits. We show two forms.

$$\begin{array}{r} 85 \\ -\ 32 \\ \hline \textbf{53} \end{array} \qquad 85 - 32 = \textbf{53}$$

Missing two-digit addends The missing addend in this problem has two digits. We can find the missing addend one digit at a time.

Tens' column ⌐⌐ Ones' column

Five plus what number is nine?
Answer: 4

$$\begin{array}{r} 56 \\ +\ \_\_ \\ \hline 98 \end{array}$$

Six plus what number is eight?
Answer: 2

The missing digits are 4 and 2. So the missing addend is 42.

Example 3
$$\begin{array}{r} 36 \\ +\ W \\ \hline 87 \end{array}$$

Solution The letter W stands for a two-digit number. We find the missing digit in the ones' place, and then the missing digit in the tens' place.

$$\begin{array}{r} W \\ +\ 36 \\ \hline 87 \end{array}$$

One plus six is seven.
Five plus three is eight.

The missing addend is **51**.

Practice

a. 485 − 242   243   **b.** $56 − $33 $23

c. Subtract 53 from 97.   44

d. Subtract twenty-three from fifty-four.   31

e.
$$\begin{array}{r} 24 \\ + \ Q \\ \hline 65 \end{array}$$ 41

f.
$$\begin{array}{r} M \\ + 31 \\ \hline 67 \end{array}$$ 36

Problem set 18

42 red surfboards
+ 17 red surfboards
 N red surfboards

4 green grasshoppers
+ N green grasshoppers
11 green grasshoppers

1. Forty-two red surfboards were on the first wave.
(12) Seventeen red surfboards were on the second wave. How many red surfboards were on the first two waves? Draw a SSM pattern.   59 red surfboards

2. Mindy saw four green grasshoppers in the first hour.
(17) In the second hour she saw some more green grasshoppers. She saw eleven green grasshoppers in all. How many green grasshoppers did she see in the second hour? Draw a SSM pattern.   7 green grasshoppers

3. Use the digits 1, 2, and 3 once each to name an even
(11) number less than 200.   132

4. Use words to write the number 915.
(8) nine hundred fifteen

5. Subtract seven hundred thirteen from eight hundred
(18) twenty-four.   111

6. Compare: 704 ⃝> 407
(15)

7. What is the total number of days in the first two
(6) months of a common year?   59 days

8. To what number is the arrow pointing?   45
(13)

9.
(16)
$$\begin{array}{r} \$346 \\ + \$298 \\ \hline \$644 \end{array}$$

10.
(16)
$$\begin{array}{r} 499 \\ + 275 \\ \hline 774 \end{array}$$

11.
(16)
$$\begin{array}{r} \$421 \\ + \$389 \\ \hline \$810 \end{array}$$

12.
(16)
$$\begin{array}{r} 506 \\ + 210 \\ \hline 716 \end{array}$$

13. $\quad$ $438 $\quad$ **14.** $\quad$ 17 $\quad$ **15.** $\quad$ 7 $\quad$ **16.** $\quad$ 5
(18) $\quad$ − $206 $\quad\quad$ (14) $\quad$ − A $\quad$ 8 $\quad$ (1) $\quad$ + B $\quad$ 7 $\quad$ (14) $\quad$ − C $\quad$ 3
$\qquad$ $232 $\qquad\qquad$ 9 $\qquad\qquad$ 14 $\qquad\qquad$ 2

17. $\quad$ 8 $\quad$ **18.** $\quad$ 15 $\quad$ **19.** $\quad$ 3 $\quad$ **20.** $\quad$ 476
(1) $\quad$ + D $\quad$ 7 $\quad$ (14) $\quad$ − K $\quad$ 6 $\quad$ (2) $\quad$ N $\quad$ 8 $\quad$ (18) $\quad$ − 252
$\qquad$ 15 $\qquad\qquad$ 9 $\qquad\qquad$ + 2 $\qquad\qquad$ 224
$\qquad\qquad\qquad\qquad\qquad\qquad\qquad$ 13

21. $\quad$ 47 $\quad$ **22.** $\quad$ 28 $\quad$ **23.** $\quad$ 75 $\quad$ **24.** $\quad$ 24
(18) $\quad$ − 16 $\quad$ (18) $\quad$ − 13 $\quad$ (18) $\quad$ + T $\quad$ 12 $\quad$ (18) $\quad$ + E $\quad$ 43
$\qquad$ 31 $\qquad\qquad$ 15 $\qquad\qquad$ 87 $\qquad\qquad$ 67

25. Write the next three numbers in this sequence:
(3)
$$81, 72, 63, \underline{\quad 54 \quad}, \underline{\quad 45 \quad}, \underline{\quad 36 \quad}, \ldots$$

LESSON 19

a. 650
b. 75
c. 94
d. 83
e. 66
f. 627
Patterns:

Subtracting Two-Digit Numbers with Regrouping

Facts Practice: 100 Subtraction Facts (Test B in Test Masters)

Mental Math: Review.

a. 250 + 300 + 100 $\quad$ **b.** 20 + 36 + 19 $\qquad$ **c.** 76 + 9 + 9
d. 64 + 9 + 10 $\qquad\quad$ **e.** 27 + 19 + 20 $\qquad$ **f.** 427 + 200

Patterns: On this hundred number chart we began circling the multiples of three. We drew an "X" on the multiples of four. The number 12 has both a circle and an X. On another chart, finish the pattern. Then shade the boxes that have numbers with both a circle and an X.

Roberto had $53. He spent $24 to buy a jacket. Then how much money did Roberto have?

We will use pictures of bills to help us understand this problem.

Roberto had $53.

He spent

Then he had .

This picture shows tha⎯⎯⎯⎯⎯⎯⎯⎯⎯⎯⎯⎯⎯⎯⎯⎯es and that he needs to take fr⎯⎯⎯⎯⎯⎯⎯⎯⎯⎯⎯⎯⎯ones. We see that Roberto has enough ⎯⎯⎯⎯⎯⎯⎯⎯enough ones. To get more ones, Roberto needs ⎯⎯⎯e 1 ten for 10 ones.

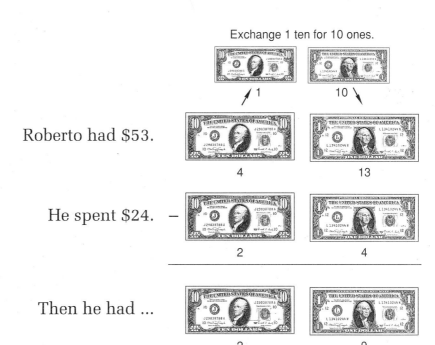

Exchange 1 ten for 10 ones.

Roberto had $53.

He spent $24. —

Then he had ...

After trading 1 ten for 10 ones, Roberto has 4 tens and 13 ones. Then he could take 2 tens and 4 ones from his money to pay for the jacket. That leaves him with 2 tens and 9 ones, which is $29.

Trading 1 ten for 10 ones is an example of **regrouping** or **exchanging** or **borrowing**. We often need to regroup when we subtract using pencil and paper.

Example   Find the difference: 56 − 29

Solution   We write the first number on top and see that we need to regroup.

$$\begin{array}{r} 56 \\ -\ 29 \\ \hline ? \end{array}$$

We understand that 56 means 50 and 6 and that 29 means 20 and 9. Since 6 is less than 9, we need to regroup before we subtract. We take 10 from 50 and add that 10 to the 6.

Take 10 from 50, leaving 40.

Add 10 to 6, making 16.

$$\begin{array}{r} \overset{40}{\cancel{5}0} \text{ and } \overset{1}{6} \\ -\ 20 \text{ and } 9 \\ \hline 20 \text{ and } 7 \end{array}$$

This makes 56 into 40 and 16, which is still equal to 56. Now we subtract and get 20 and 7, which is **27.** This is how we usually show the regrouping.

$$\begin{array}{r} \overset{4}{\cancel{5}}\,\overset{1}{6} \\ -\ 2\ 9 \\ \hline 2\ 7 \end{array}$$

Practice   Use bills or draw pictures to show these subtractions:

a. $\begin{array}{r} \$53 \\ -\ \$29 \\ \hline \$24 \end{array}$ (see lesson for illustration)

b. $\begin{array}{r} \$56 \\ -\ \$27 \\ \hline \$29 \end{array}$ (see lesson for illustration)

Use pencil and paper to find each difference:

c. 63 − 36   27

d. 40 − 13   27

Problem set 19

618 acorns
+ 117 acorns
 N acorns

16 knights
+ N knights
76 knights

1. Jimmy found six hundred eighteen acorns under one
(12) tree. He found one hundred seventeen acorns under
another tree. How many acorns did Jimmy find in all?
Draw a SSM pattern.   735 acorns

2. On the first day Richard the Lion-Hearted had sixteen
(17) knights. On the second day some more knights came.
Then he had seventy-six knights. How many knights
came on the second day? Draw a SSM pattern.
60 knights

3. Use the digits 3, 6, and 7 once each to write an even
(11) number less than 400.   376

4. Use words to write the number 605.   six hundred five
(8)

5. The smallest odd two-digit number is 11. What is the
(11) smallest even two-digit number?   10

6. Compare: 75 (>) 57
(15)

7. Subtract 245 from 375.   130
(18)

8. To what number is the arrow pointing?   34
(13)

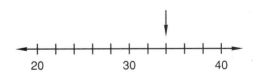

9. $426
(16) + $298
       —————
       $724

10. $278
(16)   + $456
        —————
        $734

11.   721
(16) + 189
      ————
      910

12.   409
(16) + 198
      ————
      607

13.   D   5
(1)   + 7
      ————
      12

14.   18
(14)   − A   9
       ————
       9

15.   8
(1)   + B   4
      ————
      12

16.   C   5
(14)   − 4
       ————
       1

17. $456
(18)   − $120
        —————
        $336

18. $54
(19)   − $27
        —————
        $27

19.   46
(19)   − 28
       ————
       18

20.   35
(19)   − 16
       ————
       19

21. What is the total number of days in the last two
(6) months of the year?   61 days

22. The numbers 5, 6, and 11 are a fact family. Write four
 (7)   addition/subtraction facts using these three numbers.
      5 + 6 = 11, 6 + 5 = 11, 11 − 6 = 5, 11 − 5 = 6

23. 3 + 6 + 7 + 5 + 4 + 8   33
 (1)

Write the next three numbers in each sequence:

24. 81, 72, 63, __54__, __45__, __36__, ...
 (3)

25. 14, 21, 28, __35__, __42__, __49__, ...
 (3)

**LESSON
20**

a. 127
b. 263
c. 348
d. 245
e. 164
f. 377
g. 8; 5; 4; 7; 9
Problem Solving:
   3 nickels and
   1 dime

Expanded Form • More on Missing Numbers in Subtraction

Facts Practice: 100 Addition Facts (Test A in Test Masters)

Mental Math: Add a number ending in two zeros to a two-
              digit number.

a. 27 + 100   **b.** 63 + 200
c. 28 + 20 + 300   **d.** 36 + 9 + 200
e. 45 + 19 + 100   **f.** 48 + 29 + 300
g. What number should be added to each of these numbers
    for the total to be 10: 2, 5, 6, 3, 1?

Problem Solving: Bob had four coins in his pocket totaling
                25¢. What coins did Bob have in his
                pocket?

**Expanded
form**

The number 365 means

   3 hundreds and 6 tens and 5 ones

We can write this as

$$300 + 60 + 5$$

This is the expanded form of 365.

Example 1   Write 275 in expanded form.

Solution   **200 + 70 + 5**

Example 2 Write 407 in expanded form.

Solution There are no tens. We write

$$400 + 7$$

More on missing numbers in subtraction We have found missing numbers in subtraction problems by "subtracting down" or "adding up." We can use these methods when subtracting numbers with one, two, or more digits.

SUBTRACTING DOWN:

$$\begin{array}{r} 56 \\ - W \\ \hline 14 \end{array}$$

We ask ourselves:

"Six minus what number is four?"

"Five minus what number is one?"

We find that the missing number is 42.

ADDING UP:

$$\begin{array}{r} N \\ - 56 \\ \hline 23 \end{array}$$

We add up:

"Three plus six is nine."

"Two plus five is seven."

The missing number is 79.

In this lesson we will practice another method for finding missing numbers in subtraction problems. Look for a pattern in each pair of subtraction facts shown here.

$$\begin{array}{cc} 12 & 12 \\ -\ 5 & -\ 7 \\ \hline 7 & 5 \end{array} \qquad \begin{array}{cc} 15 & 15 \\ -\ 6 & -\ 9 \\ \hline 9 & 6 \end{array} \qquad \begin{array}{cc} 23 & 23 \\ -\ 11 & -\ 12 \\ \hline 12 & 11 \end{array}$$

Notice that in each subtraction fact two numbers can be reversed. We may use this pattern to help us find missing numbers in subtraction problems.

Example 3 Find the missing number:
$$\begin{array}{r} 64 \\ - W \\ \hline 36 \end{array}$$

Solution We will reverse the two lower numbers.

$$\begin{array}{r} 64 \\ - W \\ \hline 36 \end{array} \times \begin{array}{r} 64 \\ - 36 \\ \hline W \end{array}$$

Then we will subtract to find the missing number.

$$\begin{array}{r} \overset{5}{\cancel{6}}\overset{1}{4} \\ -\ 3\ 6 \\ \hline 2\ 8 \end{array}$$

We find that the missing number is **28.** Now we check 28 in the original problem.

$$\begin{array}{r} 64 \\ -\ W \\ \hline 36 \end{array} \qquad \begin{array}{r} \overset{5}{\cancel{6}}\overset{1}{4} \\ -\ 2\ 8 \\ \hline 3\ 6 \end{array}$$ Sixty-four minus 28 is 36.
The answer checks.
The missing number is 28.

Practice   Write each of these numbers in expanded form:

a. 86   80 + 6   **b.** 325   **c.** 507   500 + 7
300 + 20 + 5

Find the missing numbers:

d. $\begin{array}{r} 36 \\ -\ P \\ \hline 19 \end{array}$ 17   **e.** $\begin{array}{r} 41 \\ -\ Q \\ \hline 24 \end{array}$ 17   **f.** $\begin{array}{r} 50 \\ -\ T \\ \hline 17 \end{array}$ 33

Problem set 20

1. Twenty-three horses grazed in the pasture. The rest of
$^{(17)}$ the horses were in the corral. If there were eighty-nine horses in all, how many horses were in the corral? Draw a SSM pattern.   66 horses; $\begin{array}{r} 23\ \text{horses} \\ +\ N\ \text{horses} \\ \hline 89\ \text{horses} \end{array}$

2. Three hundred seventy-five students stood silently in
$^{(12)}$ the hall. The other one hundred seven students in the hall were shouting and jumping up and down. Altogether, how many students were in the hall? Draw a SSM pattern.   482 students; $\begin{array}{r} 375\ \text{students} \\ +\ 107\ \text{students} \\ \hline N\ \text{students} \end{array}$

3. Use the digits 1, 2, and 8 once each to write an odd
$^{(11)}$ number less than 300.   281

4. Write 782 in expanded form.   700 + 80 + 2
$^{(20)}$

5. The largest odd three-digit number is 999. What is the
$^{(11)}$ smallest three-digit even number?   100

6. Compare: 918 $\big(>\big)$ 819
(15)

7. How many days are in 6 weeks? Count by sevens.
(3) 42 days

8. To what number is the arrow pointing?   475
(13)

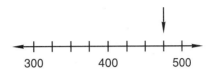

9. (16)	$576 + $128	**10.** (16)	$243 + $578	**11.** (16)	186 + 285	**12.** (16)	329 + 186
	$704		$821		471		515

9. $576
(16) + $128
      $704

10. $243
(16) + $578
      $821

11. 186
(16) + 285
      471

12. 329
(16) + 186
      515

13. *D* 5
(18) + 12
      17

14. 17
(14) − *A* 8
      9

15. 8
(1) + *B* 6
     14

16. *C* 9
(14) − 7
      2

17. 25
(19) − 19
      6

18. 42
(19) − 28
      14

19. 46
(19) − 18
      28

20. 42
(19) − 16
      26

21. 68
(20) − *D* 34
      34

22. *B* 49
(20) − 34
      15

23. 62
(20) − *H* 34
      28

24. *L* 82
(20) − 46
      36

25. Write the next three numbers in this sequence:
(3)
16, 20, 24, __28__, __32__, __36__, …

LESSON 21

Adding Columns of Numbers

a. 456
b. 354
c. 83
d. 244
e. 267
f. 477
g. 1; 3; 5; 6; 2
Patterns:

1	2	3	4	5	6	7	8	9	10
11	12	13	14	15	16	17	18	19	20
21	22	23	24	25	26	27	28	29	30
31	32	33	34	35	36	37	38	39	40
41	42	43	44	45	46	47	48	49	50
51	52	53	54	55	56	57	58	59	60
61	62	63	64	65	66	67	68	69	70
71	72	73	74	75	76	77	78	79	80
81	82	83	84	85	86	87	88	89	90
91	92	93	94	95	96	97	98	99	100

30; 60; 90

Facts Practice: 100 Subtraction Facts (Test B in Test Masters)

Mental Math: Review.

a. 56 + 400
b. 154 + 200
c. 54 + 29
d. 35 + 9 + 200
e. 48 + 19 + 200
f. 400 + 39 + 38
g. What number should be added to each of these numbers for the total to be 10: 9, 7, 5, 4, 8?

Patterns: The multiples of six are 6, 12, 18, and so on. On a hundred number chart, shade the squares that contain a multiple of six. Which of the shaded squares also contain a multiple of five?

Sometimes the sum of the digits in the ones' column is a number greater than 19. When this happens, we bring a group of 2 tens or 3 tens or more to the tens' column.

Example 1 Add: 28 + 16 + 39 + 29

Solution We write the numbers in a column and add the ones. The sum is 32, which is 3 tens and 2 ones. We write the 3 tens either above or below the tens' column and finish adding.

```
      3 above      or    3 below
         3                   28
        28                   16
        16                   39
        39                 + 29
      + 29                    3
      ─────               ─────
       112                  112
```

Example 2 Add: 227 + 88 + 6

Solution We line up the last digits of the numbers. Then we add the digits in the ones' column and get 21.

```
    227
     88
  +   6
  ─────
   (21)
```

The number 21 is 2 tens plus 1 one. We record the 1 in the ones' column and write the 2 in the tens' column, and then we add the tens. The sum is 12 tens.

$$
\begin{array}{r}
2 \\
227 \\
88 \\
+6 \\
\hline
\textcircled{12}1
\end{array}
$$

We record a 2 in the tens' place and write the 1, which is 1 hundred, in the next column. Then we add in the hundreds' column.

$$
\begin{array}{r}
12 \\
227 \\
88 \\
+6 \\
\hline
\mathbf{321}
\end{array}
$$

Practice

a.
$$
\begin{array}{r}
47 \\
29 \\
46 \\
+\,95 \\
\hline
217
\end{array}
$$

b.
$$
\begin{array}{r}
28 \\
47 \\
+\,65 \\
\hline
140
\end{array}
$$

c.
$$
\begin{array}{r}
38 \\
22 \\
31 \\
+\,46 \\
\hline
137
\end{array}
$$

d.
$$
\begin{array}{r}
438 \\
76 \\
+5 \\
\hline
519
\end{array}
$$

e. $15 + 24 + 11 + 25 + 36$ 111

Problem set 21

1. [17] One doctor put in twenty-four stitches. A second doctor put in some more stitches. There were seventy-five stitches in all. How many stitches did the second doctor put in? Draw a SSM pattern.   51 stitches

$$
\begin{array}{r}
24 \text{ stitches} \\
+\,N \text{ stitches} \\
\hline
75 \text{ stitches}
\end{array}
$$

2. [12] Four hundred seven roses were in front. Three hundred sixty-two roses were behind. How many roses were there in all? Draw a SSM pattern.
769 roses

$$
\begin{array}{r}
407 \text{ roses} \\
+\,362 \text{ roses} \\
\hline
N \text{ roses}
\end{array}
$$

3. [11] Use the digits 9, 2, and 8 once each to write an even number less than 300.   298

4. [20,8] Write 813 in expanded form. Then use words to write the number. $800 + 10 + 3$; eight hundred thirteen

5. The largest two-digit even number is 98. What is the
(11) smallest two-digit odd number?   11

6. To what number is the arrow pointing?   125
(13)

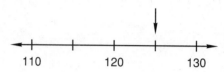

7.
(21)
$$\begin{array}{r} 294 \\ 312 \\ +5 \\ \hline 611 \end{array}$$

8.
(16)
$$\begin{array}{r} \$189 \\ +\$298 \\ \hline \$487 \end{array}$$

9.
(16)
$$\begin{array}{r} \$378 \\ +\$496 \\ \hline \$874 \end{array}$$

10.
(16)
$$\begin{array}{r} 109 \\ +486 \\ \hline 595 \end{array}$$

11.
(21)
$$\begin{array}{r} 14 \\ 28 \\ 35 \\ 16 \\ +227 \\ \hline 320 \end{array}$$

12.
(14)
$$\begin{array}{r} 14 \\ -A \\ \hline 7 \end{array}\quad 7$$

13.
(1)
$$\begin{array}{r} 8 \\ +B \\ \hline 14 \end{array}\quad 6$$

14.
(14)
$$\begin{array}{r} C \\ -13 \\ \hline 5 \end{array}\quad 18$$

15.
(14)
$$\begin{array}{r} 11 \\ -D \\ \hline 9 \end{array}\quad 2$$

16.
(14)
$$\begin{array}{r} E \\ -5 \\ \hline 8 \end{array}\quad 13$$

17.
(19)
$$\begin{array}{r} 38 \\ -29 \\ \hline 9 \end{array}$$

18.
(19)
$$\begin{array}{r} 57 \\ -38 \\ \hline 19 \end{array}$$

19.
(18)
$$\begin{array}{r} 34 \\ +B \\ \hline 86 \end{array}\quad 52$$

20.
(20)
$$\begin{array}{r} 48 \\ -O \\ \hline 25 \end{array}\quad 23$$

21.
(20)
$$\begin{array}{r} D \\ -46 \\ \hline 15 \end{array}\quad 61$$

22.
(20)
$$\begin{array}{r} Y \\ -15 \\ \hline 17 \end{array}\quad 32$$

Write the next three numbers in each sequence:

23. 48, 44, 40, __36__ , __32__ , __28__ , ...
(3)

24. 12, 15, 18, __21__ , __24__ , __27__ , ...
(3)

25. The numbers 6, 9, and 15 are a fact family. Write four
(7) addition/subtraction facts using these three numbers.
6 + 9 = 15, 9 + 6 = 15, 15 − 6 = 9, 15 − 9 = 6

LESSON
22

a. 73
b. 98
c. 69
d. 89
e. 94
f. 95
g. 7; 2; 9; 5; 6
Problem Solving:
   1 quarter and 4
   nickels

Facts Practice: 100 Subtraction Facts (Test B in Test Masters)

Mental Math: Add tens and then ones. For example, 32 + 43
is 70 and 5, which is 75.

a.	32	**b.**	56	**c.**	45	**d.**	67	**e.**	41	**f.**	64
	+ 41		+ 42		+ 24		+ 22		+ 53		+ 31

g. What number should be added to each of these numbers
for the total to be 10: 3, 8, 1, 5, 4?

Problem Solving: Sam had five coins in his pocket totaling
less than 50 cents. He didn't have any
pennies, but he did have a quarter. What
coins did Sam have in his pocket?

A **scale** is a type of number line often used for measuring.
Scales are found on rulers, gauges, thermometers,
speedometers, and many other instruments. The trick to
reading a scale is to determine the distance between the
marks on the scale. Then we can find the values of all the
marks on the scale.

We use a thermometer to measure temperature.
Temperature is usually measured in degrees Fahrenheit
(abbreviated °F) or in degrees Celsius (abbreviated °C). On
a Fahrenheit thermometer, tick marks are often two
degrees apart.

Example 1 What temperature is shown on this
Fahrenheit thermometer?

Solution There are five spaces between 50° and
60° on this scale, so each space cannot
equal one degree. If we try counting
by twos, we find our count matches
the scale. We count up by twos from
50° and find that the temperature is
54°F.

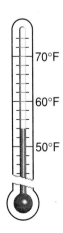

Example 2 This speedometer shows speed in miles per hour (mph). The speedometer shows that the car is going how fast?

Solution By trying different counts on the scale, we find that each space equals five. If we count up by fives from 40, we see that the pointer points to 55. The car is going **55 mph**.

Practice What number is indicated on each of these scales?

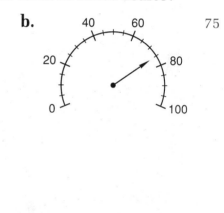

Problem set 22

1. The first flower had twenty-four petals. The second flower had more petals. There were fifty-six petals in all. How many petals did the second flower have? Draw a SSM pattern.   32 petals
(17)

$$\begin{array}{r} 24 \text{ petals} \\ + \ N \text{ petals} \\ \hline 56 \text{ petals} \end{array}$$

2. Four hundred seventy-two soldiers strutted proudly in front. Two hundred seven soldiers walked sadly behind them. How many soldiers were there in all? Draw a SSM pattern.   679 soldiers
(12)

$$\begin{array}{r} 472 \text{ soldiers} \\ + \ 207 \text{ soldiers} \\ \hline N \text{ soldiers} \end{array}$$

3. Use the digits 2, 5, and 7 once each to write an even number that is greater than 700.   752
(11)

4. The tens' digit is 4. The ones' digit is 9. The number is
(5) between 200 and 300. What is the number?   249

5. Which of these numbers is an odd number that is
(11) greater than 750?   C. 903

A. 846   B. 864   C. 903   D. 309

6. To what number is the arrow pointing?   475
(13)

7. $392   **8.** $439   **9.**   774   **10.**   389
(16) + $278   (16) + $339   (16) + 174   (16) + 398
─────────   ─────────   ─────   ─────
      $670 $778   948   787

11.   13   **12.**   18   **13.**   8   **14.**   C   8
(21)   25   (20)   − A   6   (1)   + B   8   (14) − 5
          46   ────   ────   ───
          25   12   16   3
       + 29
       ─────
         138

15.   62   **16.**   82   **17.**   28   **18.**   35
(19)   − 48   (19)   − 58   (21)   36   (20)   − Y   21
        ─────   ─────   57   ────
          14   24   + 47   14
                                          ─────
                                            168

19.   45   **20.**   75   **21.**   C   82   **22.**   E   22
(18)   + P   10   (20)   − L   28   (20)   − 47   (18) + 15
       ────   ────   ────   ────
         55   47   35   37

23. Write 498 in expanded form.   400 + 90 + 8
(20)

24. Compare: 423 ⊙< 432
(15)

25. 4 + 7 + 3 + 5 + 2 + 3 + 2 + 7 + 8   41
(1)

LESSON 23

Reading Time from a Clock

a. 76
b. 77
c. 76
d. 175
e. 289
f. 185
g. 3; 8; 1; 5; 4

Patterns:

1	2	3	4	5	6	7	8	9	10
11	12	13	14	15	16	17	18	19	20
21	22	23	24	25	26	27	28	29	30
31	32	33	34	35	36	37	38	39	40
41	42	43	44	45	46	47	48	49	50
51	52	53	54	55	56	57	58	59	60
61	62	63	64	65	66	67	68	69	70
71	72	73	74	75	76	77	78	79	80
81	82	83	84	85	86	87	88	89	90
91	92	93	94	95	96	97	98	99	100

70

Facts Practice: 100 Subtraction Facts (Test B in Test Masters)

Mental Math: Review.

a. 44 + 32
b. 57 + 20
c. 57 + 19
d. 32 + 43 + 100
e. 58 + 31 + 200
f. 56 + 29 + 100
g. What number should be added to each of these numbers for the total to be 10: 7, 2, 9, 5, 6?

Patterns: The multiples of seven are 7, 14, 21, and so on. On a hundred number chart, shade the squares that contain a multiple of seven. Which of the shaded squares contain an even number that is a multiple of five?

The scale on a clock is actually two number lines in one. One number line marks hours and is usually numbered. The other number line marks minutes and usually is not numbered. We have numbered the minute number line outside this clock. Notice that each big mark is five minutes. So counting by fives can help us find the number of minutes before or after the hour.

To tell time, we read the location of the short hand on the hour number line and the location of the long hand on the minute number line.

To write the time of day, we write the hour followed by a colon. Then we write two digits to show the number of minutes after the hour. We use the abbreviation a.m. for the 12 hours before noon and p.m. for the 12 hours after noon. This form is referred to as *digital form*. Noon is written as 12:00 p.m. and midnight is 12:00 a.m.[†]

Example 1   If it is evening, what time is shown by the clock?

Solution   Since the short hand is between the 9 and the 10, we know it is after 9 p.m. We count 5, 10, 15, 20 minutes after 9:00 p.m. It is **9:20 p.m.**

Since sixty minutes is one hour, thirty minutes is half an hour. So if the time is 7:30, we might say that the time is half past seven. Fifteen minutes is a quarter of an hour. At 6:15 we might say that the time is a quarter after six.

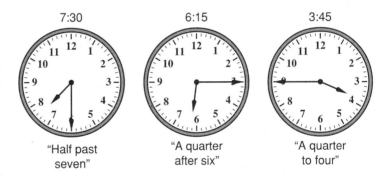

| 7:30 | 6:15 | 3:45 |

"Half past seven"   "A quarter after six"   "A quarter to four"

Sometimes when it is getting close to the next hour, we say how many minutes it is until the next hour. When the time is 5:50, we might say, "It is ten minutes to six." When it is 3:45, we might say, "It is a quarter to four."

Example 2   Use the digital form to show what time it is at a quarter to eight in the evening.

Solution   A quarter to eight is 15 minutes before eight, which is **7:45 p.m.**

[†]The use of p.m. and a.m. to designate 12:00 is unclear. To avoid confusion, we refer to these times as *noon* and *midnight*.

Practice   If it is morning, what time is shown by each clock?

a.   b.   c.

8:30 a.m.   7:12 a.m.   10:40 a.m.

d. Use the digital form to show what time it is at ten minutes to nine in the evening.   8:50 p.m.

Problem set 23

51 pencils
+ *N* pencils
76 pencils

1. On the first day Sarah sharpened fifty-one pencils.
   (17) Then she sharpened some more pencils on the second day. She sharpened seventy-six pencils in all. How many pencils did she sharpen on the second day? Draw a SSM pattern.   25 pencils

270 ambassadors
302 ambassadors
+ 111 ambassadors
   N ambassadors

2. Two hundred seventy ambassadors came on Monday.
   (12) Three hundred two ambassadors came on Tuesday. One hundred eleven ambassadors came on Wednesday. How many ambassadors came in all? Draw a SSM pattern.   683 ambassadors

3. The hundreds' digit is 5. The ones' digit is 7. The
   (5) number is greater than 540 and less than 550. What is the number?   547

4. Write 905 in expanded form.   900 + 5
   (20)

5. Use digits and a comparison symbol to write "One
   (15) hundred twenty is greater than one hundred twelve."
   120 > 112

6. This clock shows that it is half
   (23) past four. It is afternoon. Write the time shown in digital form.
   4:30 p.m.

7. What temperature is shown on the
(22) thermometer?　76°F

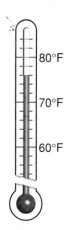

8.　$468　　　**9.**　468　　　**10.**　$187
(16)　+ $293　　　(16)　+ 185　　　(16)　+ $698
　　——————　　　　——————　　　　——————
　　$761　　　　　653　　　　　　$885

11.　14　　**12.**　8　　**13.**　C　15　**14.**　14
(14)　− A　7　(1)　+ B　8　(14)　− 8　　(14)　− D　5
　　————　　　————　　　————　　　————
　　7　　　　16　　　　7　　　　9

15.　74　　**16.**　$44　　**17.**　23　　**18.**　$62
(19)　− 58　　(19)　− $28　　(19)　− 18　　(19)　− $43
　　————　　　————　　　————　　　————
　　16　　　$16　　　5　　　　$19

19.　25　　**20.**　45　　**21.**　13　　**22.**　F　77
(21)　28　　(20)　− P　24　(18)　+ B　24　(20)　− 45
　　46　　　————　　　————　　　————
　　+ 88　　21　　　37　　　32
　　————
　　187

23. How many quarters are equal to four dollars? Count by
(3)　fours.　16 quarters

24. Write a number sentence for this
(1)　picture.　3 + 6 = 9

25. Write the next three numbers in this sequence:
(3)
　　　　8, 16, 24, __32__ , __40__ , __48__ , ...

LESSON 24

Reading a Centimeter Scale

a. 84
b. 68
c. 95
d. 267
e. 95
f. 630
g. 2; 6; 7; 1; 5
Problem Solving:
    14 times

Facts Practice: 100 Addition Facts (Test A in Test Masters)

Mental Math: Review.

a. 63 + 21   b. 45 + 23
c. 65 + 30   d. 48 + 19 + 200
e. 36 + 29 + 30   f. 130 + 200 + 300
g. What number should be added to each of these numbers for the total to be 10: 8, 4, 3, 9, 5?

Problem Solving: The hour hand moves around the face of a clock once in twelve hours. How many times does the hour hand move around the face of the clock in a week?

The scale on a ruler is used to measure length. One kind of scale used on a ruler is a **centimeter** scale. A centimeter is this long.

———

We use the letters "cm" to abbreviate the word *centimeter*. To measure lengths in centimeters, we match the length of the object we are measuring with the marks on the scale.

Example   How long is this nail?

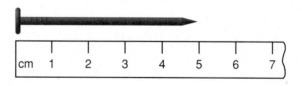

Solution   The head of the nail is lined up on the "zero" of the centimeter scale. The point of the nail is closest to the 5-centimeter mark of the scale, so the nail is 5 centimeters long. We abbreviate this by writing **5 cm.**

Practice Find the length of each object to the nearest centimeter:

a. 3 cm

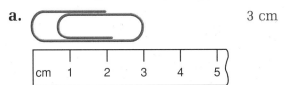

b. 5 cm

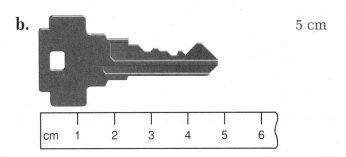

c. Use the centimeter scale on your ruler to draw a line segment 10 cm long.

_____

d. Use the centimeter scale on your ruler to measure how long this book is. 26 cm

Problem set 24

$\begin{array}{r} N \text{ eggs} \\ + 21 \text{ eggs} \\ \hline 72 \text{ eggs} \end{array}$

1. Martine gathered a "whole bunch" of eggs one day. She gathered twenty-one eggs on the second day. If she gathered seventy-two eggs in all, how many were in the whole bunch? Draw a SSM pattern. 51 eggs
(17)

$\begin{array}{r} 476 \text{ children} \\ + 397 \text{ children} \\ \hline N \text{ children} \end{array}$

2. Four hundred seventy-six children stood quietly in one line. Three hundred ninety-seven children stood quietly in another line. Altogether, how many children stood quietly in line? Draw a SSM pattern. 873 children
(12)

3. The ones' digit is 5. The tens' digit is 6. The number is between 600 and 700. What is the number? 665
(5)

4. Write 509 in expanded form. 500 + 9
(20)

5. Use digits and a comparison symbol to compare 493 and 439. 493 > 439
(15)

6. What temperature is shown on
(22) this thermometer?   70°F

7. It is a quarter after four in the
(23) afternoon. Write the time shown
in digital form.   4:15 p.m.

8. How long is the pin?   3 cm
(24)

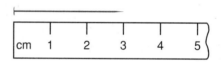

9. $476
(16) + $285
       ―――――
       $761

10. $185
(16) + $499
        ―――――
        $684

11.   568
(16)   + 397
        ―――――
        965

12.   478
(16)   + 196
        ―――――
        674

13.   17
(14) − A   8
       ――――
        9

14.   14
(14) − B   0
       ――――
        14

15.   13
(14) − C   7
       ――――
        6

16. $35
(19) − $28
       ―――――
        $7

17.   23
(19) − 15
       ――――
        8

18.   63
(19) − 36
       ――――
        27

19.   74
(19) − 59
       ――――
        15

20.   M   23
(18) + 22
       ――――
        45

21.   K   47
(20) − 15
       ――――
        32

22.   47
(20) − K   13
       ――――
        34

23.   28
(21)   36
        44
      + 58
       ―――
       166

24.   49
(21)   28
        32
      + 55
       ―――
       164

25. Without a ruler, try to draw a line segment that is 3 cm
(24) long. Then use the centimeter scale on your ruler to
check your drawing.   answer varies

LESSON
25

Triangles, Rectangles, Squares, and Circles

a. 576   b. 677
c. 395   d. 687
e. 296   f. 599
g. 8; 4; 3; 9; 5
Patterns:

1	2	3	4	5	6	7	8	9	10
11	12	13	14	15	16	17	18	19	20
21	22	23	24	25	26	27	28	29	30
31	32	33	34	35	36	37	38	39	40
41	42	43	44	45	46	47	48	49	50
51	52	53	54	55	56	57	58	59	60
61	62	63	64	65	66	67	68	69	70
71	72	73	74	75	76	77	78	79	80
81	82	83	84	85	86	87	88	89	90
91	92	93	94	95	96	97	98	99	100

9, 18, 27, 36, 45, 54, 63, 72, 81, 90; The tens' digit goes up one each time, the ones' digit goes down one, and the sum of the digits is nine.

Facts Practice: 100 Subtraction Facts (Test B in Test Masters)

Mental Math: Add hundreds, then tens, and then ones.

a.   320   b.   645   c.   145   d.   632   e.   86   f.   360
   + 256   + 32   + 250   + 55   + 210   25
                                                                      + 214

g. What number should be added to each of these numbers for the total to be 10: 2, 6, 7, 1, 5?

Patterns: On a hundred number chart, shade the squares that contain a multiple of 9. Then write these shaded numbers from 9 to 90 in a column. What patterns can you find in the column of numbers?

In this lesson we will practice drawing triangles, rectangles, squares, and circles.

Example 1   Draw a triangle that has all sides the same length.

Solution   You may need to practice on scratch paper until you find out how to draw this triangle. A triangle has three sides. If you start out with a "square" corner, the third side will be too long.

This side is longer than the other two sides.

A triangle that has all sides the same length looks like this.

Example 2   Draw a rectangle that has all sides the same length.

Solution   A rectangle does not have to be longer than it is wide. A rectangle does have "square corners" and four sides. A rectangle with all sides the same length looks like this.

This may look like a square to you. It **is** a square. It is also a rectangle. **A square is a special kind of rectangle.**

Example 3   Draw a circle that is about 1 centimeter across the center.

Solution   First we will draw a line segment one centimeter long. Then we will draw a circle around the segment.

Circle drawing improves with practice.

Practice   **a.** Draw a triangle that has two sides that are the same length.   answer varies

b. Draw a rectangle that is about twice as long as it is wide.   answer varies

c. Draw a square. Inside the square draw a circle that just touches all four sides of the square.

Problem set 25

1. Roger had four hundred seventeen marbles. Harry had two hundred twenty-two marbles. How many marbles did Roger and Harry have in all? Draw a SSM pattern.   639 marbles
(12)

$$\begin{array}{r} 417 \text{ marbles} \\ + 222 \text{ marbles} \\ \hline N \text{ marbles} \end{array}$$

2. Susie put forty jacks into a pile. Jane put all of her jacks in the pile. Then there were seventy-two jacks in the pile. How many jacks did Jane put in? Draw a SSM pattern.   32 jacks
(17)

$$\begin{array}{r} 40 \text{ jacks} \\ + N \text{ jacks} \\ \hline 72 \text{ jacks} \end{array}$$

3. The ones' digit is 5. The number is greater than 640 and less than 650. What is the number?   645
(5)

4. Write seven hundred fifty-three in expanded form.
(20) $700 + 50 + 3$

5. Use digits and a comparison symbol to compare four
(15) hundred seventy-seven and five hundred forty-two.
$477 < 542$

6. The needle is pointing to what
(22) number on this scale?   350

7. How long is the pencil?   11 cm
(24)

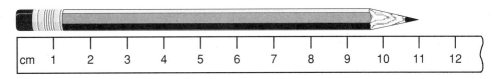

8.   493
(16) $+ 278$
  771

9. $486
(16) $+ \$378$
  $864

10. $524
(16) $+ \$109$
  $633

2 cm
2 cm
2 cm

11. Draw a triangle in which each side is 2 cm long.
(25)

12. Draw a square. Then draw a circle around the square
(25) so that the circle just touches each corner of the
square.

13.   17
(14) $- \; A$ 8
   9

14.   45
(19) $- 29$
  16

15.   15
(14) $- \; B$ 9
   6

16.   62
(19) $- 45$
  17

17.   24
(18) $+ \; D$ 21
  45

18.   14
(14) $- \; B$ 12
   2

19. Y 92
(20) $- 36$
  56

20.   75
(20) $- \; P$ 27
  48

21.   46
(21)   35
  27
$+ 39$
 147

22.   14
(21)   28
  77
$+ 23$
 142

23.   14
(21)   23
  38
$+ 64$
 139

24.   15
(21)   24
  36
$+ 99$
 174

25. Write the next three numbers in this sequence:
(3)

28, 35, 42, __49__ , __56__ , __63__ , ...

LESSON 26

Rounding Whole Numbers to the Nearest Ten

a. 686
b. 695
c. 365
d. 556
e. 362
f. 491
g. 5
Problem Solving:
  2 and 7; 3 and 6;
  4 and 5

Facts Practice: 100 Subtraction Facts (Test B in Test Masters)

Mental Math: Add hundreds, then tens, and then ones.

  a. 365 + 321   **b.** 650 + 45
  c. 40 + 300 + 25   **d.** 500 + 40 + 16
  e. 300 + 50 + 12   **f.** 400 + 80 + 11
  g. Seven can be split into 3 + 4. Seven can also be split into
     2 + ☐.

Problem Solving: The pair of numbers 1 and 8 have the sum
                of 9. List three more pairs of counting
                numbers that have a sum of 9.

One of the sentences below uses an **exact number.** The other sentence uses a **rounded number.** Can you tell which sentence uses the rounded number?

• The radio cost about $70.

• The radio cost $68.47.

The first sentence uses a rounded number. Rounded numbers usually end with a zero. Rounded numbers are often used in place of exact numbers because they are easy to understand and easy to work with.

    To round an exact number to the nearest ten, we choose the closest number that ends in zero. The number line can help us understand rounding.

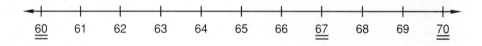

We see that 67 is between 60 and 70. Since 67 is closer to 70 than it is to 60, we say that 67 is "about 70." When we say this, we have rounded 67 to the nearest ten.

Example   Round 82 to the nearest ten.

Solution Rounding to the nearest ten means to round to a number we would say when counting by tens (10, 20, 30, 40, and so on). We will use a number line marked off in tens to picture this problem.

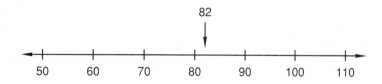

We see that 82 is between 80 and 90. Since 82 is closer to 80 than it is to 90, we round 82 to **80.**

Practice Round each number to the nearest ten. For each problem, draw a number line to show your work.

a. 78   80   **b.** 43   40   **c.** 61   60   **d.** 49   50

Problem set 26

44 dogs
76 dogs
+ 23 dogs
N dogs

1. Forty-four dogs were in front. Seventy-six dogs were
(12) in the middle. Twenty-three dogs brought up the rear. How many dogs were there in all? Draw a SSM pattern.   143 dogs

2. The smallest three-digit whole number is subtracted
(18) from two hundred twenty-four. What is the answer?
124

3. Amelda had twenty-six books. Then Grant gave her
(17) some more books. Now she has ninety-nine books. How many books did Grant give to Amelda? Draw a SSM pattern.   73 books

26 books
+ N books
99 books

4. List the odd numbers between 740 and 750.
(11)   741, 743, 745, 747, 749

5. Write four hundred eleven in expanded form.
(20)   400 + 10 + 1

6. Use digits and a comparison symbol to write "Five
(15) hundred eighty is greater than five hundred eighteen."
580 > 518

7. Round 71 to the nearest ten.   70
(26)

8. How long is the AA battery?   5 cm
(24)

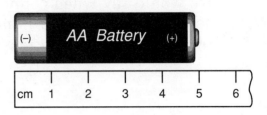

9. Draw a triangle that has all sides the same length. *(25)* Then draw a circle around the triangle that just touches the "corners" of the triangle.

10. *(16)*	**11.** *(16)*	**12.** *(16)*	**13.** *(16)*
387 + 196 ——— 583	$496 + $503 ——— $999	762 + 109 ——— 871	$458 + $385 ——— $843

14. *(16)*	**15.** *(19)*	**16.** *(19)*	**17.** *(20)*
129 + 548 ——— 677	$43 − $27 ——— $16	42 − 15 ——— 27	52 − Y 25 ——— 27

18. *(20)*	**19.** *(20)*	**20.** *(21)*	**21.** *(21)*
X 47 − 29 ——— 18	73 − C 27 ——— 46	14 28 47 + 33 ——— 122	21 38 46 + 93 ——— 198

22. Write four addition/subtraction facts using the three *(7)* numbers 5, 8, and 13.

8 + 5 = 13, 5 + 8 = 13, 13 − 8 = 5, 13 − 5 = 8

Write the next three numbers in each sequence:

23. 14, 21, 28, __35__ , __42__ , __49__ , ...
(3)

24. 20, 24, 28, __32__ , __36__ , __40__ , ...
(3)

25. Without a ruler, try to draw a line segment that is 2 cm *(24)* long. Then use your ruler to check your drawing.

answer varies

LESSON 27

Metric Units of Length

a. 590
b. 682
c. 785
d. 275
e. 187
f. 45
g. 4; 3
Problem Solving:
14 hours of
sunlight

Facts Practice: 100 Subtraction Facts (Test B in Test Masters)

Mental Math: Add hundreds, then tens, and then ones.

   a. 340 + 50 + 200   **b.** 200 + 50 + 432

   c. 560 + 200 + 25

Review:

   d. 56 + 19 + 200   **e.** 48 + 39 + 100   **f.** 36 + 9

   g. Complete each split: 6 = 2 + ☐   6 = 3 + ☐

Problem Solving: If the sun rose at 5:00 a.m. and then set at 7:00 p.m., how many hours of sunlight were there?

The centimeter is a unit we use to measure short distances. To measure longer distances, we use the **meter** or the **kilometer.**

A meter is exactly 100 centimeters. An easy way to remember this fact is that there are 100 centimeters in 1 meter just as there are 100 cents in one dollar. Perhaps you have a meterstick in your classroom. A meterstick is a ruler that is 1 meter long. Notice it is also 100 centimeters long. If you took a **big step,** your step would be about **1 meter.**

From the word *meter* comes the word *metric.* The **metric system** of measurement uses meters, fractions of meters, and multiples of meters to measure distances.

A much larger unit of length in the metric system is the kilometer. *Kilo-* means "1000." **A kilometer is 1000 meters.** If you took **1000 big steps,** you would walk about **1 kilometer.**

We often use the abbreviations "cm," "m," and "km" to stand for "centimeters," "meters," and "kilometers."

Metric Units of Length

100 cm = 1 m
1000 m = 1 km

Activities   (a) Use a meterstick to measure the height and width of a classroom door.

(b) Estimate the length and width of the classroom by "pacing off" the distance between opposite walls. Then measure the distance using a meterstick.

Practice   **a.** If Simon said, "Take 5 giants steps," about how many meters would you walk?   5 m

b. One meter is how many centimeters?   100 cm

c. One kilometer is how many meters?   1000 m

Problem set 27

342 students
+ 214 students
‾‾‾‾‾‾‾‾‾‾‾‾
N students

1. When the bell rang, three hundred forty-two students came. When the bell rang again, two hundred fourteen students came. How many students came in all? Draw a SSM pattern.   556 students
(12)

46 times
+ N times
‾‾‾‾‾‾‾‾‾
98 times

2. The small horn sounded 46 times. The big horn sounded many times. If the horns sounded a total of 98 times, how many times did the big horn sound? Draw a SSM pattern.   52 times
(17)

3. Write seven hundred forty-two in expanded form.   700 + 40 + 2
(20)

4. Simon was twelfth in line. Mandy was seventh in line. How many people were between Simon and Mandy?   4 people
(6)

5. Round sixty-eight to the nearest ten.   70
(26)

6. A door is about how many meters wide?   1 m
(27)

7. What temperature is shown on the thermometer?   86°F
(22)

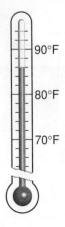

2 cm
[rectangle] 1 cm

8. Draw a rectangle that is 2 centimeters long and 1
(25) centimeter wide.

9. Use digits and a comparison symbol to write "Three
(15) hundred twenty-seven is less than three hundred
thirty."   327 < 330

| **10.** (19) | $43
− $27
─────
$16 | **11.** (16) | $278
+ $569
─────
$847 | **12.** (19) | 61
− 37
────
24 | **13.** (19) | 72
− 29
────
43 |

| **14.** (16) | 389
+ 256
─────
645 | **15.** (20) | 47
− Q   33
────
14 | **16.** (18) | 43
+ S   31
────
74 | **17.** (18) | 389
− 256
─────
133 |

18. 486 + 276   762   **19.** 91 − 76   15
(16)   (19)

20. 42 + 23 + 86 + 98   **21.** 95 + 87 + 24 + 38
(21) 249   (21) 244

Write the next three numbers in each sequence:

22. 24, 30, 36, __42__, __48__, __54__, ...
(3)

23. 28, 32, 36, __40__, __44__, __48__, ...
(3)

24. 24 + 26 + 35 + 27 + 15   127
(21)

25. 36 + 15 + 43 + 55 + 23   172
(21)

LESSON
28

Naming Fractions • Adding Dollars and Cents

a. 80
b. 62
c. 70
d. 82
e. 380
f. 482
g. 7; 5
Problem Solving:
1 half-dollar,
1 dime, and
1 nickel

Facts Practice: 100 Subtraction Facts (Test B in Test Masters)

Mental Math: Add from the left with regrouping. For example, 35 + 26 is 50 plus 11, which is 61.

a.	55	b.	36	c.	48	d.	37	e.	235	f.	156
	+ 25		+ 26		+ 22		+ 45		+ 145		+ 326

g. Complete each split: 8 = 1 + ☐   8 = 3 + ☐

Problem Solving: Jennifer has three coins in her left pocket that total 65¢. What coins does Jennifer have in her left pocket?

Naming fractions

Part of a whole can be named with a fraction. A fraction is written with two numbers. The bottom number of a fraction is called the **denominator.** The denominator tells how many equal parts are in the whole. The top number of a fraction is called the **numerator.** The numerator tells how many of the parts are being counted. When naming fractions, we name the numerator first; then we name the denominator using the ordinal number. Some fractions and their names are given here.

$\frac{1}{2}$ one half $\frac{3}{5}$ three fifths

$\frac{1}{3}$ one third $\frac{5}{6}$ five sixths

$\frac{2}{3}$ two thirds $\frac{7}{8}$ seven eighths

$\frac{1}{4}$ one fourth $\frac{1}{10}$ one tenth

Example 1   What fraction of the circle is shaded?

Solution   There are four equal parts, and three are shaded. Therefore, the fraction of the circle that is shaded is three fourths, which we write

$$\frac{3}{4}$$

Adding dollars and cents

We add dollars and cents just like we add whole numbers. The dot, called a **decimal point,** separates dollars from cents. To add dollars to dollars and cents to cents, we align the decimal points. We remember the dollar sign and the decimal point when we write the sum.

Example 2 Add: $3.56
+ $2.75

Solution We add the pennies, add the dimes, and add the dollars. Since ten pennies equal a dime and ten dimes equal a dollar, we regroup when the total in any column is ten or more.

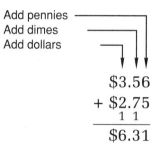

```
Add pennies
Add dimes
Add dollars
                $3.56
              + $2.75
                1 1
                ─────
                $6.31
```

Practice What fraction of each shape is shaded?

a. $\frac{1}{3}$

b. $\frac{5}{9}$

c. $\frac{3}{8}$

d. $\frac{1}{4}$

Add:

e. $2.75
+ $2.75
─────
$5.50

f. $3.65
+ $4.28
─────
$7.93

Problem set 28

1. The first four odd numbers are 1, 3, 5, and 7. What is
(1) their sum?   16

2. James was 49 inches tall at the beginning of summer.
(12) He grew 2 inches over the summer. How tall was James at the end of summer? Draw a SSM pattern.
51 inches

```
  49 inches
+  2 inches
─────────────
   N inches
```

3. Use the digits 1, 2, and 3 once each to make an odd
(11) number less than 200.   123

Write the next three numbers in each sequence:

4. 80, 72, 64, __56__ , __48__ , __40__ , ...
(3)

5. 60, 54, 48, __42__ , __36__ , __30__ , ...
(3)

Find the missing number in each sequence:

6. 18, __27__ , 36, 45, ...   **7.** 18, __20__ , 22, 24, ...
(3)   (3)

8. What is the place value of the 9 in 891?   tens'
(5)

9. Write 106 in expanded form.   100 + 6
(20)

10. Write 160 using words.   one hundred sixty
(8)

11. Use digits and symbols to write that eighteen minus
(15) nine equals five plus four.
18 − 9 = 5 + 4

12. Round 28 to the nearest ten.   30
(26)

13. A bicycle is about how many meters long?   2 m
(27)

14. The needle is pointing to what
(22) number on this scale?   96

15. Draw a circle that is 2 centimeters
(25) across the center.

16. What fraction of the rectangle is
(28) shaded? $\frac{1}{6}$

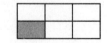

17. The door was two meters high. Two meters is how
(27) many centimeters?   200 cm

18. 51 − 43   8   **19.** 70 − 44   26   **20.** 37 − 9   28
(19)   (19)   (19)

21. $8.79 + $0.64 $9.43   **22.** $5.75 + $2.75 $8.50
(28)   (28)

23.
(18)
$$\begin{array}{r} N \quad 4 \\ + 13 \\ \hline 17 \end{array}$$

24.
(20)
$$\begin{array}{r} X \quad 69 \\ - 42 \\ \hline 27 \end{array}$$

25.
(20)
$$\begin{array}{r} 31 \\ - O \quad 17 \\ \hline 14 \end{array}$$

LESSON 29

Parallel and Perpendicular Lines • Right Angles

a. 61
b. 372
c. 81
d. 382
e. 84
f. 392
g. 6; 5
Problem Solving:
  27, 36, 45, 54,
  63, 72

Facts Practice: 100 Subtraction Facts (Test B in Test Masters)

Mental Math: Add hundreds, then tens, and then ones, re-grouping ones.

a. 25 + 36

b. 147 + 225

c. 30 + 25 + 26

d. 356 + 26

e. 46 + 10 + 28

f. 350 + 35 + 7

g. Complete each split: 9 = 3 + ☐   9 = 4 + ☐

Problem Solving: The two-digit numbers 18 and 81 are written with digits whose sum is nine. On your paper, list in order the eight two-digit numbers which have the sum of nine, from 18 to 81.

18, ___ , ___ , ___ , ___ , ___ , ___ , 81

Parallel and perpendicular lines

Lines that go in the same direction and stay the same distance apart are **parallel lines.**

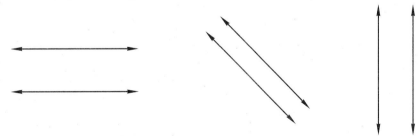

Pairs of parallel lines

When lines cross, we say they **intersect.**

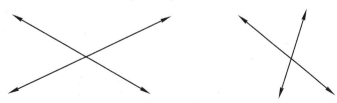

Pairs of intersecting lines

Intersecting lines that form "square corners" are **perpendicular.**

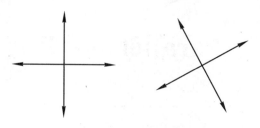

Pairs of perpendicular lines

Right angles   The corners are called **angles.** Square corners are called **right angles.**

Example 1   Which of these angles is a right angle?

A.   B.   C.

Solution   Angle B makes a square corner, so **angle B is a right angle.**

Example 2   Which shape below has four right angles?

A.   B.   C.

Solution   The shape labeled "B" has four square corners. Thus **shape B has four right angles.**

Example 3   Draw a triangle that has one right angle.

Solution   We begin by drawing two line segments to make a right angle. Then we draw the third side.

Practice   **a.** Draw two lines that intersect but are not perpendicular.   answer varies

b. Draw two lines that are perpendicular. $\times$

c. Are train tracks parallel or perpendicular?   parallel

d. A triangle has how many angles?   3

e. Which of these angles is not a right angle?   2. $\angle$

1. $\lfloor$ 2. $\diagup$ 3. $\lrcorner$

Problem set 29

28 children
+ 42 children
N children

1. Twenty-eight children were in the first line. Forty-two children were in the second line. How many children were in both lines? Draw a SSM pattern.   70 children
(12)

12 books
+ N books
28 books

2. Tina knew that there were 28 books in two stacks. In the first stack Tina counted 12 books. Then she figured out how many books were in the second stack. How many books were in the second stack? Draw a SSM pattern.   16 books
(17)

3. Use the digits 1, 2, and 3 once each to make an odd number greater than 300.   321
(11)

Write the next three numbers in each sequence:

4. 40, 36, 32, __28__, __24__, __20__, ...
(3)

5. 30, 27, 24, __21__, __18__, __15__, ...
(3)

6. Use digits and a comparison symbol to write that six hundred thirty-eight is less than six hundred eighty-three.   638 < 683
(15)

7. Round 92 to the nearest ten.   90
(26)

8. A nickel is 2 centimeters across the center. If 10
(3) nickels are laid in a line, how long will the line be?
Count by twos.   20 cm

9. How long is this rectangle?   3 cm
(24)

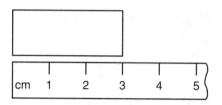

10. Draw a pair of perpendicular lines.
(29)

11. What fraction of this triangle is
(28) shaded? $\frac{1}{3}$

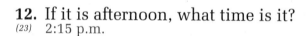

12. If it is afternoon, what time is it?
(23) 2:15 p.m.

13. (19)	$\begin{array}{r} \$83 \\ -\ \$27 \\ \hline \$56 \end{array}$	**14.** (19)	$\begin{array}{r} 42 \\ -\ 27 \\ \hline 15 \end{array}$	**15.** (19) $\begin{array}{r} 72 \\ -\ 36 \\ \hline 36 \end{array}$ **16.** (28) $\begin{array}{r} \$4.28 \\ +\ \$1.96 \\ \hline \$6.24 \end{array}$

17. $\begin{array}{r} \$4.36 \\ +\ \$2.95 \\ \hline \$7.31 \end{array}$ **18.** $\begin{array}{r} 57 \\ +\ K \\ \hline 88 \end{array}$ 31   **19.** $\begin{array}{r} 67 \\ -\ B \\ \hline 48 \end{array}$ 19   **20.** $\begin{array}{r} K \\ -\ 22 \\ \hline 22 \end{array}$ 44
(28)   (18)   (20)   (20)

21. 42 − 27   15   **22.** 55 − 48   7   **23.** 31 − 14   17
(19)   (19)   (19)

24. 4 + 3 + 2 + 5 + 7 + 6 + 3 + 8 + 5 + 4   47
(1)

25. 25 + 25 + 25 + 25   100
(21)

LESSON
30

a. 90
b. 73
c. 174
d. 580
e. 270
f. 77
g. 4; 2
Problem Solving:
 3:00, 9:00

More About Missing Addends

Facts Practice: 100 Addition Facts (Test A in Test Masters)

Mental Math: Review.
   a. 54 + 36   **b.** 54 + 19   **c.** 54 + 120
   d. 350 + 30 + 200   **e.** 210 + 25 + 35   **f.** 48 + 29
   g. Complete each split: 5 = 1 + ☐   5 = 3 + ☐

Problem Solving: At 12:00 the hands of the clock point in the same direction. At 6:00 the hands point in opposite directions. At what hours do the hands of a clock form right angles?

We have found missing addends by asking an addition question. We can also find missing addends by asking a subtraction question.

What number plus
 five equals
 fourteen?

$$\begin{array}{r} N \\ + 5 \\ \hline 14 \end{array}$$

Fourteen minus
 five equals what
 number?

Sometimes the subtraction question is easier to answer.

Example 1   Find the missing addend:
$$\begin{array}{r} W \\ + 26 \\ \hline 63 \end{array}$$

Solution   We will ask the subtraction question "Sixty-three minus twenty-six equals what number?"

$$\begin{array}{r} \overset{5}{\cancel{6}}\overset{1}{}3 \\ - 2\,6 \\ \hline 3\,7 \end{array}$$

We find that the missing addend is **37**. Now we try 37 in the original problem to check our answer.

$$\begin{array}{r} \overset{1}{} \\ 37 \\ + 26 \\ \hline 63 \end{array}$$

The answer checks.

Example 2   Find the missing addend: 37
                                           $\underline{+\ M}$
                                            84

Solution   Remember that with subtraction problems we may "subtract down" or "add up." With addition problems we may "add down" or "subtract up." Some people just remember that we can turn addition or subtraction problems and do the opposite operation.

ADD, OR TURN AND SUBTRACT   SUBTRACT, OR TURN AND ADD

$$\begin{array}{r} 5 \\ + 3 \\ \hline 8 \end{array} \qquad \begin{array}{r} 8 \\ - 3 \\ \hline 5 \end{array} \qquad\qquad \begin{array}{r} 15 \\ - 7 \\ \hline 8 \end{array} \qquad \begin{array}{r} 8 \\ + 7 \\ \hline 15 \end{array}$$

For this problem we may add, or turn and subtract.

$$\begin{array}{r} 37 \\ + M \\ \hline 84 \end{array} \qquad\qquad \begin{array}{r} 84 \\ - M \\ \hline 37 \end{array}$$

We will answer the subtraction problem as we have practiced.

$$\begin{array}{r} 84 \\ - M \\ \hline 37 \end{array} \quad\Large\times\quad \begin{array}{r} \overset{7}{\cancel{8}}{}^{1}4 \\ - 3\ 7 \\ \hline 4\ 7 \end{array}$$

Now we try 47 in the original problem.

$$\begin{array}{r} \overset{1}{} \\ 37 \\ + 47 \\ \hline 84 \end{array}$$

The answer checks. The missing addend is **47.**

Practice   Find the missing addends:

a.   23   **b.**   Q   28   **c.**   28   **d.**   Y   18
         $\underline{+\ M}$ 19 $\underline{+\ 17}$ $\underline{+\ W}$ 25 $\underline{+\ 36}$
         42   45   53   54

**Problem set
30**
(12)

275 fans
+ 362 fans
  N fans

47 apples
+ N apples
 82 apples

1. Two hundred seventy-five fans sat in the first row.
Three hundred sixty-two fans sat in the second row.
How many fans sat in the first two rows? Draw a SSM
pattern.   637 fans

2. There were 47 apples in the big tree. There was a total
(17) of 82 apples in the big tree and in the little tree. How
many apples were in the little tree? Draw a SSM
pattern.   35 apples

3. All the students lined up in two equal rows. Which
(11) could not be the total number of students?   B. 45

A. 36   B. 45   C. 60

Find the missing numbers in each sequence:

4. 9, 18, __27__, __36__, 45, __54__, ...
(3)

5. 7, 14, __21__, __28__, 35, __42__, ...
(3)

6. Compare: 15 − 9 ⊘ 13 − 8
(15,7)

7. Round 77 to the nearest ten.   80
(26)

8. A professional basketball player is about how many
(27) meters tall?   2 m

9. If it is morning, what time is
(23) shown on this clock?   7:10 a.m.

10. Which street is parallel to Elm?
(29) Oak

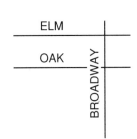

11. What fraction of this shape is
(28) shaded? $\frac{1}{2}$

12. Draw a rectangle that is 3 centimeters long and 2
(25) centimeters wide.

13. Which of these angles is a right angle? A. ⌐
(29)
A. ⌐   B. ╲   C. ╲

14. $31   **15.** $468   **16.**   57   **17.** $4.97
(19) − $14   (16) + $247   (18) − 37   (28) + $2.58
      ———   ————   ——   ————
      $17 $715   20 $7.55

18.   36   **19.**   *B* 17   **20.**   87   **21.**   *N* 44
(20) − *C* 17   (30) + 65   (30) + *D* 6   (20) − 32
      ——   ——   ——   ——
      19   82   93   12

22. 48 − 28   20   **23.** 41 − 32   9   **24.** 76 − 58   18
(18)   (19)   (19)

25. 416 + 35 + 27 + 43 + 5   526
(21)

LESSON
31

"Some Went Away" Word Problems

a. 42
b. 34
c. 43
d. 53
e. 75
f. 53
Problem Solving:
  Lowest value:
    $0.07
  Highest value:
    $1.75

Facts Practice: 100 Subtraction Facts (Test B in Test Masters)

Mental Math: We can split numbers to help us add. Adding 35
and 8, we may notice that 35 needs 5 more to
make 40, and that 8 splits into 5 + 3. So to add
35 and 8, we could add 35 + 5 + 3.

  a. 35 + 7   **b.** 26 + 8   **c.** 38 + 5
  d. 47 + 6   **e.** 68 + 7   **f.** 45 + 8

Problem Solving: Tom has seven coins in his right pocket. He
does not have a half dollar in his right pocket.
What is the lowest possible value of all seven
coins? What is the highest possible value of
all seven coins?

We have practiced "some and some more" story problems.
The "some and some more" pattern is an addition pattern.

In this lesson we will begin practicing **"some went away"** story problems. The "some went away" pattern is a subtraction pattern. In this book we will sometimes use the initials SWA to stand for "some went away." Read this "some went away" story:

John had 7 marbles. Then he lost 3 marbles. He has 4 marbles left.

We will write the information from this story in a "some went away" story pattern. We use a subtraction sign in this pattern.

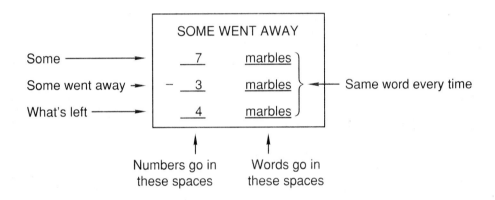

In a subtraction pattern, the top number is the largest number. The top number is the sum of the other two numbers. If we know two numbers in the pattern, we can find the missing number.

Example 1   Jimmy had some marbles. Then he lost 15 marbles. He has 22 marbles left. How many marbles did he have in the beginning?

Solution   He had some marbles. Then **some marbles went away.** The pattern for a "some went away" problem is a subtraction pattern. To make a subtraction pattern, we use six lines and a minus sign.

The same word goes in the three spaces on the right. This problem is about marbles, so the word is "marbles."

$$
\begin{array}{r}
\underline{} \quad \text{marbles} \\
- \ \underline{} \quad \text{marbles} \\
\underline{} \quad \text{marbles}
\end{array}
$$

He began with some marbles. Then 15 marbles went away. **In a "some went away" problem, the number that went away has the minus sign.** Then he had 22 marbles left.

Some	N	marbles
Some went away	$-$ 15	marbles
What's left	22	marbles

We can find the missing number in this subtraction pattern by asking an **addition question.**

22 marbles + 15 marbles = how many marbles?

The answer is **37 marbles.**

Now we check the answer.

$$
\begin{array}{r}
37 \text{ marbles} \\
- \ 15 \text{ marbles} \\
\hline
22 \text{ marbles} \quad \text{check}
\end{array}
$$

Example 2   Celia had 42 marbles. She lost some marbles. She has 29 marbles left. How many marbles did she lose?

Solution   **Some marbles went away.** "Some went away" problems have a subtraction pattern. Since some marbles were lost, the minus sign goes with those "some went away" marbles.

Some	42	marbles
Some went away	$-$ N	marbles
What's left	29	marbles

Now we must find the missing number in the pattern. To find the middle number, we subtract. Let's subtract 29 from 42.

$$\begin{array}{r} 42 \\ -\ 29 \\ \hline 13 \end{array}$$

Now let's see if **13 marbles** makes the pattern correct.

$$\begin{array}{r} 42 \text{ marbles} \\ -\ 13 \text{ marbles} \\ \hline 29 \text{ marbles} \end{array}$$

Now we check. We can check two ways.

$$42 - 13 = 29 \quad \text{check}$$

$$29 + 13 = 42 \quad \text{check}$$

Example 3 Rebecca had 65 marbles. Then she lost 13 marbles. How many marbles does she have left?

Solution This problem has the thought that **some went away.** This problem has a subtraction pattern. The number that went away has the minus sign.

Some	65	marbles
Some went away	$-$ 13	marbles
What's left	W	marbles

Now we have the pattern. To find the missing number, we subtract 13 from 65 and get 52.

$$\begin{array}{r} 65 \text{ marbles} \\ -\ 13 \text{ marbles} \\ \hline \mathbf{52 \text{ marbles}} \end{array}$$

To check, we note that 52 plus 13 equals 65. This means that our answer is correct.

Practice Draw a "some went away" pattern for each problem. Then answer each question.

a. Marko had 42 marbles. Then he lost some marbles. Now he has 26 marbles. How many marbles did he lose? 16 marbles; $\begin{array}{r} 42 \text{ marbles} \\ -\ N \text{ marbles} \\ \hline 26 \text{ marbles} \end{array}$

$\begin{array}{r} N \text{ marbles} \\ -\ 42 \text{ marbles} \\ \hline 26 \text{ marbles} \end{array}$ **b.** Karen lost 42 marbles. Now she has 26 marbles. How many marbles did she have in the beginning? 68 marbles

c. Barbara had 75 cents. Then she spent 27 cents. Now how many cents does Barbara have?   48 cents; $\begin{array}{r} 75 \text{ cents} \\ - 27 \text{ cents} \\ \hline N \text{ cents} \end{array}$

Problem set 31

1. Micky had 75 rocks. Then she lost some rocks. Now
(31) she has 27 rocks. How many rocks did she lose? Draw a "some went away" pattern.   48 rocks; $\begin{array}{r} 75 \text{ rocks} \\ - N \text{ rocks} \\ \hline 27 \text{ rocks} \end{array}$

2. Sixty-three birds sat in the tree. Then fourteen birds
(31) flew away. How many birds remained in the tree? Draw a SWA pattern.   49 birds; $\begin{array}{r} 63 \text{ birds} \\ - 14 \text{ birds} \\ \hline N \text{ birds} \end{array}$

3. There were many cats in the alley at noon. Seventy-
(31) five cats ran away. Forty-seven cats remained. How many cats were in the alley at noon? Draw a SWA pattern.   122 cats; $\begin{array}{r} N \text{ cats} \\ - 75 \text{ cats} \\ \hline 47 \text{ cats} \end{array}$

4. There are 12 months in a whole year. How many
(6) months are in half of a year?   6 months

5. Find the missing numbers in this sequence:
(3)
$$5, 10, \underline{\hspace{0.5em} 15 \hspace{0.5em}}, \underline{\hspace{0.5em} 20 \hspace{0.5em}}, 25, \underline{\hspace{0.5em} 30 \hspace{0.5em}}, \ldots$$

6. Use digits and a comparison symbol to write that
(15) seven hundred sixty-two is less than eight hundred twenty-six.   762 < 826

7. Round 78 to the nearest ten.   80
(26)

8. Use a centimeter scale to measure the width of the
(24) cover of this book.   19 cm or 20 cm

9. If it is afternoon, what time is it?
(23) 1:20 p.m.

10. Which street is perpendicular to
(29) Elm?   Broadway

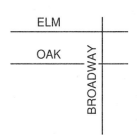

11. What fraction of this shape is
(28) shaded? $\frac{5}{12}$

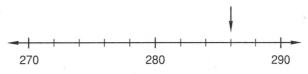

12. Draw a square whose sides are 2 cm long.
(25)

13. To what number is the arrow pointing?   286
(13)

14. $52   **15.**   476   **16.**   62   **17.** $4.97
(19) − $14   *(16)* + 177   *(19)* − 38   *(28)* + $2.58
       ―――――   ―――――   ―――――   ――――――
         $38   653   24 $7.55

18.   36   18   **19.**   55   32   **20.**   D   81 **21.**   Y   18
(20) − G   *(18)* + B   *(20)* − 23   *(30)* + 14
       ――――   ――――   ――――   ――――
         18   87   58   32

22. 42 − 37   5   **23.** 52 − 22   30
(19)   *(18)*

24. 73 − 59   14   **25.** 900 + 90 + 9   999
(19)   *(21)*

LESSON 32

Drawing Pictures of Fractions

a. 44
b. 54
c. 56
d. 186
e. 590
f. 283
Patterns:
25, 36, 49, 64, 81, 100

Facts Practice: 100 Subtraction Facts (Test B in Test Masters)

Mental Math: Practice splitting the second number to add.

   a. 36 + 8   **b.** 48 + 6   **c.** 47 + 9

Review:

   d. 67 + 19 + 100   **e.** 350 + 40 + 200   **f.** 38 + 45 + 200

Patterns: In some sequences the count from one number to the next increases. In this sequence, from 1 to 4 is 3, from 4 to 9 is 5, and from 9 to 16 is 7. (Notice that the increase itself forms a sequence.) Continue this sequence to the tenth term, which is 100.

1, 4, 9, 16, ...

We can understand fractions better if we learn to draw pictures that represent fractions.

Example 1 Draw a rectangle and shade two thirds of it.

Solution On the left, we draw a rectangle. In the center, we divide the rectangle into **3 equal parts.**

Rectangle   3 equal parts   2 parts shaded

On the right, we shade any two of the equal parts. We have shaded two thirds of the rectangle.

There are many ways to divide the rectangle into three parts. Here is another way.

Rectangle   3 equal parts   2 parts shaded

Again we have shaded two thirds of the rectangle.

Example 2   Draw a circle and shade one fourth of it.

Solution   First we draw a circle. Then we divide the circle into **four equal parts.** Then we shade any one of the parts. We have shaded one fourth of the circle.

Circle   4 equal parts   1 part shaded

Practice   Follow your teacher's example as you do these exercises:

    a. Draw a square and shade one half of it.

b. Draw a rectangle and shade one third of it.

    c. Draw a circle and shade three fourths of it.

d. Draw a circle and shade two thirds of it.

**Problem set
32**

$$\begin{array}{r} 42 \text{ pebbles} \\ -\ N \text{ pebbles} \\ \hline 27 \text{ pebbles} \end{array}$$

$$\begin{array}{r} N \text{ pebbles} \\ -\ 17 \text{ pebbles} \\ \hline 46 \text{ pebbles} \end{array}$$

1. Mary had 42 pebbles. She threw some in the lake. Then she had 27 pebbles left. How many pebbles did she throw in the lake? Draw a SWA pattern.
(31)
15 pebbles

2. Demosthenes had a bag of pebbles when the sun came up. He put 17 pebbles in his mouth. Then there were 46 pebbles left in the bag. How many pebbles were in the bag when the sun came up? Draw a SWA pattern.
(31)
63 pebbles

3. Franklin saw one hundred twelve stars. Eleanor looked the other way and saw some more. If they saw three hundred seventeen stars in all, how many did Eleanor see? Draw a SSM pattern.   205 stars;
(17)
$$\begin{array}{r} 112 \text{ stars} \\ +\ N \text{ stars} \\ \hline 317 \text{ stars} \end{array}$$

4. Use the digits 4, 5, and 6 once each to write an even number less than 500.   456
(11)

Find the missing numbers in each sequence:

5. 14, 21, __28__, 35, __42__, __49__, …
(3)

6. 16, 24, __32__, 40, __48__, __56__, …
(3)

7. Use digits and symbols to show that twenty-seven
(15) plus eleven equals eleven plus twenty-seven.
27 + 11 = 11 + 27

8. Round 19 to the nearest ten. 20
(26)

9. One meter equals how many centimeters? 100 cm
(27)

10. If it is before noon, what time is
(23) shown by this clock? 11:35 a.m.

11. Which street makes a right angle
(29) with Oak? Broadway

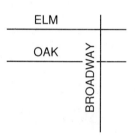

12. What fraction of this figure is
(28) shaded? $\frac{3}{10}$

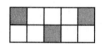

13. This scale shows weight in
(22) pounds. How many pounds does
the needle show? 360 pounds

14. (30) $\begin{array}{r} Y \\ + 63 \\ \hline 81 \end{array}$ 18	**15.** (16) $\begin{array}{r} \$486 \\ + \$277 \\ \hline \$763 \end{array}$	**16.** (19) $\begin{array}{r} \$68 \\ - \$39 \\ \hline \$29 \end{array}$	**17.** (28) $\begin{array}{r} \$5.97 \\ + \$2.38 \\ \hline \$8.35 \end{array}$

18. $\begin{array}{r} 71 \\ - 42 \\ \hline 29 \end{array}$ **19.** $\begin{array}{r} 87 \\ - N \\ \hline 65 \end{array}$ 22 **20.** $\begin{array}{r} 27 \\ + C \\ \hline 48 \end{array}$ 21 **21.** $\begin{array}{r} E \\ - 14 \\ \hline 25 \end{array}$ 39
(19)   (20)   (18)   (20)

22. 42 − 29 13 **23.** 77 − 37 40 **24.** 41 − 19 22
(19)   (18)   (19)

25. 4 + 7 + 15 + 21 + 5 + 4 + 3 59
(21)

**LESSON
33**

Multiplication as Repeated Addition • Elapsed Time

a. 65
b. 74
c. 43
d. 175
e. 885
f. 590
Problem Solving:
   Lowest value:
      $0.44
   Highest value:
      $1.16

> **Facts Practice:** 100 Subtraction Facts (Test B in Test Masters)
>
> **Mental Math:** Practice splitting the second number to add.
>   **a.** 58 + 7   **b.** 65 + 9   **c.** 37 + 6
>
> **Review:**
>   **d.** 46 + 29 + 100   **e.** 650 + 35 + 200   **f.** 340 + 43 + 207
>
> **Problem Solving:** Johnna has seven coins in her right pocket. She does not have a half dollar, but she does have at least one penny, one nickel, one dime, and one quarter. What is the lowest possible value of all seven coins? What is the highest possible value of all seven coins?

Multiplication as repeated addition

Suppose we want to find the total number of dots shown on these four number cubes.

There are several ways we can find the total number of dots. One way is to count the number of dots one by one. Another way is to recognize that there are five dots in each group and that there are four groups. We can find the answer by adding four fives.

$$5 + 5 + 5 + 5 = 20$$

We can also use multiplication to show that we want to add five four times.

$$4 \times 5 = 20 \qquad \text{or} \qquad \begin{array}{r} 5 \\ \times\ 4 \\ \hline 20 \end{array}$$

If we find the answer this way, we are using multiplication. We call the × a **multiplication sign.** We read 4 × 5 as "Four times five."

Example 1   Change this addition problem to a multiplication problem:

$$6 + 6 + 6 + 6 + 6$$

Solution   We see five sixes. We can change this addition problem to a multiplication problem by writing either

$$5 \times 6 \qquad \text{or} \qquad \begin{array}{r} 6 \\ \times\, 5 \\ \hline \end{array}$$

Elapsed time   Elapsed time is time that has gone by. To find elapsed time, we must find the difference between two times.

Example 2   If it is afternoon, what time will it be in 3 hours and 20 minutes?

Solution   First we count forward on the clock face 20 minutes. From that point we count forward 3 hours.

> **Step 1.** From 1:45 p.m. we count forward 20 minutes. This makes it 2:05 p.m.
>
> **Step 2.** From 2:05 p.m. we count forward 3 hours. This makes it **5:05 p.m.**

Example 3   If it is afternoon, what time was it 4 hours and 25 minutes ago?

Solution   First count back the number of minutes. Then count back hours.

> **Step 1.** We count back 25 minutes from 1:15 p.m. This makes it 12:50 p.m.
>
> **Step 2.** From 12:50 p.m. we count back 4 hours. This makes it **8:50 a.m.**

Practice Change each addition problem to a multiplication problem:

a. 3 + 3 + 3 + 3   4 × 3   **b.** 9 + 9 + 9   3 × 9

c. 7 + 7 + 7 + 7 + 7 + 7   6 × 7

d. 5 + 5 + 5 + 5 + 5 + 5 + 5 + 5   8 × 5

Use this clock to answer these questions.

e. If it is morning, what time will it be in 2 hours and 25 minutes?
1:00 p.m.

f. If it is morning, what time was it 6 hours and 30 minutes ago?
4:05 a.m.

Problem set 33

78 elves
− N elves
42 elves

1. Just before high noon, Nancy saw seventy-eight elves playing in the valley. At high noon, there were only forty-two elves playing in the valley. How many elves had left the valley by high noon? Draw a SWA pattern.
(31)
36 elves

2. According to the ancient Greeks, dryads were wood nymphs. Penelope went one way and saw forty-six dryads. Perseus went the other way and saw some more dryads. Altogether, they saw seventy-three dryads. How many dryads did Perseus see? Draw a SSM pattern.   27 dryads;   46 dryads / + N dryads / 73 dryads
(17)

3. List the even numbers between 31 and 39.
(11) 32, 34, 36, 38

Find the missing numbers in each sequence:

4. 8, __12__, __16__, 20, 24, __28__, ...
(3)

5. 24, __21__, __18__, 15, 12, __9__, ...
(3)

6. Write 265 in expanded form.   200 + 60 + 5
(20)

7. Use words to write 613.   six hundred thirteen
(8)

8. Round 63 to the nearest ten.   60
(26)

9. Compare: $392 \gtrdot 329$
(15)

10. The arrow is pointing to what number?   550
(13)

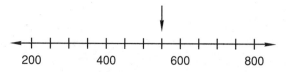

200   400   600   800

11. Draw a square and shade one fourth of it.
(32)

12. What fraction of this figure is
(28)   shaded? $\frac{2}{5}$

13. It is afternoon. What will be the
(33)   time 3 hours from now?   4:20 p.m.

14. $67
(19) $-\ 29
$38

15.   483
(16) $+\ 378$
861

16.   71
(19) $-\ 39$
32

17. $5.88
(28) $+\ 2.39
$8.27

18. D 17
(30) $+\ 19$
36

19.   66
(18) $+\ F$ 21
87

20.   87
(20) $-\ R$ 20
67

21. B 41
(20) $-\ 14$
27

22. $400 - 300$ 100
(18)

23. $663 - 363$ 300
(18)

24. Change this addition problem to a multiplication
(33)   problem: 4×9

$$9 + 9 + 9 + 9$$

25. $5 + 7 + 3 + 6 + 4 + 8 + 7 + 2 + 5 + 6 + 4 + 8$
(1)   65

LESSON
34

a. 65
b. 84
c. 53
d. 890
e. 282
f. 592
Patterns:

25

36

The Multiplication Table

Facts Practice: 100 Subtraction Facts (Test B in Test Masters)

Mental Math: Practice splitting the second number to add.

   a. 57 + 8   **b.** 78 + 6   **c.** 49 + 4

Review:

   d. 300 + 520 + 70   **e.** 63 + 19 + 200   **f.** 354 + 220 + 18

Patterns: Here we show 4 squares. The smallest is 1 small square. The next have 4, 9, and 16 small squares, respectively. Draw the next 2 squares in the pattern.

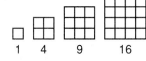

1   4   9   16

If we count by zeros, ones, twos, and threes, we get the sequences shown below.

Zeros	0	0	0	0	0	0	0	0	0	0	0	0
Ones	1	2	3	4	5	6	7	8	9	10	11	12
Twos	2	4	6	8	10	12	14	16	18	20	22	24
Threes	3	6	9	12	15	18	21	24	27	30	33	36

If we count by fours, fives, sixes, sevens, eights, and nines,[†] and put all these sequences in a box, we have a **multiplication table**.

Multiplication Table

	0	1	2	3	4	5	6	7	8	9
0	0	0	0	0	0	0	0	0	0	0
1	0	1	2	3	4	5	6	7	8	9
2	0	2	4	6	8	10	12	14	16	18
3	0	3	6	9	12	15	18	21	24	27
4	0	4	8	12	16	20	24	28	32	36
5	0	5	10	15	20	25	30	35	40	45
6	0	6	12	18	24	30	36	42	48	54
7	0	7	14	21	28	35	42	49	56	63
8	0	8	16	24	32	40	48	56	64	72
9	0	9	18	27	36	45	54	63	72	81

[†]Multiplication by tens, elevens, and twelves is considered in Appendix A.

From a multiplication table we can find the answer to multiplications such as 3 × 4 by using rows and columns. Rows run left to right and columns run top to bottom. We start by finding the row which begins with the 3 and the column which begins with the 4. Then we look for the number where that row and column meet.

Column

	0	1	2	3	4	5	6	7	8	9
0	0	0	0	0	0	0	0	0	0	0
1	0	1	2	3	4	5	6	7	8	9
2	0	2	4	6	8	10	12	14	16	18
3	0	3	6	9	(12)	15	18	21	24	27
4	0	4	8	12	16	20	24	28	32	36
5	0	5	10	15	20	25	30	35	40	45
6	0	6	12	18	24	30	36	42	48	54
7	0	7	14	21	28	35	42	49	56	63
8	0	8	16	24	32	40	48	56	64	72
9	0	9	18	27	36	45	54	63	72	81

Row →

Each of the two numbers multiplied is called a **factor.** The answer to a multiplication problem is called a **product.** In this problem, 3 and 4 are factors and 12 is the product. In multiplication problems, the order of the factors does not matter. Thus, the product of 4 × 3 also equals 12.

Practice   Use the multiplication table to find the following products:

a. $\begin{array}{r} 9 \\ \times\, 3 \\ \hline 27 \end{array}$ **b.** $\begin{array}{r} 3 \\ \times\, 9 \\ \hline 27 \end{array}$ **c.** $\begin{array}{r} 6 \\ \times\, 4 \\ \hline 24 \end{array}$ **d.** $\begin{array}{r} 4 \\ \times\, 6 \\ \hline 24 \end{array}$

e. $\begin{array}{r} 7 \\ \times\, 8 \\ \hline 56 \end{array}$ **f.** $\begin{array}{r} 8 \\ \times\, 7 \\ \hline 56 \end{array}$ **g.** $\begin{array}{r} 5 \\ \times\, 8 \\ \hline 40 \end{array}$ **h.** $\begin{array}{r} 8 \\ \times\, 5 \\ \hline 40 \end{array}$

**Problem set
34**

72 pieces of gingerbread
+ 342 pieces of gingerbread
N pieces of gingerbread

1. Hansel ate seventy-two pieces of gingerbread. Then
(12) Gretel ate three hundred forty-two pieces of
gingerbread. How many pieces of gingerbread did they
eat in all? Draw a SSM pattern.   414 pieces of gingerbread

2. Sherry needs $35 to buy a baseball glove. She has
(17) saved $18. How much more money does she need?
Draw a SSM pattern. $17; $\begin{array}{r}\$18 \\ + \ N \\ \hline \$35\end{array}$

3. All of the men walked to the meeting. Then forty-two
(31) men got mad and went home. Only twenty-three men
were left at the meeting. How many men walked to the
meeting? Draw a SWA pattern.   65 men; $\begin{array}{r}N \text{ men} \\ -42 \text{ men} \\ \hline 23 \text{ men}\end{array}$

Find the missing numbers in each sequence:

4. 12, __18__, __24__, 30, 36, __42__, ...
(3)

5. 36, __32__, __28__, 24, 20, __16__, ...
(3)

6. Use words to write 265.   two hundred sixty-five
(8)

7. Round 28 to the nearest ten.   30
(26)

8. A right triangle has one right angle. Draw a right
(29,24) triangle. Draw the two perpendicular sides 3 cm long
and 4 cm long.

3 cm   4 cm

9. It is morning. What time will it be
(33) 10 minutes from now?   10:25 a.m.

10. What fraction of the group is
(28) shaded? $\frac{5}{12}$

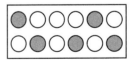

11. Write 417 in expanded form.   400 + 10 + 7
(20)

12. How long is this arrow?   4 cm
(24)

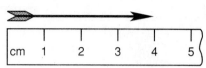

13. 76   **14.** $286   **15.** $73   **16.** $5.87
(19) − 29   (16) + $388   (19) − $39   (28) + $2.43
───   ──────   ─────   ──────
  47       $674 $34 $8.30

17. 46   **18.** N   39   **19.** 29   **20.**   D   51
(20) − C 27   (30) + 48   (30) + Y 28   (20) − 14
───   ──   ──   ──
  19   87   57   37

21. 78 − 43   35   **22.** 77 − 17   60   **23.** 53 − 19   34
(18)   (18)   (19)

24. Change this addition problem to a multiplication
(33) problem: 7 × 6

6 + 6 + 6 + 6 + 6 + 6 + 6

25. 4 + 3 + 6 + 5 + 2 + 3 + 7 + 4 + 5 + 2 + 8 + 9
(1)   58

LESSON 35

a. 55
b. 73
c. 46
d. 965
e. 186
f. 890
Problem Solving:
 $0.57; $0.72; $0.77;
 $0.81

Multiplication Facts (0, 1, 2, 5)

Facts Practice: 100 Subtraction Facts (Test B in Test Masters)

Mental Math: Practice splitting the second number to add.

 a. 49 + 6   **b.** 65 + 8   **c.** 38 + 8

Review:

 d. 920 + 38 + 7   **e.** 57 + 29 + 100   **f.** 350 + 40 + 500

Problem Solving: Tom has seven coins in his right pocket. He does not have a half dollar, but he has at least one penny, one nickel, one dime, and one quarter. However, Tom has no more than two of any one kind of coin. What are the possible values of all seven coins? (There are four possibilities.)

We must memorize all the multiplication facts. Sixty-four of the 100 multiplication facts in the multiplication table shown in Lesson 34 have 0, 1, 2, or 5 as one of the factors. These facts are the easiest to learn.

Zero times any number equals zero.

$$0 \times 5 = 0 \quad\quad 5 \times 0 = 0 \quad\quad 7 \times 0 = 0 \quad\quad 0 \times 7 = 0$$

One times any number equals the number.

$$1 \times 5 = 5 \quad\quad 5 \times 1 = 5 \quad\quad 7 \times 1 = 7 \quad\quad 1 \times 7 = 7$$

Two times any number doubles the number.

$$2 \times 5 = 10 \quad 2 \times 7 = 14 \quad 2 \times 6 = 12 \quad 2 \times 8 = 16$$

Until we have memorized the facts, we can find multiples of 2 by counting by twos. So 6×2 is the sixth number we say when counting by twos: 2, 4, 6, 8, 10, 12. **Counting by twos is not a substitute for memorizing the facts.**

Five times any number equals a number that ends in zero or in five.

$$5 \times 1 = 5 \quad 5 \times 3 = 15 \quad 5 \times 8 = 40 \quad 5 \times 7 = 35$$

Until we have memorized the facts, we can find multiples of 5 by counting by fives. The sixth number we say when counting by fives is 30, so $6 \times 5 = 30$.

Practice   Do the Facts Practice "Multiplication Facts: 0, 1, 2, 5" (Test C in Test Masters).

Problem set 35

1. Two hundred sixty-two soldiers were in the vanguard.
   $^{(12)}$ Three hundred seventy-five were in the main body. One hundred seven were in the rear guard. How many soldiers were there in all? Draw a SSM pattern.
   744 soldiers

   $$\begin{array}{r} 262 \text{ soldiers} \\ 375 \text{ soldiers} \\ + 107 \text{ soldiers} \\ \hline N \text{ soldiers} \end{array}$$

2. Ninety-two blackbirds squawked noisily in the tree.
   $^{(31)}$ Then some flew away. Twenty-four blackbirds remained. How many blackbirds flew away? Draw a SWA pattern.   68 blackbirds;

   $$\begin{array}{r} 92 \text{ blackbirds} \\ - N \text{ blackbirds} \\ \hline 24 \text{ blackbirds} \end{array}$$

3. Robill threw 42 rocks. Then Buray threw some rocks.
   $^{(17)}$ They threw 83 rocks in all. How many rocks did Buray throw? Draw a SSM pattern.   41 rocks;

   $$\begin{array}{r} 42 \text{ rocks} \\ + N \text{ rocks} \\ \hline 83 \text{ rocks} \end{array}$$

Find the missing numbers in each sequence:

4. 8, __16__ , __24__ , 32, 40, __48__ , ...
(3)

5. 14, __21__ , __28__ , 35, 42, ...
(3)

6. Use the digits 4, 5, and 6 once each to write a three-
(11) digit odd number that is less than 640.   465

7. Use digits and a comparison symbol to write that two
(15) hundred nine is greater than one hundred ninety.
209 > 190

8. It is afternoon. What time will it
(33) be in 6 hours?
9:25 p.m.

9. Draw a rectangle and shade two
(32) thirds of it.

10. 2 × 8   **11.** 5 × 7   **12.** 2 × 7   **13.** 5 × 8
(35,34) 16   (35,34) 35   (35,34) 14   (35,34) 40

14. $83   **15.** $286   **16.**   72   **17.** $5.87
(19) − $19   (16) + $387   (19) − 38   (28) + $2.79
    $64 $673   34 $8.66

18.   19   **19.**   88   **20.**   88   **21.** G 33
(30) + Q 27   (20) − N 51   (20) − M 41   (18) + 14
    46   37   47   47

22. 870 − 470   400   **23.** 525 − 521   4
(18)   (18)

24. Change this addition problem to a multiplication
(33) problem: 3 × 8

8 + 8 + 8

25. 2 + 5 + 3 + 7 + 8 + 5 + 6 + 4 + 3 + 2 + 1 + 5 + 4
(1)   55

LESSON
36

Multiplication Patterns

a. 20
b. 50
c. 500
d. 74
e. 186
f. 490

Patterns:

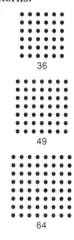

36

49

64

Facts Practice: Multiplication Facts: 0, 1, 2, 5 (Test C in Test Masters)

Mental Math: Subtract numbers ending in one or two zeros.

   a. 60 − 40   **b.** 80 − 30   **c.** 800 − 300

Review:

   d. 67 + 7   **e.** 67 + 19 + 100   **f.** 340 + 35 + 115

Patterns: These dots are arranged in square patterns of 2 rows of 2, 3 rows of 3, and so on. Copy these patterns and continue the sequence to 8 rows of 8.

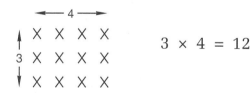

4   9   16   25

We can draw patterns that help us understand multiplication. The patterns have the shapes of rectangles. The patterns have rows and columns. One of the numbers in the multiplication pattern is the number of rows. The other number is the number of columns.

To make our first pattern, we will use X's to show the multiplication of 3 times 4. We will use 3 rows and 4 columns. The total number of X's is the answer.

$$\begin{array}{cccc} X & X & X & X \\ X & X & X & X \\ X & X & X & X \end{array} \qquad 3 \times 4 = 12$$

We do not have to use X's. Another method is to draw a rectangle with small squares. We will use 3 rows of small squares. There are 4 columns of small squares.

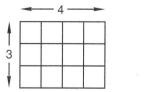 $3 \times 4 = 12$

Example 1   Draw a pattern of X's to show the multiplication of 4 × 5.

Solution   One of the numbers is the number of rows, and the other number is the number of columns. It does not matter which is which. We show both patterns.

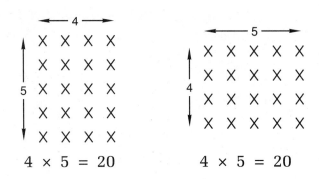

$$4 \times 5 = 20 \qquad\qquad 4 \times 5 = 20$$

Example 2   Draw a rectangle to show the multiplication fact 2 × 4 = 8.

Solution   We will draw a rectangle that is 2 small squares wide and 4 small squares long.

$$2 \times 4 = 8$$

Practice   **a.** Draw a pattern of X's to show the multiplication fact 6 × 3 = 18.

b. Draw a rectangle to show the multiplication fact 2 × 5 = 10.

Write a multiplication fact for each pattern below:

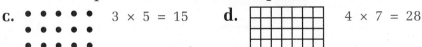

c.   3 × 5 = 15   **d.**   4 × 7 = 28

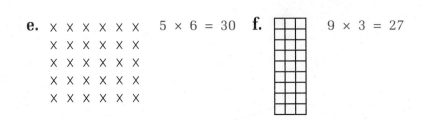

e. X X X X X X   5 × 6 = 30   **f.**   9 × 3 = 27

**Problem set
36**

28 boys
35 boys
+ 50 boys
N boys

40 crayons
− N crayons
19 crayons

N crayons
+ 36 crayons
72 crayons

1. Twenty-eight boys sat in the first row. Thirty-five boys
(12) sat in the second row. Fifty boys sat in the third row.
How many boys sat in the first three rows? Draw a
SSM pattern.   113 boys

2. Forty crayons were in the box. Fran took some crayons
(31) out of the box. Nineteen crayons were left in the box.
How many crayons did Fran take out of the box? Draw
a SWA pattern.   21 crayons

3. William had some crayons when he came to school.
(17) Then Fran gave him 36 crayons. William now has 72
crayons. How many crayons did William have when
he came to school? Draw a SSM pattern.   36 crayons

4. The first eight counting numbers are 1, 2, 3, 4, 5, 6, 7,
(1) and 8. What is the sum of the first eight counting
numbers?   36

5. Find the missing numbers in this sequence:
(3)
45, __54__, __63__, 72, 81, __90__, ...

6. It is evening. What time was it 10
(33) hours ago?   9:15 a.m.

7. Write 703 in expanded form. Then use words to write
(20,8) this number.   700 + 3; seven hundred three

8. Use digits and symbols to write that eight times zero
(15) equals nine times zero.   8 × 0 = 9 × 0

9. This metal object was found in a park. About how long
(24) is it?   3 cm

10. A 2 is in the ones' place. The number is between 742
(5) and 762. What is the number?   752

x x x x x x x   **11.** Draw a pattern of X's to show the multiplication of
x x x x x x x (36) 2 × 7.

12. 4 × 5   20   **13.** 2 × 5   10   **14.** 5 × 8   40
(35,34)   (35,34)   (35,34)

15.   93   **16.** $386   **17.** $61   **18.** $5.86
(19)   − 29   (16)   + $275   (19)   − $38   (28)   + $3.76
         64              $661 $23 $9.62

19.   C   23 **20.**   84   **21.**   C   90 **22.**   N   35
(18)   + 14   (20)   − A   47 (20)   − 76   (30)   + 28
         37   37   14   63

23. 486 + 294 + 8   788
(21)

24. Change this addition problem to a multiplication
(33) problem: 6 × 7

7 + 7 + 7 + 7 + 7 + 7

25. 2 + 3 + 5 + 7 + 4 + 8 + 5 + 3 + 7 + 6 + 5 + 4
(1)   59

LESSON 37

Subtracting Three-Digit Numbers with Regrouping

a. 300
b. 35
c. 350
d. 162
e. 265
f. 682
Problem Solving:
  $0.72

Facts Practice: 100 Addition Facts (Test A in Test Masters)

Mental Math: Subtract numbers ending in one or two zeros.
  a. 600 − 300   **b.** 65 − 30   **c.** 650 − 300
Review:
  d. 58 + 4 + 100   **e.** 36 + 29 + 200   **f.** 520 + 36 + 126

Problem Solving: Refer to Lesson 35 for information about the coins in Tom's pocket. Although he has an odd number of coins in his right pocket, their total value is an even number of cents. What is the value of the coins?

Up to this point, we have subtracted three-digit numbers without regrouping. In this lesson we will discuss subtracting three-digit numbers with regrouping.

Example 1   Find the difference: $365 − $187

Solution   We write the first number on top. We line up the last digits. We cannot subtract 7 ones from 5 ones.

$$\begin{array}{r} \$365 \\ -\ \$187 \\ \hline (?) \end{array}$$

We exchange 1 ten for 10 ones. Now there are 15 ones, and we can subtract the ones.

$$\begin{array}{r} {}^{5}_{}{}^{1} \\ \$\,3\,\cancel{6}\,5 \\ -\ \$\,1\,8\,7 \\ \hline 8 \end{array}$$

We cannot subtract 8 tens from 5 tens. This time we exchange 1 hundred for 10 tens. Now we have 15 tens and we can subtract.

$$\begin{array}{r} {}^{2}{}^{15}{}^{1} \\ \$\,\cancel{3}\,\cancel{6}\,5 \\ -\ \$\,1\,8\,7 \\ \hline 7\,8 \end{array}$$

We subtract 1 hundred from 2 hundreds to finish. The difference is **$178.**

$$\begin{array}{r} {}^{2}{}^{15}{}^{1} \\ \$\,\cancel{3}\,\cancel{6}\,5 \\ -\ \$\,1\,8\,7 \\ \hline \$\,1\,7\,8 \end{array}$$

Example 2
$$\begin{array}{r} \$4.10 \\ -\ \$1.12 \\ \hline \end{array}$$

Solution   We subtract pennies, then dimes, and then dollars.

$$\begin{array}{r} {}^{0}{}^{1} \\ \$\,4.\cancel{1}\,0 \\ -\ \$\,1.1\,2 \\ \hline 8 \end{array} \qquad \begin{array}{r} {}^{3}{}^{10}{}^{1} \\ \$\,\cancel{4}.\cancel{1}\,0 \\ -\ \$\,1.1\,2 \\ \hline .9\,8 \end{array} \qquad \begin{array}{r} {}^{3}{}^{10}{}^{1} \\ \$\,\cancel{4}.\cancel{1}\,0 \\ -\ \$\,1.1\,2 \\ \hline \$\,2.9\,8 \end{array}$$

Practice   **a.**
$$\begin{array}{r} \$365 \\ -\ \$287 \\ \hline \$78 \end{array}$$
b.
$$\begin{array}{r} \$4.30 \\ -\ \$1.18 \\ \hline \$3.12 \end{array}$$
c.
$$\begin{array}{r} 563 \\ -\ 356 \\ \hline 207 \end{array}$$

d. 240 − 65   175   **e.** 459 − 176   283 **f.** 157 − 98   59

Problem set 37   **1.** The room was full of students when the bell rang.
(31)   Then forty-seven students ran away. Twenty-two students remained. How many students were there when the bell rang? Draw a SWA pattern.   69 students

$$\begin{array}{r} N \text{ students} \\ -\ 47 \text{ students} \\ \hline 22 \text{ students} \end{array}$$

2. Fifty-six children peered through the window of the
(17) pet shop. Then the store owners brought the puppies out. Now there were seventy-three children peering through the window. How many children came to the window when the store owners brought the puppies out? Draw a SSM pattern.   17 children; $\begin{array}{r} 56 \text{ children} \\ + \underline{N \text{ children}} \\ 73 \text{ children} \end{array}$

3. A nickel is worth 5¢. Gilbert has an even number of
(11) nickels in his pocket. Which of the following **could not be** the value of his nickels?   A. 45¢

   A. 45¢   B. 70¢   C. 20¢

4. It is morning. What time will it be
(33) in 15 minutes?   9:35 a.m.

5. Draw a rectangle and shade one fifth of it.
(32)

6. To what number is the arrow pointing?   480
(13)

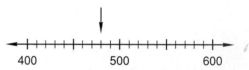

7. Write a multiplication fact for this
(36) pattern.   4 × 8 = 32

8. Write 843 in expanded form. Then use words to write
(20,8) 843.   800 + 40 + 3; eight hundred forty-three

9. 6 × 8   **10.** 4 × 2   **11.** 4 × 5   **12.** 6 × 5
(34) 48   *(35,34)* 8   *(35,34)* 20   *(35,34)* 30

13.   746   **14.** $3.86   **15.**   61   **16.** $4.86
(37) − 295   *(28)* + $2.78   *(19)* − 48   *(37)* − $2.75
        451               $6.64   13 $2.11

17.   51   **18.**   86   **19.**   25   **20.**   Q   61
(30) + M   19   *(20)* − A   43   *(18)* + Y   11   *(20)* − 24
        70   43   36   37

21. Write four addition/subtraction facts using the three
₍₇₎ numbers 8, 3, and 11.
3 + 8 = 11, 8 + 3 = 11, 11 − 3 = 8, 11 − 8 = 3

22. 25¢ + 25¢ + 25¢ + 25¢ $1.00
₍₂₁₎

23. There are 100 cents in a dollar. How many cents are in
₍₂₈₎ half of a dollar?   50 cents

24. Change this addition problem to a multiplication
₍₃₃₎ problem: 7 × 7

$$7 + 7 + 7 + 7 + 7 + 7 + 7$$

25. 4 + 3 + 8 + 4 + 2 + 5 + 7 + 6 + 3 + 7 + 2 + 5
₍₁₎   56

LESSON
38

"Larger-Smaller-Difference" Word Problems

a. 550
b. 36
c. 45
d. 95
e. 162
f. 885
Patterns:
25, 36, 49, 64, 81

Facts Practice: Multiplication Facts: 0, 1, 2, 5 (Test C in Test
Masters)

Mental Math: Subtract numbers ending in one or two zeros.
  a. 750 − 200   **b.** 86 − 50   **c.** 245 − 200
Review:
  d. 78 + 7 + 10   **e.** 43 + 9 + 110   **f.** 630 + 45 + 210

Patterns: This multiplication pattern sequence is 1 × 1, 2 × 2,
3 × 3,.... Use a multiplication table to help you
continue this pattern sequence to 100.

1, 4, 9, 16, ___, ___, ___, ___, ___, 100

There are 43 apples in the large basket.

There are 19 apples in the small basket.

When we compare the number of apples in the two baskets, we see that 43 is **greater than** 19. To find **how much greater** 43 is than 19, we can subtract.

$$
\begin{array}{r}
43 \\
-\ 19 \\
\hline
24
\end{array}
$$

As we think about this problem, we realize that it is not a "some went away" problem because nothing went away. This is a different kind of problem. In this problem we are **comparing** two numbers. The thinking pattern we use to help us compare numbers is called the **"larger-smaller-difference"** pattern. We will sometimes use the abbreviation L-S-D to stand for "larger-smaller-difference."

The "larger-smaller-difference" pattern is a subtraction pattern. We write the two numbers we are comparing on the first two lines with the larger number on top. The smaller number is written on the second line. **The smaller number has a minus sign.** The bottom number tells us **how much larger** the top number is than the middle number. The bottom number also tells us **how much smaller** the middle number is than the top number.

Below we have drawn a "larger-smaller-difference" pattern box. Inside we have written the number of apples in the two baskets.

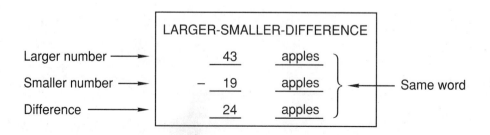

The difference tells us how many more. It also tells us how many fewer. There are **24 more** apples in the large basket than there are in the small basket. We can say this comparison another way. There are **24 fewer** apples in the small basket than there are in the large basket.

Example 1 Forty-two apples is how many more than 13 apples?

Solution To find out **how many more,** we use the "larger-smaller-difference" thinking pattern. The two numbers we are comparing are 42 and 13. We write these on the first two lines with the larger number on top. The minus sign goes with the smaller number.

Larger number	42	apples
Smaller number	− 13	apples
Difference	N	apples

To find the bottom number in this pattern, we subtract.

$$\begin{array}{r} 42 \text{ apples} \\ - 13 \text{ apples} \\ \hline 29 \text{ apples} \end{array} \qquad \begin{array}{r} 29 \\ + 13 \\ \hline 42 \end{array} \text{ check}$$

Forty-two apples is **29 apples** more than 13 apples.

Example 2 Seventeen apples is how many fewer than 63 apples?

Solution Whether we are finding how many more or how many fewer, we still use the "larger-smaller-difference" thinking pattern. We are comparing 17 and 63. We write "63" on top.

Larger number	63	apples
Smaller number	− 17	apples
Difference	N	apples

To find the bottom number, we subtract.

$$\begin{array}{r} 63 \text{ apples} \\ - 17 \text{ apples} \\ \hline 46 \text{ apples} \end{array} \qquad \begin{array}{r} 46 \\ + 17 \\ \hline 63 \end{array} \text{ check}$$

Seventeen apples is **46 apples** fewer than 63 apples.

Example 3   Seventeen is how much less than 42?

Solution   Problems about numbers that ask **how much less** or **how much greater** also have a "larger-smaller-difference" pattern. Since we are just comparing numbers, there are no words to write in the pattern.

Larger number	42 ____
Smaller number	− 17 ____
Difference	N ____

We find the bottom number by subtracting.

$$\begin{array}{r} 42 \\ -\ 17 \\ \hline 25 \end{array} \qquad \begin{array}{r} 25 \\ +\ 17 \\ \hline 42 \end{array} \ \text{check}$$

Seventeen is **25** less than 42.

Practice   Draw a "larger-smaller-difference" pattern for each problem. Then answer each question.

$$\begin{array}{r} 43 \ \_\_ \\ -\ 27 \ \_\_ \\ \hline N \ \_\_ \end{array}$$

a. Forty-three is how much greater than twenty-seven?   16

$$\begin{array}{r} 42 \text{ peanuts} \\ -\ 22 \text{ peanuts} \\ \hline N \text{ peanuts} \end{array}$$

b. Mary has 42 peanuts. Frank has 22 peanuts. How many fewer peanuts does Frank have?   20 peanuts

$$\begin{array}{r} 95 \text{ shells} \\ -\ 53 \text{ shells} \\ \hline N \text{ shells} \end{array}$$

c. Roger had 53 shells. Juanita had 95 shells. How many more shells did Juanita have?   42 shells

Problem set 38

$$\begin{array}{r} 43 \text{ parrots} \\ -\ N \text{ parrots} \\ \hline 27 \text{ parrots} \end{array}$$

1. There were 43 parrots in the tree. Some flew away.
(31) Then there were 27 parrots in the tree. How many flew away? Draw a SWA pattern.   16 parrots

$$\begin{array}{r} 150 \ \_\_ \\ -\ 23 \ \_\_ \\ \hline N \ \_\_ \end{array}$$

2. One hundred fifty is how much greater than twenty-
(38) three? Draw a "larger-smaller-difference" pattern.
127

$$\begin{array}{r} 75 \text{ apples} \\ -\ 23 \text{ apples} \\ \hline N \text{ apples} \end{array}$$

3. Twenty-three apples is how many fewer than seventy-
(38) five apples? Draw a L-S-D pattern.   52 apples

4. It is evening. What time will it be 3
(33) hours from now?   11:05 p.m.

5. Write 412 in expanded form. Then use words to write
(20,8) the number 412.   400 + 10 + 2; four hundred twelve

6. What fraction of this figure is
(28) shaded? $\frac{7}{18}$

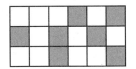

7. Matt drew a triangle that had two sides each 3 cm
(29,24) long. These sides made a right angle. Draw this
triangle.

3 cm

3 cm

8. 2 × 5 10   **9.** 5 × 7 35   **10.** 2 × 7 14
(35,34)   (35,34)   (35,34)

11. To what number is the arrow pointing?   110
(13)

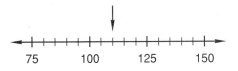

75   100   125   150

12. 5 × 8 40   **13.** 2 × 8 16   **14.** 5 × 9 45
(35,34)   (35,34)   (35,34)

15. $4.22   **16.**   909   **17.** $422   **18.**   703
(37)   − $2.95   (37)   − 27   (37)   − $144   (37)   − 471
      ────────   ─────   ────────   ─────
       $1.27   882 $278   232

19. $4.86   **20.**   370   **21.**   22   **22.**   76
(28)   + $2.95   (37)   − 209   (18)   + N 15   (20)   − C 48
      ────────   ─────   ────   ────
       $7.81   161   37   28

23. 24 + 48 + 65 + 93   230
(21)

24. Change this addition problem to a multiplication
(33) problem: 5 × 2

2 + 2 + 2 + 2 + 2

25. Draw a pattern of X's to show 3 × 5.   x x x x x
(36)   x x x x x
                                              x x x x x

LESSON 39

Multiplication Facts (Squares)

a. 640
b. 820
c. 625
d. 282
e. 85
f. 970
Problem Solving:
    6 squares

Facts Practice: Multiplication Facts: 0, 1, 2, 5 (Test C in Test Masters)

Mental Math: Subtract numbers ending in one or two zeros.
  a. 840 − 200   **b.** 840 − 20   **c.** 845 − 220

Review:
  d. 75 + 7 + 200   **e.** 36 + 39 + 10   **f.** 300 + 620 + 50

Problem Solving: A checkerboard has 64 small squares. There are 8 squares along each side. If a square checkerboard had only 36 small squares, how many squares would there be along each side?

Squares are the multiplication facts that have the same factor twice: 1 × 1, 2 × 2, 3 × 3, and so on. They are called **squares** because squares can be used to illustrate these facts.

1 × 1 = 1   2 × 2 = 4   3 × 3 = 9   4 × 4 = 16   5 × 5 = 25

These are squares that we will memorize:

       0 × 0 = 0   7 × 7 = 49

       1 × 1 = 1   8 × 8 = 64

       2 × 2 = 4   9 × 9 = 81

       3 × 3 = 9   10 × 10 = 100

       4 × 4 = 16   11 × 11 = 121

       5 × 5 = 25   12 × 12 = 144

       6 × 6 = 36

To memorize facts, it is helpful to practice saying the facts out loud. Say these facts out loud two or three times a day. Get used to the sounds. The sounds help us remember the facts.

Example What multiplication fact is illustrated by this square?

Solution The length is 6 and the width is 6. Counting, we find there are 36 squares. This is a picture of **6 × 6 = 36**.

Practice **a.** 3 × 3   9   **b.** 6 × 6   36   **c.** 9 × 9   81

d. 4 × 4   16   **e.** 8 × 8   64   **f.** 7 × 7   49

g. Draw a square to show 3 × 3.

Problem set 39

1. Forty-two is how much greater than twenty-seven?
$^{(38)}$ Draw a L-S-D pattern.   15; $\frac{42}{-27}$ ___ N ___

2. Forty-six is how much less than seventy? Draw a
$^{(38)}$ "larger-smaller-difference" pattern.   24; $\frac{70}{-46}$ ___ N ___

715 cheerful hikers
− _N_ cheerful hikers
317 cheerful hikers

3. Seven hundred fifteen cheerful hikers began the long
$^{(31)}$ march. Three hundred seventeen cheerful hikers finished the long march. How many cheerful hikers did not finish the long march? Draw a SWA pattern.
398 cheerful hikers

4. Write 483 in expanded form. Then use words to write
$^{(20,8)}$ this number.   400 + 80 + 3; four hundred eighty-three

5. Draw a rectangle whose length is 5 cm and whose
$^{(25,24)}$ width is 3 cm.

3 cm
5 cm

6. It is evening. What time will it be
$^{(33)}$ 13 hours from now?   10:25 a.m.

7. What fraction of this shape is shaded? $\frac{2}{5}$
(28)

8. The addition problem 5 + 5 + 5 can be written as a
(33) multiplication problem by writing 3 × 5. Write a multiplication problem for 7 + 7 + 7 + 7.   4 × 7

9. Round 38 to the nearest ten. Round 44 to the nearest
(26) ten. Then add the rounded numbers.
40; 40; 40 + 40 = 80

10. The digit in the tens' place is 4. The digit in the ones'
(5) place is 2. The number is greater than 500 and less than 600. What is the number?   542

11. To what number is the needle
(22) pointing?   650

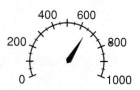

12. 4 × 4   **13.** 6 × 6   **14.** 7 × 7   **15.** 9 × 9
(39) 16   (39) 36   (39) 49   (39) 81

16.   433   **17.**   807   **18.**   406   **19.** $7.22
(37) − 268   (37)   − 45   (37) − 241   (37) − $4.44
       165   762   165 $2.78

20.   C 238 **21.** $3.27 **22.**   747   **23.**   85
(30) + 248   (28) + $4.68 (20) −   B 333 (20) −   B 58
       486          $7.95   414   27

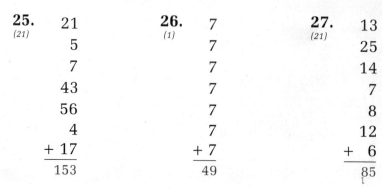

24. Draw a square to show 4 × 4.
(36)

25.   21   **26.**   7   **27.**   13
(21)   5   (1)   7   (21)   25
            7   7   14
           43   7   7
           56   7   8
            4   7   12
         + 17   + 7   + 6
          153   49   85

LESSON
40

Squares and Square Roots

a. 580
b. 640
c. 428
d. 64
e. 176
f. 670
Problem Solving:
  A is $\frac{1}{2}$, B is $\frac{1}{4}$, C is $\frac{1}{8}$,
  and D is $\frac{1}{8}$.

Facts Practice: Multiplication Facts: 2, 5, Squares (Test D in Test Masters)

Mental Math: Subtract numbers ending in one or two zeros.
  a. 780 − 200   **b.** 870 − 230   **c.** 458 − 30

Review:
  d. 58 + 6   **e.** 157 + 19   **f.** 435 + 35 + 200

Problem Solving: The rectangle is divided into four areas, A, B, C, and D. Area C is the same size as Area D. Areas C and D together are the same size as Area B. Areas B, C, and D together are the same size as Area A. What fraction of the whole rectangle is each area?

To **square** a number, we multiply the number by itself. If we square five, we get 25 because 5 × 5 is 25. Likewise, six squared is 36 since 6 × 6 is 36. A picture of a square can help us understand this idea.

Five squared is 25.   Six squared is 36.

A side is 5.   A side is 6.

25 squares in all   36 squares in all

To find a **square root** of a number, we find a number which, when multiplied by itself, equals the original number. A square root of 25 is five. A square root of 36 is six. Again, a picture of a square can help us understand the idea. When searching for a square root, we know the number of squares in all, and we are looking for the length of a side.

A square root
of 25 is 5.

A square root
of 36 is 6.

25 squares in all

36 squares in all

A side is 5.

A side is 6.

We can show that we mean the square root of a number by using a square root symbol.

We can read this symbol as "the square root of."

$$\sqrt{25} = 5$$

"The square root of twenty-five equals five."

Example   (a) What is the square of 9?

(b) What is a square root of 9?

Solution   Carefully read both questions and understand the difference between them.

(a) We square a number by multiplying the number by itself. It is like knowing the length of a side of a square and finding the number of squares in all. Since $9 \times 9 = 81$, the square of 9 is **81.**

(b) A square root of 9 is a number which, when multiplied by itself, equals 9. Since $3 \times 3 = 9$, a square root of 9 is **3.**

Practice   Square each number:

    a. 4   16   **b.** 7   49   **c.** 10   100

Find each square root:

    d. $\sqrt{4}$ 2   **e.** $\sqrt{16}$ 4   **f.** $\sqrt{64}$ 8

**Problem set
40**

1. Two hundred thirty-three is how much greater than seventy-six? Draw a L-S-D pattern.   157; $\begin{array}{r} 233 \\ -\ 76 \\ \hline N \end{array}$
(38)

$\begin{array}{r} 572 \\ -\ 123 \\ \hline N \end{array}$

2. One hundred twenty-three is how much less than five hundred seventy-two? Draw a L-S-D pattern.   449
(38)

223 beds
243 beds
+ 175 beds
_____
N beds

3. The first shipment contained 223 beds. The second
(12) shipment contained 243 beds. The third shipment
contained only 175 beds. What was the total number
of beds in all three shipments? Draw a SSM pattern.
641 beds

4. Write the number 780 in expanded form.   700 + 80
(20)

5. Draw two perpendicular lines.
(29)

6. It is early in the morning. What
(33) time will it be in 30 minutes?
2:50 a.m.

7. What fraction of this shape is
(28) shaded? $\frac{3}{8}$

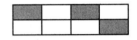

8. Change this addition problem to a multiplication
(33) problem: 7 × 8

$$8 + 8 + 8 + 8 + 8 + 8 + 8$$

9. Compare: three squared ⊘ the square root of 36
(40,15)

10. The digit in the hundreds' place is 4. The digit in the
(5) ones' place is 2. The number is between 450 and 460.
What is the number?   452

11. To what number is the arrow pointing?   170
(13)

12. 7 × 7   **13.** 9 × 9   **14.** 6 × 6   **15.** $\sqrt{64}$
(39) 49   (39) 81   (39) 36   (40) 8

16. $444   **17.**   927   **18.**   345   **19.** $7.25
(37) − $268   (37) − 48   (30) + C   76 (37) − $5.66
         $176   879   421 $1.59

20.   478   **21.** $4.28   **22.**   B   85 **23.**   Z   732
(37) − 259   (37) − $3.29   (20) − 48   (20) − 328
         219          $0.99   37   404

24. 88 + 24 + 35 + 66 + 58 + 229   500
(21)

25. Draw a rectangle to show 3 × 4.
(36)

**LESSON
41**

Multiplication Facts (9's)

a. $4.45
b. $7.75
c. $2.85
d. 245
e. 173
f. 275

Problem Solving:
   1 half dollar,
   1 quarter, 2 dimes,
   and 1 nickel

Facts Practice: Multiplication Facts: 2, 5, Squares (Test D in Test Masters)

Mental Math: Add dollars to another amount of money.
   a. $3.45 + $1.00   **b.** $5.75 + $2.00   **c.** $0.85 + $2.00

Review:
   d. 365 − 120   **e.** 45 + 8 + 120   **f.** 56 + 19 + 200

Problem Solving: We can make a dollar with two coins—two half dollars. We can make a dollar with three coins—a half dollar and two quarters. We can make a dollar with four coins—four quarters. What coins do we need to make a dollar with five coins?

The 9's multiplication facts have patterns that can help us learn these facts.

Below we have listed some 9's multiplication facts. **Notice that the first digit of each answer is one less than the number that is multiplied by nine.**

$$9 \times 2 = 18 \qquad (1 + 8 = 9)$$
$$9 \times 3 = 27 \qquad (2 + 7 = 9)$$
$$9 \times 4 = 36 \qquad (3 + 6 = 9)$$
$$9 \times 5 = 45 \qquad (4 + 5 = 9)$$
$$9 \times 6 = 54 \qquad (5 + 4 = 9)$$
$$9 \times 7 = 63 \qquad (6 + 3 = 9)$$
$$9 \times 8 = 72 \qquad (7 + 2 = 9)$$
$$9 \times 9 = 81 \qquad (8 + 1 = 9)$$

Notice also that the two digits of the answer add up to nine.

These two patterns can help us quickly find the answer to a 9's multiplication. The first digit of the answer is one less than the number multiplied. The two digits add up to nine.

Example 1 What is the **first digit** of each answer?

(a)   9   (b)   3   (c)   9   (d)   4   (e)   9
     × 6   × 9   × 7   × 9   × 8
     ? __   ? __   ? __   ? __   ? __

Solution The first digit is one less than the number multiplied by nine.

(a)   9   (b)   3   (c)   9   (d)   4   (e)   9
     × 6   × 9   × 7   × 9   × 8
     5 __   **2** __   **6** __   **3** __   **7** __

Example 2 Complete these two-digit numbers so that the sum of the digits is nine:

(a) 3 __   (b) 6 __   (c) 4 __   (d) 5 __

(e) 8 __   (f) 1 __   (g) 2 __   (h) 7 __

Solution We find the second digit so that the two digits add up to nine.

(a) 3**6**   (b) 6**3**   (c) 4**5**   (d) 5**4**

(e) 8**1**   (f) 1**8**   (g) 2**7**   (h) 7**2**

Practice Find the answer to each multiplication fact. Remember, the first digit is one less than the number multiplied, and the two digits add up to nine.

a.   9   b.   5   c.   9   d.   3
    × 6   × 9   × 8   × 9
    ____   ____   ____   ____
     54   45   72   27

e.   9   f.   7   g.   9   h.   9
    × 4   × 9   × 2   × 9
    ____   ____   ____   ____
     36   63   18   81

Problem set
41

1. There are two hundred fifteen pages in the book. Ted
(31) has read eighty-six pages. How many more pages are
left to read? Draw a SWA pattern.   129 pages;   215 pages
                                                  − 86 pages
                                                  _____ N pages

2. Use the digits 7, 8, and 9 once each to make an even
(11) number greater than 800.   978

3. Use digits and a comparison symbol to show that four
(15) hundred eighty-five is less than six hundred ninety.
   485 < 690

4. This is a sequence of square numbers. What are the
(39,3) next three numbers in the sequence?

   1, 4, 9, 16, __25__ , __36__ , __49__ , ...

5. If it is morning, what time is
(23) shown on this clock?   6:06 a.m.

6. Use words to write 697.
(8) six hundred ninety-seven

7. Write 729 in expanded form.
(20) 700 + 20 + 9

8. Round 66 to the nearest ten.   70
(26)

9. Each side of this square is how long?   2 cm
(24)

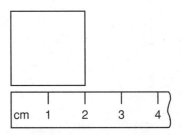

10. Find a letter of the alphabet formed with just two
(29) perpendicular line segments.   T or L

11. $12 - W = 7$ 5
(14)

12. What fraction of this rectangle is
(28) shaded? $\frac{7}{8}$

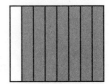

x x x x x **13.** Draw a pattern of X's to show the multiplication
x x x x x (36) 5 × 5.
x x x x x
x x x x x
x x x x x

14. Is the value of three nickels and two dimes an even
(11) number of cents or an odd number of cents?   odd

15. The arrow is pointing to what number on this number
(13) line?   125

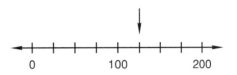

16. 9 × 6   54   **17.** 9 × 8   72   **18.** 9 × 4   36
(41)   (41)   (41)

19. √81   9   **20.** $3.60 − $1.37 $2.23
(40)   (37)

21. 413 − 380   33   **22.** 875 − 218   657
(37)   (37)

23. Compare: 47 + 36 ⊜ 57 + 26
(15)

24. Five squared is how much more than the square root
(40,38) of 25?   20

25. Change this addition problem to a multiplication
(33) problem: 7 × 6

6 + 6 + 6 + 6 + 6 + 6 + 6

LESSON 42

Writing Numbers Through 999,999: Part 1

a. $4.44
b. $6.73
c. $1.80
d. 418
e. 264
f. 387
Problem Solving:
$\frac{3}{4}$

Facts Practice: Multiplication Facts: 2, 5, 9, Squares (Test E in Test Masters)

Mental Math: To add 99¢ or 98¢ or 95¢ to another amount of money, add a dollar; then subtract 1¢ or 2¢ or 5¢.

  a. $3.45 + $0.99   **b.** $5.75 + $0.98   **c.** $0.85 + $0.95

Review:

  d. 438 − 20   **e.** 58 + 6 + 200   **f.** 78 + 9 + 300

Problem Solving: Jill's mom cut an orange in half. Then she cut each half in half. Jill ate three of the orange slices. What fraction of the orange did Jill eat?

We remember that the places in a three-digit number are the hundreds' place, the tens' place, and the ones' place. The places to the left of the hundreds' place are the thousands' place (1,000s), the ten-thousands' place (10,000s), and the hundred-thousands' place (100,000s). We notice that as we move to the left, each new place has one more zero.

hundred-thousands' place 100,000 | ten-thousands' place 10,000 | thousands' place 1,000 | , | hundreds' place 100 | tens' place 10 | ones' place 1

Example 1 Write 75,634 in expanded form.

Solution The 7 is in the ten-thousands' place and has a value of 70,000. So we write

$$70,000 + 5000 + 600 + 30 + 4$$

We usually use a comma to write a number equal to or greater than one thousand. A comma helps us read numbers that have four, five, or six digits. It is not necessary, but we often use a comma to write four-digit numbers. However, a comma should be inserted when writing numbers with five or more digits. To read

4507   34507   234507

we place a comma three digits from the right-hand end of the numbers.

4,507   34,507   234,507

The comma is the thousands' comma. **The digits to the left of this comma tell the number of thousands.** First we read the part of the number to the left of the comma. Then we read the thousands' comma by saying "thousand." Then we read the part of the number to the right of the comma.

4,507	is read	four **thousand,** five hundred seven
34,507	is read	thirty-four **thousand,** five hundred seven
234,507	is read	two hundred thirty-four **thousand,** five hundred seven

When we write the number in words, we must remember to place a comma after the word *thousand*, as we did in these examples.

Example 2   Use words to write 123456.

Solution   First we place a comma three places from the right-hand end of the number.

123,456

Now we write the part of the number to the left of the comma.

One hundred twenty-three

Next we write **"thousand"** and **put a comma after this word.**

One hundred twenty-three thousand,

Finally, we write the part of the number to the right of the comma.

> **One hundred twenty-three thousand, four hundred fifty-six**

Practice   Use words to write:

a. 907,411   nine hundred seven thousand, four hundred eleven

b. 223,512
   two hundred twenty-three thousand, five hundred twelve

c. 14,518   fourteen thousand, five hundred eighteen

d. Write 5,280 in expanded form.   5000 + 200 + 80

Problem set 42

1. Wilbur saw that there were one hundred forty-two goldfish in the first tank. There were three hundred fifteen goldfish in the second tank. How many more goldfish were in the second tank? Draw a L-S-D pattern.   173 goldfish; $\frac{315 \text{ goldfish}}{- 142 \text{ goldfish}}$
   $\overline{N \text{ goldfish}}$
(38)

2. The square root of 49 is how much less than four squared?   9
(40,38)

3. When Linda looked the first time, she saw 211 elves frolicking in the glen. When she looked the second time, there were 272 elves frolicking in the glen. How many more elves did she see the second time? Draw a L-S-D pattern.   61 elves; $\frac{272 \text{ elves}}{- 211 \text{ elves}}$
   $\overline{N \text{ elves}}$
(38)

4. Write the number 3,425 in expanded form. Then write this number using words.   3000 + 400 + 20 + 5;
   three thousand, four hundred twenty-five
(42)

5. Draw two parallel lines. Then draw a line that makes right angles when it crosses the parallel lines.
(29)

6. It is evening. What time will it be 2 hours and 25 minutes from now?   8:00 p.m.
(33)

7. What fraction of this figure is
(28) shaded? $\frac{5}{18}$

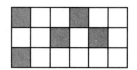

8. Change this addition problem to a multiplication
(33) problem: 5 × 9

$$9 + 9 + 9 + 9 + 9$$

9. Compare: 9 × 4 ⬡> √36
(15)

10. The digit in the thousands' place is 4. The digit in the
(42) ones' place is 6. The digit in the tens' place is 7. The
number is between 4200 and 4300. What is the
number? 4276

11. To what number is the arrow pointing? 2260
(13)

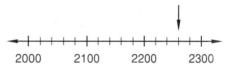

| 2000 | 2100 | 2200 | 2300 |

12. 5 × 8   **13.** 8 × 8   **14.** 9 × 3   **15.** 9 × 4
(35)   40   (39)   64   (41)   27   (41)   36

16. $7.37   **17.**   921   **18.**   464
(37) − $2.68   (37)   − 58   (16) + 247
      ———————   ————   ————
        $4.69   863   711

19.   329   **20.** $4.88   **21.**   555
(30) +   Z   218   (28) + $2.69   (20) −   C   333
      ————   ————————   ————
        547                       $7.57   222

22. Janet's birth date is 5/23/54. In what month was she
(6) born? May

23. Use words to write 416,803.
(42) four hundred sixteen thousand, eight hundred three

24.   4   **25.**   5
(21)   8   (21)   8
           12   7
           16   14
           14   6
           28   21
        + 37   + 15
        ——————   ——————
          119   76

LESSON 43

Writing Numbers Through 999,999: Part 2

a. $6.84
b. $9.61
c. $5.93
d. 374
e. 193
f. 784
Problem Solving:
    65 to 66 minutes

Facts Practice: Multiplication Facts: 2, 5, Squares (Test D in Test Masters)

Mental Math: Practice adding 99¢, 98¢, or 95¢.
  a. $5.85 + $0.99   **b.** $8.63 + $0.98   **c.** $4.98 + $0.95
Review:
  d. 574 − 200   **e.** 77 + 6 + 110   **f.** 460 + 300 + 24

Problem Solving: The two hands of a clock are together at noon. The next time the hands of a clock are together is about how many minutes later?

In Lesson 42, we practiced using words to write numbers through 999,999. In this lesson we will use digits to write numbers through 999,999.

We use a comma to help us write thousands. We write the number of thousands in front of the comma and the rest of the number behind the comma. The form looks like this.

_____ , _____

Example 1 Use digits to write eight hundred ninety-five thousand, two hundred seventy.

Solution It is a good idea to read the entire number before we begin writing it. We see the word *thousand*, so we know it will have a **thousands' comma** after the digits that tell how many thousands.

_____ , _____

Then we go back and read the part of the number in front of the word *thousand* and write this number in front of the comma. For "eight hundred ninety-five thousand" we write:

895, _____

Now, to the right of the comma, we write the last part of the number.

895,270

When writing thousands, we must be sure there are **three digits after** the thousands' comma. Sometimes it may be necessary to use one or more zeros to be sure there are three digits after the comma.

Example 2   Use digits to write thirty-five thousand.

Solution   We see the word *thousand*, so it will have this form.

_____ , _____

In front of the word *thousand*, we read "thirty-five," so for thirty-five thousand we write

35, _____

There is nothing written after the word *thousand*—no hundreds, no tens, no ones. However, we need to have three digits, so we write three zeros.

35,000

Example 3   Use digits to write seven thousand, twenty-five.

Solution   For "seven thousand," we write

7, _____

After the word *thousand*, we read "twenty-five." It would not be correct to write

7,25   NOT CORRECT

We need to write three digits after the thousands' comma because there are three whole number places after the comma: hundreds, tens, and ones. Since there are no hundreds, we put a zero in the hundreds' place.

7,025   CORRECT

Practice Use digits to write each number:

        a. One hundred twenty-one thousand, three hundred forty   121,340

        b. Twelve thousand, five hundred seven   12,507

        c. Five thousand, seventy-five   5,075

        d. Eighty-two thousand, five hundred   82,500

        e. Seven hundred fifty thousand   750,000

        f. Two thousand, one   2,001

Problem set 43

1. Four hundred sixty-five is how much greater than twenty-four? Draw a L-S-D pattern.   441;
(38)
$$\begin{array}{r} 465 \\ -\ 24 \\ \hline N \end{array}$$

2. Marcie had four hundred twenty marbles. Robert had one hundred twenty-three marbles. How many fewer marbles did Robert have? Draw a L-S-D pattern.
(38)
297 marbles

$$\begin{array}{r} 420 \text{ marbles} \\ -\ 123 \text{ marbles} \\ \hline N \text{ marbles} \end{array}$$

3. Terry has forty-two marbles. Mary has one hundred thirty marbles. How many marbles do Mary and Terry have together? Draw a SSM pattern.   172 marbles
(12)

$$\begin{array}{r} 42 \text{ marbles} \\ +\ 130 \text{ marbles} \\ \hline N \text{ marbles} \end{array}$$

4. Write the number 25,463 in expanded form.
(42)   20,000 + 5000 + 400 + 60 + 3

5. Draw a circle that is about 3 centimeters across the center.
(25)

3 cm

6. It is afternoon. What time will it be in four and a half hours?
(33)
8:40 p.m.

7. What fraction of the circles is shaded? $\frac{4}{11}$
(28)

8. Change this addition problem to a multiplication
(33) problem: 5 × 8

$$8 + 8 + 8 + 8 + 8$$

9. Round 76 to the nearest ten. Round 59 to the nearest
(26,15) ten. Use digits and a symbol to compare the rounded
numbers.   80; 60; 80 > 60

10. The digit in the ones' place is 5. The digit in the tens'
(5) place is 6. The number is between 166 and 364. What
is the number?   265

11. To what number is the arrow pointing?   2140
(13)

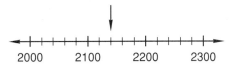

12. 9 × 9   **13.** 5 × 7   **14.** 6 · × 6   **15.** $\sqrt{16}$
(39) 81   (35) 35   (39) 36   (40) 4

16.   535   **17.**   908   **18.**   471
(37) − 268   (37) − 43   (37) − 346
     ⎯⎯⎯   ⎯⎯⎯   ⎯⎯⎯
     267   865   125

19.   *C* 386   **20.**   *C* 525   **21.** $3.49
(30) + 329   (20) − 127   (28) + $4.28
     ⎯⎯⎯   ⎯⎯⎯   ⎯⎯⎯⎯⎯
     715   398 $7.77

22. Five squared is how much more than 5 + 5?   15
(40)

23. How many sides are on eight triangles? Count by
(3) threes.   24 sides

24. Use words to write 365,123.
(42)   three hundred sixty-five thousand, one hundred twenty-three

25. Use digits to write nine hundred forty thousand, ten.
(43)   940,010

LESSON
44

Naming Mixed Numbers

a. $7.83
b. $8.72
c. $6.80
d. 337
e. 184
f. 290
Patterns:
$3\frac{1}{2}$, 4, $4\frac{1}{2}$, 5, $5\frac{1}{2}$, 6, $6\frac{1}{2}$, 7, $7\frac{1}{2}$, 8

Facts Practice: Multiplication Facts: 2, 5, Squares (Test D in Test Masters)

Mental Math: To add $1.99 to an amount of money, we may add two dollars, and then subtract one cent. Practice adding $1.99, $1.98, and $1.95.

   a. $5.85 + $1.98   **b.** $6.73 + $1.99   **c.** $4.85 + $1.95

Review:

   d. 687 − 350   **e.** 36 + 8 + 140   **f.** 56 + 34 + 200

Patterns: This is the sequence of numbers we say when we count by halves. Copy this sequence on your paper and continue the sequence to the whole number 8.

$$\frac{1}{2}, 1, 1\frac{1}{2}, 2, 2\frac{1}{2}, 3, \ldots$$

A **mixed number** is a **whole number** followed by a **fraction.** The mixed number $3\frac{1}{2}$ is read "three and one half."

Example 1 How many circles are shaded?

Solution Two whole circles are shaded and one fourth of another circle is shaded. The total number of shaded circles is two and one fourth, which we write as

$$2\frac{1}{4}$$

Example 2 Use words to write $21\frac{1}{2}$.

Solution We *do* use the word *and* when naming mixed numbers.

Twenty-one and one half

Practice What mixed numbers are pictured here?

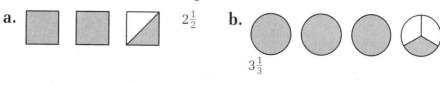

a. $2\frac{1}{2}$ b. $3\frac{1}{3}$

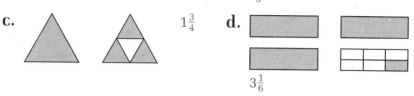

c. $1\frac{3}{4}$ d. $3\frac{1}{6}$

e. Use words to name $34\frac{3}{4}$.   thirty-four and three fourths

Problem set 44

1. There were seventy-one birds in the first tree. There
(38) were forty-two birds in the second tree. How many
more birds were in the first tree? Draw a L-S-D pattern.
29 birds

$$\frac{\begin{array}{r} 71 \text{ birds} \\ - 42 \text{ birds} \end{array}}{N \text{ birds}}$$

2. At first there were four hundred ten screaming
(31) students. Then some quieted down, and only two
hundred eighty-seven students were screaming. How
many students quieted down? Draw a SWA pattern.
123 students

$$\frac{\begin{array}{r} 410 \text{ students} \\ - \quad N \text{ students} \end{array}}{287 \text{ students}}$$

3. Ninety-seven oranges were in the first bunch, fifty-
(12) seven oranges were in the second bunch, and forty-
eight oranges were in the third bunch. How many
oranges were in all three bunches? Draw a SSM
pattern.   202 oranges

$$\frac{\begin{array}{r} 97 \text{ oranges} \\ 57 \text{ oranges} \\ + 48 \text{ oranges} \end{array}}{N \text{ oranges}}$$

4. What mixed number is pictured
(44) in this figure? $2\frac{2}{3}$

5. Write the number 506,148 in expanded form.
(42) 500,000 + 6000 + 100 + 40 + 8

6. Use words to write $56\frac{5}{6}$.   fifty-six and five sixths
(44)

7. Which letter below has no right angles?   N
(29)

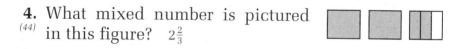

T   H   E   N

8. It is morning. What time will it be
(33) 5 hours and 20 minutes from
now?   4:00 p.m.

9. Change this addition problem to a multiplication
(33) problem: 8 × 4

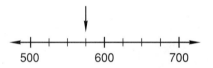

$$4 + 4 + 4 + 4 + 4 + 4 + 4 + 4$$

10. Round 176 to the nearest ten.   180
(26)

11. To what number is the arrow pointing?   575
(13)

```
              ↓
  ←—+—+—+—+—+—+—+—+—+→
     500      600      700
```

12. 9 × 7   **13.** 9 × 6   **14.** 6 × 7   **15.** √36
(41) 63   (41) 54   (34) 42   (40) 6

16. $7.32   **17.** $4.89   **18.**   464
(37) − $3.45   (28) + $2.57   (37) − 238
—————   —————   —————
      $3.87 $7.46   226

19.   548   **20.**   487   **21.**   250
(16) + 999   (30) + Z   234   (20) − C   128
—————   —————   —————
     1,547   721   122

22.   C   576   **23.**   87
(20) − 338   (20) − B   33
—————   ————
      238   54

24. 22 + 46 + 84 + 97 + 96 + 47   392
(21)

25. Use digits to write nine hundred seven thousand,
(43) seventy.   907,070

LESSON
45

a. $7.64
b. $5.81
c. $9.22
d. 400
e. 785
f. 286
Problem Solving:

Two Forms of Money

Facts Practice: Multiplication Facts: 2, 5, 9, Squares (Test E in Test Masters)

Mental Math: Practice adding amounts ending in 99¢, 98¢, or 95¢.
  a. $4.65 + $2.99   **b.** $3.86 + $1.95   **c.** $6.24 + $2.98
Review:
  d. 520 − 120   **e.** 350 + 400 + 35   **f.** 37 + 29 + 220

Problem Solving: We can quickly add or subtract some numbers on a calendar. Select a number from the middle part of a monthly calendar. If we move straight up from that number, we subtract 7. If we move straight down, we add 7. We can add or subtract two other numbers if we move diagonally. Which numbers do we add or subtract when we move in these directions?

We can tell how much money there is by using a number and a cent sign (¢). If we put the cent sign behind the number, we are telling how many cents.

(a) 324¢   (b) 20¢   (c) 4¢

We can also use a dollar sign ($) to tell how much money there is. We always put the dollar sign in front of the number. Then we put a **decimal point** two places from the end of the number. The number to the left of the decimal point tells how many dollars. The number to the right of the decimal point tells how many cents.

(a) $3.24   (b) $0.20   (c) $0.04

The first amount is three dollars and twenty-four cents. The second amount is twenty cents. Since there were no dollars, we wrote a zero for dollars. We do not read the zero. The third amount is four cents.

The decimal point must be two digits from the end. If there is just one digit, we insert another zero in front of that digit.

$0.04 means the same as 4¢

We do not read the zeros in $0.04. We just say "Four cents."

Example 1   Write three hundred fifteen dollars and twenty-five cents using a dollar sign and a decimal point.

Solution   When we use a dollar sign, we put a decimal point two places from the end.

$315.25

Example 2   Use words to write $30.76.

Solution   We write the number of dollars, write "and," and then write the number of cents.

Thirty dollars and seventy-six cents

Example 3   Use a dollar sign and a decimal point to write seven cents.

Solution   To show cents with a dollar sign, we use a decimal point. The decimal point goes two places from the end. If we write the seven,

7

we have only one digit, so we put a zero between the seven and the decimal point.

$.07

We may put another zero in front of the decimal point because there are no dollars.

$0.07

Example 4   Tommy has one quarter, one dime, and one nickel. Write how much money he has using a cent sign. Then write the amount again using a dollar sign and a decimal point.

Solution First we find how many cents. A quarter is twenty-five cents, a dime is ten cents, and a nickel is five cents.

$$25¢ + 10¢ + 5¢ = \mathbf{40¢}$$

Now we write forty cents using a dollar sign and a decimal point.

$0.40

Practice Write these amounts with a cent sign instead of a dollar sign:

a. $0.17 17¢ **b.** $0.05 5¢ **c.** $4.60 460¢

Write these amounts with a dollar sign instead of a cent sign:

d. 195¢ $1.95 **e.** 8¢ $0.08 **f.** 30¢ $0.30

g. Write the value of two quarters, two dimes, and one nickel with a dollar sign. Then use a cent sign to write this amount again. $0.75; 75¢

Use words to write each amount:

h. $0.77 seventy-seven cents

i. $12.25 twelve dollars and twenty-five cents

j. $20.05 twenty dollars and five cents

Problem set
45
(38)

1. The king saw two hundred seventy peasants. The queen saw one hundred fifty-five peasants. How many more peasants did the king see? Draw a L-S-D pattern. 115 peasants

270 peasants
− 155 peasants
  N peasants

2. The king saw five hundred sixty-seven peasants the first time he looked. Then he saw eight hundred forty-two peasants the second time he looked. How many fewer peasants did he see the first time he looked? Draw a L-S-D pattern. 275 peasants;

842 peasants
− 567 peasants
  N peasants

3. Jimbo had four dollars and sixty-five cents. Use a
(45) dollar sign and a decimal point to write this amount.
Then write this amount again using a cent sign.
$4.65; 465¢

4. What temperature is shown on
(22) this thermometer?   38°F

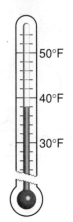

5. Which one of these angles does not look like a right
(29) angle?

C. ∠

    A. ⌐   B. ∧   C. ∠   D. ⌐

6. What mixed number is pictured?
(44) $3\frac{2}{3}$

7. The square root of 81 is how much less than seven
(40,38) squared?   40

8. Write 250,516 in expanded form. Then use words to
(42) write this number.   200,000 + 50,000 + 500 + 10 + 6;
two hundred fifty thousand, five hundred sixteen

9. It is evening. What time will it be
(33) 2 hours and 20 minutes from
now?   11:45 p.m.

10. The digit in the ones' place is 5. The digit in the tens'
(5) place is 6. The number is between 390 and 490. What
is the number?   465

11. To what number is the arrow pointing?   4200
(13)

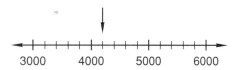

3000   4000   5000   6000

12. Use words to write $1.43. Then use a cent sign to write
(45) the same amount.   one dollar and forty-three cents; 143¢

13. 6 × 9   **14.** 4 × 9   **15.** 8 × 9   **16.** 3 × 9
(41) 54   *(41)* 36   *(41)* 72   *(41)* 27

17. $6.05   **18.**   489   **19.** $5.32
(37)   − $2.53   *(30)*   + Z   277   *(28)*   + $3.44
         ───────   ─────   ───────
          $3.52   766 $8.76

20.   C   576   **21.**   423   **22.**   670
(30)   + 294   *(37)*   − 245   *(20)*   −   Z   318
         ─────   ─────   ─────
          870   178   352

23. 46 + 24 + 87 + 96   253
(21)

24. Draw a rectangle that shows 2 × 5. Shade three tenths
(36,32) of the rectangle.

25. Use digits to write four hundred twenty-seven
(43) thousand, five hundred two.   427,502

LESSON 46

Reading Fractions and Mixed Numbers from a Number Line

a. 321
b. $3.25
c. $8.26
d. $6.84
e. 75
f. 393
Problem Solving:
1:05, 2:11, 3:16,
4:22, 5:27, 7:38,
8:44, 9:49, 10:55
(approximate
times)

Facts Practice: Multiplication Facts: 2, 5, 9, Squares (Test E in Test Masters)

Mental Math: Subtract without regrouping.
  a. 563 − 242   **b.** $5.75 − $2.50   **c.** $8.98 − $0.72
Review:
  d. $4.85 + $1.99   **e.** 48 + 7 + 20   **f.** 54 + 19 + 320

Problem Solving: The hands of a clock are together at 12:00. The hands of a clock are not together at 6:30, because the hour hand is halfway between the 6 and the 7 at 6:30. The hands come together at about 6:33. Name nine more times that the hands of a clock come together.

To find mixed numbers on a number line, we must find the number of **spaces** between consecutive whole numbers. If there are four spaces between the whole numbers, each space equals $\frac{1}{4}$. If there are six spaces between the whole numbers, each space equals $\frac{1}{6}$.

Example 1   The arrow points to what number?

Solution   There are three **spaces** between 5 and 6. Each space equals $\frac{1}{3}$. The arrow points to **$5\frac{2}{3}$**.

Example 2   The arrow points to what number on each number line?

(a)   (b)

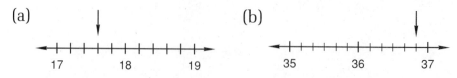

Solution   (a) There are five spaces between the whole numbers. Each space equals $\frac{1}{5}$. The arrow points to **$17\frac{3}{5}$**.

(b) There are six spaces between the whole numbers. Each space equals $\frac{1}{6}$. The arrow points to **$36\frac{5}{6}$.**

Practice Name the fraction or mixed number marked by the arrows on these number lines: **a.** $\frac{3}{4}$ **b.** $2\frac{1}{4}$ **c.** $\frac{2}{3}$ **d.** $2\frac{1}{3}$ **e.** $26\frac{3}{7}$ **f.** $1\frac{1}{4}$

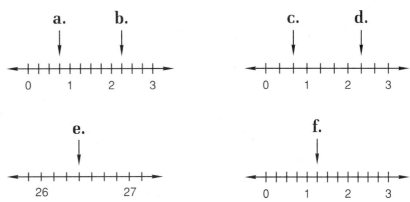

Problem set
46

715 petunia blossoms
$-$ 427 petunia blossoms
$\quad N$ petunia blossoms

1. On the way to school, Ted saw four hundred twenty-seven petunia blossoms. Karen saw seven hundred fifteen petunia blossoms. How many more petunia blossoms did Karen see? Draw a L-S-D pattern.
(38)
288 petunia blossoms

2. Circe had two hundred seventy-five pigs. After Odysseus came, Circe had four hundred sixty-two pigs. How many pigs did she get from Odysseus? Draw a SSM pattern.   187 pigs; $\begin{array}{r} 275 \text{ pigs} \\ + \ N \text{ pigs} \\ \hline 462 \text{ pigs} \end{array}$
(17)

3. Four hundred seventy-five thousand, three hundred forty-two is a big number. Use digits to write this number.   475,342
(43)

4. The money in the piggy bank was worth seven dollars and sixty-five cents. Use a dollar sign to write this amount. Then use a cent sign to write this amount.
(45)
$7.65; 765¢

5. The arrow is pointing to what number? $11\frac{3}{8}$
(46)

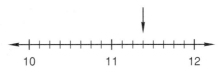

6. Draw a rectangle whose length is 5 cm and whose
(25) width is 3 cm.

7. What mixed number is shown by
(44) the shaded rectangles? $5\frac{1}{2}$

8. Use words to write $32\frac{2}{3}$.   thirty-two and two thirds
(44)

9. Write 257,026 in expanded form. Then use words to
(42) write this number.   200,000 + 50,000 + 7000 + 20 + 6;
two hundred fifty-seven thousand, twenty-six

10. It is early morning. What time
(33) will it be 2 hours and 35 minutes
from now?   7:00 a.m.

11. Write each amount using a dollar sign. Then write
(45) each amount again using a cent sign.

    (a) One dollar and forty-seven cents $1.47; 147¢

    (b) Seven cents $0.07; 7¢

12. Draw a rectangle pattern to show 4 × 6.
(36)

13. 7 × 9   **14.** 6 × 9   **15.** 4 × 9
(41)   63   (41)   54   (41)   36

16. $\sqrt{81}$ 9   **17.** $6.63 − $3.55 $3.08
(40)   (37)

18. $4.99 + $2.88 $7.87   **19.** $A − 247 = 321$ 568
(28)   (20)

20. $Z + 296 = 531$ 235   **21.** $523 − Z = 145$ 378
(30)   (20)

22. 28 + 46 + 48 + 64 + 32 + 344   562
(21)

23. Y 51   **24.**   74   **25.**   67
(20)   − 14   (20)   − B 26   (30)   + Y 16
      37   48   83

LESSON 47

Multiplication Facts (Memory Group)

LESSON
47

a. 75
b. 55
c. $9.21
d. 582
e. 273
Patterns:

Sequence:

$\frac{1}{2}$, 1, $1\frac{1}{2}$, 2, $2\frac{1}{2}$, 3,

$3\frac{1}{2}$, 4, $4\frac{1}{2}$, 5, $5\frac{1}{2}$, 6,

$6\frac{1}{2}$, 7, $7\frac{1}{2}$, 8, $8\frac{1}{2}$, 9,

$9\frac{1}{2}$, 10

Between 2 and 5:

$3\frac{1}{2}$

Facts Practice: Multiplication Facts: 2, 5, 9, Squares (Test E in Test Masters)

Mental Math: Subtract a number ending in five from a number ending in zero.

a. 80 − 5   **b.** 80 − 25 (Subtract 20. Then subtract 5 more.)

Review:

c. $6.23 + $2.98   **d.** 340 + 26 + 216   **e.** 65 + 8 + 200

Patterns: Counting by halves we say, "One half, one, one and one half, two." Count by halves from one half to ten. Then write this sequence on a piece of paper. What number is halfway between two and five?

There are only 10 multiplication facts we have not practiced. We call these facts the **memory group.**

$$3 \times 4 = 12 \qquad 4 \times 7 = 28$$

$$3 \times 6 = 18 \qquad 4 \times 8 = 32$$

$$3 \times 7 = 21 \qquad 6 \times 7 = 42$$

$$3 \times 8 = 24 \qquad 6 \times 8 = 48$$

$$4 \times 6 = 24 \qquad 7 \times 8 = 56$$

These facts must be memorized. Sounds are often helpful when we memorize things. If we say these facts out loud in a sing-song manner, the sounds become familiar. When you practice facts, you should say the facts softly to yourself.

The multiplication facts should be practiced by doing **timed written tests** on a daily basis. A suggested goal is to complete a 100-facts written test in 4 minutes with no more than three errors. Then you should continue to practice often so you remember the facts.

Practice Multiplication Facts: Memory Group (Test F in Test Masters)

Problem set
47

$$\begin{array}{r} 405 \text{ toys} \\ -\ 220 \text{ toys} \\ \hline N \text{ toys} \end{array}$$

1. There were two hundred twenty toys in the first pile.
(38) There were four hundred five toys in the second pile.
How many more toys were in the second pile? Draw a
L-S-D pattern.   185 toys

2. Five hundred seventy-five thousand, five hundred
(43) forty-two people lived in the city. Use digits to write
this number.   575,542

3. Write 472,503 in expanded form. Then use words to
(42) write this number.   400,000 + 70,000 + 2000 + 500 + 3;
four hundred seventy-two thousand, five hundred three

$$\begin{array}{r} 432 \text{ boys} \\ +\ N \text{ girls} \\ \hline 918 \text{ boys and girls} \end{array}$$

4. There were four hundred thirty-two boys. There were
(17) nine hundred eighteen boys and girls. How many girls
were there? Draw a SSM pattern. (*Hint*: The number
of boys is one part. The number of girls is another part.
The number of boys and girls is the total.)   486 girls

5. The arrow is pointing to what number? $8\frac{3}{4}$
(46)

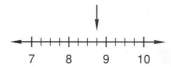

6. Which street is parallel to Broad
(29) Street?   Main Street

7. What mixed number is shown by
(44) the shaded circles? $2\frac{1}{8}$

8. Round 624 to the nearest ten.   620
(26)

9. It is morning. What time will it be
(33) 5 hours and 15 minutes from
now?   12:40 p.m.

10. Use a dollar sign and a decimal point to write each of
(45) these amounts:

(a) 1256¢ $12.56   (b) 4¢ $0.04

11. Draw shaded circles to show $2\frac{3}{4}$.
(44)

x x x x x x x
x x x x x x x
x x x x x x x   **12.** Draw a pattern of X's to show 4 × 7.
x x x x x x x   (36)

13. 4 × 7   **14.** 4 × 8   **15.** 4 × 6   **16.** 7 × 8
(47) 28   (47) 32   (47) 24   (47) 56

17. $7.23   **18.** $5.42   **19.**   943
(37)   − $2.54   (28)   + $2.69   (37)   − 276
      ───────   ───────   ─────
       $4.69 $8.11   667

20.   478   **21.**   Z   803   **22.**   C   117
(16)   + 249   (20)   − 581   (30)   + 843
      ───────   ─────   ─────
       727   222   960

23. 28 + 36 + 78 + $\sqrt{49}$ 149
(40,21)

24.   14   **25.**   29
(21)   18   (21)   5
         6   13
         4   27
        18   63
      + 15   + 76
      ─────   ─────
        75   213

LESSON 48

Reading an Inch Scale to the Nearest Fourth

a. 65
b. 25
c. 245
d. $9.91
e. 285
f. 890
Vocabulary:

| factor |
| × factor |
| product |

factor × factor = product

Facts Practice: Multiplication Facts: Memory Group (Test F in Test Masters)

Mental Math: Subtract a number ending in five from a number ending in zero.

   a. 70 − 5   **b.** 70 − 45   **c.** 370 − 125

Review:

   d. $5.96 + $3.95   **e.** 76 + 9 + 200   **f.** 560 + 24 + 306

Vocabulary: Copy these two patterns on a piece of paper. In each of the six boxes write either "factor" or "product."

An **inch** is a unit used for measuring length. An inch is this long.

We use the letters "in." to abbreviate the word *inch*. To avoid confusing the abbreviation for *inch* with the word *in*, we write the abbreviation with a period. To measure lengths in inches, we use an inch scale. Inch scales are found on rulers and on tape measures. An inch scale has marks between the inch marks. These marks let us read the inch scale to the nearest half inch, nearest quarter inch, or nearest eighth inch. One quarter inch is the same as one fourth inch. In this lesson we will practice reading to the nearest quarter inch.

When reading an inch scale, we should remember that $\frac{2}{4}$ is equal to $\frac{1}{2}$. The two circles below show that equal parts of the circles are shaded.

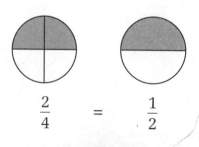

$$\frac{2}{4} \quad = \quad \frac{1}{2}$$

The fraction $\frac{1}{2}$ is the reduced form of $\frac{2}{4}$. Instead of naming a fraction $\frac{2}{4}$, we will use the fraction $\frac{1}{2}$. Half inch marks are usually drawn slightly longer than quarter inch marks.

Example   How long is the toothpick to the nearest quarter inch?

Solution   The toothpick is 2 inches plus a fraction. It is closest to $2\frac{2}{4}$ inches. Instead of writing $\frac{2}{4}$, we use $\frac{1}{2}$. The toothpick is $2\frac{1}{2}$ inches long. We abbreviate this by writing **$2\frac{1}{2}$ in.**

Practice   **a.** Draw a picture that shows that $\frac{2}{4}$ equals $\frac{1}{2}$.

Name each point marked by an arrow on this inch scale:
b. $\frac{3}{4}$ in.   **c.** $1\frac{1}{2}$ in.   **d.** $2\frac{1}{4}$ in.   **e.** $3\frac{3}{4}$ in.

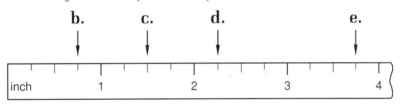

Problem set 48

1. Ann is twelve years old. Ann's mother is thirty-five
   $^{(38)}$ years old. Ann's mother is how many years older than Ann? Draw a L-S-D pattern.   23 years older; $\begin{array}{r} 35 \\ -\ 12 \\ \hline N \end{array}$

2. Four hundred sixty-eight thousand, five hundred two
   $^{(43)}$ boxes were in the warehouse. Use digits to write this number.   468,502

3. Write the number 3,905 in expanded form. Then use
   $^{(42)}$ words to write this number.
   3000 + 900 + 5; three thousand, nine hundred five

4. Dan smashed two hundred forty-three pop cans with
   $^{(12,11)}$ his right foot and smashed three hundred sixty-four pop cans with his left foot. Was the total number of smashed cans an even number or an odd number?
   odd

5. Use words to write the mixed number $102\frac{1}{2}$.
(44) one hundred two and one half

6. Use digits and a comparison symbol to show that
(15) seven hundred eighty-six is greater than seven
hundred sixty-eight.   786 > 768

7. Use a dollar sign to write the value of two dollars, one
(45) quarter, two dimes, and three nickels. Write the value
again using a cent sign. $2.60; 260¢

8. It is morning. What time will it be
(33) 10 minutes from now?   8:27 a.m.

9. One kilometer is how many meters?   1000 m
(27)

10. How many of these circles are
(44) shaded? $2\frac{2}{3}$

11. Find the length of this screw to the nearest quarter
(48) inch.   1 inch

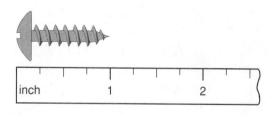

12. $\begin{array}{r} 9 \\ \times\ 8 \\ \hline 72 \end{array}$
(41)

13. $\begin{array}{r} 6 \\ \times\ 7 \\ \hline 42 \end{array}$
(47)

14. $\begin{array}{r} 8 \\ \times\ 6 \\ \hline 48 \end{array}$
(47)

15. $\begin{array}{r} 6 \\ \times\ 4 \\ \hline 24 \end{array}$
(47)

16. $\begin{array}{r} 7 \\ \times\ 3 \\ \hline 21 \end{array}$
(47)

17. $\begin{array}{r} \$4.86 \\ +\ \$2.47 \\ \hline \$7.33 \end{array}$
(28)

18. $\begin{array}{r} \$4.86 \\ -\ \$2.47 \\ \hline \$2.39 \end{array}$
(37)

19. $\begin{array}{r} 293 \\ +\ 678 \\ \hline 971 \end{array}$
(16)

20. $\begin{array}{r} 893 \\ -\ 678 \\ \hline 215 \end{array}$
(37)

21. $\begin{array}{r} 463 \\ -\ Y \\ \hline 411 \end{array}$ 52
(20)

22. $\begin{array}{r} 463 \\ +\ Q \\ \hline 527 \end{array}$ 64
(30)

23. 418
(20) $-\quad T$ 202
      216

24. 24
(21) 36
      84
      125
    + 127
      396

25. Draw a rectangle that shows 3 × 5. Then shade four
(36,32) fifteenths of it.

LESSON
49

U.S. Units of Length

a. $0.45
b. $1.35
c. $3.35
d. $7.27
e. 94
f. 382
Patterns:
$\frac{1}{4}$, $\frac{1}{2}$, $\frac{3}{4}$, 1, $1\frac{1}{4}$, $1\frac{1}{2}$, $1\frac{3}{4}$,
2, $2\frac{1}{4}$, $2\frac{1}{2}$, $2\frac{3}{4}$, 3, $3\frac{1}{4}$,
$3\frac{1}{2}$, $3\frac{3}{4}$, 4, $4\frac{1}{4}$, $4\frac{1}{2}$, $4\frac{3}{4}$,
5

Facts Practice: Multiplication Facts: Memory Group (Test F in Test Masters)

Mental Math: Subtract a number ending in five from a number ending in zero.

  a. $0.80 − $0.35   **b.** $1.60 − $0.25   **c.** $4.50 − $1.15

Review:

  d. $6.28 + $0.99   **e.** 68 + 6 + 20   **f.** 43 + 29 + 310

Patterns: This is the sequence of numbers we say when we count by fourths. Copy this sequence on your paper and continue the sequence to the whole number 5.

$$\frac{1}{4},\ \frac{1}{2},\ \frac{3}{4},\ 1,\ 1\frac{1}{4},\ 1\frac{1}{2},\ 1\frac{3}{4},\ 2,\ \dots$$

In Lesson 27 we described some units of length in the metric system. In the United States we also use other units of length. Some of these are inches, feet, yards, and miles. In Lesson 48, we said that an inch is this long.

———————

Twelve inches equal 1 **foot.** You may have a 1-foot ruler for use at your desk. A **yard** is 3 feet. One *big* step is about 1 yard. So a yard is about the same length as a meter. Actually, a yard is about $3\frac{1}{2}$ inches less than a meter. A **mile** is 1760 yards, which is 5280 feet.

We often use the abbreviations "in.," "ft," "yd," and "mi" to stand for *inches, feet, yards,* and *miles.*

U. S. Units of Length

12 in. = 1 ft
36 in. = 1 yd
3 ft = 1 yd
5280 ft = 1 mi
1760 yd = 1 mi

Activity   Use a yardstick and a 1-foot ruler to measure objects in the classroom. How tall and how wide is the door? How long and how wide is the room? Tables, desks, cabinets, and countertops can be measured. Compare a yardstick and a meterstick. Which is longer and by how much? A 1-foot ruler is about how many centimeters long?

Example 1   How many 1-foot rulers laid end to end would it take to equal 2 yards?

Solution   A yard is 3 feet long. So it would take 3 one-foot rulers to reach 1 yard. To reach another yard would take 3 more one-foot rulers. Therefore, to reach 2 yards would take **6 one-foot rulers.**

Example 2   How many *big* steps would it take to walk a mile?

Solution   A mile is 1760 yards, which is about **1760 *big* steps.**

Practice   **a.** How many 1-foot rulers laid end to end would it take to reach 3 yards?   9 one-foot rulers

b. A mile is how many feet?   5280 ft

c. One yard is how many inches?   36 in.

Problem set 49

1. Use the digits 4, 5, and 6 once each to make an even
$^{(11)}$ number greater than 600.   654

2. Myrtle the Turtle laid one hundred fifty eggs in the
$^{(12)}$ sand. Her friend Gertle laid one hundred seventy-five
eggs. Together, how many eggs did they lay? Draw a
SSM pattern.   325 eggs; $\begin{array}{r} 150 \text{ eggs} \\ + 175 \text{ eggs} \\ \hline N \text{ eggs} \end{array}$

$\begin{array}{r} 15 \quad\underline{} \\ - 6 \quad\underline{} \\ \hline N \quad\underline{} \end{array}$
3. Jill is 6 years younger than her brother. If her brother
$^{(38)}$ is 15 years old, how old is Jill? Draw a L-S-D pattern.
9 years old

4. What numbers are missing in this sequence?
$^{(3)}$
    __32__ , 40, __48__ , __56__ , 64, 72, ...

5. Use words to write the mixed number $23\frac{2}{3}$.
$^{(44)}$ twenty-three and two thirds

6. $219 = N + 10 + 9$ 200
$^{(2)}$

7. Write 809,742 in expanded form. Then use words to
$^{(42)}$ write this number. $800,000 + 9000 + 700 + 40 + 2$;
eight hundred nine thousand, seven hundred forty-two

8. Compare: three squared $\boxed{=}$ $\sqrt{81}$
$^{(40,15)}$

9. Round 128 to the nearest ten.   130
$^{(26)}$

10. Write the value of three quarters and three dimes with
$^{(45)}$ a dollar sign. Then use words to write this amount of
money. $1.05; one dollar and five cents

11. Find the length of this rectangle to the nearest quarter
$^{(48)}$ inch. $1\frac{1}{2}$ in.

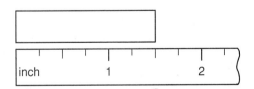

12. Draw a square and shade one ninth of it. (*Hint:* Draw a
$^{(32)}$ square. Then draw an evenly spaced tic-tac-toe pattern
inside the square.)

13. Three one-foot rulers laid end to end reach how many
(49) inches?   36 in.

14. Compare: one mile $\bigcirc>$ 1000 yards
(49,15)

15. (47)	**16.** (47)	**17.** (47)	**18.** (47)	**19.** (41)
3 $\times 7$	4 $\times 6$	6 $\times 7$	7 $\times 8$	8 $\times 9$
21	24	42	56	72

20. (37)	**21.** (28)	**22.** (37)	**23.** (37)
$7.20 − $4.25	$4.26 + $1.57	463 − 286	436 − 147
$2.95	$5.83	177	289

24. $36 + 42 + 8 + \sqrt{81} + N = 100$ 5
(40,2)

x x x x x x x
x x x x x x x
x x x x x x x   **25.** Draw a pattern of X's to show 6 × 7.
x x x x x x x   (36)
x x x x x x x
x x x x x x x

LESSON 50

Lines and Segments • Missing Factors

a. 250
b. $3.50
c. $3.50
d. $9.85
e. 581
f. 275
Problem Solving:
    56 = 7 × 8

Facts Practice: Multiplication Facts: Memory Group (Test F in Test Masters)

Mental Math: Subtract a number ending in 50 from a number ending in two zeros.
 a. 300 − 50   **b.** $4.00 − $0.50   **c.** $5.00 − $1.50

Review:
 d. $7.90 + $1.95   **e.** 536 + 45   **f.** 59 + 6 + 210

Problem Solving: The digits 1, 2, 3, and 4, in order, can be written with an equal sign and a times sign to make a multiplication fact.
                12 = 3 × 4
Write another multiplication fact using four different digits written in order.

Lines and segments   A pencil line has two ends. We say that a mathematical line has no ends. A mathematical line just goes on and on in both directions. Sometimes we draw arrowheads on a pencil line to show this idea.

$\longleftrightarrow$

A line never ends.

Part of a mathematical line is a **line segment** or just a **segment.** A segment has two endpoints.

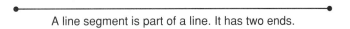

A line segment is part of a line. It has two ends.

Sometimes the endpoints of a segment are labeled with letters, and the segment is named using the letters. When we write the name of a segment, either letter can come first.

This is segment *AB*. This is also segment *BA*.

We can also write segment *AB* as $\overline{AB}$ and segment *BA* as $\overline{BA}$. Notice that the bar replaces the word *segment*. When there is more than one segment in a picture, we use the letters to make it clear which segment we are talking about.

Example 1   The length of $\overline{AB}$ is 3 cm. The length of $\overline{BC}$ is 4 cm. What is the length of $\overline{AC}$?

Solution   Two short segments can form a longer segment. From *A* to *B* is one segment. From *B* to *C* is a second segment. Together they form the third segment, segment *AC*. We are told the lengths of $\overline{AB}$ and $\overline{BC}$. If we add these lengths together, the sum will equal the length of $\overline{AC}$.

$$3 \text{ cm} + 4 \text{ cm} = 7 \text{ cm}$$

The length of $\overline{AC}$ is **7 cm.**

Since this problem is drawn to scale, we can check our answer with a ruler. However, we should not assume that all problems are drawn to scale. Therefore, we should always find the length mathematically instead of measuring with a ruler.

Missing factors   Recall that numbers that are multiplied are called *factors* and the answer is called the *product*.

$$\text{Factor} \times \text{factor} = \text{product}$$

If we know one factor and the product, we can figure out the other factor.

Example 2   Find the missing factors:

(a) $5 \times N = 40$ 　　　　　　　　 (b) $A \times 4 = 36$

Solution   (a) Five times what number is 40? Since $5 \times 8 = 40$, the missing factor is **8.**

(b) Since $9 \times 4 = 36$, the missing factor is **9.**

Practice   **a.** The length of segment *AB* is 5 cm. The length of segment *BC* is 4 cm. What is the length of segment *AC*?
9 cm

$$\overset{\textstyle A}{\bullet}\rule{6cm}{0.4pt}\overset{\textstyle B}{\bullet}\rule{3cm}{0.4pt}\overset{\textstyle C}{\bullet}$$

b. The length of $\overline{RS}$ is 4 cm. The length of $\overline{RT}$ is 10 cm. What is the length of $\overline{ST}$? (*Hint:* This time you will need to subtract.)   6 cm

$$\overset{\textstyle R}{\bullet}\rule{5cm}{0.4pt}\overset{\textstyle S}{\bullet}\rule{5cm}{0.4pt}\overset{\textstyle T}{\bullet}$$

Find each missing factor:

c. $8 \times W = 32$ 4 　　　　　 **d.** $P \times 3 = 12$ 4

Problem set 50

1. A group of quail is called a *covey*. A group of cows is called a *herd*. A group of fish is called a *school*. There are twenty-five fish in the small school. There are one hundred twelve fish in the big school. How many fewer fish are in the small school? Draw a L-S-D pattern.   87 fish; $\begin{array}{r} 112 \text{ fish} \\ -\ 25 \text{ fish} \\ \hline N \text{ fish} \end{array}$
⁽³⁸⁾

2. A 36-inch yardstick was divided into two pieces. One piece was 12 inches long. How many inches long was the other piece? Draw a SWA pattern.   24 inches
⁽³¹⁾

$\begin{array}{r} 36 \text{ inches} \\ -\ 12 \text{ inches} \\ \hline N \text{ inches} \end{array}$

47 postcards
62 postcards
+ 75 postcards
N postcards

3. Mrs. Green mailed forty-seven postcards from Paris.
(12) Her husband mailed sixty-two postcards from Paris.
Her son mailed seventy-five postcards from Paris. In
all, how many postcards did the Greens mail from
Paris? Draw a SSM pattern.   184 postcards

4. Write the number 416,528 in expanded form. Then
(42) use words to write this number.   400,000 + 10,000 + 6000 +
500 + 20 + 8; four hundred sixteen thousand, five hundred twenty-eight

5. Use digits and a comparison symbol to write that one
(15) thousand, four hundred sixty is less than one
thousand, six hundred forty.   1,460 < 1,640

6. Use a dollar sign and a decimal point to write the
(45) value of three dollars, two quarters, one dime, and two
nickels. Then write this amount of money using
words. $3.70; three dollars and seventy cents

7. Find each missing factor:
(50)
(a) 5 × N = 20   4   (b) W × 3 = 21   7

8. How many squares are shaded? $4\frac{1}{2}$
(44)

9. Find the length of the segment to the nearest quarter
(48) inch. $1\frac{1}{2}$ in.

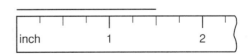

10. The length of segment *AB* is 3 cm. The length of seg-
(50) ment *BC* is 4 cm. What is the length of segment *AC*?
7 cm

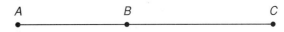

11. It is evening. What time will it be
(33) 1 hour and 50 minutes from now?
12:00 a.m.

12. Use a comparison symbol to compare 294 and 302.
(15) 294 < 302

13. Draw a circle that is about 2 centimeters across the
(25) center.

14.   9   **15.**   7   **16.**   6   **17.**   6   **18.**   4
(41)   × 7   (47)   × 3   (47)   × 8   (39)   × 6   (47)   × 8
      ----   ----   ----   ----   ----
       63   21   48   36   32

19.   416   **20.** $4.98   **21.**   536
(20)   −   Z   237   (28) + $7.65   (30)   +   Z   185
      -----   -------   -----
       179                   $12.63   721

22. $\sqrt{1} + \sqrt{4} + \sqrt{9} + N = 10$ 4
(40,2)

23. Draw a pattern of X's to show 3 × 7.   X X X X X X X
(36)   X X X X X X X
                                                  X X X X X X X

24. Use digits to write four hundred fifteen thousand,
(43) seven.   415,007

25.   4   **26.**   9   **27.**   7
(1)   5   (21)   3   (1)   2
          8   14   8
          9   7   9
          6   8   4
          5   5   7
        + 4   + 24   + 6
        ----   -----   ----
         41   70   43

LESSON
51

Subtracting Across Zero

a. 605

b. 708

c. 625

d. $4.50

e. $6.55

f. 176

Problem Solving:

Sequence:

$\frac{1}{4}, \frac{1}{2}, \frac{3}{4}, 1, 1\frac{1}{4}, 1\frac{1}{2},$

$1\frac{3}{4}, 2, 2\frac{1}{4}, 2\frac{1}{2}, 2\frac{3}{4},$

$3, 3\frac{1}{4}, 3\frac{1}{2}, 3\frac{3}{4}, 4$

Between $2\frac{1}{2}$ and 3:

$2\frac{3}{4}$

Between 3 and 4:

$3\frac{1}{2}$

Facts Practice: Multiplication Facts: Memory Group (Test F in Test Masters)

Mental Math: Add hundreds, then tens, and then ones, regrouping tens.

   a. $365 + 240$ **b.** $456 + 252$ **c.** $584 + 41$

Review:

   d. $6.00 - $1.50   **e.** $4.56 + $1.99   **f.** $47 + 29 + 100$

Problem Solving: Counting by fourths we say, "One fourth, one half, three fourths, one." Count by fourths from one fourth to four. Write this sequence on a sheet of paper. What number is between $2\frac{1}{2}$ and 3? What number is halfway between 3 and 4?

In the problem below we must regroup twice before we can subtract the first time.

$$\begin{array}{r} \$405 \\ - \$126 \\ \hline \end{array}$$

We cannot exchange a ten for ones because there are no tens. The first step is to exchange 1 hundred for 10 tens.

$$\begin{array}{r} \overset{3}{\cancel{4}}\overset{1}{0}\,5 \\ \$\,\cancel{4}\,0\,5 \\ -\$\,1\,2\,6 \\ \hline \end{array}$$

Now we have 10 tens. The next step is to exchange 1 of the tens for 10 ones.

$$\begin{array}{r} \overset{3}{\cancel{4}}\overset{9}{\cancel{0}}\overset{1}{5} \\ \$\,\cancel{4}\,\cancel{0}\,5 \\ -\$\,1\,2\,6 \\ \hline \end{array}$$

Now we subtract.

$$\begin{array}{r} \overset{3}{\cancel{4}}\overset{9}{\cancel{0}}\overset{1}{5} \\ \$\,\cancel{4}\,\cancel{0}\,5 \\ -\$\,1\,2\,6 \\ \hline \$\,2\,7\,9 \end{array}$$

We check by adding.

$$\begin{array}{r} \$126 \\ + \$279 \\ \hline \$405 \quad \text{check} \end{array}$$

Example   Tom had $3.00 and spent $1.23. How much money did he have left?

Solution   First we change 3 dollars to 2 dollars and 10 dimes. Next we change 10 dimes to 9 dimes and 10 pennies. Then we subtract.

$$\begin{array}{r} \$\ 3.0\ 0 \\ -\ \$\ 1.2\ 3 \\ \hline \end{array} \qquad \begin{array}{r} \overset{2}{\$\ \cancel{3}.0\ 0} \\ -\ \$\ 1.2\ 3 \\ \hline \end{array} \qquad \begin{array}{r} \overset{2\ \ 9}{\$\ \cancel{3}.\cancel{0}\ 0} \\ -\ \$\ 1.2\ 3 \\ \hline \$\ 1.7\ 7 \end{array}$$

Now we check by adding.

$$\begin{array}{r} \$1.23 \\ + \$1.77 \\ \hline \$3.00 \quad \text{check} \end{array}$$

Practice   **a.** $\begin{array}{r} \$3.00 \\ - \$1.32 \\ \hline \$1.68 \end{array}$ **b.** $\begin{array}{r} \$405 \\ - \$156 \\ \hline \$249 \end{array}$ **c.** $\begin{array}{r} 201 \\ - 102 \\ \hline 99 \end{array}$

d. $4.00 - $0.86   **e.** $304 - $128   **f.** 703 - 198
$3.14 $176   505

Problem set 51

1. There were one hundred forty-seven birds in the first
(38) flock. There were six hundred forty-three birds in the second flock. How many more birds were in the second flock? Draw a L-S-D pattern.   496 birds

$$\begin{array}{r} 643 \text{ birds} \\ - 147 \text{ birds} \\ \hline N \text{ birds} \end{array}$$

2. Kevin had a dime, a quarter, and a penny. Write this
(45) amount with a dollar sign and a decimal point. $0.36

3. San Francisco is 400 miles north
(50) of Los Angeles, as shown. Santa Barbara is 110 miles north of Los Angeles. How far is it from Santa Barbara to San Francisco?   290 mi

• San Francisco

• Santa Barbara
• Los Angeles

4. Use the digits 5, 6, and 7 once each to make an odd
(11) number greater than 700.   765

5. Use digits and a comparison symbol to show that five
(15) hundred ninety-four is greater than five hundred
forty-nine.   594 > 549

6. It is dark now. What time will it
(33) be 7 hours from now?   5:17 a.m.

7. Find the missing factor:
(50) $W \times 5 = 40$ 8

8. Draw a rectangle and shade one fourth of it.
(32)

9. There is a 6 in the ones' place and a 7 in the tens'
(42) place. The number is between 4000 and 4100. What is
the number?   4076

10. Which letter below has no right angles?   Z
(29)
F   E   Z   L

11. Find the length of segment *BC*.   6 cm
(50)

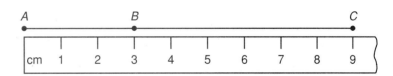

12. The arrow points to what number on this inch scale?
(48) $1\frac{3}{4}$ in.

13.   7
(47) × 8
   ——
   56

14.   9
(41) × 6
   ——
   54

15.   *M*   8
(50) × 8
   ——
   64

16.   6
(47) × 7
   ——
   42

17.   9
(41) × 8
   ——
   72

18.   *Z*   317
(30) + 179
   ——
   496

19. 251
(30) $+\quad C$ 175
       ——
       426

20. 405
(20) $-\quad P$ 282
       ——
       123

21. W 783
(20) $-\ 297$
       ——
       486

22. Six squared $+ \sqrt{64} + N = 50$ 6
(40,2)

23. Use digits to write seven hundred thousand,
(43) seventeen.   700,017

24. 27
(21)   4
       16
       28
        7
      $+ 15$
       ——
       97

25. 19
(21)   81
        5
        7
       14
      $+ 21$
       ——
       147

26. 31
(21)   14
       28
       15
        6
      $+\ 7$
       ——
       101

**LESSON
52**

Rounding Numbers to the Nearest Hundred • Multiplying by Multiples of 10 and 100

a. 538
b. $6.09
c. 758
d. 590
e. $7.05
f. $9.22

Problem Solving:
7:05, 8:11, 9:16,
10:22, 11:29, 1:38,
2:44, 3:49, 4:55
(approximate
times)

Facts Practice: Multiplication Facts: Memory Group (Test F in Test Masters)

Mental Math: Add hundreds, then tens, and then ones, regrouping tens.

  a. 466 + 72   **b.** $3.59 + $2.50   **c.** 572 + 186

Review:

  d. 400 + 160 + 30   **e.** $4.60 + $2.45   **f.** $6.24 + $2.98

Problem Solving: The hands of a clock point in opposite directions at 6:00. They also point in opposite directions at about 12:33. Name nine more times the hands of a clock point in opposite directions.

**Rounding
numbers to
the nearest
hundred**

We have practiced rounding numbers to the nearest ten. Now we will learn to round numbers to the nearest hundred. To round numbers to the nearest hundred, we find the hundred number to which the number is nearest.

The hundred numbers are the numbers in this sequence.

$$100, 200, 300, 400, \ldots$$

A number line can help us understand rounding to the nearest hundred.

Example 1 Round 472 to the nearest hundred.

Solution The number 472 is between the hundred numbers 400 and 500. Halfway between 400 and 500 is 450. Since 472 is greater than 450, it is nearest 500. We see this on the number line below.

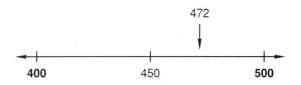

Rounding 472 to the nearest hundred gives us **500.**

Example 2 Round 362 and 385 to the nearest hundred. Then use a comparison symbol to compare the rounded numbers.

Solution The number 362 is closer to 400 than it is to 300. The number 385 is closer to 400 than it is to 300. Both 362 and 385 round to **400.** If we compare the rounded numbers, we get

$$400 \; = \; 400$$

Multiplying by multiples of 10 and 100 The multiples of 10 are the numbers we say when we count by 10.

Multiples of 10: 10, 20, 30, 40, 50, ...

Likewise, the multiples of 100 are the numbers we say when we count by 100.

Multiples of 100: 100, 200, 300, 400, 500, ...

When multiplying by multiples of 10 and 100, we focus our attention on the first digit of the multiple of 10 or 100.

Example 3   Find the product: 3×200

Solution   We will show three ways.

$$
\begin{array}{r}
200 \\
200 \\
+\ 200 \\
\hline
600
\end{array}
\qquad
\begin{array}{r}
2 \text{ hundred} \\
\times \qquad\quad 3 \\
\hline
6 \text{ hundred}
\end{array}
\qquad
\begin{array}{r}
200 \\
\times \quad 3 \\
\hline
600
\end{array}
$$

We will look closely at the method on the right.

$$
\begin{array}{r}
2\,0\,0 \quad \longleftarrow \text{Two zeros here} \\
\times \quad 3 \\
\hline
2 \times 3 = 6 \longrightarrow 6\,0\,0 \quad \longleftarrow \text{Two zeros here}
\end{array}
$$

By focusing on the first digit and by counting ending zeros, we can multiply by multiples of 10 and 100 mentally.

Example 4   Multiply: 6×40

Solution   We will practice two mental math methods.

$$
6 \times 4\,0 = \mathbf{240}
\qquad
\begin{array}{r}
4\,0 \\
\times \quad 6 \\
\hline
2\,4\,0
\end{array}
$$

Practice   Round each number to the nearest hundred:

a. 813   800   **b.** 685   700   **c.** 427   400   **d.** 573   600

Find each product:

e.
$$
\begin{array}{r}
50 \\
\times\ 7 \\
\hline
350
\end{array}
$$
f.
$$
\begin{array}{r}
600 \\
\times\ 3 \\
\hline
1800
\end{array}
$$
g. 7×40
280
h. 4×800
3200

Problem set 52

1. ⁽¹⁷⁾ Two hundred fifty-two cowboys came when the bell rang once. Then some more cowboys came when the bell rang twice. Four hundred two cowboys came in all. How many cowboys came when the bell rang twice? Draw a SSM pattern.   150 cowboys;
$$
\begin{array}{r}
252 \text{ cowboys} \\
+\ \ N \text{ cowboys} \\
\hline
402 \text{ cowboys}
\end{array}
$$

2. Wilbur had sixty-seven grapes. He ate some grapes.
(31) Then he had thirty-eight grapes. How many grapes did
he eat? Draw a SWA pattern.   29 grapes; $\begin{array}{r} 67 \text{ grapes} \\ - \ N \text{ grapes} \\ \hline 38 \text{ grapes} \end{array}$

3. The distance from Whery to Radi-
(50) cal is 42 km. The distance from
Whery to Appletown through
Radical is 267 km. How far is it
from Radical to Appletown?
225 km

4. It is afternoon. What time will it
(33) be in half an hour?   4:42 p.m.

5. Write the next three numbers in this sequence of
(39,3) square numbers:

1, 4, 9, 16, 25, 36, 49, __64__ , __81__ , __100__ , ...

6. Round 673 to the nearest hundred.   700
(52)

7. How many squares are shaded?
(44) $3\frac{3}{4}$

8. Find the length of the screw to the nearest quarter
(48) inch. $1\frac{1}{4}$ in.

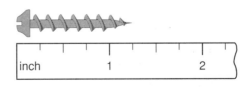

9. The length of $\overline{AB}$ is 7 cm. The length of $\overline{AC}$ is 12 cm.
(50) How long is $\overline{BC}$?   5 cm

A   B   C

10. One way to remember the difference between the
(29) words *parallel* and *perpendicular* is to look at the
three l's in *parallel*. The l's are parallel. Now here's
the question. Are the line segments in a plus sign
parallel or perpendicular?   perpendicular

11. To what number is the arrow pointing?   1425
(13)

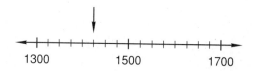

12. Use the digits 4, 7, and 8 once each to write an odd
(11) number greater than 500.   847

13. 6 × 80   **14.** 7 × 700   **15.** 9 × 80   **16.** 7 × 600
(52)   480   (52)   4900   (52)   720   (52)   4200

17.   Z   169   **18.** $4.06   **19.**   705
(30)   + 338   (51)   − $2.28   (20)   −   N   289
           507   _____   416
                                   $1.78

20.   N   727   **21.** 55 + 555 + 378   988
(20)   − 422   (21)
           305

22. 293 + 58 + 681   1032
(21)

23. 8 + 56 + 78 + 24 + 55 + 387   608
(21)

x x x x x x x x
x x x x x x x x
x x x x x x x x   **24.** Draw a pattern of X's to show 6 × 8.
x x x x x x x x   (36)
x x x x x x x x
x x x x.x x x x

25. Write each amount of money with a dollar sign and a
(45) decimal point.

(a) 77¢ $0.77   (b) 8¢ $0.08   (c) 430¢ $4.30

26. Use words to write 703,742.
(42)   seven hundred three thousand, seven hundred forty-two

27. Use digits to write nine hundred two thousand, five
(43) hundred seven.   902,507

LESSON
53

More Adding and Subtracting Money

a. 412
b. $632
c. 941
d. 183
e. 775
f. 365

Problem Solving:
$\frac{3}{4}$ in.

Facts Practice: 64 Multiplication Facts (Test G in Test Masters)

Mental Math: Add hundreds, then tens, and then ones, regrouping tens and ones.

    a. 258 + 154   **b.** $367 + $265   **c.** 587 + 354

Review:

    d. 54 + 19 + 110   **e.** 620 + 40 + 115   **f.** 480 − 115

Problem Solving: From Point A to Point B is $1\frac{1}{4}$ inches. How far is it from Point B to Point C?

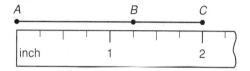

To add or subtract money written with a dollar sign, we first line up the decimal points.

Example 1   (a) $3.45 + $0.75   (b) $5.35 − $2

Solution   (a) First we line up the decimal points.

$$\begin{array}{r} \$3.45 \\ + \ \$0.75 \\ \hline \end{array}$$

Now we add, remembering to write the dollar sign and decimal point.

$$\begin{array}{r} \$3.45 \\ + \ \$0.75 \\ \hline \mathbf{\$4.20} \end{array}$$

(b) First we use a decimal point to write $2. To do this, we put a decimal point and two zeros behind the $2.

$$\$2 \text{ means } \$2.00$$

Now we line up the decimal points and subtract.

$$\begin{array}{r} \$5.35 \\ - \ \$2.00 \\ \hline \mathbf{\$3.35} \end{array}$$

Example 2　(a) 67¢ − 59¢ 　　　　　　(b) 45¢ + 80¢

Solution　To add or subtract money in cent form, we line up the last digits and add or subtract as the sign shows. If the answer equals $1 or more, we usually change from cent form to dollar form.

$$(a) \quad \overset{5}{\cancel{6}}\overset{1}{7}¢ \qquad (b) \quad 45¢$$
$$\underline{-\ 5\ 9¢} \qquad\qquad \underline{+\ 80¢}$$
$$8¢ \qquad\qquad 125¢ = \mathbf{\$1.25}$$

Example 3　$3.75 + $4 + 15¢

Solution　If both forms of money are in the problem, we change to one form first. Most people change the cent form to the dollar form. We make these changes.

$4　　　　means　　　　$4.00

15¢　　　means　　　　$0.15

Then we line up the decimal points and add.

$$\$3.75$$
$$\$4.00$$
$$\underline{+\ \$0.15}$$
$$\mathbf{\$7.90}$$

Practice　**a.** $6.32 + $5　$11.32　　　　**b.** $3.25 − $1.75　$1.50

c. 46¢ + 64¢　$1.10　　　　　　　**d.** 98¢ − 89¢　9¢

e. $1.46 + 87¢　$2.33　　　　　　**f.** 76¢ − $0.05　71¢

Problem set 53

1. One hundred pennies are separated into two piles. In one pile there are thirty-five pennies. How many pennies are in the other pile? Draw a SWA pattern.
(31)
65 pennies

$$\begin{array}{r} 100 \text{ pennies} \\ -\ 35 \text{ pennies} \\ \hline N \text{ pennies} \end{array}$$

2. Maria skied three hundred forty-two kilometers the first month. She skied seven hundred fifteen kilometers the second month. How many more kilometers did she ski the second month? Draw a L-S-D pattern.
(38)
373 kilometers;

$$\begin{array}{r} 715 \text{ kilometers} \\ -\ 342 \text{ kilometers} \\ \hline N \text{ kilometers} \end{array}$$

3. The apple cost 35¢. Harry gave the vendor a dollar
(53) bill. How much change did he get back?   65¢

4. Purcell is a town between Chickasha and Konawa. It is
(50) 61 miles from Chickasha to Konawa through Purcell. It
is 24 miles from Chickasha to Purcell. How far is it
from Purcell to Konawa? Draw a sketch of this
problem.   37 miles

5. Round 572 to the nearest hundred.   600
(52)

6. Write the number 7,284 in expanded form. Then use
(42) words to write the number.   7000 + 200 + 80 + 4;
seven thousand, two hundred eighty-four

7. Are railroad tracks parallel or perpendicular?
(29) parallel

8. Draw a square to show 3 × 3. Then shade two ninths
(36,32) of the square.

9. It is morning. What time was it 2
(33) hours ago?   6:05 a.m.

10. To what number is the arrow pointing?   154
(13)

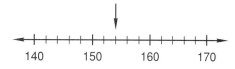

11. $2.45 + $3 $5.45   **12.** $3.25 − $2.47 $0.78
(53)   *(53)*

13. $2.15 + $3 + 7¢   **14.** 4¢ + 23¢ + 7¢   34¢
(53) $5.22   *(53)*

15.   507   **16.** N 630   **17.** $4.86
(20)   − N 51   *(20)*   − 207   *(28)*   + $9.57
          456   423 $14.43

18. 6 × 80 480   **19.** 4 × 300 1200   **20.** 7 × 90 630
(52)   *(52)*   *(52)*

21. $4 \times N = 32$ 8   **22.** $\sqrt{100}$ 10
(50)   (40)

23. Use digits to write four hundred two thousand, five
(43) hundred two.   402,502

24. (21)		**25.** (21)	
	5		19
	7		42
	5		17
	14		5
	17		2
	17		8
	21		9
	8		5
+	6	+	6
	100		113

LESSON 54

Multiplying Two-Digit Numbers, Part 1

a. 635
b. 800
c. $7.10
d. $584
e. 95
f. 807

Problem Solving:
3 quarters, 2 dimes, and 1 nickel or 1 half dollar, 1 quarter, 1 dime, and 3 nickels

Facts Practice: 64 Multiplication Facts (Test G in Test Masters)

Mental Math: Add hundreds, then tens, and then ones, regrouping tens and ones.

  a. 589 + 46   **b.** 375 + 425   **c.** $5.64 + $1.46

Review:

  d. $389 + $195   **e.** 76 + 9 + 10   **f.** 500 + 43 + 264

Problem Solving: One way to make a dollar with six coins is with a half dollar and five dimes. Find two more ways to make a dollar with six coins.

If there are 23 children in each classroom, then how many children are in 3 classrooms?

One way to find the answer to this question is to multiply 3 × 23. Here are two ways to multiply using pencil and paper.

23 is 20 + 3

MULTIPLY 3 × 20.   MULTIPLY ONES.

MULTIPLY 3 × 3.   MULTIPLY TENS.

$\begin{array}{r} 20 + 3 \\ \times\qquad 3 \\ \hline 60 + 9 = 69 \end{array}$	$\begin{array}{r} 23 \\ \times\ 3 \\ \hline 69 \end{array}$

⟶

THEN ADD.

The method on the left is helpful when multiplying mentally. The method on the right is a quick way to multiply using pencil and paper.

Example Multiply: 42 × 3

Solution We put 42 above and 3 below, under the 2. First we multiply 2 by 3 and get 6. Then we multiply 4 (for 40) by 3 and get 12. The product is 126.

$\begin{array}{r} 42 \\ \times\ 3 \\ \hline \mathbf{126} \end{array}$

Practice

a. $\begin{array}{r} 31 \\ \times\ 2 \\ \hline 62 \end{array}$	b. $\begin{array}{r} 31 \\ \times\ 4 \\ \hline 124 \end{array}$	c. $\begin{array}{r} 42 \\ \times\ 4 \\ \hline 168 \end{array}$
d. $\begin{array}{r} 30 \\ \times\ 2 \\ \hline 60 \end{array}$	e. $\begin{array}{r} 30 \\ \times\ 4 \\ \hline 120 \end{array}$	f. $\begin{array}{r} 24 \\ \times\ 0 \\ \hline 0 \end{array}$

Problem set 54

1. *(43,15)* Juan compared two numbers. The first number was forty-two thousand, three hundred seventy-six. The second number was forty-two thousand, eleven. Use digits and a comparison symbol to show the comparison.   42,376 > 42,011

496 pinecones
− 243 pinecones
N pinecones

2. Sally found two hundred forty-three pinecones. Jane found four hundred ninety-six pinecones. How many more pinecones did Jane find? Draw a L-S-D pattern.
(38)
253 pinecones

3. The ticket cost $3.25. The man paid for the ticket with a $5 bill. How much change did he get? $1.75
(53,51)

4. Nine squared is how much more than the square root of nine? 78
(40,38)

5. Find the missing factor: $8 \times M = 48$ 6
(50)

6. The length of segment *RT* is 9 cm. The length of segment *ST* is 5 cm. What is the length of segment *RS*? 4 cm
(50)

7. How many circles are shaded? $3\frac{1}{3}$
(44)

8. Find the length of this bottle to the nearest quarter inch. $2\frac{1}{4}$ in.
(48)

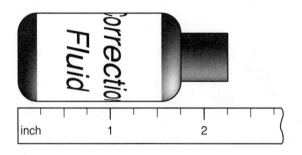

9. Compare: $4 \times 60 \, \bigcirc\!\!= \, 3 \times 80$
(52,15)

10. (51)	**11.** (28)	**12.** (37)	**13.** (51)
$4.03 − $1.68	$4.33 + $5.28	$5.22 − $2.46	$7.08 − $0.59
$2.35	$9.61	$2.76	$6.49

14. (54)	**15.** (52)	**16.** (54)	**17.** (54)
21 × 6	40 × 7	73 × 2	51 × 6
126	280	146	306

18. $2 + 47¢ + 21¢
(53) $2.68

19. $3.42 + 75¢ + 68¢
(53) $4.85

20.   462
(20) −   N   319
     ―――
      143

21.   N   718
(20) − 472
     ―――
      246

22. Write this addition problem as a multiplication
(33) problem: 6 × 21

$$21 + 21 + 21 + 21 + 21 + 21$$

23. Use words to write 815,002.
(42) eight hundred fifteen thousand, two

24.   426
(30) +   N   95
     ―――
      521

25.   N   165
(30) + 628
     ―――
      793

LESSON
55

a. 541
b. $5.50
c. $9.24
d. $3.25
e. $6.85
f. 287
Problem Solving:

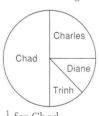

$\frac{1}{2}$ for Chad,
$\frac{1}{4}$ for Charles,
$\frac{1}{8}$ for Diane, and
$\frac{1}{8}$ for Trinh

Parentheses

Facts Practice: 100 Multiplication Facts (Test H in Test Masters)

Mental Math: Add hundreds, then tens, and then ones, regrouping tens and ones.

  a. 396 + 145   **b.** $2.75 + $2.75   **c.** $6.38 + $2.86

Review:

  d. $4.80 − $1.55   **e.** $3.90 + $2.95   **f.** 48 + 39 + 200

Problem Solving: Chad bought a pizza and gave half of it to Charles. Charles gave half of his portion to Diane. Diane gave half of hers to Trinh. Draw a diagram of the divided pizza. Each person ended up with what fraction of the pizza?

When parentheses are in an arithmetic problem, we do the work inside the parentheses first.

$$2 × (3 + 4)$$

In this problem, we first add 3 and 4 and get 7. Then we multiply 2 times 7. The answer is 14.

Example 1   (3 × 4) + 5

Solution   First we multiply 3 × 4 and get 12. Then we add 5 to 12.

$$12 + 5 = \mathbf{17}$$

Example 2   3 × (4 + 5)

Solution   We add 4 + 5 and get 9. Then we multiply 9 by 3.

$$3 × 9 = \mathbf{27}$$

Practice   **a.** 8 − (4 + 2)   2   **b.** (8 − 4) + 2   6

c. 9 − (6 − 3)   6   **d.** (9 − 6) − 3   0

e. 10 + (2 × 3)   16   **f.** 3 × (10 + 20)   90

Problem set 55

1. There were four hundred twenty-four carrots in the
$^{(17)}$ first bunch. There were seven hundred forty-two
carrots in the first two bunches combined. How many
carrots were in the second bunch? Draw a SSM
pattern.   318 carrots; $\begin{array}{r} 424 \text{ carrots} \\ + \quad N \text{ carrots} \\ \hline 742 \text{ carrots} \end{array}$

2. A whole hour is 60 minutes. How many minutes is
$^{(23)}$ half of an hour?   30 minutes

$\begin{array}{r} 155 \text{ miles} \\ - \quad 25 \text{ miles} \\ \hline N \text{ miles} \end{array}$ **3.** The space shuttle orbited 155 miles above the earth.
$^{(38)}$ The weather balloon floated 25 miles above the earth.
The space shuttle was how much higher than the
weather balloon? Draw a L-S-D pattern.   130 miles

4. How much change should you get back if you give the
$^{(53,51)}$ clerk $5.00 for a box of cereal that costs $2.85? $2.15

5. Use the digits 4, 5, 6, and 7 once each to write an odd
$^{(11)}$ number between 4700 and 4790.   4765

6. Use digits and a comparison symbol to show that five
$^{(15)}$ hundred sixteen is less than five hundred sixty.
516 < 560

7. It is morning. What time was it 20
(33) minutes ago?   5:50 a.m.

8. Write 72,856 in expanded form. Then use words to
(42) write this number.   70,000 + 2000 + 800 + 50 + 6;
seventy-two thousand, eight hundred fifty-six

9. How many circles are shaded? $2\frac{1}{4}$
(44)

10. Use shaded circles to show the mixed number $4\frac{3}{4}$.
(44)

11. Use a ruler to measure this line segment to the nearest
(48) quarter inch.   2 in.

12. Use a centimeter scale to measure the segment in
(24) Problem 11 to the nearest centimeter.   5 cm

13. 8 × (40 + 30)   560
(55)

14. (8 × 4) + 3   35
(55)

15.
(37)
$4.07
− $2.26
―――
$1.81

16.
(51)
$5.02
− $2.47
―――
$2.55

17.
(37)
$5.83
− $2.97
―――
$2.86

18.
(28)
$3.92
+ $5.14
―――
$9.06

19.
(54)
42
× 3
―――
126

20.
(54)
83
× 2
―――
166

21.
(52)
40
× 4
―――
160

22.
(54)
41
× 6
―――
246

23. $2 + 42¢ + 7¢ $2.49
(53)

24. $5.24 + 23¢ + 2¢
(53) $5.49

25. $\sqrt{36}$ + 18 + 26 + 200 + N = 300   50
(40,2)

26. Write this addition problem as a multiplication
(33) problem: 4 × 40

$$40 + 40 + 40 + 40$$

27. Eight times four is how much less than six squared?
(39,38) 4

28. Find the missing factor: 6 × W = 42   7
(50)

LESSON
56

a. 60
b. 30
c. 80
d. 640
e. $2.15
f. 375
g. 3, 5, 2, 8
Problem Solving:
   June 25, 1994

Facts Practice: 100 Multiplication Facts (Test H in Test Masters)

Mental Math: Subtract a multiple of 10 from 100.

  a. 100 − 40   **b.** 100 − 70   **c.** 100 − 20

Review:

  d. 465 + 175   **e.** $3.50 − $1.35   **f.** 346 + 29

  g. What number should be added to each of these numbers for the total to be 9: 6, 4, 7, 1?

Problem Solving: On Christmas Day, 1995, Stacy's brother turned eighteen months old. What was the date of her brother's birth?

Remember that multiplication problems have three numbers. The multiplied numbers are **factors.** The answer is the **product.**

$$\text{Factor} \times \text{factor} = \text{product}$$

If we know the two factors, we multiply to find the product. If the factors are 4 and 3, the product is 12.

$$4 \times 3 = 12$$

If we know one factor and the product, we can find the other factor.

$$4 \times W = 12 \qquad N \times 3 = 12$$

The process of finding the missing factor is called *division.*

We know how to use a multiplication table to find the product of 3 and 4. We locate the proper row and column. Where they meet, we find the product.

	0	1	2	3	④
0	0	0	0	0	0
1	0	1	2	3	4
2	0	2	4	6	8
③	0	3	6	9	⑫
4	0	4	8	12	16

We may also use a multiplication table to find a missing factor. If we know that one factor is 3 and the product is 12, we move across the row that starts with 3 until we get to 12. Then we look up to the top of the column with 12 and find 4, which is the missing factor.

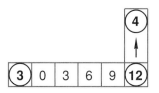

We write the numbers 3, 4, and 12 with a division box this way.

$$\begin{array}{r} 4 \\ 3\overline{)12} \end{array}$$

We say "Twelve divided by three is four."

Example 1   Divide: $4\overline{)32}$

Solution   The problem is to find the missing factor. We think, "Four times what number is thirty-two?" We show how to find the missing factor in the multiplication table below. First we find the row beginning with 4. Then we follow this row across until we see 32. Then we go up this column and find that the answer is **8**.

Multiplication Table

	0	1	2	3	4	5	6	7	8	9
0	0	0	0	0	0	0	0	0	0	0
1	0	1	2	3	4	5	6	7	8	9
2	0	2	4	6	8	10	12	14	16	18
3	0	3	6	9	12	15	18	21	24	27
4	0	4	8	12	16	20	24	28	32	36
5	0	5	10	15	20	25	30	35	40	45
6	0	6	12	18	24	30	36	42	48	54
7	0	7	14	21	28	35	42	49	56	63
8	0	8	16	24	32	40	48	56	64	72
9	0	9	18	27	36	45	54	63	72	81

Example 2 $2\overline{)18}$

Solution We search for the number that goes above the box. We think, "Two times what number is eighteen?" We remember that $2 \times 9 = 18$, so the answer is **9**. We write "9" above the 18.

$$\begin{array}{r} 9 \\ 2\overline{)18} \end{array}$$

Practice Find the answer to each division:

a. $2\overline{)12}$ = 6   **b.** $3\overline{)21}$ = 7   **c.** $4\overline{)20}$ = 5   **d.** $5\overline{)30}$ = 6

e. $6\overline{)42}$ = 7   **f.** $7\overline{)28}$ = 4   **g.** $8\overline{)48}$ = 6   **h.** $9\overline{)36}$ = 4

Problem set 56

1.
(17)
Four hundred ninety-five oil drums were on the first train. Seven hundred sixty-two oil drums were on the first two trains combined. How many oil drums were on the second train? Draw a SSM pattern.
267 oil drums

$$\begin{array}{r} 495 \text{ oil drums} \\ +\ N \text{ oil drums} \\ \hline 762 \text{ oil drums} \end{array}$$

2.
(38)
There were one hundred twenty-five fish in the first tank. There were three hundred forty-two fish in the second tank. How many fewer fish were in the first tank? Draw a L-S-D pattern. 217 fish;

$$\begin{array}{r} 342 \text{ fish} \\ -\ 125 \text{ fish} \\ \hline N \text{ fish} \end{array}$$

3.
(12)
Cyrus baled 82 bales of hay on the first day. He baled 92 bales of hay on the second day. He baled 78 bales of hay on the third day. How many bales of hay did he bale in all three days? Draw a SSM pattern.
252 bales of hay

$$\begin{array}{r} 82 \text{ bales of hay} \\ 92 \text{ bales of hay} \\ +\ 78 \text{ bales of hay} \\ \hline N \text{ bales of hay} \end{array}$$

4.
(11)
Use the digits 6, 7, and 8 once each to write an odd number greater than 856. 867

5.
(44)
Draw shaded rectangles to picture the mixed number $4\frac{1}{3}$.

6.
(1)
The first five odd numbers are 1, 3, 5, 7, and 9. What is their sum? 25

7. It is morning. What time was it 12
(33) hours ago?   10:00 p.m.

8. To the nearest quarter inch, how long is this rectangle?
(48) $1\frac{1}{4}$ in.

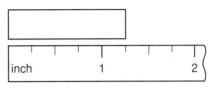

9. Martin took two dozen *big* steps. About how many
(27) meters did he walk?   24 meters

10. To what number is the arrow pointing? $10\frac{5}{6}$
(46)

11. 64 + (9 × 40)   424   **12.** $6.25 + 39¢ + $3
(55)   (53) $9.64

13. $4.02   **14.** $5.07   **15.**   N   492
(51)   − $2.47   (51)   − $2.48   (30)   + 223
     ‾‾‾‾‾‾   ‾‾‾‾‾‾   ‾‾‾‾‾
       $1.55 $2.59   715

16.   938   **17.**   42   **18.**   81
(20) −   C   715   (54) ×   3   (54) ×   5
    ‾‾‾‾‾   ‾‾‾‾‾   ‾‾‾‾‾
      223   126   405

                              5   3   7
19.   30   **20.** 6)‾3‾0   **21.** 7)‾2‾1   **22.** 8)‾5‾6
(52) ×   4   (56)   (56)   (56)
    ‾‾‾‾‾
      120
              9   4   5
23. 9)‾8‾1   **24.** 7)‾2‾8   **25.** 3)‾1‾5
(56)   (56)   (56)
              6   3   8
26. 4)‾2‾4   **27.** 8)‾2‾4   **28.** 5)‾4‾0
(56)   (56)   (56)

LESSON 57

Other Ways to Show Division

a. 170
b. 240
c. 310
d. $5.47
e. 551
f. 83
g. 1, 7, 4, 6
Problem Solving:
Sal scored 26 points. Cheryl scored 30 points.

Facts Practice: 100 Multiplication Facts (Test H in Test Masters)

Mental Math: Subtract a multiple of 10 from a multiple of 100.
  a. 200 − 30   **b.** 300 − 60   **c.** 400 − 90

Review:
  d. $2.48 + $2.99   **e.** 384 + 167   **f.** 46 + 7 + 30
  g. What number should be added to each of these numbers for the total to be 9: 8, 2, 5, 3?

Problem Solving: A loop is worth five points and a tip is worth three points. Sal made four loops and two tips. Cheryl made three loops and five tips. How many points did each person score?

We have different ways to show division. Here we show "fifteen divided by three" three different ways.

$$3\overline{)15} \qquad 15 \div 3 \qquad \frac{15}{3}$$

The first way uses a division box. The second way uses a division sign. The third way uses a division bar. We should be able to solve problems in any form and be able to change from one form to another form.

Example 1 Use digits and division symbols to show "twenty-four divided by six" in three ways.

Solution $6\overline{)24} \qquad 24 \div 6 \qquad \frac{24}{6}$

Example 2 Solve: (a) 28 ÷ 4   (b) $\frac{27}{3}$

Solution (a) We read this as "Twenty-eight divided by four." It means the same as $4\overline{)28}$.

$$28 \div 4 = 7$$

(b) We read this as "Twenty-seven divided by three." It means the same as $3\overline{)27}$.

$$\frac{27}{3} = \textbf{9}$$

A multiplication fact has three numbers. The same three numbers form a division fact. Multiplication facts and division facts should be practiced together. Frequent timed written tests on multiplication and division facts will help you memorize these facts.

Practice   **a.** $49 \div 7$ 7   **b.** $45 \div 9$ 5   **c.** $40 \div 8$ 5

d. $\dfrac{36}{6}$ 6   **e.** $\dfrac{32}{8}$ 4   **f.** $\dfrac{27}{3}$ 9

Use digits and three different division symbols to show:

g. Twenty-seven divided by nine $9\overline{)27}; 27 \div 9; \frac{27}{9}$

h. Twenty-eight divided by seven $7\overline{)28}; 28 \div 7; \frac{28}{7}$

Problem set 57

1. Frank hit the target two hundred forty-three times.
$^{(38)}$ Vanessa hit the target five hundred seven times. How many more times did Vanessa hit the target than Frank hit the target? Draw a L-S-D pattern.   264 times

$$\begin{array}{r} 507 \text{ times} \\ - 243 \text{ times} \\ \hline N \text{ times} \end{array}$$

2. The numbers 3, 4, and 12 are a multiplication and
$^{(57)}$ division fact family.

$$\begin{array}{cc} 3 & 4 \\ \times\ 4 & \times\ 3 \\ \hline 12 & 12 \end{array} \qquad \begin{array}{l} 12 \div 4 = 3 \\ 12 \div 3 = 4 \end{array}$$

Write the four multiplication/division facts using the numbers 4, 5, and 20.
$4 \times 5 = 20, 5 \times 4 = 20, 20 \div 4 = 5, 20 \div 5 = 4$

3. Altogether, how many days are there in the last three
$^{(6)}$ months of the year?   92 days

4. Use the digits 1, 5, 6, and 8 once each to write an even
$^{(11)}$ number greater than 8420.   8516

5. Draw shaded circles to picture the mixed number $4\frac{2}{3}$.
(44)

6. To the nearest quarter inch, how long is the stick of
(48) gum? $1\frac{1}{2}$ in.

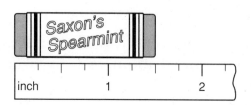

7. It is evening. What time was it 2
(33) hours and 25 minutes ago?
7:00 p.m.

8. One sixth of this rectangle is
(32) shaded. Draw another rectangle
and shade five sixths of it.

9. The length of segment PQ is 2 cm. The length of
(50) segment PR is 11 cm. How long is segment QR?   9 cm

P   Q   R

10. $95 - \left(7 \times \sqrt{64}\right)$ 39   **11.** $2.53 + 45¢ + $3
(55,40)   (53) $5.98

12. $3.04   **13.** $8.46   **14.**   842
(37) $- $1.22   (37) $- $3.58   (20) $-$ Z 627
     $1.82 $4.88   215

15. N 809   **16.**   40   **17.**   51
(20) $- 516$ (52) $\times$ 3   (54) $\times$ 5
    293   120   255

18. $28 \div 7$ **19.** $81 \div 9$ **20.** $35 \div 7$ **21.** $16 \div 4$
(57) 4   (57) 9   (57) 5   (57) 4

22. $\frac{28}{4}$ 7   **23.** $\frac{42}{7}$ 6   **24.** $\frac{48}{8}$ 6   **25.** $\frac{45}{5}$ 9
(57)   (57)   (57)   (57)

26. Five squared is how much less than 28?   3
(40,38)

LESSON
58

Multiplying Two-Digit Numbers, Part 2

a. 54¢
b. 36¢
c. 72¢
d. 48¢
e. 83¢
f. 15¢
Problem Solving:
$1\frac{3}{4}$ in.

Facts Practice: 90 Division Facts (Test I in Test Masters)

Mental Math: Nine dimes plus ten pennies total one dollar. We can use this fact to find change back from a dollar. For example, if you pay a dollar for an item that costs 47¢, you should get back 53¢. Notice that the 4 of 47¢ and the 5 of 53¢ equal 9 dimes. The 7 and the 3 equal 10 pennies. Find the change back from a dollar for items with these prices.

  a. 46¢   **b.** 64¢   **c.** 28¢   **d.** 52¢   **e.** 17¢   **f.** 85¢

Problem Solving: From Point *A* to Point *B* is $1\frac{1}{4}$ inches. From Point *B* to Point *C* is how many inches?

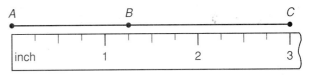

We have practiced multiplying two-digit numbers by multiplying the digit in the ones' place and then multiplying the digit in the tens' place.

MULTIPLY ONES	MULTIPLY TENS
12	12
× 4	× 4
——	——
8	48

Often when we multiply the ones, the result is a two-digit number. We do not write both digits below the line. Instead we write the last digit below the line in the ones' column and **carry** the first digit above the tens' column.

$$\begin{array}{r} 1 \\ 12 \\ \times\ 8 \\ \hline 6 \end{array}$$

Then we multiply the tens' digit and **add** the digit we wrote above this column.

We think, "Eight times one is eight, plus one is nine."

$$\begin{array}{r} 1 \\ 12 \\ \times\ 8 \\ \hline 96 \end{array}$$

Example   Find the product: 8 × $64

Solution   We write the two-digit number over
the one-digit number. We think of $64
as 6 tens and 4 ones. We multiply
8 × 4 ones and get 32 ones ($32). We
write the 2 of $32 below the line. The
3 of $32 is 3 tens. We write the 3
above the tens' column.

$$\begin{array}{r} 3 \\ \$64 \\ \times\ \ \ 8 \\ \hline 2 \end{array}$$

   Then we multiply 8 × 6 tens,
which is 48 tens. We add the 3 tens to
this, making 51 tens. We write "51"
below the line. The product is **$512.**

$$\begin{array}{r} 3 \\ \$64 \\ \times\ \ \ 8 \\ \hline \$512 \end{array}$$

Practice   **a.** $\begin{array}{r} 16 \\ \times\ \ 4 \\ \hline 64 \end{array}$ **b.** $\begin{array}{r} 24 \\ \times\ \ 3 \\ \hline 72 \end{array}$ **c.** $\begin{array}{r} 45 \\ \times\ \ 6 \\ \hline 270 \end{array}$

   d. 53 × 7   371   **e.** 35 × 8   280   **f.** 64 × 9   576

Problem set
58

1. Write four multiplication/division facts using the
   (57) numbers 3, 5, and 15.
   3 × 5 = 15, 5 × 3 = 15, 15 ÷ 5 = 3, 15 ÷ 3 = 5

   $\begin{array}{r} 472\ \text{birds} \\ -\ 147\ \text{birds} \\ \hline N\ \text{birds} \end{array}$

2. There were four hundred seventy-two birds in the first
   (38) flock. There were one hundred forty-seven birds in the
   second flock. How many fewer birds were in the
   second flock? Draw a L-S-D pattern.   325 birds

3. Rae hiked forty-two miles. Then she hiked seventy-
   (12) five more miles. How many miles did she hike in all?
   Draw a SSM pattern.   117 miles; $\begin{array}{r} 42\ \text{miles} \\ +\ 75\ \text{miles} \\ \hline N\ \text{miles} \end{array}$

4. Use the digits 1, 3, 6, and 8 once each to write an odd
   (11) number between 8000 and 8350.   8163

5. Write 306,020 in expanded form. Then use words to
   (42) write this number.
   300,000 + 6000 + 20; three hundred six thousand, twenty

6. Draw shaded circles to picture the number $2\frac{1}{8}$.
(44)

7. How many feet are in 1 mile?   5280 ft
(49)

8. To what number is the arrow pointing on this inch
(48) scale? $10\frac{3}{4}$ in.

9. How many centimeters are in a meter?   100 cm
(27)

10. To what mixed number is the arrow pointing? $14\frac{5}{9}$
(46)

11. 100 + (4 × 50)   300
(55,52)

12. $3.25 + 37¢ + $3   **13.** $\sqrt{4} \times \sqrt{9}$ 6
(53) $6.62   *(40)*

14.   33   **15.**   24   **16.**   90   **17.**   42
(58) × 6   *(58)* × 5   *(52)* × 6   *(58)* × 7
───────   ───────   ───────   ───────
   198   120   540   294

18. $5.06   **19.** $3.28   **20.** $5.27   **21.**   14
(51) − $2.28   *(28)* + $4.33   *(37)* − $3.68   *(21)*   28
──────────   ──────────   ──────────   45
   $2.78 $7.61 $1.59   36
                                        92
22. 28 ÷ 7   4   **23.** 5$\overline{)35}$ +47
(57)   *(56)*   ──────
                                       262

24. 6$\overline{)54}$ **25.** $\frac{63}{7}$ 9
(56)   *(57)*

LESSON 59

"Equal Groups" Problems, Part 1

a. 59¢
b. 11¢
c. 81¢
d. 66¢
e. 38¢
f. 656
g. $9.60
h. 833

Problem Solving:
  3 quarters, 1 dime,
  and 3 nickels
  or 1 half dollar,
  1 quarter, and
  5 nickels or 1 half
  dollar, 4 dimes,
  and 2 nickels

Facts Practice: 90 Division Facts (Test I in Test Masters)

Mental Math: Find the change back from a dollar for items with
these prices.

   a. 41¢   **b.** 89¢   **c.** 19¢   **d.** 34¢   **e.** 62¢

Review:

   f. 537 + 100 + 19   **g.** $5.62 + $3.98   **h.** 396 + 437

Problem Solving: One way to make a dollar with seven coins is
with two quarters and five dimes. Can you
find three more ways to make a dollar with
seven coins?

We have found that some story problems have an addition
pattern. The addition pattern has three numbers. If we
know two of the numbers, we can find the third number.

$$
\begin{array}{r}
5 \text{ marbles} \\
+\ 7 \text{ marbles} \\
\hline
12 \text{ marbles}
\end{array}
$$

Some story problems have a subtraction pattern. The
subtraction pattern has three numbers. If we know two of
the numbers, we can find the third number.

$$
\begin{array}{r}
12 \text{ marbles} \\
-\ 7 \text{ marbles} \\
\hline
5 \text{ marbles}
\end{array}
$$

Some story problems have a multiplication pattern. The
multiplication pattern has three numbers. If we know two
of the numbers, we can find the third number.

$$
\begin{array}{r}
5 \text{ marbles in each bag} \\
\times\ 7 \text{ bags} \\
\hline
35 \text{ marbles}
\end{array}
$$

Stories that have a multiplication pattern are often
"equal groups" stories. We will often use the abbreviation
EG to stand for "equal groups." Look at this pattern
carefully. It looks different from the other patterns we

have practiced. The top number of the pattern is the number in each equal group. The second number of the pattern is the number of groups. The bottom number is the total number in all the groups.

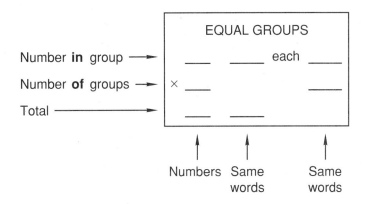

To find the bottom number in the "equal groups" pattern, we multiply. To find the first or second number, we divide.

Example   Ted has 5 cans of tennis balls. There are 3 balls in each can. How many tennis balls does he have?

Solution   The words *in each* are a clue to this problem. The words *in each* usually mean that the problem is an "equal groups" problem. We write the number and the words that go with *in each* on the first line. This is the number in each group.

Number **in** group   ___3 balls each can___
×   _____   _____

___   _____

The other number and word in the problem is *5 cans*. This is the number of groups. The word *cans* lines up with the word *can* in the first line of the pattern.

Number **in** group   ___3 balls each can___
Number **of** groups   × _5_   cans___
_N_ balls

To find the bottom number, we multiply the first two numbers. The word on the bottom line is the same as the word above it on the first line. We complete the "equal groups" pattern and answer the question. Ted has **15 tennis balls.**

Number **in** group		3	balls each can
Number **of** groups	×	5	cans
Total		15	balls

Practice

a. There were 8 birds in each flock. There were 6 flocks in all. How many birds were there in all?   48 birds

b. There are 6 people in each car. There are 9 cars. How many people are there in all?   54 people

Problem set 59

1. There were 8 boys in each row. There were 4 rows.
(59) How many boys were there? Draw an "equal groups" pattern.   32 boys;   8 boys each row / × 4 / N boys   rows

2. There were 7 girls in each row. There were 9 rows.
(59) How many girls were in all 9 rows? Draw an EG pattern.   63 girls;   7 girls each row / × 9 / N girls   rows

3. Write four multiplication/division facts using the
(57) numbers 5, 6, and 30.
$5 \times 6 = 30, 6 \times 5 = 30, 30 \div 6 = 5, 30 \div 5 = 6$

4. The big animal weighed four hundred seventy-five
(38) pounds. The small animal weighed one hundred eleven pounds. How much more did the big animal weigh? Draw a L-S-D pattern.   364 pounds;   475 pounds / − 111 pounds / N pounds

5. Shade circles to picture the number $6\frac{3}{4}$.
(44)

6. To what number is the arrow pointing? $452\frac{5}{7}$
(46)

452   453

7. It is evening. What time will it be 7
(33) hours and 22 minutes from now?
3:57 a.m.

8. Draw a rectangle and shade $\frac{7}{8}$ of it.
(32)

9. Use digits to write three hundred forty-nine thousand,
(43) eight hundred eleven.   349,811

10. Seven times eight is how much less than eight
(39,38) squared?   8

11. $4.63 + 23¢ + $6 + 6¢ $10.92
(53)

12. $3.07
(51) − $2.28
─────────
         $0.79

13. $4.78
(28) + $3.96
─────────
         $8.74

14.   707
(20) −   *N*   222
─────────
         485

15.   *C*   71
(20) − 23
─────────
         48

16. 403 − (5 × 80)   3
(55,54)

17. (4 + 3) × $\sqrt{64}$ 56
(55,40)

18. *N* × 6 = 30   5
(50)

19. (587 − 238) + 415   764
(55)

20.   45
(58) ×   6
─────────
         270

21.   23
(58) ×   7
─────────
         161

22.   34
(58) ×   8
─────────
         272

23.   83
(58) ×   5
─────────
         415

24. 56 ÷ 7
(57)   8

25. 64 ÷ 8
(57)   8

26. $\overset{5}{6\overline{)30}}$
(57)

27. $\frac{45}{9}$ 5
(57)

LESSON 60

Perimeter

a. 74¢
b. 8¢
c. 86¢
d. 24¢
e. 69¢
f. $3.50
g. 287
h. 600
Problem Solving:
    60

Facts Practice: 90 Division Facts (Test I in Test Masters)

Mental Math: Find the change back from a dollar for items with these prices.

    a. 26¢   **b.** 92¢   **c.** 14¢   **d.** 76¢   **e.** 31¢

Review:

    f. $4.00 − $0.50   **g.** 48 + 29 + 210   **h.** 300 + 260 + 40

Problem Solving: Martin was thinking of a two-digit number. He gave this clue: "You say the number when you count by threes from three, by fours from four, and by fives from five." What was Martin's number?

The distance around a shape is its **perimeter.** To find the perimeter of a shape, we add the lengths of all of its sides.

Example 1 Claudia ran around the perimeter of the block. How far did Claudia run?

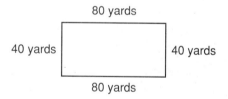

Solution We are told Claudia ran around the perimeter, so we know that she ran all the way around. We find that distance by adding all four sides.

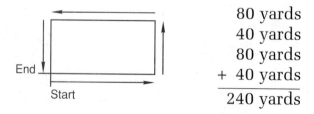

$$
\begin{array}{r}
80 \text{ yards} \\
40 \text{ yards} \\
80 \text{ yards} \\
+ \ 40 \text{ yards} \\
\hline
240 \text{ yards}
\end{array}
$$

Claudia ran **240 yards.**

Example 2   What is the perimeter of this square?

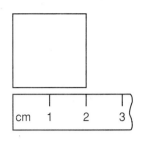

Solution   We are told the shape is a square. That means all four sides are the same length. We see that each side is 2 centimeters long. The perimeter is the distance all the way around. We add all four sides.

$$2 \text{ cm} + 2 \text{ cm} + 2 \text{ cm} + 2 \text{ cm} = 8 \text{ cm}$$

The perimeter of the square is **8 cm.**

Practice   Find the perimeter of each shape:

a.

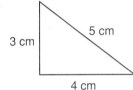

12 cm

b.   8 m

5 m   26 m

c.

6 in.   22 in.

3 in.

5 in.

3 in.

5 in.

d. What is the perimeter of this square?   4 cm

e. What does the word *perimeter* mean?   the distance around a shape

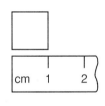

Problem set 60

1. Each of the 3 lifeboats carried 12 people. How many people were in the 3 lifeboats? Draw an EG pattern. 36 people
(59)

12 people each lifeboat
× 3
N people

lifeboats

2. The tape cost $6.98. The tax was 42¢. What was the total price? Draw a SSM pattern. $7.40;
(12)

$6.98
+ $0.42
N

3. Sarah did six hundred twenty sit-ups. Syd did four hundred seventeen sit-ups. Sarah did how many more sit-ups than Syd? Draw a L-S-D pattern.   203 sit-ups
(38)

620 sit-ups
− 417 sit-ups
N sit-ups

4. The coach separated 28 players into 4 equal teams.
(56) How many players were on each team? (*Hint*: Four
times what number is 28?)   7 players

5. Justin ran the perimeter of the block. How far did
(60) Justin run?   300 yd

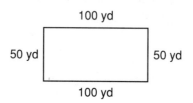

6. Shade circles to draw a picture of $3\frac{3}{8}$.
(44)

7. Use the digits 1, 2, 3, and 4 once each to write an odd
(11) number between 4205 and 4223.   4213

8. Six times seven is how much less than nine times
(38) five?   3

9. It is evening. What time will it be
(33) 9 hours and 30 minutes from
now?   8:05 a.m.

10. To what number is the arrow pointing? $72\frac{3}{4}$
(46)

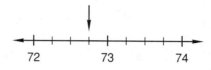

11. $(4 \times 50) + 203$ 403
(55)

12. $4.63 + $2 + 47¢ + 65¢ $7.75
(53)

13.   43   **14.**   54   **15.**   37   **16.**   40
(58) × 6   (58) × 8   (58) × 3   (54) × 4
        ——   ——   ——   ——
       258   432   111   160

17. $47 + 55 + 84 + 63 + 24 + 27$ 300
(21)

18. $\$6.08 - \$4.29$ $1.79   **19.** $\$7.03 - \$4.26$ $2.77
(53)   (53)

20. $\$3.25$ **21.** 472 **22.** N 763
(28) $+ \ \$1.98$ (16) $+ \ 348$ (20) $- \ 279$
        $\$5.23$ 820 484

23. 462 **24.** $3\overline{)24}$ **25.** $4\overline{)24}$
(30) $+ \ \ C$ 67   (57)   (57)
       529

26. $36 \div 6$ 6   **27.** $\dfrac{36}{9}$ 4
(57)   (57)

LESSON 61

Adding Numbers with More Than Three Digits • Checking One-Digit Division

a. 58¢
b. 33¢
c. $1.75
d. $8.10
e. 235
f. 195
Problem Solving:
   1 quarter, 1 dime, and 2 pennies

Facts Practice: 90 Division Facts (Test I in Test Masters)

Mental Math: Subtract cents from dollars.
  a. $\$1.00 - \$0.42$ **b.** $\$1.00 - \$0.67$ **c.** $\$2.00 - \$0.25$

Review:
  d. $\$3.45 + \$4.65$ **e.** $370 - 135$ **f.** $76 + 19 + 100$

Problem Solving: Sarah paid a dollar for an item that cost 63 cents. What four coins did she get back in change?

Adding numbers with more than three digits

To add numbers that have more than three digits, we add in the ones' column first. Then we add in the tens' column, the hundreds' column, the thousands' column, the ten-thousands' column, and so forth. When the sum of the digits in one column is a two-digit number, we record the second digit below the line. We write the first digit above or below the column to the left.

Example 1   Add: 43,287
              + 68,595

Solution   We add the digits in the ones' column first. When the sum is a two-digit number, we write the last digit below the line and the first digit above or below the next column. The sum is **111,882**.

$$
\begin{array}{r}
1 \quad 11 \\
43,287 \\
+\ 68,595 \\
\hline
111,882
\end{array}
$$

Example 2   Add: 456 + 1327 + 52 + 3624

Solution   When we write the numbers in a column, we are careful to line up the last digit in each number. We add the digits one column at a time, starting from the right. The sum is **5459**.

$$
\begin{array}{r}
111 \\
456 \\
1327 \\
52 \\
+\ 3624 \\
\hline
5459
\end{array}
$$

Checking one-digit division   We can check division by multiplying. We multiply the numbers outside the division box.

$$
\text{DIVISION: } 3\overline{)12}^{\,4} \qquad\qquad \begin{array}{r} 4 \\ \times\ 3 \\ \hline 12 \end{array} \quad \text{check}
$$

We see that the multiplication answer matches the number inside the division box. We usually show this by writing the multiplication answer under the number in the division box.

$$
3\overline{)12}^{\,4}
$$
   ← **Step 1.** Divide 12 by 3 and write "4."
12   ← **Step 2.** Multiply 4 by 3 and write "12."

Example 3   Divide. Check the answer by multiplying.

(a) 3$\overline{)18}$ (b) 4$\overline{)32}$

Solution   First we divide and write the answer above the box. Then we multiply and write the product below the box.

(a) 3$\overline{)18}^{\,6}$ (b) 4$\overline{)32}^{\,8}$
       18   32

Practice   **a.**   4356
    + 5644
    10,000

b.   46,027
    + 39,682
    85,709

c.   360,147
    + 96,894
    457,041

d. 436 + 5714 + 88   6238   **e.** 43,284 + 572 + 7635
    51,491

Divide. Check the answer by multiplying.

f. 3)‾21   7   **g.** 7)‾42   6   **h.** 6)‾48   8

Problem set   **1.** The coach had forty-two players. The coach wanted to
61   *(56)*   make six equal teams. How many players should be on
    each team? (*Hint*: Six times what number is 42?)
    7 players

7 pancakes each stack   **2.** There were 7 pancakes in each stack. There were 6
× 6   stacks   *(59)*   stacks of pancakes. How many pancakes were there in
N pancakes   all? Draw an EG pattern.   42 pancakes

3. Five hundred forty-two clowns laughed out loud.
(12)   Nine hundred thirty-three clowns merely smiled.
    What was the total of the smilers and the laughers?
    Draw a SSM pattern.   1475 clowns;   542 clowns
                + 933 clowns
                    N clowns

4. Write four multiplication/division facts using the
(57)   numbers 6, 7, and 42.
    6 × 7 = 42, 7 × 6 = 42, 42 ÷ 6 = 7, 42 ÷ 7 = 6

5. Compare: 1 + 3 + 5 + 7 + 9 ⊜ five squared
(40,15)

6. What is the smallest four-digit odd number that has
(11)   the digits 1, 2, 3, and 4 once each?   1243

7. How many circles are shaded? $3\frac{3}{8}$
(44)

8. Which of these angles does not appear to be a right
(29)   angle?

D. ∠

    A. ⌊   B. ⌉   C. ∨   D. ∠

9. This is a rectangle.
(60,25)

(a) What is the length?   4 ft

(b) What is the width?   2 ft

(c) What is the perimeter?
    12 ft

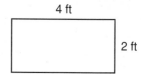

10. Thirty is how much more than four times seven?   2
(38)

11. 3864 + 598 + 4237 + 12   8711
(61)

12.   63,285
(61)   + 97,642
           ‾‾‾‾‾‾‾
           160,927

13. $5.00
(51)   − $4.81
           ‾‾‾‾‾‾
           $0.19

14. N 216
(30)   + 398
           ‾‾‾‾‾
           614

15.   85
(58)   × 5
           ‾‾‾
           425

16.   37
(58)   × 7
           ‾‾‾
           259

17.   40
(54)   × 8
           ‾‾‾
           320

18. F 9
(50)   × 8
           ‾‾‾
           72

19.   478
(20)   − C 275
           ‾‾‾‾‾
           203

20.   462,586
(61)   + 39,728
           ‾‾‾‾‾‾‾
           502,314

21. Z 741
(20)   − 478
           ‾‾‾‾‾
           263

22. Compare: 7 × 6 $<$ 44
(15)

Divide. Check each answer by multiplying.

23. 2)‾18   (9)
(61)

24. 7)‾21   (3)
(61)

25. $\frac{56}{8}$ 7
(61)

LESSON 62

Subtracting Numbers with More Than Three Digits • "Equal Groups" Problems, Part 2

a. 15¢
b. $1.37
c. $3.75
d. 872
e. $7.42
f. 370
Problem Solving:

$$\begin{array}{r} 56\underline{3} \\ +\ 2\underline{8}7 \\ \hline \underline{8}50 \end{array}$$

Facts Practice: 90 Division Facts (Test J in Test Masters)

Mental Math: Subtract dollars and cents from dollars.
  a. $1.00 − $0.85   **b.** $2.00 − $0.63   **c.** $5.00 − $1.25

Review:
  d. 340 + 500 + 32   **e.** $5.47 + $1.95   **f.** 400 − 30

Problem Solving: In this addition problem some digits are missing. Copy this problem on your paper and fill in the missing digits.

$$\begin{array}{r} 5\_3 \\ +\ 28\_ \\ \hline \_50 \end{array}$$

Subtracting numbers with more than three digits

To subtract numbers with more than three digits, we begin by subtracting in the ones' column. We regroup if it is necessary. Then we move one column to the left and subtract in the tens' column, regrouping if necessary. Then we move one column at a time to the hundreds' column, the thousands' column, the ten-thousands' column, and so on. Sometimes we must subtract across several zeros.

Example 1   Subtract: 36,152 − 9,415

Solution   We write the first number on top. We write the second number below. We line up digits with the same place value. We begin by subtracting in the ones' column. Then we subtract in the other columns.

$$\begin{array}{r} 2\ ^15\ \ \ 4 \\ \cancel{3}\,\cancel{6},^1\cancel{5}^12 \\ -\ \ \ 9,4\,1\,5 \\ \hline 2\,6,7\,3\,7 \end{array}$$

Example 2   Subtract: $\begin{array}{r} 5000 \\ -\ 2386 \\ \hline \end{array}$

Solution   We need to find some ones for the ones' place before we can subtract. We can only get ones from the tens' place, but there are no tens. We can only get tens from the hundreds' place, but

$$\begin{array}{r} 4\ ^19\ ^19\ ^1 \\ \cancel{5}\,\cancel{0}\,\cancel{0}\,0 \\ -\ 2\,3\,8\,6 \\ \hline 2\,6\,1\,4 \end{array}$$

there are no hundreds. To get hundreds, we go to the thousands' place. We exchange 1 thousand for 10 hundreds, 1 hundred for 10 tens, and 1 ten for 10 ones. Then we can subtract.

"Equal groups" problems, part 2

"Equal groups" stories have a multiplication pattern. If we know the number of groups and the number in each group, then we multiply to find the total. However, if we know the total, then we need to divide to find the number of groups or the number in each group. Carefully follow the following examples.

Example 3

Ted has 21 tennis balls in cans. There are 3 balls in each can. How many cans does he have?

Solution

There are two numbers in this problem. The words *in each* are a clue. They show us the number and words to write on the first line.

Number **in** group		3	balls	each	can
Number **of** groups	×				
Total					

The other number is 21 and the other word is *balls*. We need to decide if this is the number of groups or the total. The pattern shows us how the words should line up. Altogether, Ted had 21 tennis balls. This is the total.

Number **in** group		3	balls	each	can
Number **of** groups	×	N			cans
Total		21	balls		

Now we need to find the missing number. **To find the first or second number of an "equal groups" pattern, we divide.**

$$\begin{array}{r} 7 \\ 3\overline{)21} \end{array}$$

We complete the pattern, matching the words, and then answer the question.

Number **in** group		3	balls each	can
Number **of** groups	×	7		cans
Total		21	balls	

Seven times 3 balls is 21 balls, so our answer is correct. Ted has **7 cans.**

Example 4 Ted has 5 cans of rubber balls. He has 40 rubber balls in all. How many balls are in each can if the same number of balls is in each can?

Solution The words *in each* shows us that this is an "equal groups" problem. We are not given an *in each* number, but we are given the other words that go with *in each*, which we can write on the first line.

Number **in** group		N	balls each	can
Number **of** groups	×	5		cans
Total		40	balls	

Now we need to find the missing number on the first line. **To find the first or second number in an "equal groups" pattern, we divide.**

$$5\overline{)40}^{\,8}$$

We complete the pattern and answer the question.

Number **in** group		8	balls each	can
Number **of** groups	×	5		cans
Total		40	balls	

We see that 5 times 8 balls equals 40 balls, so our answer is correct. There are **8 rubber balls in each can.**

"Equal groups" problems are easy after we find out where to put the numbers in the pattern.

Practice

a.
$$\begin{array}{r} 4783 \\ -\ 2497 \\ \hline 2286 \end{array}$$

b.
$$\begin{array}{r} 4000 \\ -\ 527 \\ \hline 3473 \end{array}$$

c. There were 35 people. There were 7 cars. The number of people in each car was the same. How many people were in each car?   5 people

Problem set 62

1. There were 8 buses. Each bus could seat 60 students.
$^{(59)}$ How many students could ride in all the buses? Draw an EG pattern.   480 students;
$$\begin{array}{r} 60 \text{ students each bus} \\ \times\ 8 \qquad\qquad \text{buses} \\ \hline N \text{ students} \end{array}$$

2. Each van could carry 9 students. There were 63
$^{(62)}$ students. How many vans were needed? Draw an EG pattern.   7 vans;
$$\begin{array}{r} 9 \text{ students each van} \\ \times\ N \qquad\qquad \text{vans} \\ \hline 63 \text{ students} \end{array}$$

3. Fifty-six Easter eggs were to be divided into 7 equal
$^{(62)}$ piles. How many eggs would be in each pile? Draw an EG pattern.   8 eggs;
$$\begin{array}{r} N \text{ eggs each pile} \\ \times\ 7 \qquad\qquad \text{piles} \\ \hline 56 \text{ eggs} \end{array}$$

4. There are 10 swimmers in the race. Only 3 can win
$^{(31)}$ medals. How many swimmers will not win a medal? Draw a SWA pattern.   7 swimmers;
$$\begin{array}{r} 10 \text{ swimmers} \\ -\ 3 \text{ swimmers} \\ \hline N \text{ swimmers} \end{array}$$

5. There were two hundred sixty-seven apples in the first
$^{(38)}$ bin. There were four hundred sixty-five apples in the second bin. How many fewer apples were in the first bin? Draw a L-S-D pattern.   198 apples;
$$\begin{array}{r} 465 \text{ apples} \\ -\ 267 \text{ apples} \\ \hline N \text{ apples} \end{array}$$

6. Write four multiplication/division facts using the
$^{(57)}$ numbers 7, 8, and 56.
$7 \times 8 = 56, 8 \times 7 = 56, 56 \div 7 = 8, 56 \div 8 = 7$

7. Compare: $1 + 2 + 3 + 4 \;\ominus\; \sqrt{100}$
$^{(40,15)}$

8. Use shaded circles to draw a picture of $3\frac{3}{4}$.
$^{(44)}$

9. This shape has four sides, but it is
$^{(60)}$ not a rectangle. What is the perimeter of this shape in meters?   65 m

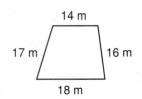

10. 849 + 73 + 615   1537
(61)

11.   47,586   **12.** $5.00   **13.**   N   346
(61) + 23,491   *(51)* − $3.26   *(30)* + 258
         ───────   ──────   ─────
         71,077 $1.74   604

14.   49   **15.**   84   **16.**   70   **17.**   35
(58) × 6   *(58)* × 5   *(54)* × 8   *(58)* × 9
        ───   ───   ───   ───
        294   420   560   315

18. $\sqrt{64}$ 8   **19.**   400   **20.**   4000
(40)   *(20)* −   N   144   *(62)* − 2468
                                         ─────   ──────
                                          256   1532

21. Use a dollar sign and a decimal point to show each
(45) amount of money.

(a) 54¢ $0.54   (b) 6¢ $0.06   (c) 340¢ $3.40

22. Thirteen is how much more than four times three?   1
(38)

23. Compare: 4 × 8 $\textcircled{>}$ 31
(15)

Divide, and then check each answer by multiplying:

          9   4   9
24. 3)‾2‾7‾   **25.** 7)‾2‾8‾   **26.** 8)‾7‾2‾   **27.** $\frac{54}{6}$ 9
(61)   *(61)*   *(61)*   *(61)*

LESSON
63

One-Digit Division with a Remainder

a. $2.75
b. $3.37
c. $1.65
d. 360
e. 194
f. $7.30
Problem Solving:
$1\frac{1}{2}$ in.

Facts Practice: 90 Division Facts (Test J in Test Masters)

Mental Math: Subtract dollars and cents from dollars.
  a. $5.00 − $2.25   **b.** $5.00 − $1.63   **c.** $5.00 − $3.35

Review:
  d. 560 − 200   **e.** 35 + 49 + 110   **f.** $6.58 + $0.72

Problem Solving: From Point A to Point B is $1\frac{1}{4}$ inches. From Point B to Point C is how many inches?

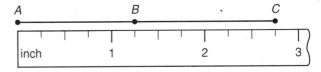

We can divide 12 objects into equal groups of four. Here we show 12 dots divided into equal groups of four.

    12 dots   3 equal groups

However, we cannot divide 13 dots into equal groups of four because there is one dot too many. We call the extra dot the **remainder.**

   13 dots   3 equal groups   Remainder

We can show that 13 is to be divided into groups of four by writing

$$4\overline{)13}$$

As we look at this problem, we may wonder what to write for the answer. The answer is not exactly three because 3 × 4 is 12, which is less than 13. However, the answer is not four because 4 × 4 is 16, which is more than 13. Since we *can* make three groups of four, we write "3" for our answer. Then we multiply 3 × 4 and write "12" below the 13.

$$\begin{array}{r} 3 \\ 4\overline{)13} \\ 12 \end{array}$$ ← three groups

We see that 13 is more than 12. Now we find out how much is left over after making three groups of four. To do this, we subtract 12 from 13.

$$\begin{array}{r} 3 \\ 4\overline{)13} \\ -12 \\ \hline 1 \end{array}$$ ← three groups

subtract

← 1 left over (remainder)

There is one left over. The amount left over is the **remainder.** We use the letter *r* to stand for **remainder.** We can write the answer as

$$\begin{array}{r} \mathbf{3\,r\,1} \\ 4\overline{)13} \\ -12 \\ \hline 1 \end{array}$$

Example 1   Divide: $3\overline{)16}$

Solution   This problem tells us to divide 16 into three groups. Three groups of six is 18. This is too much. Three groups of five is 15. This is less than 16. We write "5."

$$\begin{array}{r} 5 \\ 3\overline{)16} \end{array}$$

Since three groups of five is 15, we write "15" below the 16. Then we subtract and find that the remainder is 1.

$$\begin{array}{r} 5 \\ 3\overline{)16} \\ -15 \\ \hline 1 \end{array}$$ ← remainder

The answer is **5 r 1.**

Example 2 Divide: $20 \div 6$

Solution First we write the problem using a division box.

$$6\overline{)20}$$

Now we think, "Six times four equals twenty-four." This is too much. We think "Six times three equals eighteen." This is less than 20. We will use three.

$$\overset{3}{6\overline{)20}}$$

Next we multiply, and then we subtract.

$$\begin{array}{r} 3 \\ 6\overline{)20} \\ -18 \\ \hline 2 \end{array} \leftarrow \text{remainder}$$

We write the answer as **3 r 2.**

Practice Divide and write the answer with a remainder:

a. $3\overline{)17}$ 5 r 2   b. $5\overline{)12}$ 2 r 2   c. $4\overline{)23}$ 5 r 3

d. $15 \div 2$ 7 r 1   e. $20 \div 6$ 3 r 2   f. $25 \div 3$ 8 r 1

Problem set 63

1. (62) Harry had 56 washers. He wanted to put them into equal piles of 8 washers. How many piles would he have? Draw an EG pattern.   7 piles; $\begin{array}{r} 8 \text{ washers each pile} \\ \times N \\ \hline 56 \text{ washers} \end{array} \begin{array}{l} \\ \text{piles} \end{array}$

2. (62) There were 42 children waiting for a ride. There were 7 cars available. If the same number rode in each car, how many children would be in each car? Draw an EG pattern.   6 children; $\begin{array}{r} N \text{ children each car} \\ \times 7 \\ \hline 42 \text{ children} \end{array} \begin{array}{l} \\ \text{cars} \end{array}$

3. (57) Write four multiplication/division facts using the numbers 4, 7, and 28. $4 \times 7 = 28, 7 \times 4 = 28, 28 \div 4 = 7, 28 \div 7 = 4$

4. (6) Which months have exactly 30 days? September, April, June, November

5. (40,38) Six squared is how much more than $\sqrt{64}$?   28

6. Round 4725 to the nearest hundred.   4700
(52)

7. Write the time for a quarter after four in the afternoon
(23) in digital form.   4:15 p.m.

8. One side of a square is 4 feet long. What is the
(60) perimeter of the square?   16 ft

9. How many circles are shaded? $4\frac{1}{8}$
(44)

10. $\sqrt{64} + (42 \div 6)$ 15   **11.** $6.35 + $12.49 + 42¢
(55)   *(53)* $19.26

12. $100.00 − $59.88   **13.** 51,438 − 47,495
(53) $40.12   *(62)* 3943

14.   60   **15.**   57
(54) × 9   *(58)* × 4
      540   228

Divide and write the answer with a remainder:

16. 25 ÷ 4   **17.** 22 ÷ 5   **18.** 6)39   **19.** 7)30   4 r 2
(63) 6 r 1   *(63)* 4 r 2   *(63)* 6 r 3   *(63)*

20.   46   **21.**   38   **22.**   Z   567
(58) × 8   *(58)* × 7   *(20)* − 165
      368   266   402

23.   400   **24.** Use words to write 87,906.
(20) − C   117   *(42)* eighty-seven thousand, nine hundred six
      283

25.   48   **26.**   43
(21)   76   *(21)*   58
         25   9
        336   6
         98   454
       + 75   + 28
        658   598

LESSON 64

Years, Decades, Centuries

a. $1.05
b. $3.61
c. $1.25
d. $7.34
e. 350
f. 566
Problem Solving:
1 half dollar,
3 dimes, and
4 nickels or
2 quarters,
4 dimes, and
2 nickels, or
3 quarters and
5 nickels

Facts Practice: 90 Division Facts (Test J in Test Masters)

Mental Math: Subtract dollars and cents from dollars.
  a. $5.00 − $3.95   **b.** $5.00 − $1.39   **c.** $10.00 − $8.75

Review:
  d. $4.36 + $2.98   **e.** 475 − 125   **f.** 46 + 320 + 200

Problem Solving: Can you find three ways to make a dollar with eight coins?

A year is the number of days it takes for the earth to go around the sun. It takes the earth almost exactly $365\frac{1}{4}$ days to go around the sun. To make the days come out even, we have 3 years in a row that have 365 days each. These years are called **common years.** Then we have a year that has 366 days. The year with 366 days is called a **leap year.** We put the extra day in February.

February has 28 or 29 days. Four months have 30 days. All the rest have 31 days. If we say the four months that have 30 days, we can remember the number of days in the other months. The following jingle helps us remember which months have 30 days.

> Thirty days hath September,
> April, June, and November.
> All the rest have 31, except February.
> February has 28 or 29.

A **decade** is ten years. A **century** is one hundred years.

Example 1 How many days does December have?

Solution "Thirty days hath September, April, June, and November." This tells us that December does not have 30 days. December must have **31 days.**

Example 2   According to this calendar, May 10, 2014, is what day of the week?

		MAY	2014			
S	M	T	W	T	F	S
				1	2	3
4	5	6	7	8	9	10
11	12	13	14	15	16	17
18	19	20	21	22	23	24
25	26	27	28	29	30	31

Solution   The letters across the top of the calendar stand for "Sunday," "Monday," "Tuesday," "Wednesday," "Thursday," "Friday," and "Saturday." We see that May 10 is a **Saturday,** the second Saturday of the month.

Example 3   How many years were there from 1620 to 1776?

Solution   To find the number of years from one date to another, we may subtract.[†] This is like a "larger-smaller-difference" problem except we use the words "later-earlier-difference" (L-E-D). We subtract the earlier date from the later date. In this problem we subtract 1620 from 1776.

$$\begin{array}{r} 1776 \\ -\ 1620 \\ \hline 156 \end{array}$$

We find that there were **156 years** from 1620 to 1776.

Practice   **a.** How many days long is a leap year?   366 days

b. According to the calendar in Example 2, what is the date of the fourth Friday of the month?   May 23, 2014

c. How many years were there from 1918 to 1943?
25 years

d. A century is how many decades?   10 decades

[†]Years have been numbered forward (A.D.) and backward (B.C.) from the birth of Jesus of Nazareth. In this book, all year dates should be considered years A.D.

Problem set 64

1. There were 7 students in each row. If there were 56
(62) students in all, how many rows were there? (Use the EG pattern.)   8 rows

2. There were 7 nails in each board. If there were 42
(59) boards, how many nails were there? (Use the EG pattern.)   294 nails

3. How many years is 5 decades?   50 years
(64)

4. How many years were there from 1921 to 1938? (Use
(64) the "later-earlier-difference pattern.")   17 years

5. According to this calendar, what
(64) day of the week was December 25, 1957?   Wednesday

DECEMBER 1957						
S	M	T	W	T	F	S
1	2	3	4	5	6	7
8	9	10	11	12	13	14
15	16	17	18	19	20	21
22	23	24	25	26	27	28
29	30	31				

6. Round 523 to the nearest hundred. Round 692 to the
(52) nearest hundred. Then add the rounded numbers.
500; 700; 1200

7. One side of a rectangle is 10 kilometers long. Another
(60,25) side is 20 kilometers long. Draw a picture of the rectangle and show the lengths of the sides. What is the perimeter of the rectangle?   20 km $\boxed{}$ 10 km ; 60 km

8. How many circles are shaded? $3\frac{2}{3}$
(44)

9. To what number is the arrow pointing? $486\frac{4}{5}$
(46)

10. When Elmer emptied his bank, he found 17 pennies, 4
(45) nickels, 5 dimes, and 2 quarters. What was the value of the coins in his bank? $1.37

11. 794,150
(61) + 9,863
    ———————
    804,013

12. $51,786
(61) + $36,357
    ———————
    $88,143

13. 876
(21) 40
    317
    55
    11
  + 5
  ———
  1304

14. $20.00
(51) − $18.47
    ———————
    $1.53

15. 41,315
(62) − 29,418
    ———————
    11,897

16. 46
(58) × 7
    ———
    322

17. 54
(58) × 8
    ———
    432

18. 39
(58) × 9
    ———
    351

19. 58
(58) × 6
    ———
    348

20. 30
(54) × 4
    ———
    120

21. $\dfrac{36}{4}$ 9
(57)

22. 43 ÷ 7 6 r 1
(63)

23. $9\overline{)64}$ 7 r 1
(63)

24. $\sqrt{64}$ 8
(40)

25. $Y \times 4 = 32$
(50) 8

26. $6 \times N = 42$
(50) 7

27. Use digits to write four hundred forty-two thousand,
(43) nine hundred seventy-six. 442,976

LESSON
65

a. $1.11
b. $2.75
c. $1.33
d. 175
e. $9.71
f. 255
Problem Solving:
What day is this?
(Answer varies.)

Multiples • Percent

Facts Practice: 90 Division Facts (Test J in Test Masters)

Mental Math: Subtract dollars and cents from dollars.
  a. $5.00 − $3.89 **b.** $10.00 − $7.25 **c.** $10.00 − $8.67

Review:
  d. 126 + 49 **e.** $5.95 + $3.76 **f.** 480 − 225

Problem Solving: This question is written in code: 1 is A, 2 is B, 3 is C, and so on. Write the answer to this question in the same code.
    23-8-1-20 4-1-25 9-19 20-8-9-19?

Multiples If we multiply 4 by the numbers 1, 2, 3, 4, 5, 6, …, we get

4, 8, 12, 16, 20, 24, …

These numbers are **multiples of 4.** The multiples of 4 are the numbers we get if we count by fours.

The following numbers are the multiples of 6.

6, 12, 18, 24, 30, 36, …

The multiples of any number are the answers we get when we multiply the number by 1, 2, 3, 4, 5, 6, ….

Example 1 List the first four multiples of 7.

Solution To find the first four multiples of 7, we multiply 7 by 1, then by 2, then by 3, and then by 4.

$$
\begin{array}{cccc}
7 & 7 & 7 & 7 \\
\times\,1 & \times\,2 & \times\,3 & \times\,4 \\
\hline
7 & 14 & 21 & 28
\end{array}
$$

The first four multiples of 7 are **7, 14, 21,** and **28.** The multiples of 7 are the numbers we say when we count by 7.

Example 2 (a) What is the fourth multiple of 6?

(b) What is the third multiple of 8?

Solution (a) To find the fourth multiple of 6, we multiply 6 by 4. The fourth multiple of 6 is **24.**

(b) To find the third multiple of 8, we multiply 8 by 3. The third multiple of 8 is **24.**

Percent We use fractions and percents to describe parts of a whole. We often use the symbol % to stand for *percent*. If your score on a test is 100%, that means you have every answer right since 100% means the whole thing. If 50% of the children in the class are girls, then half of the children are girls since 50% is half of 100%. So 50% is half of the whole group.

We can use shaded squares to illustrate percentages.

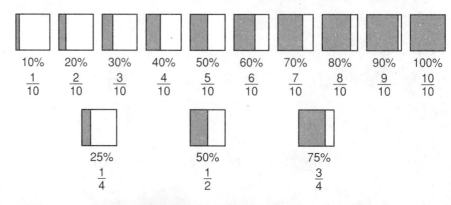

Thinking about money can help us understand percents. Twenty-five cents is $\frac{1}{4}$ of a whole dollar and it is 25% of a whole dollar. Likewise, seventy-five cents is $\frac{3}{4}$ of a whole dollar and it is 75% of a whole dollar.

Example 3   Draw a square and shade 50% of it.

Solution   Since 50% is half of 100%, we shade half of the square. Here are three ways.

Fifty percent of each square is shaded.

Example 4   Forty percent of the children in the class are girls. Are there more boys or more girls in the class?

Solution   Since 50% is half, 40% must be less than half. Since girls are less than half of the class, there must be **more boys than girls in the class.**

Practice   **a.** List the first five multiples of 6.   6, 12, 18, 24, 30

b. List the third, fourth, and fifth multiples of 9.
27, 36, 45

c. What is the seventh multiple of 8?   56

d. Draw a square and shade 25% of it.

e. The chance of rain is 20%. What is the chance that it will not rain?   80%

Problem set 65   **1.** Kent bought a toy for $1.85 and sold it for 75¢ more. For what price did he sell the toy? (Use the SSM pattern.) $2.60
(12)

2. Two thousand people entered the contest. Only seven will win prizes. How many will not win prizes? Draw a SWA pattern.   1993 people
(31)

$$\begin{array}{r} 2000 \text{ people} \\ - \underline{\quad 7 \text{ people}} \\ \underline{N \text{ people}} \end{array}$$

3. Sixty percent of the students in the class were boys.
(65) Were there more girls or more boys in the class?
more boys

4. Twenty-seven thousand people lived in the big town.
(38) Only eight thousand, four hundred seventy-two people lived in the small town. How many more people lived in the big town? (Use the L-S-D pattern.)
18,528 people

5. Draw a rectangle that is 4 cm long and 3 cm wide.
(60,25) What is the perimeter of the rectangle?   4 cm   ; 14 cm
                                                   ▭ 3 cm

6. Fiona found the third multiple of 4. Then she
(65) subtracted two from this number. What was her answer?   10

7. Compare: $\frac{1}{2}$ ⊜ 50%
(65,15)

8. If it is afternoon, what time was it
(33) 30 minutes ago?   3:19 p.m.

9. How many years were there from
(64) 1776 to 1789? (Use the L-E-D pattern.)   13 years

10. What is the length of $\overline{ST}$?   5 cm
(50)

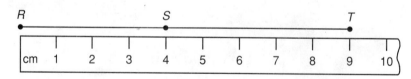

11.   400
(51) − 222
        178

12.   705
(37) − 423
        282

13.   4587
(61) + 2364
        6951

14. $25.42
(37) − $7.25
        $18.17

15.   64
(58) × 5
        320

16.   70
(54) × 6
        420

17. 89
(58)   × 4
       356

18. 63
(58)   × 7
       441

19.   46
(21)   295
          329
          746
          761
        + 356
         2533

        1 r 7
20. 8)15
(63)

        6 r 2
21. 5)32
(63)

22. $\frac{63}{7}$ 9
(57)

23. 33 ÷ 6   5 r 3
(63)

24. 44 ÷ 7   6 r 2
(63)

25. $\sqrt{64}$ ÷ 8   1
(56,40)

26. Use digits to write seventy thousand, seven hundred
(43)   two.   70,702

27. 7 + 5 + 4 + 3 + 2 + 6 + 9 + 5 + N = 44   3
(2)

LESSON
66

Using Pictures to Compare Fractions

a. 60
b. 160
c. 1600
d. $3.42
e. $6.63
f. 385
Problem Solving:
  1 quarter, 2 dimes,
  and 1 penny

Facts Practice: 64 Multiplication Facts (Test G in Test Masters)

Mental Math: Multiply by ten.
  a. 6 × 10   **b.** 16 × 10   **c.** 160 × 10

Review:
  d. $5.00 − $1.58   **e.** $4.64 + $1.99   **f.** 56 + 29 + 300

Problem Solving: Marco paid a dollar for an item that cost 54¢.
    What four coins did he get back in change?

We have practiced comparing whole numbers using comparison symbols. In this lesson we will compare fractions. To begin, we will compare one half and one third.

$$\frac{1}{2} \bigcirc \frac{1}{3}$$

One way to compare fractions is to draw pictures of the fractions and compare the pictures. We will draw two circles of the same size. We shade $\frac{1}{2}$ of one circle and $\frac{1}{3}$ of the other circle.

As we study the pictures, we see that more of the circle is shaded when $\frac{1}{2}$ is shaded than when $\frac{1}{3}$ is shaded. So $\frac{1}{2}$ is greater than $\frac{1}{3}$.

$$\frac{1}{2} > \frac{1}{3}$$

When drawing pictures to compare fractions, the figures that we draw should be **congruent.** Congruent figures are the same shape and size.

Example Compare: $\frac{1}{4} \bigcirc \frac{1}{3}$. Draw two rectangles to show the comparison.

Solution We draw two congruent rectangles. We shade $\frac{1}{4}$ of one rectangle and $\frac{1}{3}$ of the other rectangle. We see that $\frac{1}{4}$ is slightly less than $\frac{1}{3}$.

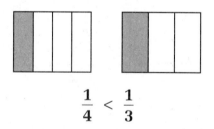

$$\frac{1}{4} < \frac{1}{3}$$

Practice Compare these fractions. Draw a pair of congruent figures to illustrate each comparison.

a. $\frac{1}{2} \,\boxed{<}\, \frac{2}{3}$ ▢ < ▥   **b.** $\frac{1}{2} \,\boxed{>}\, \frac{1}{4}$ ▢ > ▥   **c.** $\frac{2}{5} \,\boxed{>}\, \frac{1}{3}$ ▥ > ▢

Problem set 66

1. James had fifty-six pies. Seven pies would fit on one tray. How many trays did he need? Use the EG pattern.
$^{(62)}$
8 trays

2. Five hundred forty-seven birds were on the lake. At
(31) sunrise some flew away. Then only two hundred
fourteen birds were left. How many flew away? Use
the SWA pattern.   333 birds

3. Three hundred forty-two rabbits munched grass in the
(17) meadow. That afternoon some more rabbits came.
Then seven hundred fifty-two rabbits munched grass
in the meadow. How many rabbits came in the
afternoon? Use the SSM pattern.   410 rabbits

4. Write four multiplication/division facts using the
(57) numbers 3, 8, and 24.
$3 \times 8 = 24, 8 \times 3 = 24, 24 \div 3 = 8, 24 \div 8 = 3$

5. List the seven months of the year that have 31 days.
(64) January, March, May, July, August, October, December

6. Find the eighth multiple of six. Then add one. What is
(65,40) the square root of the answer?   48; 49; 7

7. Compare these fractions. Shade two congruent
(66) rectangles to show the fractions.   ▮⯑⯑⯑ > ⯑⯑⯑⯑

$$\frac{1}{4} \, \bigcirc\!\!\!> \, \frac{1}{6}$$

8. Round 497 to the nearest hundred.   500
(52)

9. What is the perimeter of this
(60) rectangle?   22 miles

7 miles

4 miles

10. $10.00   **11.**   36,024   **12.**   43,675
(51) − $5.46   *(62)* − 15,539   *(61)* + 52,059
─────────   ─────────   ─────────
  $4.54   20,485   95,734

13.   73   **14.**   46   **15.**   84   **16.**   40
(58) × 9   *(58)* × 7   *(58)* × 6   *(54)* × 5
─────   ─────   ─────   ─────
  657   322   504   200

17. 56 ÷ 5   11 r 1   **18.** 7)48̄   6 r 6   **19.** $\dfrac{63}{7}$ 9
(63)   *(63)*   *(57)*

$$\overset{3 \text{ r } 4}{7)25}$$

20.
(63)

$$\overset{6 \text{ r } 6}{9)60}$$

21.
(63)

22. $N \times 6 = 54$
(50)   9

23. N 1459
(20) $- 942$
    $\overline{517}$

24.   4
(2)   7
    8
    21
    $+ N$ 9
    $\overline{49}$

25.   5
(2)   8
    13
    14
    $+ N$ 7
    $\overline{47}$

26. Draw a rectangle and shade 50% of it.
(65)

LESSON
67

Rate Word Problems

a. 120
b. 1200
c. 100
d. 298
e. 64¢
f. $7.50
Problem Solving:
Percent shaded:
25%
Percent not shaded:
75%

> **Facts Practice:** 90 Division Facts (Test I in Test Masters)
>
> **Mental Math:** Multiply by ten.
>   **a.** 12×10 **b.** 120×10 **c.** 10×10
> **Review:**
>   **d.** $48 + 250$ **e.** $1.00 - 0.36$ **f.** $3.75 + 3.75$
>
> **Problem Solving:** The whole circle has been divided into quarters. What percent of the circle is shaded? What percent is not shaded?
>
>

A **rate** tells **how far** or **how many are in one time group.**

The car went 30 miles per hour.

This statement tells us that the car's rate is 30 miles each hour. **Rate problems have the same pattern that "equal groups" problems have.**

Example 1   Brad drove the car 30 miles per hour for 4 hours. How far did Brad drive in 4 hours?

Solution This is a rate problem. A rate problem is an "equal groups" problem. Let's draw the pattern.

Number **in** time group			each	
Number **of** time groups	×	___		___
Total		___	___	

We do not see the words *in each* in a rate problem, but there are words that mean *in each*. The words *miles per hour* mean *miles **each** hour*.

Number **in** time group		30	miles each	hour
Number **of** time groups	×	4		hours
Total		N	miles	

Now we find the missing number. To find the bottom number of an "equal groups" pattern, we multiply.

$$\begin{array}{r} 30 \\ \times\ 4 \\ \hline 120 \end{array}$$

We complete the pattern and answer the question.

Number **in** time group		30	miles each	hour
Number **of** time groups	×	4		hours
Total		120	miles	

Brad drove **120 miles** in 4 hours.

Example 2 Nalcomb earns 3 dollars a week for doing chores. How much money does he earn in 7 weeks?

Solution This is a rate problem. A rate problem is an "equal groups" problem. The words *3 dollars a week* mean *3 dollars **each** week*.

Number **in** time group		3	dollars each	week
Number **of** time groups	×	7		weeks
Total		N	dollars	

We need to find the missing number. We find the bottom number of an "equal groups" pattern by multiplying.

$$\begin{array}{r} 3 \\ \times\ 7 \\ \hline 21 \end{array}$$

We complete the pattern and answer the question.

Number **in** time group		3 dollars each	week
Number **of** time groups	×	7	weeks
Total		21 dollars	

Nalcomb earns **21 dollars** in 7 weeks.

Practice

a. Tammy drove 55 miles in one hour. At that rate, how far can she drive in 6 hours?   330 miles

b. Jeff swims 20 laps every day. How many laps will he swim in 1 week?   140 laps

Problem set 67

1. Marybeth could jump 42 times each minute. How
(67) many times could she jump in 8 minutes? Use the EG pattern.   336 times

2. Robo could run 7 miles in 1 hour. At that rate, how far
(67) could Robo run in 3 hours? Use the EG pattern.
21 miles

3. Write four multiplication/division facts using the
(57) numbers 8, 9, and 72.
$8 \times 9 = 72, 9 \times 8 = 72, 72 \div 8 = 9, 72 \div 9 = 8$

4. What is the sum of $\sqrt{36}$ and $\sqrt{64}$?   14
(40)

5. Compare: $\frac{1}{3}$ ⟨<⟩ 50%
(66,65)

6. Round 582 to the nearest hundred. Then subtract 18.
(52) What is the answer?   600; 582

7. It is afternoon. What time was it 6
(33) hours and 5 minutes ago?
9:00 a.m.

8. Find the fourth multiple of 6.
(65) Then find the third multiple of 8.
What is the sum of these two
numbers?   24; 24; 48

9. How many years were there from 1492 until 1800? Use
(64) the "later-earlier-difference" pattern.   308 years

10. A square has one side that is 7 inches long. What is the
(60) perimeter of the square?   28 inches

11.   70,003
(62) − 36,418
───────
33,585

12. N 689
(20) − 432
─────
257

13. $861.34
(28) + $764.87
─────────
$1626.21

14.   93
(58) × 5
────
465

15.   84
(58) × 6
────
504

16.   77
(58) × 7
────
539

17.   80
(54) × 8
────
640

18. $\dfrac{56}{8}$ 7
(57)

19. $\overset{9\ r\ 2}{7\overline{)65}}$
(63)

20. 45 ÷ 6   7 r 3
(63)

21. $\overset{7\ r\ 2}{7\overline{)51}}$
(63)

22. 7 × N = 42
(50)   6

23. R × 8 = 48
(50)   6

24. Compare these fractions. Draw a picture to show each
(66) fraction.   ▨ < ▩

$$\frac{2}{3} \overset{<}{\bigcirc} \frac{3}{4}$$

25.   423
(2)   7
          8
         15
    + N 5
    ─────
       458

26.   2
(2)   24
          36
         N 6
    +   14
    ─────
        82

27.   7
(2)   5
          4
          3
    + N 11
    ─────
        30

LESSON 68

Multiplying Three-Digit Numbers

a. 420
b. 400
c. 1200
d. $8.32
e. 647
f. $3.13
Patterns:
   21, 28, 36

Facts Practice: 90 Division Facts (Test I in Test Masters)

Mental Math: Multiply three numbers, including ten.
   a. $6 \times 7 \times 10$ **b.** $5 \times 8 \times 10$ **c.** $12 \times 10 \times 10$

Review:
   d. $6.47 + $1.85   **e.** 400 + 37 + 210   **f.** $10.00 − $6.87

Patterns: In this sequence the count from one number to the next increases. Copy this sequence and find the next three terms.

$$1, 3, 6, 10, 15, \underline{\quad}, \underline{\quad}, \underline{\quad}$$

When we multiply three-digit numbers, we multiply the ones' digit first. Then we multiply the tens' digit. Then we multiply the hundreds' digit.

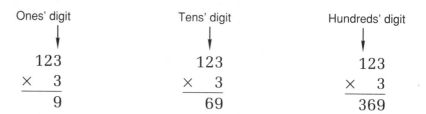

In the next problem, we get 18 when we multiply the ones' digit. We write the eight in the ones' column and write the one above the tens' column. Then we multiply the tens' digit.

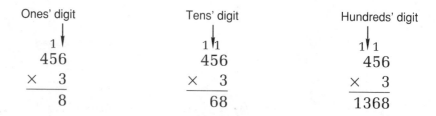

Three times five is 15, plus one is 16. We write the six below the line and write the one above the hundreds' column. Then we multiply the hundreds. Three times four is 12, plus one equals 13. The product is 1368.

Example 1   Multiply: 654 × 7

Solution
$$\begin{array}{r} \overset{3\,2}{654} \\ \times\ \ \ 7 \\ \hline \mathbf{4578} \end{array}$$

Example 2
$$\begin{array}{r} \$3.75 \\ \times\ \ \ \ \ \ 3 \\ \hline \end{array}$$

Solution   Imagine multiplying pennies, dimes, and dollars. We multiply three times five pennies and get 15 pennies, which equals one dime and five pennies. We write "5" below the line and "1" above the dimes.

$$\begin{array}{r} \overset{1}{} \\ \$3.75 \\ \times\ \ \ \ \ \ 3 \\ \hline 5 \end{array}$$

Next we multiply three times seven dimes and get 21 dimes. We add the one dime from multiplying pennies for a total of 22 dimes. Since 22 dimes equals two dollars and two dimes, we write a two below the line and a two above the dollars.

$$\begin{array}{r} \overset{2\ 1}{} \\ \$3.75 \\ \times\ \ \ \ \ \ 3 \\ \hline 25 \end{array}$$

Finally, we multiply three times three dollars and get nine dollars. We add the two dollars, making 11 dollars. The total is **$11.25.**

$$\begin{array}{r} \overset{2\ 1}{} \\ \$3.75 \\ \times\ \ \ \ \ \ 3 \\ \hline \$11.25 \end{array}$$

Practice   **a.**
$$\begin{array}{r} 234 \\ \times\ \ \ 3 \\ \hline 702 \end{array}$$
b.
$$\begin{array}{r} \$340 \\ \times\ \ \ \ 4 \\ \hline \$1360 \end{array}$$
c.
$$\begin{array}{r} \$4.25 \\ \times\ \ \ \ \ \ 5 \\ \hline \$21.25 \end{array}$$

d. Explain the steps of multiplying 5 × $4.25 by imagining multiplying dollars, dimes, and pennies.   answer varies

Problem set 68   **1.** Elizabeth pays 9 dollars every week for karate lessons.
(67)   How much does she pay for 4 weeks of karate lessons? Use the EG pattern.   36 dollars

2. It takes 4 apples to make 1 pie. How many apples does
(59) it take to make 5 pies? Use the EG pattern.   20 apples

3. Elmer has to get up at 6 a.m. What time should he go
(33) to bed in order to get 8 hours of sleep?   10 p.m.

4. Nine hundred seventy-three raccoons were hiding in
(31) the forest. Hoover found three hundred eighty-eight of
them. How many raccoons were still hiding in the
forest? Use the SWA pattern.   585 raccoons

5. Write the number 8,402 in expanded form. Then use
(42) words to write the number.
8000 + 400 + 2; eight thousand, four hundred two

6. Find the fourth multiple of 7. Then find the sixth
(65,40) multiple of 6. Add these multiples. What is the square
root of the answer?   28; 36; 64; 8

7. According to this calendar, what
(64) is the date of the second Tuesday
in September 2042?
September 9, 2042

SEPTEMBER 2042

S	M	T	W	T	F	S
		1	2	3	4	5	6
7	8	9	10	11	12	13
14	15	16	17	18	19	20
21	22	23	24	25	26	27
28	29	30				

8. If $5 + N = 23$, what number is N?   18
(30)

9. What is the perimeter of this fig-
(60) ure? Dimensions are in feet.   26 ft

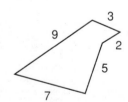

10. Compare these fractions. Shade two circles to show
(66) the fractions.

$$\frac{1}{2} \bigcirc \frac{2}{4}$$

11. The arrow points to what number on this number
(46) line? $7\frac{7}{10}$

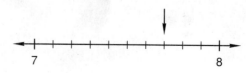

12. Draw a rectangle and shade about 30% of it.
(65)

13. $3 + $4.39 + $12.62   **14.** 47 + 362 + 85 + 454
(53) $20.01   (21) 948

15. $20.00 − $7.29 $12.71 **16.** 41,059 − 36,275 4784
(51)   (62)

17.   768   **18.** $2.80   **19.**   436
(68)   × 3   (68)   × 4   (20)   − Z 184
     ‾‾‾‾‾‾‾   ‾‾‾‾‾‾‾   ‾‾‾‾‾‾
      2304 $11.20   252

                7 r 1   6 r 3   8 r 3
20. 5)‾3‾6   **21.** 7)‾4‾5   **22.** 4)‾3‾5
(63)   (63)   (63)

23. 17 ÷ 3 5 r 2   **24.** 49 ÷ 6 8 r 1   **25.** 57 ÷ 8 7 r 1
(63)   (63)   (63)

26.   6   **27.**   N 9   **28.**   4
(2)   5   (2)   5   (2)   7
       N 6   7   8
         4   3   N 6
         7   2   3
       + 3   + 12   + 16
      ‾‾‾‾‾   ‾‾‾‾‾   ‾‾‾‾‾
        31   38   44

LESSON
69

a. 2400
b. 1200
c. 2000
d. $1.75
e. $8.54
f. 440
Problem Solving:
  Students in class:
    No
  More boys or girls:
    Yes
    (same number)
  Odd or even:
    Yes (even)

Two-Step Equations

Facts Practice: 90 Division Facts (Test J in Test Masters)

Mental Math: Multiply four numbers, including two tens.
  a. 6 × 4 × 10 × 10   **b.** 3 × 4 × 10 × 10
  c. 4 × 5 × 10 × 10

Review:
  d. $5.00 − $3.25   **e.** $7.59 + $0.95   **f.** 470 − 30

Problem Solving: Fifty percent of the students in Gabriel's class are girls. Do we know how many students are in this class? Do we know whether there are more boys or more girls in the class? Do we know if the number of students in the class is an odd or even number?

We have used letters to stand for numbers in arithmetic problems. Problems like we have practiced are sometimes called *equations*. Some equations can be solved in one step while others require several steps to solve.

Example $3 \times 5 = 2 + N$

Solution   The equal sign shows that the answer to 3×5 equals the answer to $2 + N$. For the first step, we multiply 3×5 and find that the left-hand side of the equation is 15.

STEP 1 $3 \times 5 = 2 + N$
$15 = 2 + N$

Since the left-hand side of the equation is 15, the right-hand side must also total 15. So the second step is to find this missing addend.

STEP 2 $15 = 2 + N$
$15 = 2 + 13$

So N is **13**.

Practice   **a.** $2 + 17 = N + 5$ 14   **b.** $W + 3 = 5 \times 3$ 12

Problem set
69

1. There were forty-two apples in each big basket. There
(59) were seven big baskets. How many apples were in the seven big baskets? Use the EG pattern.   294 apples

2. There were forty-eight pears in all. Six pears were in
(62) each box. How many boxes were there? Use the EG pattern.   8 boxes

3. One thousand, nine hundred forty-two ducks were in
(12) the first flight. Two thousand, seven hundred five ducks were in the second flight. How many ducks were in both flights? Use the SSM pattern.   4647 ducks

4. Write four multiplication/division facts using the
(57) numbers 3, 9, and 27.
$3 \times 9 = 27, 9 \times 3 = 27, 27 \div 3 = 9, 27 \div 9 = 3$

5. Compare: 50% of $16 \bigcirc\!\!> \sqrt{16}$
(65,40)

6. Find the sum of the fourth multiple of 10, the third
(65) multiple of 7, and the second multiple of 100.   261

7. How many years were there from 1492 to 1701? Use
(64) the L-E-D pattern.   209 years

8. It is dark outside. What time was
(33) it 3 hours and 10 minutes ago?
9:18 p.m.

9. Compare these fractions. Shade rectangles to show the
(66) fractions.   ▥ > ▥

$$\frac{2}{5} \; \bigcirc\!\!> \; \frac{1}{4}$$

10. Janine could pack 40 packages in 1 hour. How many
(67) packages could she pack in 5 hours? Use the EG
pattern.   200 packages

11. If $25 + N = 5 \times 7$, what number is N?   10
(69)

12. One side of a rectangle is 2 miles long. Another side is
(60,25) 3 miles long. Draw a picture of the rectangle and show
the length of each side. What is the perimeter of the
rectangle?   10 mi

13. $37.75
(28) + $45.95
─────────
   $83.70

14.   43,793
(61) + 76,860
─────────
  120,653

15.   480
(61)   97
      126
       53
  + 2362
  ─────────
     3118

16. $50.00
(51) − $42.87
─────────
   $7.13

17.   43,793
(62) − 26,860
─────────
  16,933

18. 483 × 4 1932
(68)

19. 360 × 4 1440
(68)

20. 207 × 8 1656
(68)

21. 8)43   5 r 3
(63)

22. 5)43   8 r 3
(63)

23. 7)43   6 r 1
(63)

24. 29 ÷ 4   7 r 1
(63)

25. $\frac{32}{8}$ 4
(57)

26. 55 ÷ 9   6 r 1
(63)

27. $5 + 7 + N + 4 + 7 + 8 + 7 + 6 + 3 = 52$ 5
(2)

LESSON 70

Estimating Arithmetic Answers • More About Rate

a. 1600
b. 1500
c. 4200
d. 2000

Problem Solving:

Which coin equals half of a dime?
14-9-3-11-5-12
(nickel)

Facts Practice: 90 Division Facts (Test J in Test Masters)

Mental Math: Multiply two numbers ending in zero.
Example: 30 × 40 equals 3 × 10 times 4 × 10. This equals 3 × 4 × 10 × 10, which is 1200.

a. 40 × 40   **b.** 30 × 50   **c.** 60 × 70   **d.** 40 × 50

Problem Solving: This question is written in code. When you figure out the question, write the answer in the same code.
23-8-9-3-8   3-15-9-14   5-17-21-1-12-19
8-1-12-6   15-6   1   4-9-13-5?

Estimating arithmetic answers

We can **estimate** arithmetic answers by using round numbers instead of exact answers to do the arithmetic. Estimating does not give us the exact answer, but it gives us an answer that is close to the exact answer. Estimating is a way to find if our exact answer is **reasonable.**

Example 1   Estimate the sum of 396 and 512.

Solution   To estimate, we first change the exact numbers to round numbers. We round 396 to 400. We round 512 to 500. Then we do the arithmetic with the round numbers. We find the sum by adding, so we add 400 and 500.

$$
\begin{array}{r}
400 \\
+\ 500 \\
\hline
900
\end{array}
$$

The estimated sum of 396 and 512 is **900.** The exact sum of 396 and 512 is 908. The estimated answer is not exact, but it is close to the exact number.

Example 2   Estimate the product of 72 and 5.

Solution   We round the two-digit number but not the one-digit number. The estimated product of 72 and 5 is **350.**

$$
\begin{array}{r}
70 \\
\times\ 5 \\
\hline
350
\end{array}
$$

More about rate   In Lesson 67, we learned that rate problems have the same pattern as "equal groups" problems. The rate tells how many are in each time group. If we know two numbers in the problem, we can find the third number. We have practiced problems in which we were given the rate and time. We multiplied to find the total. In this lesson we will practice problems in which we are given the total. We will divide to find the number we are not given.

Example 3   Stanley can read 2 pages in 1 minute. How long will it take him to read 18 pages?

Solution   This is a rate problem. A rate problem is an "equal groups" problem. Let's draw the pattern.

Number **in** time group	___ _____	each	_____
Number **of** time groups	× ___		_____
Total	. ___ _____		

We are told that the rate is 2 pages in 1 minute. This means 2 pages each minute. We are told that the total number of pages is 18.

Number **in** time group	2	pages each	minute
Number **of** time groups	× N		minutes
Total	18	pages	

Now we find the missing number. **To find the first or second number in an "equal groups" pattern, we divide.**

$$2)\overline{18} \quad 9$$

We complete the pattern and answer the question.

Number **in** time group	2	pages each	minute
Number **of** time groups	× 9		minutes
Total	18	pages	

It would take Stanley **9 minutes** to read 18 pages.

Practice   Estimate the answer to each arithmetic problem. Then find the exact answer.

a. 59 + 68 + 81   210; 208   **b.** 607 + 891   1500; 1498

c. 585 − 294   300; 291   **d.** 82 − 39   40; 43

e. 59 × 6   360; 354   **f.** 397 × 4   1600; 1588

g. Miguel can sharpen 5 pencils in a minute. How long will it take Miguel to sharpen 40 pencils?   8 minutes

Problem set 70

1. Fifty percent of an hour is how many minutes?
(65)   30 minutes

2. There were two hundred fourteen parrots, seven hundred fifty-two crows, and two thousand, forty-two blue jays. How many birds were there in all? Use the SSM pattern.   3008 birds
(12)

3. Letha could make four burritos with one pound of beans. How many pounds of beans would she need to make a dozen burritos? Use the EG pattern.
(62)   3 pounds of beans

4. Harry could paint 36 signs in 3 hours. How many signs could he paint in 1 hour? Use the EG pattern.
(70)   12 signs

5. Round each number to the nearest hundred; then add to estimate the sum of 286 and 415.   300; 400; 700
(70)

6. What is the sum of the fourth multiple of 100 and the seventh multiple of 10?   470
(65)

7. Write the digital form for a quarter to seven in the morning.   6:45 a.m.
(23)

8. $140 + N = 28 \times 5$ 0
(69)

9. The product of 6 and 7 is how much greater than the sum of 6 and 7?   29
(38)

10. What is the length of segment *BC*?   3 cm
(50)

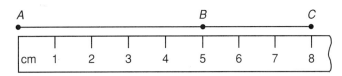

11. Compare: $(32 \div 8) \div 2$ $\textcircled{<}$ $32 \div (8 \div 2)$
(57,55)

12. $6.49 + $12 + $7.59 + 8¢ $26.16
(53)

13. 3742 + 5329 + 8415   **14.** $30.00 − $29.17
(61)   17,486   (51) $0.83

15.   350   **16.**   204   **17.**   463
(68) × 5   (68) × 7   (68) × 6
─────   ─────   ─────
1750   1428   2778

         9 r 1   6 r 3   9 r 1
18. 4$\overline{)37}$ **19.** 6$\overline{)39}$ **20.** 3$\overline{)28}$
(63)   (63)   (63)

21. $\sqrt{49} \div 7$ 1   **22.** 48 ÷ 5 9 r 3   **23.** $\dfrac{48}{8}$ 6
(56,40)   (63)   (57)

24.   5   **25.**   4   **26.**   5
(1)   1   (2)   2   (2)   2
        2   N 3   42
        3   15   3
        8   12   N 3
        4   3   16
      + 7   + 5   + 4
      ─────   ─────   ─────
       30   44   75

LESSON
71

Remaining Fraction

a. 600
b. 2400
c. 1200
d. $0.76
e. $8.87
f. 355
Problem Solving:
  2 quarters,
  1 nickel and
  1 penny

Facts Practice: 90 Division Facts (Test J in Test Masters)

Mental Math: Multiply three numbers, including numbers ending in zero.

  a. $3 \times 10 \times 20$ **b.** $4 \times 20 \times 30$ **c.** $3 \times 40 \times 10$

Review:

  d. $10.00 - $9.24   **e.** $6.48 + $2.39   **f.** $480 - 125$

Problem Solving: Joan paid a dollar for an item that cost 44¢. What four coins did she get back in change?

If a whole has been divided into parts and we know the size of one part, then we can figure out the size of the other parts.

Example 1 (a) What fraction of the circle is shaded?

(b) What fraction of the circle is **not** shaded?

Solution We see that the whole circle has been divided into eight parts. Three of the parts are shaded, so five of the parts are not shaded.

(a) The fraction that is shaded is $\frac{3}{8}$.

(b) The fraction that is **not** shaded is $\frac{5}{8}$.

Example 2 The pizza was cut into eight equal slices. After Bill, Tony, and Jenny each took a slice, what fraction of the pizza was left?

Solution The whole pizza was cut into eight equal parts. Since three of the eight parts were taken, five of the eight parts remained. The fraction that was left was $\frac{5}{8}$.

Example 3 Two fifths of the crowd cheered. What fraction of the crowd did not cheer?

Solution We think of the crowd as though it were divided into five parts. We are told that two of the five parts cheered. So there were three parts that did not cheer. The fraction that did not cheer was $\frac{3}{5}$.

Practice **a.** What fraction of this rectangle is not shaded? $\frac{5}{6}$

b. Three fifths of the race was over. What fraction of the race was left? $\frac{2}{5}$

Problem set 71

1. The first number was one thousand, three hundred
(38) forty-two. The second number was five hundred fourteen. The second number was how much less than the first number? Use the L-S-D pattern. 828

2. Five little people could crowd into each one of the
(59) spaces. If there were thirty-five spaces, how many little people could crowd in? Use the EG pattern.
175 little people

3. Only two big people could crowd into one of the
(62) spaces. If there were sixty-four big people standing in line, how many spaces would it take to hold them? Use the EG pattern. 32 spaces .

4. The Gilbreth family drank 39 quarts of milk in 3 days.
(70) That amounts to how many quarts of milk each day? Use the EG pattern. 13 quarts of milk

5. Carl weighed 88 pounds. He put on his clothes, which
(12) weighed 2 pounds, and his shoes, which weighed 1 pound each. Finally, he put on a jacket that weighed 3 pounds and stepped on the scale again. Then how much did the scale show that he weighed? Use the SSM pattern. 95 pounds

6. What fraction of this rectangle is
(71) not shaded? $\frac{7}{10}$

7. The pumpkin pie was sliced into 6 equal parts. After 1
(71) slice was taken, what fraction of the pie was left? $\frac{5}{6}$

8. Compare these fractions. Shade parts of circles to
(66) show each fraction.

$$\frac{2}{3} \enspace \text{\textcircled{<}} \enspace \frac{3}{4} \qquad \text{◐} < \text{⊕}$$

9. Use rounded numbers to estimate the sum of 507 and
(70) 384.   900

10. If 60% of the answers were true, then were there more
(65) true answers or more false answers?   more true answers

11. What is the perimeter of this
(60) rectangle?   24 cm

```
┌──────────────┐
│              │ 4 cm
└──────────────┘
      8 cm
```

12. $62.59
(28) + $17.47
─────────
   $80.06

13. Z 685
(20) − 417
─────────
     268

14.   976
(61)   434
             129
              85
         + 1140
         ──────
           2764

15. $1000 - (110 \times 9)$ 10
(55)

16.   413,216
(62) − 127,159
──────────
     286,057

17.   670
(68) ×   4
─────────
    2680

18.   703
(68) ×   6
─────────
    4218

19.   346
(68) ×   9
─────────
    3114

20. $5\overline{)39}$ 7 r 4
(63)

21. $7\overline{)39}$ 5 r 4
(63)

22. $4\overline{)39}$ 9 r 3
(63)

23. $16 \div 3$ 5 r 1
(63)

24. $26 \div 6$ 4 r 2
(63)

25. $36 \div \sqrt{36}$ 6
(57,40)

a. 2000
b. 6000
c. 20,000
d. 2500
e. $1.29
f. $7.42
Patterns:
  2, 7, 12, 17, 22, 27, ...

LESSON
72

Multiplying Three Factors • Exponents

Facts Practice: 90 Division Facts (Test J in Test Masters)

Mental Math: Multiply numbers ending in two zeros by numbers ending in one zero.

a. 200 × 10   b. 300 × 20   c. 400 × 50

Review:

d. 250 × 10   e. $1.00 + $0.29   f. $4.47 + $2.95

Patterns: Counting by fives from five, we say this sequence:

5, 10, 15, 20, 25, 30, ...

If we count by fives from **one,** we say this sequence:

1, 6, 11, 16, 21, 26, ...

What sequence do we say when we count by fives from **two?**

Multiplying three factors

To multiply three numbers, we first multiply two of the numbers. Then we multiply the answer we get by the third number.

Example 1   3 × 4 × 5

Solution   First we multiply two numbers and get an answer. Then we multiply that answer by the third number. If we multiply 3 × 4 first, we get 12. Then we multiply 12 × 5 and get 60.

$$
\begin{array}{cc}
\text{FIRST} & \text{THEN} \\
3 & 12 \\
\times\,4 & \times\,5 \\
\hline
12 & \mathbf{60}
\end{array}
$$

It does not matter which numbers we multiply first. If we multiply 5 × 4 first, we get 20. Then we multiply 20 × 3 and get 60 again.

$$
\begin{array}{cc}
\text{FIRST} & \text{THEN} \\
5 & 20 \\
\times\,4 & \times\,3 \\
\hline
20 & \mathbf{60}
\end{array}
$$
← same answer

Exponents An exponent is a number that shows how many times another number is to be used as a factor. An exponent is written above and to the right of the other number.

$$5^2 \leftarrow \text{exponent}$$

$$5^2 \text{ means } 5 \times 5.$$

$$5^2 \text{ equals } 25.$$

We read 5^2 as "five squared."

Example 2 $5^2 + 2^3$

Solution We read 2^3 as "two cubed." We will find the value of 5^2 and 2^3 and then add.

$$5^2 \text{ means } 5 \times 5, \text{ which is } 25.$$

$$2^3 \text{ means } 2 \times 2 \times 2, \text{ which is } 8.$$

Now we add 25 and 8.

$$5^2 + 2^3$$

$$25 + 8 = \mathbf{33}$$

Practice **a.** $2 \times 3 \times 4$ 24 **b.** $2 \times 4 \times 6$ 48

c. 8^2 64 **d.** 3^3 27

Problem set 72

1. There were twice as many peacocks as peahens. If there were 12 peacocks, how many peahens were there? 6 peahens
(56)

2. Beth's dance class begins at 6 p.m. It takes 20 minutes to drive to dance class. What time should she leave home to get to dance class on time? 5:40 p.m.
(33)

3. Samantha bought a package of paper for $1.98 and 2 pens for $0.49 each. The tax was 18¢. What was the total price? Use the SSM pattern. $3.14
(12)

4. Nalcomb earns $3 a week for washing the car. How
(67) much money does he earn in a year? (There are 52
weeks in a year.) Use the EG pattern. $156

5. Two thirds of the race was over. What fraction of the
(71) race was left? $\frac{1}{3}$

6. Estimate the difference: 887 − 291   600
(70)

7. In the equation 9 × 11 = 100 − *y*, the letter *y* stands
(69) for what number?   1

8. Compare: $\frac{2}{4}$ ⊜ $\frac{4}{8}$. Draw and shade two circles to show
(66) the comparison.   ⊕ = ⊛

9. What is the sum of the eighth multiple of 5 and the
(65) fourth multiple of 10?   80

10. According to this calendar, the
(64) Fourth of July, 2014, is what day
of the week?   Friday

JULY 2014						
S	M	T	W	T	F	S
		1	2	3	4	5
6	7	8	9	10	11	12
13	14	15	16	17	18	19
20	21	22	23	24	25	26
27	28	29	30	31		

11. Write four multiplication/divi-
(57) sion facts using the numbers 6, 3,
and 18.
6 × 3 = 18; 3 × 6 = 18; 18 ÷ 3 = 6; 18 ÷ 6 = 3

12. 5 × 6 × 7   210   **13.** 4^3 64
(72)   *(72)*

14.   476,385   **15.** $20.00   **16.** C 65,013
(61) + 259,518   *(51)* − $17.84   *(20)*   − 19,434
       735,903 $2.16   45,579

17.   417   **18.**   470   **19.**   608
(68) ×   8   *(68)* ×   7   *(68)* ×   4
       3336   3290   2432

                7 r 1   8 r 1   5 r 4
20. 4$\overline{)29}$ **21.** 8$\overline{)65}$ **22.** 5$\overline{)29}$
(63)   *(63)*   *(63)*

23. 65 ÷ 7   9 r 2   **24.** 29 ÷ 5   5 r 4   **25.** 65 ÷ 9   7 r 2
(63)   (63)   (63)

26. If 40% of the students are boys, then what percent of
(65) the students are girls?   60%

LESSON   **Polygons**
73

a. 1000
b. 6000
c. 24,000
d. $9.32
e. 580
f. $1.21
Problem Solving:
  Exercised:
    30 minutes
  Running:
    15 minutes

Facts Practice: 90 Division Facts (Test I in Test Masters)

Mental Math: Multiply three numbers ending in zero.
  a. 10 × 10 × 10   **b.** 10 × 20 × 30   **c.** 20 × 30 × 40
Review:
  d. $6.48 + $2.84   **e.** 320 + 200 + 60   **f.** $5.00 − $3.79

Problem Solving: Mathea exercised for 50% of an hour. For 50% of her exercise time she was running. For how many minutes was Mathea exercising? For how many minutes was she running?

Polygons are closed, flat shapes formed by straight lines.

Example 1   Which of these shapes is a polygon?

A.   B.    C.   D.

Solution   Figure A is not a polygon because it is not closed. Figure B is not a polygon because it is not flat. Figure C is not a polygon because not all of its sides are straight. **Figure D is a polygon.**

The name of a polygon tells how many sides the polygon has. The sides do not have to have the same lengths. If the sides do have the same lengths and all angles are the same size, they are called **regular** polygons. The right-most figure in each row illustrates a regular polygon.

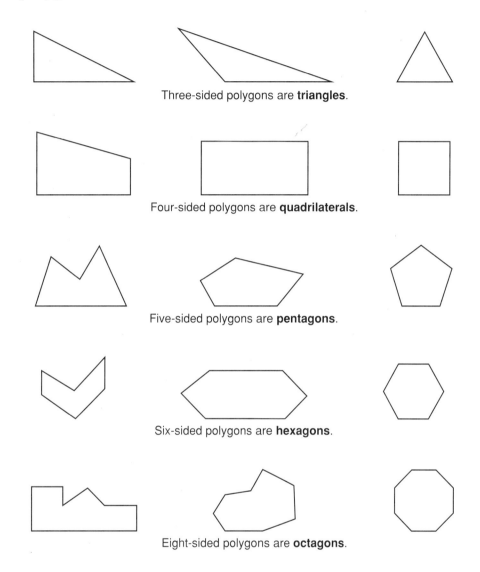

Three-sided polygons are **triangles**.

Four-sided polygons are **quadrilaterals**.

Five-sided polygons are **pentagons**.

Six-sided polygons are **hexagons**.

Eight-sided polygons are **octagons**.

Example 2 What kind of a polygon is a square?

Solution A square has four sides, so a square is a **quadrilateral.**

Practice Draw an example of each kind of polygon:

    a. triangle answer varies   **b.** quadrilateral
                                                               answer varies

    c. pentagon   **d.** hexagon   **e.** octagon
       answer varies   answer varies   answer varies

Problem set
73

1. Three feet equals one yard. A car that is 15 feet long is
(62) how many yards long? Use the EG pattern.   5 yards

2. Write four multiplication/division facts using the
(57) numbers 3, 10, and 30.
$3 \times 10 = 30$; $10 \times 3 = 30$; $30 \div 3 = 10$; $30 \div 10 = 3$

3. Roberta had six quarters, three dimes, and fourteen
(45) pennies. How much money did she have in all? $1.94

4. What is the sum of the even numbers that are greater
(11) than 10 but less than 20?   60

5. Estimate the sum of 715 and 594 by rounding these
(70) numbers to the nearest hundred before adding.   1300

6. Seven bugs could fit into one small space. There were
(62) 56 bugs in all. How many small spaces were needed to
hold them all? Use the EG pattern.   8 small spaces

7. The arrow points to what number? $6\frac{5}{8}$
(46)

6   7

8. The cake was cut into 12 pieces. Seven of the pieces
(71) were eaten. What fraction of the cake was left? $\frac{5}{12}$

9. The product of 4 and 3 is how much greater than the
(38) sum of 4 and 3?   5

10. What is the sum of 9^2 and $\sqrt{9}$?   84
(40,1)

11. (a) What is the name of this
(73,60)   polygon?   hexagon

(b) Each side is the same length.
What is the perimeter of this
polygon?   6 cm

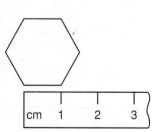

cm   1   2   3

12. Roger could pick 56 flowers in 8 minutes. How many
(70) flowers could he pick in 1 minute? Use the EG pattern.
7 flowers

13. Sarah could pick 11 flowers in 1 minute. How many
(67) flowers could she pick in 5 minutes? Use the EG
pattern.   55 flowers

14. $3 \times 5 \times 7$ **15.** 5^3 125   **16.**   2415
(72) 105   (72)   (61)   3621
                                                     157
                                                     642
17. $40.00   **18.**   64,150   +   93
(20) $-$ D $37.57 (62) $-$ 48,398   ———
       ————   ————   6928
       $2.43   15,752

                                                      5 r 4
19. 349×8 **20.** 760×7 **21.** $6\overline{)34}$
(68) 2792   (68) 5320   (63)

        7 r 6   4 r 4   63
22. $8\overline{)62}$ **23.** $5\overline{)24}$ **24.** $\dfrac{63}{7}$ 9
(63)   (63)   (57)

25. $5 \times N = 15 + \sqrt{25}$ 4   **26.**   7
(69)   (2)   8
                                                  4
                                                  3
                                                  6
27. If 60% of the flowers Sarah   5
(65) picked were red, then what per-   1
cent of the flowers Sarah picked   3
were not red?   40% $+ N$ 7
                                                 ——
                                                 44

LESSON 74

Division with Two-Digit Answers, Part 1

a. 1200
b. 240
c. 360
d. 8000
e. $7.34
f. 185
Problem Solving:

$$\begin{array}{r} 796 \\ + 149 \\ \hline 945 \end{array}$$

Facts Practice: 90 Division Facts (Test I in Test Masters)

Mental Math: Multiply three numbers.
   a. $12 \times 10 \times 10$ **b.** $12 \times 2 \times 10$ **c.** $12 \times 3 \times 10$

Review:
   d. $20 \times 20 \times 20$ **e.** $5.36 + $1.98   **f.** $56 + 9 + 120$

Problem Solving: In this addition problem some digits are missing. Copy this problem on your paper and fill in the missing digits.

$$\begin{array}{r} 7\_6 \\ + \ 4\_ \\ \hline \_45 \end{array}$$

In this lesson we will learn a pencil-and-paper method for dividing a two-digit number by a one-digit number. To show the method, we will divide 78 by 3.

$$3\overline{)78}$$

For the first step we ignore the 8 and divide 7 by 3. We write the 2 above the 7. Then we multiply 2×3 and write "6" below the 7. We subtract and write "1."

$$\begin{array}{r} 2 \\ 3\overline{)78} \\ 6 \\ \hline 1 \end{array}$$

Then we "bring down" the 8, as we show here. Together, the 1 and 8 form 18.

$$\begin{array}{r} 2 \\ 3\overline{)78} \\ 6\downarrow \\ \hline 18 \end{array}$$

Now we divide 18 by 3 and get 6. We write the 6 above the 8 in 78. Then we multiply 6 by 3 and write "18" below the 18.

$$\begin{array}{r} 26 \\ 3\overline{)78} \\ 6 \\ \hline 18 \\ 18 \\ \hline 0 \end{array}$$

When we subtract, we find the remainder is zero. This shows that if we divide 78 into 3 parts, there will be 26 in each part.

Example Divide: $3\overline{)87}$

Solution For the first step we ignore the 7. We divide 8 by 3, multiply, and then subtract. Now we bring down the 7. This forms 27. Now we divide 27 by 3, multiply, and subtract again.

$$
\begin{array}{r}
29 \\
3\overline{)87} \\
6\downarrow \\
\hline
27 \\
27 \\
\hline
0
\end{array}
$$

When we divide 87 into 3 parts, there are **29** in each part.

Practice

a. $3\overline{)51}$ (17)   b. $4\overline{)52}$ (13)   c. $5\overline{)75}$ (15)

d. $3\overline{)72}$ (24)   e. $4\overline{)96}$ (24)   f. $2\overline{)74}$ (37)

Problem set 74

1. Franco liked to run. He ran the course two thousand, (12) three hundred times the first year. He ran the course one thousand, nine hundred forty-two times the second year. How many times did he run the course in all? Use the SSM pattern.   4242 times

2. William Tell's target was one hundred thirteen paces (59) away. If each pace was 3 feet, how many feet away was the target? Use the EG pattern.   339 feet

3. Tracy's baseball card album will hold five hundred (31) cards. Tracy has three hundred eighty-four cards. How many more cards will fit in the album? Use the SWA pattern.   116 cards

4. The trip lasted 21 days. How many weeks is that? (62) 3 weeks

5. A stop sign has the shape of an octagon. How many (73) sides are on seven stop signs?   56 sides

6. Find the length of this hairpin to the nearest quarter
(48) inch. $1\frac{3}{4}$ in.

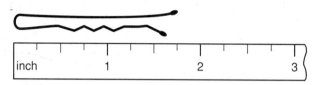

7. Write 406,912 in expanded form. Then use words to
(42) write this number.   400,000 + 6000 + 900 + 10 + 2;
four hundred six thousand, nine hundred twelve

8. One foot equals 12 inches. If each side of a square is
(60) one foot long, what is the perimeter of the square in
inches?   48 in.

9. Estimate the sum of 586 and 797 by rounding the
(70) numbers to the nearest hundred and then adding the
rounded numbers.   1400

10. Compare: $\frac{3}{6} \bigcirc \frac{1}{2}$. Draw and shade two circles to show
(66) the comparison.   ⊗ = ◒

11. Compare: 50% of 100 ⊙ $\sqrt{100}$
(65,40)

12. Some birds sat on the wire at sunup. Later, 47 more
(17) birds came. Then there were 112 birds sitting on the
wire. How many birds sat on the wire at sunup? Use
the SSM pattern.   65 birds

13. $32.47
(28)   + $67.54
        ―――――
        $100.01

14.   51,036
(62)   − 7,648
        ――――――
         43,388

15.   536
(61)   29
           974
            88
        + 4361
        ――――――
          5988

16. 5)75 $\frac{15}{}$
(74)

17. 3)84 $\frac{28}{}$
(74)

18.   257
(68)   ×   5
       ―――――
        1285

19.   709
(68)   ×   3
       ―――――
        2127

20.   334
(68)   ×   9
       ―――――
        3006

21. 4)92 $\frac{23}{}$
(74)

22. 6)58 $\frac{9\,r\,4}{}$
(63)

23. 2)36 $\frac{18}{}$
(74)

24. $N \times 4 = 36$ 9
(50)

25. $4^2 + 2^3$ 24
(72)

LESSON
75

Division with Two-Digit Answers, Part 2

a. 420
b. 500
c. 480
d. 27,000
e. $7.01
f. $9.15
Problem Solving:
    $3.75

Facts Practice: 90 Division Facts (Test I in Test Masters)

Mental Math: Multiply three numbers.

   a. $21 \times 2 \times 10$ **b.** $25 \times 2 \times 10$ **c.** $12 \times 4 \times 10$

Review:

   d. $30 \times 30 \times 30$ **e.** $\$10.00 - \$2.99$ **f.** $\$7.16 + \$1.99$

Problem Solving: The parking lot charged $1.50 for the first hour and 75¢ for each additional hour. Harold parked the car in the lot from 11 a.m. to 3 p.m. How much did he have to pay?

To perform the following division, we begin by dividing $3\overline{)23}$.

$$3\overline{)234}$$

We write "7" above the 3 of 23. Then we multiply. Then we subtract.

$$
\begin{array}{r}
7 \\
3\overline{)234} \\
\underline{21} \\
2
\end{array}
$$

Next, we bring down the 4.

$$
\begin{array}{r}
7 \\
3\overline{)234} \\
\underline{21\downarrow} \\
24
\end{array}
$$

Now we divide 24 by 3. We write the 8 above the 4. Then we multiply and finish by subtracting.

$$
\begin{array}{r}
78 \\
3\overline{)234} \\
\underline{21} \\
24 \\
\underline{24} \\
0
\end{array}
$$

We see that 234 divides into 3 equal groups of 78.

Example   Divide: $174 \div 3$

Solution   We begin by dividing $3\overline{)17}$. We write the 5 above the 7 in 17. Then we multiply. Then we subtract.

$$\begin{array}{r} 5 \\ 3\overline{)174} \\ 15 \\ \hline 2 \end{array}$$

Then we bring down the 4. Now we divide 24 by 3.

$$\begin{array}{r} 58 \\ 3\overline{)174} \\ 15\downarrow \\ \hline 24 \\ 24 \\ \hline 0 \end{array}$$

We see that 174 divides into 3 equal groups of **58**.

Practice   **a.** $3\overline{)144}^{\,48}$ **b.** $4\overline{)144}^{\,36}$ **c.** $6\overline{)144}^{\,24}$

d. $225 \div 5$ 45   **e.** $455 \div 7$ 65   **f.** $200 \div 8$ 25

Problem set 75

1. The chef used 3 eggs for each omelet. How many omelets would be made from 24 eggs? Use the EG pattern.   8 omelets
(62)

2. Seventy-two young knights met peril in the forest. Twenty-seven fought bravely, but the others fled. How many young knights fled? Use the SWA pattern.
(31)   45 young knights

3. Brian wore braces for 3 years. How many months is that?   36 months
(59)

4. Fango could walk 3 miles in 1 hour. At that rate, how many miles could he walk in 10 hours? Use the EG pattern.   30 mi
(67)

5. Fanga ran 28 miles in 4 hours. She ran at a rate of how
(70) many miles per hour?   7 miles per hour

6. Andrea bought dance shoes for $37.95 and tap shoes
(12) for $6.85. How much did she pay for both pairs of
shoes? Use the SSM pattern. $44.80

7. What fraction of this hexagon has
(71) not been shaded? $\frac{5}{6}$

8. Each side of the hexagon in prob-
(60) lem 7 is 1 cm long. What is its
perimeter?   6 cm

9. Jim began walking in the morning. He stopped
(33) walking later that morning. How long did he walk?
2 hours, 20 minutes

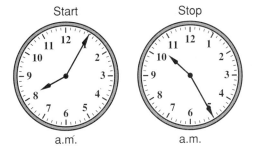

10. Use rounded numbers to estimate the difference
(70) between 903 and 395.   500

11. How long is segment *BC*?   6 cm
(50)

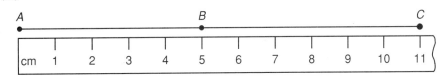

12. How much greater than two hundred ninety-seven
(38) thousand, one hundred fifteen is three hundred
eighty-four thousand, two hundred? Use the L-S-D
pattern.   87,085

13. Compare: $27 \div 3^2$ $<$ $27 \div \sqrt{9}$
(72,40)

14. $97.56
(28)   + $8.49
        $106.05

15. $60.00
(51)   − $54.78
        $5.22

16.   3764
(61)   2945
          301
        + 7538
        14,548

17. 168 ÷ 3   56
(75)

18. 378 ÷ 7   54
(75)

19. 840 × 3   2520
(68)

20. 4 × 564   2256
(68)

21. 304 × 6   1824
(68)

22. 4)‾136‾   34
(75)

23. 2)‾132‾   66
(75)

24. 6)‾192‾   32
(75)

25. N × 7 = 56   8
(50)

26. 4 × N = 56   14
(74,50)

LESSON 76

Area, Part 1

a. 9000
b. 2400
c. 440
d. $0.72
e. $6.70
f. 404
Problem Solving:
  1 half dollar,
  1 quarter,
  2 nickels, and
  5 pennies

Facts Practice: 90 Division Facts (Test I in Test Masters)

Mental Math: Review.

  a. 300 × 30   **b.** 240 × 10   **c.** 11 × 4 × 10
  d. $10.00 − $9.28   **e.** $3.75 + $2.95   **f.** 467 − 63

Problem Solving: Henry has ten coins that total one dollar, but only one of the coins is a dime. What are the other nine coins?

We can find the **area** of a shape by counting the number of squares of a certain size that are needed to cover the shape. The surface within this rectangle is covered with squares that are 1 cm on each side. By counting the squares, we see that the area of the rectangle is 12 square centimeters.

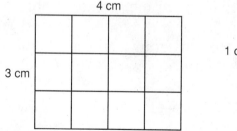

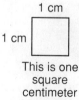

This is one square centimeter

Notice that area is not the same as perimeter. Perimeter is the measure of the distance around a shape. Area is the measure of the surface within the shape.

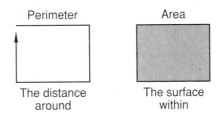

In this lesson we will practice finding areas of rectangles by counting squares.

Example   Find the perimeter and the area of this rectangle.

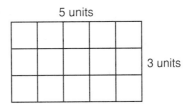

Solution   The length of the rectangle is 5 units. The width of the rectangle is 3 units. The perimeter is the distance around, so **the perimeter is 16 units.** The area is the number of square units that cover the surface within the rectangle. We count three rows of squares with five squares in each row. **The area is 15 square units.**

Practice   Find the perimeter and area of each rectangle:

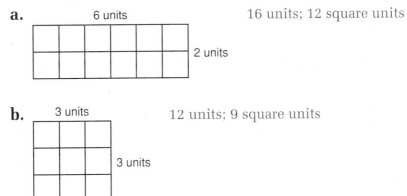

a.   6 units   16 units; 12 square units

              2 units

b.   3 units   12 units; 9 square units

       3 units

Problem set 76

1. With his bow and arrow, William Tell split 10 apples
(32) in half. How many apple halves were there?
20 apple halves

2. Every third bead on the necklace was red. There were
(62) one hundred forty-one beads in all. How many beads
were red? (Make equal groups of three.)   47 red beads

3. Twenty-five percent of this square
(71,65) is shaded. What percent of the
square is not shaded?   75%

4. Big Fox chased Little Rabbit 20 kilometers north, then
(50) 15 kilometers south. How far was Big Fox from where
he started? (Draw a diagram.)   5 km

20 km   15 km

5. At 11:45 a.m. Jason glanced at the clock. His doctor's
(33) appointment was in $2\frac{1}{2}$ hours. At what time was his
appointment?   2:15 p.m.

6. Find the perimeter and area of this rectangle.
(76) 18 units; 18 square units

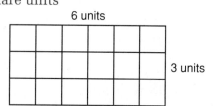

6 units

3 units

7. The car could go 30 miles on 1 gallon of gas. How far
(67) could the car go on 8 gallons of gas? Use the EG
pattern.   240 mi

8. Two sevenths of the crowd cheered wildly. The rest of
(71) the crowd stood silently. What fraction of the crowd
stood silently? $\frac{5}{7}$

9. $N + 2 = 3 \times 12$ 34
(69)

10. Forty-two glops were required to make a good glue.
(59) Jean needed nine good glues. How many glops did she
need? Use the EG pattern.   378 glops

11. Compare: $\frac{1}{2} \bigcirc \frac{2}{5}$. Draw and shade two rectangles to
(66) show the comparison.   ▭ > ▥

12. 46,278 + 148,095   194,373
(61)

13. 48 + 163 + $\sqrt{81}$ + 83 + 3425   3728
(61,40)

14. $10 − 10¢ $9.90   **15.** 43,016 − 5987   37,029
(53)   *(62)*

16. 5 × 6 × 8   240
(72)

17.   486   **18.**   307   **19.**   460
(68)   × 7   *(68)*   × 8   *(68)*   × 9
   ─────   ─────   ─────
   3402   2456   4140

          76   44   14
20. 2)152   **21.** 6)264   **22.** 4)56
(75)   *(75)*   *(74)*

23. 230 ÷ 5   46   **24.** 91 ÷ 7   13   **25.** 135 ÷ 3   45
(75)   *(74)*   *(75)*

26. Write each amount of money by using a dollar sign
(45) and decimal point:

(a) 17¢ $0.17   (b) 8¢ $0.08   (c) 345¢ $3.45

**LESSON
77**

Multiplying by Multiples of 10

a. 300
b. 10,000
c. 630
d. 250
e. $3.05
f. 543
Patterns:
  Count by fives:
    3, 8, 13, 18, 23,
    28, ...
  Final digits:
    3 and 8

Facts Practice: 90 Division Facts (Test I in Test Masters)

Mental Math: Review.

  a. 5 × 6 × 10   **b.** 500 × 20   **c.** 21 × 3 × 10

  d. 300 − 50   **e.** $5.00 − $1.95   **f.** 456 + 87

Patterns: Counting by fives from one we say this sequence:

1, 6, 11, 16, 21, 26, ...

What sequence do we say when we count by fives
from three? Which two digits appear as final digits?

We remember that the multiples of 10 are the numbers we
use when we count by tens. The last digit in every
multiple of 10 is a zero. The first five multiples of 10 are

10, 20, 30, 40, 50

To multiply a whole number by a multiple of 10, we may write the multiple of 10 so that the zero "hangs out" to the right, as we show here.

$$
\begin{array}{r}
34 \\
\times\ 20 \\
\end{array}
$$
← zero "hangs out" to the right

Next, we write a zero in the answer directly below the zero that we let hang out.

$$
\begin{array}{r}
34 \\
\times\ 20 \\
\hline
0 \\
\end{array}
$$

Then we multiply by the first digit.

$$
\begin{array}{r}
34 \\
\times\ 20 \\
\hline
680 \\
\end{array}
$$

Example 1   Multiply: 30 × 34

Solution   We set up the problem so that the multiple of 10 is the bottom number. We let the zero "hang out."

$$
\begin{array}{r}
34 \\
\times\ 30 \\
\hline
\end{array}
$$

Next, we write a zero in the answer directly below the zero in 30. Then we multiply by the first digit. Our answer is **1020.**

$$
\begin{array}{r}
1 \\
34 \\
\times\ 30 \\
\hline
1020 \\
\end{array}
$$

Example 2   Multiply: $1.43 × 20

Solution   We set up the problem so that the zero "hangs out." We write a zero below the line, and then multiply by the 2. We place the decimal point so that there are two digits after it. Finally, we write a dollar sign in front to get **$28.60.**

$$
\begin{array}{r}
\$1.43 \\
\times\ \ \ 20 \\
\hline
\$28.60 \\
\end{array}
$$

Practice   **a.** 75 × 10   750   **b.** 10 × 32   320   **c.** 10 × 53¢

                                                                    $5.30

d.   26   **e.** $1.64   **f.**   45

       × 20   ×   30   × 50

          520                          $49.20   2250

Problem set   **1.** Find the perimeter and area of this rectangle.

77   (76)   22 units; 24 square units

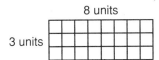

8 units

3 units

2. Seventy-five beans were equally divided into five
(62) pots. How many beans were in each pot? Use the EG
      pattern.   15 beans

3. Five thousand, seven hundred people listened to the
(31) concert. Then some went home. Three thousand,
      forty-two remained. How many people went home?
      Use the SWA pattern.   2658 people

4. James could go 7 miles on 1 sandwich. He wanted to
(70) go 84 miles. How many sandwiches did he need? Use
      the EG pattern.   12 sandwiches

5. The starting time was before dawn. The stopping time
(33) was in the afternoon. What was the difference in the
      two times?   12 hours, 5 minutes

Starting   Stopping

6. One hundred forty thousand is how much less than
(38) two hundred thousand? Use the L-S-D pattern.   60,000

7. What fraction of this pentagon is
(71) not shaded? $\frac{3}{5}$

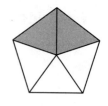

8. Is the shaded part of this pentagon
(65) more than 50% or less than 50%
of the pentagon?   less than 50%

9. According to this calendar, what
(64) is the date of the last Saturday in
July, 2019?   July 27, 2019

JULY 2019						
S	M	T	W	T	F	S
	1	2	3	4	5	6
7	8	9	10	11	12	13
14	15	16	17	18	19	20
21	22	23	24	25	26	27
28	29	30	31			

10. To what number is the arrow pointing? $7\frac{5}{13}$
(46)

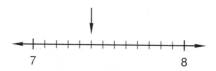

11. Estimate the product of 78 and 4 by rounding 78 to the
(70) nearest ten before multiplying by 4.   320

12. Compare: $2^3 \enclose{circle}{>} 2 \times 3$
(72,15)

13. $6.25 + $4 + $12.78 $23.03
(53)

14. 142 + 386 + 570 + 864   1962
(21)

15. $30.25   **16.**   149,384   **17.**   409
(20)   −   B $17.19 (62)   − 98,765   (77)   × 70
        $13.06   50,619   28,630

18. 5 × $3.46 $17.30   **19.** $0.79 × 6 $4.74
(68)   (68)

20. 10 × 39¢ $3.90   **21.** 6)$\overline{90}$ (15)
(77)   (74)

22. 4)$\overline{96}$ (24)   **23.** 8)$\overline{456}$ (57)
(74)   (75)

24. 95 ÷ 5   19   **25.** 234 ÷ 3   78   **26.** 364 ÷ 7   52
(74)   (75)   (75)

LESSON
78

Division with Two-Digit Answers and a Remainder

a. 240
b. 360
c. 480
d. 295
e. $8.85
f. 64¢
Problem Solving:
    1 inch longer

Facts Practice: 100 Multiplication Facts (Test H in Test Masters)

Mental Math: Multiply two-digit numbers by numbers ending in zero.

   a. 12 × 20   **b.** 12 × 30   **c.** 12 × 40

Review:

   d. 36 + 29 + 230   **e.** $4.87 + $3.98   **f.** $1.00 − 36¢

Problem Solving: Segment *AC* is how much longer than segment *AB*?

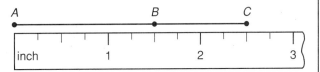

The method we use for dividing has four steps. These steps are divide, multiply, subtract, and bring down. Then we repeat the steps as necessary.

      Step 1. Divide.

      Step 2. Multiply.

      Step 3. Subtract.

      Step 4. Bring down.

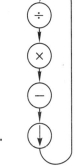

For each step we write a number. When we finish Step 4, we go back to Step 1 and repeat the steps until there are no digits left to bring down. Then whatever is left after the last subtraction is the remainder. We will continue to write the remainder after the division answer with a small "r" in front.

Example $5\overline{)137}$

Solution   **Step 1.** We divide $5\overline{)13}$ and write "2."

Step 2. We multiply 2 × 5 and write "10."

Step 3. We subtract 13 − 10 and write "3."

Step 4. We bring down 7 to make 37.

$$\begin{array}{r} 2 \\ 5\overline{)137} \\ -10\!\downarrow \\ \hline 37 \end{array}$$

Now we repeat the same four steps:

Step 1. We divide 37 by 5 and write "7."

Step 2. We multiply 7 × 5 and write "35."

Step 3. We subtract 37 − 35 and write "2."

Step 4. There are no more digits to bring down, so we are finished. We write the 2 as a remainder. Our answer is **27 r 2.**

$$\begin{array}{r} 27 \\ 5\overline{)137} \\ -10 \\ \hline 37 \\ -35 \\ \hline 2 \end{array}$$

If we divide 137 into 5 equal groups, there will be 27 in each group. There will also be 2 extra.

Practice   **a.** $3\overline{)134}$ 44 r 2   **b.** $7\overline{)240}$ 34 r 2   **c.** $5\overline{)88}$ 17 r 3

d. 259 ÷ 8 32 r 3   **e.** 95 ÷ 4 23 r 3   **f.** 325 ÷ 6 54 r 1

Problem set 78

1. Find the perimeter and area of this rectangle.
(76) 20 units; 24 square units

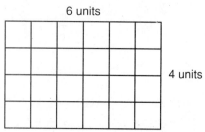

6 units

4 units

2. It took four spoonfuls to make one complete batch.
(59) How many spoonfuls were required to make 40 batches? Use the EG pattern.   160 spoonfuls

3. The first number was forty-two thousand, five
(38) hundred. The second number was eighteen thousand,
forty-two. How much greater was the first number?
Use the L-S-D pattern.   24,458

4. Olive ran $\frac{3}{5}$ of the course but walked the rest of the
(71) way. What fraction of the course did she walk? $\frac{2}{5}$

5. In problem 4, did Olive run more than 50% of the
(65) course or less than 50% of the course?   more than 50%

6. Jimmy had an octagon and a pentagon. What was the
(73) total of the number of sides in these two polygons?
13 sides

7. The arrow points to what mixed number on this
(46) number line? $7\frac{2}{5}$

8. Mount Rainier stands four thousand, three hundred
(43) ninety-two meters above sea level. Use digits to write
this number.   4,392

9. Mickey could make 35 prizes in 7 minutes. How many
(70) prizes could he make in 1 minute? Use the EG pattern.
5 prizes

10. Estimate the sum of 681 and 903 by rounding each
(70) number to the nearest hundred before adding.   1600

11. $12 + $8.95 + 75¢
(53) $21.70

12. 3627 + 5314 + 729
(61) 9670

13. $30.00 − $21.49
(51) $8.51

14. 36,157 − 29,448
(62) 6709

15.   43¢
(58)   × 8
   ———
   $3.44

16. $3.05
(68)   ×   5
   ———
   $15.25

17. $2.63
(68)   ×   7
   ———
   $18.41

18. 47 × 30 1410
(77)

19. 60 × 39 2340
(77)

20. 85 × 40 3400
(77)

21. 5)96   19 r 1
(78)

22. 7)156   22 r 2
(78)

23. 3)246   82
(75)

24. $\frac{216}{6}$ 36
(75)

25. 156 ÷ 4   39
(75)

26. 195 ÷ 8   24 r 3
(78)

LESSON 79

Millimeters

a. 420
b. 750
c. 500
d. $7.02
e. 377
f. 365
Problem Solving:
About 1000 calories

Facts Practice: 100 Multiplication Facts (Test H in Test Masters)

Mental Math: Multiply two-digit numbers by numbers ending in zero.

  a. 21 × 20   **b.** 25 × 30   **c.** 25 × 20

Review:

  d. $10.00 − $2.98   **e.** 48 + 19 + 310   **f.** 490 − 125

Problem Solving: John figures that about 50% of the calories he consumes are from carbohydrates. John consumes about 2000 calories each day. About how many of those calories are from carbohydrates?

A centimeter is this long.

———

If we divide a centimeter into 10 equal lengths, each equal length is 1 millimeter long. A dime is about 1 millimeter thick.

 ◄— 1 millimeter thick

The words *centimeter* and *millimeter* are based on Latin words. *Centum* is the Latin word for "hundred." This is why we say there are 100 cents in a dollar. The Latin word for "feet" is *pede*. A centipede looks like it has 100 feet. **There are 100 centimeters in 1 meter.**

Mille is the Latin word for "thousand." A millipede looks like it has 1000 feet. **There are 1000 millimeters in 1 meter. It takes 10 millimeters to equal 1 centimeter.**

Here we show a millimeter scale and a centimeter scale.

Millimeter

Centimeter

We use the letters "mm" to abbreviate the word *millimeter*.

Example 1   This segment is how many millimeters long?

Solution   The length of the segment is **35 mm.**

Example 2   This paper clip is 3 cm long. How many millimeters long is it?

Solution   Each centimeter is 10 mm. We multiply 3 × 10 mm and find that the length of the paper clip is **30 mm.**

Practice   **a.** The thickness of a dime is about 1 mm. How many dimes would it take to form a stack that is 1 cm high? 10 dimes

b. How long is this segment?   27 mm

c. Each side of this square is 1 cm long. What is the perimeter of this square in millimeters?   40 mm

Problem set
79

1. In the morning one hundred forty-two thousand,
(12) seven hundred fifty-three athletes came. In the
afternoon ninety-six thousand, five hundred twenty-
two athletes came. How many athletes came in all?
Use the SSM pattern.   239,275 athletes

2. Tracy has three hundred eighty-four baseball cards.
(38) Nathan has two hundred sixty baseball cards. Tracy
has how many more cards than Nathan? Use the L-S-D
pattern.   124 cards

3. Forty-two students could get on 1 bus. There were 30
(59) buses. How many students could get on all the buses?
Use the EG pattern.   1260 students

4. To what number is the arrow pointing?   260
(13)

5. Copy this hexagon and shade one
(32) sixth of it.

6. (a) This match is how many centimeters long?   4 cm
(79)
    (b) This match is how many millimeters long?   40 mm

7. Twenty-five percent of the students earned an A. What
(65) percent of the students did not earn an A?   75%

8. One yard equals 3 feet. If each side of a square is 1
(60) yard long, then what is the perimeter of the square in
feet?   12 feet

9. Estimate the sum of 412, 695, and 379 by rounding
(70) each of the three numbers to the nearest hundred
before adding.   1500

10. Segment *AB* is 35 mm long. Segment *AC* is 115 mm
(50) long. How long is segment *BC*?   80 mm

A   B   C

11. Hugo could go 125 miles in 5 hours. How many miles
(70) could Hugo go in 1 hour? Use the EG pattern.   25 mi

12. Urgo could go 21 miles in one hour. How many miles
(67) could Urgo go in 7 hours? Use the EG pattern.   147 mi

13. $96.89
(28) + $26.56
     ―――――
      $123.45

14.   *E*
(20) − 28,165   43,411
     ―――――
      15,246

15.   362
(61)   47
          159
         1484
          305
      +   60
     ―――――
         2417

16. $10.00
(51) − $1.73
     ―――――
       $8.27

17.   36,428
(62) − 27,338
     ―――――
        9090

18.   78
(77) × 60
     ―――――
      4680

19. 9 × $4.63
(68) $41.67

20. 80 × 29¢
(77) $23.20

        82
21. 4)328
(75)

        53 r 4
22. 7)375
(78)

        64
23. 5)320
(75)

24. $\frac{256}{8}$ 32
(75)

25. 250 ÷ 6
(78)   41 r 4

26. 100 ÷ 9
(78)   11 r 1

27. *A* × 5 = 25 + 25   10   **28.** 4 × *W* = 60   15
(69)   (74,50)

LESSON 80

"Fraction-of-a-Group" Problems, Part 1

a. 2500
b. 4000
c. 3600
d. 337
e. $7.50
f. $9.48
Problem Solving:
    $13.00

Facts Practice: 100 Multiplication Facts (Test H in Test Masters)

Mental Math: Multiply by 100.

  a. 25×100 **b.** 100×40 **c.** $12 \times 3 \times 100$

Review:

  d. $567 - 230$ **e.** $\$20.00 - \$12.50$ **f.** $\$6.49 + \$2.99$

Problem Solving: The charge for the taxi ride was $2.50 for the first mile and $1.50 for each additional mile. What was the charge for an 8-mile taxi ride?

We know that the fraction $\frac{1}{2}$ means that a whole has been divided into 2 parts. To find the number in $\frac{1}{2}$ of a group, we divide the total number in the group by 2. To find the number in $\frac{1}{3}$ of a group, we divide the total number in the group by 3. To find the number in $\frac{1}{4}$ of a group, we divide the total number in the group by 4.

Example 1   One half of the carrot seeds sprouted. If 84 seeds were planted, how many sprouted?

Solution   We will begin by drawing a picture. The large rectangle stands for all the seeds. We are told that $\frac{1}{2}$ of the seeds sprouted, so we divide the large rectangle into 2 parts (into halves). Then we divide 84 by 2 and find that **42 seeds sprouted.**

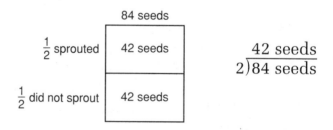

Example 2   One third of the 27 students earned an A on the test. How many students earned an A on the test?

Solution   We start with a picture. The whole rectangle stands for all of the students. Since $\frac{1}{3}$ of the students earned an A, we divide the rectangle into 3 equal parts. To find how many students are in each part, we divide 27 by 3 and find that **9 students** earned an A on the test.

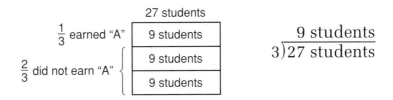

Example 3   One fourth of the team's 32 points were scored by Cliff. Cliff scored how many points?

Solution   We draw a rectangle. The whole rectangle stands for all 32 points. Cliff scored $\frac{1}{4}$ of the points, so we divide the rectangle into 4 parts. We divide 32 by 4 and find that each part is 8 points. **Cliff scored 8 points.**

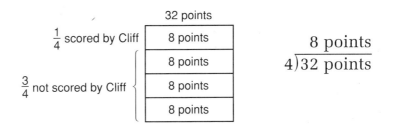

Example 4   What is $\frac{1}{5}$ of 40?

Solution   We sketch a rectangle to stand for 40. We divide the rectangle into five parts, and we divide 40 by 5. Each part is 8, so $\frac{1}{5}$ **of 40 is 8.**

$$\begin{array}{r} 8 \\ 5\overline{)40} \end{array}$$

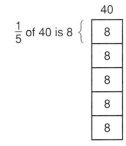

Practice   **a.** What is $\frac{1}{3}$ of 60?   20   **b.** What is $\frac{1}{2}$ of 60?   30

　　　　　c. What is $\frac{1}{4}$ of 60?   15   **d.** What is $\frac{1}{5}$ of 60?   12

Problem set
80

1. Nine hundred forty-two thousand is how much greater
(38) than two hundred forty-two thousand? Use the L-S-D
pattern.   700,000

2. There were 150 seats at the Round Table. If 128 seats
(31) were taken, how many seats were empty? Use the
SWA pattern.   22 seats

3. There were 3 surf riders for each child. How many surf
(59) riders were there for 17 children? Use the EG pattern.
51 surf riders

4. Stuart bought his lunch Monday through Friday. If
(67) each lunch cost $1.25, how much did he spend on
lunch for the week? Use the EG pattern. $6.25

5. Find the perimeter and area of this rectangle.
(76) 18 units; 20 square units

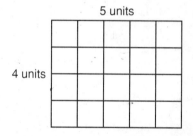

5 units

4 units

6. Rhonda read 30 pages a day on Monday, Tuesday, and
(12) Wednesday. She read 45 pages on Thursday and 26
pages on Friday. How many pages did she read in all?
161 pages

74 seeds

| 37 seeds | } ½ sprouted |
| 37 seeds | } ½ did not sprout |

7. One half of the cabbage seeds sprouted. If 74 seeds
(80) were planted, how many sprouted? Draw a picture.
37 seeds

8. In problem 7, what percent of the seeds sprouted?
(65) 50%

60
10	⅙
10	
10	
10	
10	
10	

9. What is ⅙ of 60? Draw a picture.   10
(80)

10. The machine made 39 buttons in 1 minute. How many
(67) buttons would it make in 1 hour (60 minutes)? Use the
EG pattern.   2340 buttons

11. An older machine made 160 buttons in 4 minutes.
(70) How many buttons could it make in 1 minute? Use the
EG pattern.   40 buttons

12. (a) This shirt button is how many
(79)   centimeters across?   1 cm

     (b) This shirt button is how many
     millimeters across?   10 mm

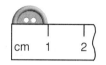

13. Segment AB is 27 mm long. Segment BC is 48 mm
(50) long. How long is segment AC?   75 mm

$$A \qquad\qquad B \qquad\qquad\qquad\qquad C$$

14. $8 + $9.48 + 79¢   **15.** 285 + 37 + 962 + 215
(53) $18.27   (21)   1499

16. $100.00   **17.**   37,102   **18.** $\sqrt{49} \times 2^3$ 56
(51) $-$ $59.47   (62) $-$ 18,590   (72,40)
      $40.53   18,512

19. $1.63 × 40   **20.** 60 × 39   **21.** 7 × $2.56
(77) $65.20   (77) 2340   (68) $17.92

        29 r 2   26 $\dfrac{90}{6}$ 15
22. 3$\overline{)89}$ **23.** 9$\overline{)234}$ **24.**
(78)   (75)   (74)

25. 243 ÷ 7   **26.** 355 ÷ 5   **27.**   7
(78) 34 r 5   (75)   71   (2)   6
                                               3
                                               4
                                               2
                                               8
                                     $+ N$ 24
                                             54

LESSON
81

a. 65
b. 72
c. 91
d. 83
Problem Solving:

   123
 $-$ 49
   74

Division Answers Ending with Zero

Facts Practice: 100 Multiplication Facts (Test H in Test Masters)

Mental Math: The sum of 38 and 17 is 55. If we make 38 larger by 2 and 17 smaller by 2, then the addition is 40 + 15. The sum is still 55, but the mental addition is easier. Before adding these numbers, make one number larger and the other number smaller so that one of the numbers ends in zero.

    a. 38 + 27   **b.** 48 + 24   **c.** 59 + 32   **d.** 57 + 26

Problem Solving: In this subtraction problem some digits are missing. Copy this problem on your paper and fill in the missing digits.

$$\begin{array}{r} 123 \\ -\ 4\_ \\ \hline \_4 \end{array}$$

Sometimes two-digit division answers have a zero in them before the division is complete. It is important to continue the division until it is completed. Look at this problem.

Two hundred pennies are separated into 4 equal piles. How many pennies are in each pile?

This problem can be answered by dividing 200 by 4. We begin by dividing 4 into 20. We put a 5 on top. Then we multiply, and then we subtract.

$$\begin{array}{r} 5 \\ 4\overline{)200} \\ 20 \\ \hline 0 \end{array}$$

It may look like the division is complete, but it is not. The answer is not "five pennies in each pile." That would total only 20 pennies. There is another zero inside the division box that we have not used. **We have not finished dividing.** So we bring down the zero and divide again. Of course, 4 goes into zero 0 times, and zero times four equals zero.

$$
\begin{array}{r}
50 \\
4\overline{)200} \\
20\downarrow \\
\hline
00 \\
0 \\
\hline
0
\end{array}
$$

The answer is 50 pennies in each pile.

Sometimes a two-digit division answer will end with a zero, yet there will be a remainder. We show this in the following example.

Example $3\overline{)121}$

Solution   We begin by dividing $3\overline{)12}$. After we subtract, we bring down the next digit, which is 1. Now we divide $3\overline{)1}$ (or $3\overline{)01}$, which means the same thing). Since 1 is less than 3, the answer is 0. We write this on top above the 1. Since 0×3 is 0, we write "0" below the 1 and subtract. The remainder is 1.

$$
\begin{array}{r}
4 \\
3\overline{)121} \\
12 \\
\hline
0
\end{array}
$$

$$
\begin{array}{r}
\mathbf{40\ r\ 1} \\
3\overline{)121} \\
12 \\
\hline
01 \\
0 \\
\hline
1
\end{array}
$$

Practice   **a.** $3\overline{)120}$ = 40   **b.** $4\overline{)240}$ = 60   **c.** $5\overline{)152}$ = 30 r 2

d. $4\overline{)121}$ = 30 r 1   **e.** $3\overline{)91}$ = 30 r 1   **f.** $2\overline{)41}$ = 20 r 1

Problem set 81

1. The first number was one hundred forty-two thousand. The second number was one hundred eight thousand. How much larger was the first number?
(38)
34,000

2. Four hundred eleven people waited to buy tickets. When the rain began, some went home. Then there were only two hundred forty-two in line. How many people went home when the rain began? 169 people
(31)

3. Each cookie contained 5 chocolate chips. How many
(59) chocolate chips would be in 115 cookies?

575 chocolate chips

4. Harry could hop 420 spaces in 7 minutes. How many
(70) spaces could he hop in 1 minute?   60 spaces

5. What is the value of 5 pennies, 3 dimes, 2 quarters,
(45) and 3 nickels? $1.00

280 students

| 70 students |
| 70 students |
| 70 students |
| 70 students |

$\frac{1}{4}$ earned an A

$\frac{3}{4}$ didn't earn an A

6. One fourth of the students earned an A. There were
(80) 280 students in all. How many students earned an A?
Draw a picture.   70 students

7. What percent of the students in problem 6 earned
(65) an A?   25%

560

| 280 |
| 280 |

$\}\frac{1}{2}$

8. What is $\frac{1}{2}$ of 560? Draw a picture.   280
(80)

9. (a) The line segment shown is how many centimeters
(79)   long?   3 cm

(b) The segment is how many millimeters long?
30 mm

10. It is evening. What time was it 6
(33) hours and 10 minutes ago?
12:07 p.m.

11. Compare: $\frac{2}{3} > \frac{2}{5}$. Draw and shade
(66) two rectangles to show the com-
parison.

12. Jenny could hop 72 spaces in 1 minute. How many
(67) spaces could she hop in 9 minutes?   648 spaces

13. *(28)* $375.48
        + $536.70
        ─────────
          $912.18

14. *(61)* 367,419
        + 90,852
        ─────────
          458,271

15. *(21)*   423
                 571
                 289
                 964
               + 380
               ─────
                2627

16. *(51)* $20.00
        − $19.39
        ─────────
          $0.61

17. *(62)* 310,419
        − 250,527
        ─────────
           59,892

18. *(68)*   608
               ×   7
               ─────
                4256

19. *(77)*   86
               × 40
               ─────
                3440

20. *(58)*   59¢
               ×   8
               ─────
                $4.72

21. *(81)* 3$\overline{)180}$ 60

22. *(81)* 8$\overline{)241}$ 30 r 1

23. *(78)* 5$\overline{)323}$ 64 r 3

24. *(81)* $184 \div 6$ 30 r 4

27. *(78)* $279 \div 4$ 69 r 3

28. *(81)* $423 \div 7$ 60 r 3

29. *(69)* $9 \times M = 27 + 72$ 11

30. *(74,50)* $N \times 6 = 90$ 15

25. *(2)*
```
  7
  6
  4
  5
  9
  4
  3
  7
+ N   11
───
 56
```

26. *(2)*
```
  8
  5
  3
  4
  7
  8
  2
  3
+ N   16
───
 56
```

LESSON 82

Finding Information to Solve Problems

a. 84
b. 92
c. 72
d. 12,000
e. $5.02
f. 597
Problem Solving:
 7 days after
 Monday:
  Monday
 71 days after
 Monday:
  Tuesday
 699 days after
 Monday:
  Sunday

Facts Practice: 100 Multiplication Facts (Test H in Test Masters)

Mental Math: Before adding, make one number larger and the other number smaller.

 a. 49 + 35   **b.** 57 + 35   **c.** 28 + 44

Review:

 d. 400 × 30   **e.** $10.00 − $4.98   **f.** 350 + 47 + 200

Problem Solving: Which day of the week is 7 days after Monday? Which day of the week is 71 days after Monday? Which day of the week is 699 days after Monday?

Part of the problem-solving process is finding the information needed to solve the problem. We may find information in graphs, tables, books, or other places. In this lesson we will practice solving problems in which we need to choose the information needed to solve the problem.

Example   Read this information. Then answer the questions.

> *The school elections were held on Friday, February 2. Kim, Dan, and Miguel ran for president. Dan received 146 votes, and Kim received 117 votes. Miguel received 35 more votes than Kim.*

(a) How many votes did Miguel receive?

(b) Who won the election?

(c) Speeches were given on the Tuesday before the election. What was the date on which the speeches were given?

Solution   (a) We read that Miguel received 35 more votes than Kim and that Kim received 117 votes. We add 35 and 117 and find that Miguel received **152 votes.**

(b) Miguel received the most votes, so the winner was **Miguel.**

(c) We read that the election was on Friday, February 2. The Tuesday before that is 3 days before that. We count back 3 days: February 1, January 31, January 30. The speeches were given on Tuesday, **January 30.**

Practice Read this information. Then answer the questions.

> *Tom did yard work on Saturday. He worked for 3 hours in the morning and 4 hours in the afternoon. He was paid $4 for every hour he worked.*

a. How many hours did Tom work in all? 7 hours

b. How much money did Tom earn in the morning? $12

c. How much money did Tom earn in all? $28

Problem set 82

1. Of the one thousand, six hundred forty-two fair
(17) maidens that Sir Lancelot rescued, only one hundred twenty-one remembered to thank him. How many did not thank Sir Lancelot? 1521 fair maidens

2. Christie's car travels 18 miles on each gallon of gas.
(67) How far can it travel on 10 gallons of gas? 180 miles

3. Humpty Dumpty weighed 160 pounds. If Humpty
(81) Dumpty broke into 8 equal pieces, how much did each piece weigh? 20 pounds

4. Soccer practice lasts for an hour and a half. If practice
(33) starts at 3:15 p.m., at what time does it end? 4:45 p.m.

5. One third of the team's 36 points were scored by Lucy.
(80) How many points were scored by Lucy? Draw a picture. 12 points

```
36 points
┌─────────┐
│12 points│ ⎫ 1
├─────────┤ ⎬ ─ scored
│12 points│ ⎭ 3 by Lucy
├─────────┤ ⎫ 2
│12 points│ ⎬ ─ not scored
└─────────┘ ⎭ 3 by Lucy
```

6. Find the perimeter and area of this rectangle.
(76) 14 units; 12 square units

4 units

3 units

7. A dime is about 1 millimeter thick. A roll of 50 dimes
(79) is about how many centimeters long?   5 cm

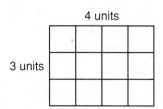

$5   DIMES $5

mm 10   20   30   40   50

8. According to this calendar, the
(64) year 1902 began on what day of
the week?   Wednesday

DECEMBER 1901						
S	M	T	W	T	F	S
1	2	3	4	5	6	7
8	9	10	11	12	13	14
15	16	17	18	19	20	21
22	23	24	25	26	27	28
29	30	31				

9. The chance of rain is 30%. What
(65) is the chance that it will not rain?
70%

10. A meter equals 100 centimeters. If each side of a
(60) square is 1 meter, then what is the perimeter of the
square in centimeters?   400 cm

11. $1.68 + 32¢ + $6.37 + $5 $13.37
(53)

12. 43 + 24 + 8 + 67 + 4327   4469
(61)

13. $10 − $8.63 $1.37   **14.** 361,420 − 23,169
(51)   (62)   338,251

15. 5 × 4 × 5   **16.** 359 × 70   **17.** 50 × 74
(72) 100   (77) 25,130   (77) 3700

18. 2)161   80 r 1   **19.** 5)400   80   **20.** 9)462   51 r 3
(81)   (81)   (78)

21. $\frac{216}{3}$ 72   **22.** 159 ÷ 4   **23.** $\frac{490}{7}$ 70
(75)   (78)   39 r 3   (81)

24. $\dfrac{126}{3}$ 42
₍₇₅₎

25. $360 \div \sqrt{36}$ 60
_(81,40)

26. $5 \times N = 120$ 24
_(75,50)

27.
₍₂₀₎
$$\begin{array}{r} 473 \\ - N \\ \hline 274 \end{array}$$ 199

28.
₍₂₎
$$\begin{array}{r} 9 \\ 5 \\ 6 \\ 4 \\ 7 \\ 8 \\ 5 \\ 7 \\ + N \\ \hline 64 \end{array}$$ 13

29.
₍₂₎
$$\begin{array}{r} 4 \\ 3 \\ 7 \\ 6 \\ 8 \\ 2 \\ 9 \\ 1 \\ + N \\ \hline 64 \end{array}$$ 24

30.
₍₂₀₎
$$\begin{array}{r} N \\ - 437 \\ \hline 943 \end{array}$$ 1380

LESSON 83

Measuring Liquids

a. 102
b. 72
c. 491
d. $8.20
e. 450
f. $0.62
Patterns:
  Count by fives:
    4, 9, 14, 19, 24,
    29, ...
  Final digits:
    4 and 9

Facts Practice: 64 Multiplication Facts (Test G in Test Masters)

Mental Math: Before adding, make one number larger and the other number smaller.

  a. 55 + 47   **b.** 24 + 48   **c.** 458 + 33

Review:

  d. $6.25 + $1.95   **e.** 15 × 30   **f.** $1.00 − $0.38

Patterns: Counting by fives from one we say this sequence:

  1, 6, 11, 16, 21, 26, ...

  What sequence do we say when we count by fives from four? Which two digits appear as final digits?

Liquids like paint, milk, juice, and soda pop are measured in **liquid units. Ounces, pints, quarts,** and **gallons** are liquid units in the U.S. system. **Liters** and **milliliters** are liquid units in the metric system.

1 gallon

$\frac{1}{2}$ gallon

1 quart

2 liters

A liter is about the same amount as a quart.

The abbreviations for units of liquid measure are as follows:

oz	ounce	L	liter
pt	pint	mL	milliliter
qt	quart		
gal	gallon		

The chart below shows the number of units needed to equal the next larger unit.

Units of Liquid Measure

U.S. Units	Metric Units
16 oz = 1 pt 2 pt = 1 qt 4 qt = 1 gal	1000 mL = 1 L

Example 1 Two liters of water is how many milliliters?

Solution From the chart we see that 1 liter is 1000 milliliters. Two liters would be twice as much. Thus, 2 liters of water equals **2000 milliliters of water.**

Example 2 A half gallon of milk is how many quarts?

Solution One gallon of milk is 4 quarts. So a half gallon is half of 4 quarts. Since half of 4 is 2, a half gallon of milk is **2 quarts of milk.**

Practice **a.** A quart is a "quarter" of a gallon. How many "quarters" make a whole?   4

b. Two pints equals a quart. How many ounces are in 2 pints?   32 oz

c. Three liters is how many milliliters?   3000 mL

Choose the most reasonable measure:

d. Would a glass of chocolate milk be about 8 oz or 8 qt?   8 oz

e. Would a can of pop be about 350 mL or 350 L?   350 mL

Problem set 83

Use this information to answer questions 1–3:

Thirty students are going on a field trip. Each car can hold five students. The field trip will cost each student $5.

1. How many cars are needed for the field trip?   6 cars
(82)

2. Altogether, how much money will be collected? $150
(82)

3. Don has saved $3.25. How much more does he need to go on the field trip? $1.75
(82)

4. During the summer the swim team practiced $3\frac{1}{2}$ hours a day. If practice started at 6:30 a.m., at what time did it end?   10:00 a.m.
(33)

5. Half of the 48 pencils were sharpened. How many were not sharpened? What percent of the pencils were not sharpened?   24 pencils; 50%
(80,65)

60	
15	$\frac{1}{4}$
15	
15	
15	

6. What number is $\frac{1}{4}$ of 60? Draw a picture.   15
(80)

7. One gallon of water will be poured into 1-quart bottles. How many 1-quart bottles can be filled?   4 one-quart bottles
(83)

1 gal   1 qt

8. Each side of a regular polygon has the same length.
(79) This is a regular hexagon. How many **millimeters** is the perimeter of this hexagon?   60 mm

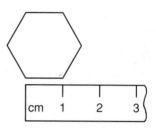

9. A mile is five thousand, two hundred eighty feet. The
(38) Golden Gate Bridge is four thousand, two hundred feet long. The Golden Gate Bridge is how many feet less than 1 mile long?   1080 ft

10. Estimate the product of 394 and 5 by rounding 394 to
(70) the nearest hundred before multiplying.   2000

11. What number is halfway between 300 and 400?
(13) (*Hint:* Use a number line.)   350

12.
(20)
$$\begin{array}{r} Z \quad 801 \\ -\ 476 \\ \hline 325 \end{array}$$

13.
(61)
$$\begin{array}{r} 37{,}156 \\ +\ 214{,}390 \\ \hline 251{,}546 \end{array}$$

14.
(61)
$$\begin{array}{r} 1534 \\ 367 \\ 29 \\ 6 \\ +\ 142 \\ \hline 2078 \end{array}$$

15.
(51)
$$\begin{array}{r} \$100.00 \\ -\ \$31.53 \\ \hline \$68.47 \end{array}$$

16.
(62)
$$\begin{array}{r} 251{,}546 \\ -\ 37{,}156 \\ \hline 214{,}390 \end{array}$$

17.
(68)
$$\begin{array}{r} 346 \\ \times\ 7 \\ \hline 2422 \end{array}$$

18.
(77)
$$\begin{array}{r} 96 \\ \times\ 30 \\ \hline 2880 \end{array}$$

19.
(68)
$$\begin{array}{r} \$0.59 \\ \times\ 8 \\ \hline \$4.72 \end{array}$$

20. $7\overline{)633}$ 90 r 3
(81)

21. $5\overline{)98}$ 19 r 3
(78)

22. $3\overline{)150}$ 50
(81)

23. 329 ÷ 6
(78)   54 r 5

24. 274 ÷ 4
(78)   68 r 2

25. 247 ÷ 8
(81)   30 r 7

26. $A \times 6 = 12 + 6$ 3
(69)

27.
(2)
```
  7
  5
  6
  4
  9
  3
  2
+ N   18
─────
 54
```

28.
(2)
```
  5
  2
  7
  9
  6
  4
  8
+ N   20
─────
 61
```

29. $\sqrt{25} \times M = 135$ 27
(75,50)

30.
(30)
```
    N   195
+ 423
─────
  618
```

LESSON
84

a. 91
b. 47
c. 3500
d. $0.64
e. $7.37
f. 1200
Problem Solving:
  $1\frac{1}{2}$ in.

Fraction of a Set

Facts Practice: 64 Multiplication Facts (Test G in Test Masters)

Mental Math: Review.

  a. 77 + 14   **b.** 87 − 40   **c.** 35 × 100

  d. $5.00 − $4.36   **e.** $4.38 + $2.99   **f.** 120 × 10

Problem Solving: Segment *AC* is how much longer than segment *AB*?

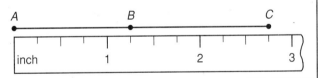

There are seven circles in the set below. Three of the circles are shaded. The fraction of the set that is shaded is $\frac{3}{7}$.

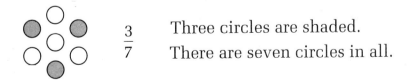

$\frac{3}{7}$ Three circles are shaded.

There are seven circles in all.

The number of members in the set is the bottom number (denominator) of the fraction. The number of members named is the top number (numerator) of the fraction.

Example 1   What fraction of the triangles is not shaded?

Solution   There are 9 triangles in all (denominator). There are 5 triangles that are not shaded (numerator). The fraction not shaded is $\frac{5}{9}$.

Example 2   In a class of 25 students, there are 12 girls and 13 boys. What fraction of the class is girls?

Solution   The total number of members in the class is 25 (denominator). The number of girls is 12 (numerator). The fraction of the class that is girls is $\frac{12}{25}$.

Practice   a. What fraction of the set is shaded? $\frac{5}{12}$

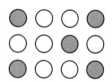

b. What fraction of the set is not shaded? $\frac{6}{7}$

c. In a class of 27 students, there are 14 girls and 13 boys. What fraction of the class is boys? $\frac{13}{27}$

d. What fraction of the letters in the word ALABAMA is made up of A's? $\frac{4}{7}$

Problem set 84

1. Michael caught sixty-two crawfish in the creek. James
(12) caught seven crawfish, and Julie and John each caught twelve crawfish. Altogether, how many crawfish did these young people catch?   93 crawfish

2. The Matterhorn is fourteen thousand, six hundred
(38) ninety-two feet high. Mont Blanc is fifteen thousand, seven hundred eighty-one feet high. How much taller is Mont Blanc than the Matterhorn?   1089 feet

3. There are 25 squares on a bingo card. How many
(59) squares are there on 4 bingo cards? 100 squares

4. Ninety-six books were placed on 4
(80) shelves so that there were the same number of books on each shelf. How many books were on each shelf? 24 books

96 books

5. One half of the 780 fans stood and cheered. How many
(65) fans stood and cheered? What percent of the fans stood and cheered? 390 fans; 50%

6. How many years is ten centuries? 1000 years
(64)

7. What fraction of this set is not
(84) shaded? $\frac{4}{7}$

8. The 2-liter bottle contains how
(83) many milliliters of beverage?
2000 mL

9. Estimate the sum of 493 and 387.
(70) 900

10. What is the perimeter of this
(60) rectangle? 20 in.

6 in.

4 in.

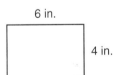

11. If this rectangle were to be cov-
(76) ered with squares with sides one inch long, how many squares would be needed? 24 squares

12. $6.15 − ($0.57 + $1.20) $4.38
(55)

13. 3746 + 2357 + 489 6592
(61)

14. 462 − Y = 205 257
(20)

15. 43,160 − 8,459 34,701
(62)

16. 8 × 8 × 8 512
(72)

17. $3.54 × 6 $21.24
(68)

18. 80×57 4560
(77)

19. 704×9 6336
(68)

20. $9\overline{)354}$ $\overset{39 \text{ r } 3}{}$
(78)

21. $7\overline{)285}$ 40 r 5
(81)

22. $5\overline{)439}$ $\overset{87 \text{ r } 4}{}$
(78)

23. $515 \div 6$ 85 r 5
(78)

24. $\dfrac{360}{4}$ 90
(81)

25. $784 \div 8$ 98
(75)

26. $50 = 5 \times R$ 10
(50)

27.
(2)

4
7
8
5
7
6
4
3
+ N 12
56

28. $6^2 - \sqrt{36}$ 30
(40)

29.
(30)

$$\begin{array}{r} 476 \\ + \ N \quad 256 \\ \hline 732 \end{array}$$

30.
(20)

$$\begin{array}{r} N \quad 852 \\ - \ 214 \\ \hline 638 \end{array}$$

LESSON 85

Pictographs and Bar Graphs • Tallying

a. 85
b. 91
c. 182
d. 24,000
e. $7.50
f. $8.44
Problem Solving:
  53¢

Facts Practice: 64 Multiplication Facts (Test G in Test Masters)

Mental Math: Before adding, make one number larger and the other number smaller.

  a. $48 + 37$ **b.** $62 + 29$ **c.** $135 + 47$

Review:

  d. $30 \times 40 \times 20$ **e.** $\$20.00 - \$12.50$ **f.** $\$6.46 + \$1.98$

Problem Solving: Robby is mailing an envelope that weighs 6 ounces. Postage costs 32¢ for the first ounce and 23¢ for each additional ounce. Robby pays the postal clerk $2.00 for postage. How much money should he get back?

A **graph** is a picture that shows number information about the topic of the graph. There are many types of graphs. In this lesson we will look at **pictographs** and **bar graphs**.

Example 1   James made a pictograph to show the number of gummy bears of a certain color that he found in one package. According to this graph, what was the total number of yellow and green gummy bears in the package?

Gummy Bears in One Package

Solution   From the pictograph we can count the number of gummy bears of each color. There were 4 yellow gummy bears and 9 green gummy bears. To find the total of yellow and green gummy bears, we add 4 and 9 to get **13 yellow and green gummy bears.**

Example 2   This bar graph shows the same information as the pictograph, but in a different form. Use the bar graph to answer each question.

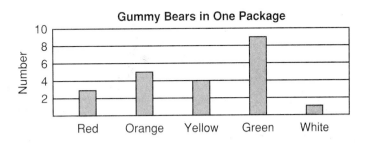

Gummy Bears in One Package

(a) How many red gummy bears were there?

(b) How many more gummy bears were green than were orange?

Solution   (a) The top of the bar showing the number of red gummy bears is halfway between 2 and 4 on the scale. So there were **3 red gummy bears.**

(b) There were 9 green gummy bears and 5 orange gummy bears. By subtracting, we find there were **4 more green gummy bears** than orange gummy bears.

Tallying   Tallying is a way of keeping track of a count. A tally mark is a short vertical mark that counts as one. Two marks count as two. Four marks with a diagonal line crossing them count as five.

| | || ||| |||| ⊬⊬ ⊬⊬ |
| one | two | three | four | five | six |

Practice   Use the information in the graphs from this lesson to answer questions a–c:

a. How many gummy bears were in the package?
22 gummy bears

b. The total of which two colors of gummy bears equals the number of green gummy bears?
orange and yellow gummy bears

c. The total of which three colors of gummy bears equals the number of green gummy bears?
red, orange, and white gummy bears

d. What number is represented by this tally?   ⊬⊬ ⊬⊬ ||
12

Problem set 85

1. Pears cost 59¢ per pound. How much would 4 pounds of pears cost? $2.36
(59)

2. Find the perimeter and area of this rectangle.
(76)   20 units; 24 square units

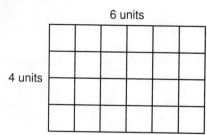

6 units

4 units

3. There were three hundred twelve books on the floor. Frankie put one fourth of the books on a table. How many books did Frankie put on the table?   78 books
(80)

4. What percent of the books in problem 3 were left on
$^{(65)}$ the floor? 75%

5. To what number is the arrow pointing? $201\frac{1}{9}$
$^{(46)}$

6. Estimate the sum of 272 and 483. Begin by rounding
$^{(70)}$ both numbers to the nearest hundred. 800

7. What fraction of this set is
$^{(84)}$ shaded? $\frac{4}{9}$

8. One quart of milk is how many
$^{(83)}$ ounces? 32 oz

9. One quart is a quarter of a gallon. So one quart is what
$^{(65)}$ percent of a gallon? 25%

Use the information in this bar graph to answer questions
10 and 11:

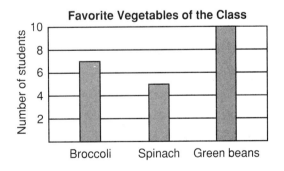

10. Spinach was the favorite vegetable of how many
$^{(85)}$ students? 5 students

11. Altogether, how many students said broccoli or
$^{(85)}$ spinach was their favorite vegetable? 12 students

12. *(28)*

$86.47
+ $47.98
$134.45

13. *(61)*

362,458
+ 179,682
542,140

14. *(61)*

2358
4715
317
2103
+ 62
9555

15. *(62)*

17,362
− 9,854
7508

16. *(20)*

N $39.02
− $17.53
$21.49

17. *(68)*

$6.95
× 8
$55.60

18. *(77)*

46
× 70
3220

19. *(68)*

460
× 9
4140

20. *(78)* 8)716   89 r 4

21. *(81)* 2)161   80 r 1

22. *(75)* 7)434   62

23. *(81)* $\dfrac{270}{9}$ 30

24. *(78)* 513 ÷ 6   85 r 3

25. *(75)* $\dfrac{267}{3}$ 89

26. *(69)* 3 × A = 30 + 30   20

27. *(72)* $3^2 - 2^3$ 1

28. *(2)* 4 + 7 + 3 + 5 + 6 + 5 + 7 + 2 + N = 43   4

**LESSON
86**

Division with Three-Digit Answers

a. 6
b. 29
c. 15
d. 47

Facts Practice: 64 Multiplication Facts (Test G in Test Masters)

Mental Math: Subtracting two-digit numbers is easier to do mentally if the second number ends in zero. By making both subtraction numbers larger, we can sometimes make subtraction easier while keeping the difference the same.

$$\text{Instead of subtracting} \quad \begin{array}{r} 45 \\ -\ 28 \\ \hline \end{array} \quad \text{we subtract} \quad \begin{array}{r} 47 \\ -\ 30 \\ \hline \end{array}$$

We added 2 to 28 so that the second number would end in zero. Then we added 2 to 45 to keep the difference the same.

a. $\begin{array}{r} 45 \\ -\ 39 \\ \hline \end{array}$	**b.** $\begin{array}{r} 56 \\ -\ 27 \\ \hline \end{array}$	**c.** $\begin{array}{r} 63 \\ -\ 48 \\ \hline \end{array}$	**d.** $\begin{array}{r} 82 \\ -\ 35 \\ \hline \end{array}$

We have practiced division problems that have two-digit answers. In this lesson we will practice division problems that have three-digit answers.

We remember that the method we use for dividing has four steps.

Step 1. Divide. $\div$

Step 2. Multiply. $\times$

Step 3. Subtract. $-$

Step 4. Bring down. $\downarrow$

For each step we write a number. When we finish Step 4, we go back to Step 1 and repeat the steps until there are no digits left to bring down.

Example 1 3)794

Solution **Step 1.** Divide 3)7 and write "2."

Step 2. Multiply 2 × 3 and write "6."

Step 3. Subtract 6 from 7 and write "1."

Step 4. Bring down the 9, making 19.

REPEAT:

Step 1. Divide 3)19 and write "6."

Step 2. Multiply 6 × 3 and write "18."

Step 3. Subtract 18 from 19 and write "1."

Step 4. Bring down the 4, making 14.

REPEAT:

Step 1. Divide 3)14 and write "4."

Step 2. Multiply 4 × 3 and write "12."

Step 3. Subtract 12 from 14 and write "2."

Step 4. There are no digits to bring down. We are finished dividing. We write "2" as a remainder for a final answer of **264 r 2.**

$$
\begin{array}{r}
264 \text{ r } 2 \\
3\overline{)794} \\
6 \\
\overline{19} \\
18 \\
\overline{14} \\
12 \\
\overline{2}
\end{array}
$$

To divide dollars and cents by a whole number, we divide the digits just like we divide whole numbers. **The decimal point in the answer is placed directly above the decimal point inside the division box.** We write the dollar sign in front of the answer.

Example 2 $8.40 ÷ 3

Solution We put a decimal point in the answer directly above the decimal point in the problem. Then we divide. We put a dollar sign in front of the answer.

$$
\begin{array}{r}
\$2.80 \\
3\overline{)\$8.40} \\
6 \\
\overline{2\ 4} \\
2\ 4 \\
\overline{00} \\
00 \\
\overline{0}
\end{array}
$$

Practice **a.** Copy this diagram and name the four steps of division.
divide, multiply, subtract, bring down

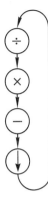

b. 4)974   243 r 2   **c.** $7.95 ÷ 5 $1.59

       252                      $6.25
d. 6)1512   **e.** 8)$50.00

Problem set 86

1. Seven thousand, three hundred ninety-six is how
(38) much less than eleven thousand, eight hundred
seventy-three?   4477

2. Shannon has five days to read a 200-page book. If she
(62) wants to read the same number of pages each day, how
many pages should she read each day?   40 pages

3. Julie ordered a book for $2.99, a dictionary for $3.99,
(12) and a set of maps for $4.99. What was the price for all
three items? $11.97

4. The prince searched 7 weeks for the princess. For how
(59) many days did he search?   49 days

5. One third of the books were placed on the first shelf.
(71) What fraction of the books were not placed on the first
shelf? $\frac{2}{3}$

6. What number is halfway between 2000 and 3000?
(13) (*Hint:* Use a number line.)   2500

7. In the word HIPPOPOTAMI, what fraction of the
(84) letters is made up of P's? $\frac{3}{11}$

8. Mary ran a 5-kilometer race. Five kilometers is how
(27) many meters?   5000 m

9. 12 + 13 + 5 + N = 9 × 8   42
(69)

10. What is the perimeter of this
(60) triangle? 60 mm

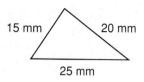

11. The length of segment *AB* is 36 mm. The length of
(50) segment *AC* is 118 mm. What is the length of
segment *BC*? 82 mm

12. $25 − ($19.71 + 98¢)   **13.** $365 + 10^2 + 3^3$ 492
(55) $4.31   *(72)*

14. $5.00 − $2.92 $2.08   **15.** 36,214 − 579 35,635
(51)   *(62)*

16. 5 × 6 × 9   **17.** 50 × 63   **18.** 478 × 6
(72) 270   *(77)* 3150   *(68)* 2868

19. 3)‾435‾ 145   **20.** 7)‾867‾ 123 r 6   **21.** 5)‾$13.65‾ $2.73
(86)   *(86)*   *(86)*

22. 453 ÷ 6   **23.** 543 ÷ 4   **24.** $4.72 ÷ 8
(78) 75 r 3   *(86)* 135 r 3   *(86)* $0.59

25. $N × 6 = 120$ 20   **26.** $4 × W = 132$ 33
(50)   *(50)*

27. $4 + 8 + 7 + 6 + 4 + N + 3 + 6 + 5 = 55$ 12
(2)

28. Find the perimeter and area of this rectangle.
(76)   16 units; 15 square units

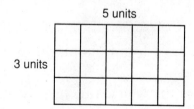

LESSON 87

Ounces, Pounds, and Tons

a. 35
b. 28
c. 34
d. 82
e. 2400
f. $4.15
Patterns:
  From two:
    2 or 7
  From three:
    3 or 8
  From four:
    4 or 9

Facts Practice: 64 Multiplication Facts (Test G in Test Masters)

Mental Math: Find each difference by first enlarging both numbers so that the second number ends in zero.

  a. 63 − 28   **b.** 45 − 17   **c.** 80 − 46

Review:

  d. 48 + 34   **e.** 24 × 100   **f.** $10.00 − $5.85

Patterns: When we count by fives from five, the numbers end with 0 or 5. When we count by fives from one, the numbers end with 1 or 6. When we count by fives from two, from three, and from four, how do the numbers end?

In Lesson 83 we used the word *ounce* to describe an amount of liquid. The word *ounce* can also describe an amount of weight. A liquid ounce of water weighs about one weight ounce. The units of weight of the U.S. system are **ounces, pounds,** and **tons.** A ton equals 2000 pounds. *Ounce* is abbreviated **oz.** *Pound* is abbreviated **lb.**

$$\boxed{\begin{array}{l} 16 \text{ oz } = 1 \text{ lb} \\ 2000 \text{ lb } = 1 \text{ ton} \end{array}}$$

Some boxes of cereal weigh 24 ounces. Some boys weigh 98 pounds. Some cars weigh 1 ton.

24 ounces

98 pounds

1 ton

Example 1   This book weighs about 2 pounds. Two pounds is how many ounces?

Solution   Each pound is 16 ounces, so 2 pounds is 2 × 16 ounces, which is **32 ounces.**

Example 2   The rhinoceros weighed 3 tons. Three tons is how many pounds?

Solution   Each ton is 2000 pounds, so 3 tons is 3 × 2000 pounds, which is **6000 pounds.**

Problem set 87   Use the information in this pictograph to answer questions 1–3:

Consumed by Matt in One Day

Water   🥤🥤🥤🥤🥤🥤

Soda   🥤

Milk   🥤🥤🥤🥤

Juice   🥤🥤🥤

🥤 = 1 cup = 8 ounces

1. How many pints of liquid did Matt drink in 1 day?
(85)   7 pints

2. Matt drank twice as much water as he did what other
(85) beverage?   juice

3. Of which beverage did he drink exactly 1 quart?   milk
(85)

4. There were 4 rooms. One fourth of the 56 guests
(80,65) gathered in each room. How many guests were in each room? What percent of the guests were in each room?
14 guests; 25%

5. Which of these arrows could be pointing to 2500?   B
(13)

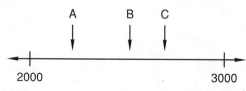

6. Estimate the sum of 682, 437, and 396.   1500
(70)

7. What fraction of this set is
(84) shaded? $\frac{1}{7}$

8. McGillicuddy weighed 9 pounds
(87) when he was born. How many
ounces is that?   144 oz

9. (a) The segment is how many centimeters long?   4 cm
(79) (b) The segment is how many millimeters long?
         40 mm

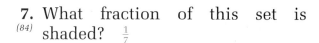

10. Four hundred forty-two thousand is how much greater
(38) than three hundred thousand?   142,000

11. If each side of a hexagon is 1 foot long, how many
(73) inches is its perimeter?   72 in.

12.   93,417   **13.**   42,718   **14.**   1307
(61)   + 8,915   *(20)*   −   K 16,664 *(61)*   638
    102,332   26,054   5219
                                     138

15. $100.00   **16.**   405,158   +   16
(51)   − $86.32   *(62)*   − 396,370   7318
     $13.68   8788

17. 567 × 8   **18.** 30 × 84¢   **19.** $2.08 × 4
(68) 4536   *(77)* $25.20   *(68)* $8.32

20. 4)$15.00   **21.** $\frac{936}{6}$ 156   **22.** 8)4537
(86) $3.75   *(86)*   *(86)* 567 r 1

23. 452 ÷ 5   **24.** 378 ÷ 9   **25.** 960 ÷ 7
(81) 90 r 2   *(75)*   42   *(86)* 137 r 1

26. $\sqrt{16} \times N = 100$ 25   **27.** $5 \times B = 10^2$ 20
(50)   *(50)*

28.
(2)

$$\begin{array}{r} 4 \\ 7 \\ 3 \\ 5 \\ 4 \\ 8 \\ + N \quad 14 \\ \hline 45 \end{array}$$

29.
(20)

$$\begin{array}{r} N \quad 677 \\ - 463 \\ \hline 214 \end{array}$$

30.
(20)

$$\begin{array}{r} 756 \\ - N \quad 294 \\ \hline 462 \end{array}$$

LESSON 88

Grams and Kilograms

a. 14
b. 23
c. 48
d. 95
e. 480
f. $8.47
Problem Solving:
12 months after May:
  May
121 months after May:
  June
1199 months after May:
  April

Facts Practice: 90 Division Facts (Test I in Test Masters)

Mental Math: Find each difference by first enlarging both numbers so that the second number ends in zero.

  a. 72 − 58   **b.** 60 − 37   **c.** 83 − 35

Review:

  d. 76 + 19   **e.** 24 × 20   **f.** $6.98 + $1.49

Problem Solving: Which month is 12 months after May? Which month is 121 months after May? Which month is 1199 months after May?

Grams and kilograms are metric units of weight.[†] Recall that the prefix *kilo-* means "1000." Thus, a kilogram is 1000 grams.

$$1000 \text{ grams} = 1 \text{ kilogram}$$

This book weighs about 1 kilogram, so one of these pages weighs more than a gram. A dollar bill weighs about 1 gram. *Gram* is abbreviated **g**. *Kilogram* is abbreviated **kg**.

[†]There is a technical difference between the terms *weight* and *mass* that will be clarified in other coursework. In this book, we will use the word *weight* to include the meaning of both terms.

Example 1 Choose the more sensible measure:

(a) A pair of shoes (b) A chicken   (c) A quarter

    1 g   1 kg   3 g   3 kg   5 g   5 kg

Solution (a) **1 kg**   (b) **3 kg**   (c) **5 g**

Example 2 Jason's rabbit weighs 4 kilograms. Four kilograms is how many grams?

Solution Each kilogram is 1000 grams. Four kilograms is 4 × 1000 grams, which is **4000 grams.**

Practice Choose the more sensible measure in these problems:

  a. Tennis ball   **b.** Cat   **c.** Bowling ball

    57 g   57 kg   6 g   6 kg   7 g   7 kg

    57 g   6 kg   7 kg

  d. Seven kilograms is how many grams? 7000 g

Problem set 88

1. Katie hit the ball seven hundred forty-two times on
(12) Monday, two hundred sixty-seven times on Tuesday, and eight hundred forty-seven times on Wednesday. How many times did she hit the ball in the 3 days?
1856 times

2. Mickey bought apples at 5 cents per pound at the sale.
(62) She spent 95 cents. How many pounds of apples did she buy? 19 lb

3. Bill placed 243 paint cans on the shelf. Ninety-five
(31) cans fell off during the earthquake. How many paint cans stayed on the shelf? 148 paint cans

4. Pamela listened to half of a 90-minute tape. How
(80) many minutes of the tape did she hear? 45 minutes

5. One fourth of the guests gathered in the living room.
(71,65) What fraction of the guests did not gather in the living room? What percent of the guests did not gather in the living room? $\frac{3}{4}$; 75%

6. Which of these arrows could be pointing to 2750?   C
(13)

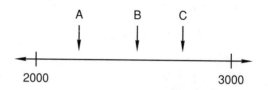

7. Half of a gallon is a half gallon. Half of a half gallon is
(83) a quart. Half of a quart is a pint. Half of a pint is a cup.
A cup is what fraction of a quart? $\frac{1}{4}$

8. Debbie weighed 3 kilograms when she was born. How
(88) many grams is that?   3000 g

9. Estimate the product of 396 and 7.   2800
(70)

10. It is afternoon. What time was it
(33) 12 hours ago?   4:56 a.m.

11. Compare: $\frac{3}{4}$ ◯ $\frac{4}{5}$. Draw and shade
(66) two rectangles to show the
comparison.   ▨ < ▨

12. 4329 + 157 + (6385 − 9)   10,862
(55)

13. $17.54 + 49¢ + $15 $33.03
(53)

14. 36,147 − 16,280   19,867
(62)

15. $50.00 − $42.60 $7.40
(51)

16. 2)567   283 r 1
(86)

17. 6)$34.56 $5.76
(86)

18. 4)978   244 r 2
(86)

19. 398 × 6   2388
(68)

20. 47 × 60   2820
(77)

21. 8 × $6.25 $50.00
(68)

22. 970 ÷ $\sqrt{25}$ 194
(86)

23. $\frac{372}{3}$ 124
(86)

24. 491 ÷ 7   70 r 1
(81)

25. 8 × N = 120   15
(50)

26. F × 3^2 = 108   12
(50)

27. $7 + 8 + 5 + 4 + N + 2 + 7 + 3 = 54$ 18
(2)

28. Find the perimeter and area of this rectangle.
(76)   24 units; 32 square units

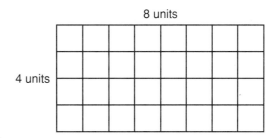

8 units

4 units

LESSON
89

Tables

a. 84
b. 91
c. 72
d. 15,000
e. $1.85
Problem Solving:
  Segment *AB*:
    $1\frac{1}{2}$ inch
  Segment *BC*:
    1 inch
  How much longer:
    $\frac{1}{2}$ inch

Facts Practice: 90 Division Facts (Test I in Test Masters)

Mental Math: Before adding, make one number larger and the other number smaller.

  a. 38 + 46   **b.** 67 + 24   **c.** 44 + 28

Review:

  d. $30 \times 50 \times 10$ **e.** $5.00 − $3.15

Problem Solving: How long is segment *AB*? How long is segment *BC*? Segment *AB* is how much longer than segment *BC*?

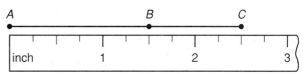

We have studied graphs that present number information in picture form. Another way of presenting number information is in a **table**.

Example   Use the information in the table to answer these questions.

Heights of Major Mountains

MOUNTAIN	FEET	METERS
Everest	29,028	8848
McKinley	20,320	6194
Kilimanjaro	19,340	5895
Matterhorn	14,691	4478
Pike's Peak	14,110	4301
Fuji	12,389	3776

(a) The Matterhorn is how many meters taller than Pike's Peak?

(b) Mount McKinley is how many feet taller than Mount Kilimanjaro?

Solution   We compare the heights by subtracting.

(a) We use the numbers from the meters column.

Matterhorn	4478 m
Pike's Peak	− 4301 m
	177 m

(b) We use the numbers from the feet column.

McKinley	20,320 ft
Kilimanjaro	− 19,340 ft
	980 ft

Practice   Use the information from the table given in the example to answer these questions:

a. Mount Kilimanjaro is how many meters taller than Mount Fuji?   2119 m

b. Mount Everest is how many feet taller than the Matterhorn?   14,337 ft

Problem set 89 Use the information in this table to answer questions 1–4:

Average Yearly Rainfall

CITY	RAINFALL IN INCHES
Boston	43
Chicago	35
Denver	16
Houston	49
San Francisco	20

1. Which cities listed in the table average less than 2 feet
(89) of rain per year?   Denver and San Francisco

2. One year Houston received 62 inches of rain. This was
(89) how much more than its yearly average?   13 in.

3. About how many inches of rain would Denver receive
(89) in 3 average years?   48 in.

4. Copy and finish this bar graph to show the
(85) information in the rainfall table:

Average Yearly Rainfall

5. One fifth of the 60 eggs were
(80) placed in each box. How many
eggs were placed in each box?
12 eggs

60 eggs

6. Which of these arrows could be pointing to 2250?   A
(13)

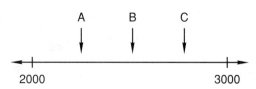

7. Estimate the sum of 427, 533, and 764 by rounding
(70) each number to the nearest hundred before adding.
1700

8. What fraction of this set is not
(84) shaded? $\frac{7}{10}$

9. Forty-two   oranges   could   be
(59) shipped in one box. Luther had 30
boxes. How many oranges could
he ship?   1260 oranges

10. Only 5 apples would fit in one small box. If Roger had
(62) 145 apples, how many boxes did he need?   29 boxes

11. What is the perimeter of this
(60) square?   20 in.

5 inches

12. If this square were to be covered
(76) with small squares one inch on
each side, how many squares
would be needed?   25 squares

13. $20.10
(51) − $16.45
‾‾‾‾‾‾‾‾‾
     $3.65

14. $98.54
(28) + $9.85
‾‾‾‾‾‾‾‾‾
     $108.39

15.   135
(61)   2416
          350
          4139
       +   67
‾‾‾‾‾‾‾‾‾
         7107

16. 380 × 4 1520
(68)

17. 97 × 80 7760
(77)

18. 5)3840   768
(86)

19. $8.63 × 7 $60.41
(68)

20. 8)$70.00 $8.75
(86)

21. 6)3795   632 r 3
(86)

22. 4 × P = 160
(50)   40

23. $\frac{\sqrt{64}}{\sqrt{16}}$ 2
(40)

24. $\frac{287}{7}$ 41
(75)

25. 10 × (6^2 + 2^3)
(55)   440

LESSON
90

Division with Zeros in Three-Digit Answers

a. 27
b. 25
c. 26
d. 92
e. 3650
f. $9.50
Patterns:

15

21

28

Facts Practice: 90 Division Facts (Test I in Test Masters)

Mental Math: Before subtracting, make both numbers larger.

   a. $56 - 29$ **b.** $43 - 18$ **c.** $63 - 37$

Review:

   d. $65 + 27$ **e.** 365×10 **f.** $7.52 + $1.98

Patterns: Copy this pattern of dot triangles on your paper. Then continue the sequence by drawing the next three triangles in the pattern.

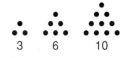

3   6   10

Recall that the method we have used for dividing numbers has four steps.

Step 1. Divide.

Step 2. Multiply.

Step 3. Subtract.

Step 4. Bring down.

Every time we bring a number down, we return to Step 1 and divide again. Sometimes the answer to the next division is zero, and we end up with a zero in the answer.

Example 1 $3\overline{)618}$

Solution   **Step 1.** Divide $3\overline{)6}$ and write "2."

            Step 2. Multiply 2×3 and write "6."

            Step 3. Subtract 6 from 6 and write "0."

            Step 4. Bring down the 1, making 01 (which is 1).

$$\begin{array}{r} 2 \\ 3\overline{)618} \\ \underline{6} \\ 01 \end{array}$$

REPEAT:

Step 1. Divide 3)⎺1 and write "0."

Step 2. Multiply 0 × 3 and write "0."

Step 3. Subtract 0 from 1 and write "1."

Step 4. Bring down the 8, making 18.

```
    206
3)618
   6
   01
    0
   18
   18
    0
```

REPEAT:

Step 1. Divide 3)⎺18 and write "6."

Step 2. Multiply 6 × 3 and write "18."

Step 3. Subtract 18 from 18 and write "0."

Step 4. There are no digits to bring down. The division is complete. The remainder is zero.

Example 2 4)⎺1483

Solution **Step 1.** Divide 4)⎺14 and write "3."

Step 2. Multiply 3 × 4 and write "12."

Step 3. Subtract 12 from 14 and write "2."

Step 4. Bring down the 8, making 28.

```
     370 r 3
4)1483
   12
   28
   28
   03
    0
    3
```

REPEAT:

Step 1. Divide 4)⎺28 and write "7."

Step 2. Multiply 7 × 4 and write "28."

Step 3. Subtract 28 from 28 and write "0."

Step 4. Bring down the 3, making 03 (which is 3).

REPEAT:

Step 1. Divide 4)⎺03 and write "0."

Step 2. Multiply 0 × 4 and write "0."

Step 3. Subtract 0 from 3 and write "3."

Step 4. There are no digits to bring down. We are finished dividing. We write "3" as the remainder.

Practice

a. List the four steps of division and draw the division diagram.   divide, multiply, subtract, bring down;

$$\begin{array}{r} 203 \text{ r } 3 \\ 4\overline{)815} \end{array}$$

b.

$$\begin{array}{r} 830 \text{ r } 2 \\ 5\overline{)4152} \end{array}$$

c.

$$\begin{array}{r} 905 \text{ r } 2 \\ 6\overline{)5432} \end{array}$$

d.

$$\begin{array}{r} 120 \text{ r } 5 \\ 7\overline{)845} \end{array}$$

e.

Problem set 90

1. If the chance of rain is 30%, then which is more
(65) likely—that it will rain or that it will not rain?
that it will not rain

2. Monty's time for running the race was 12 seconds less
(82) than Ivan's time. Monty's time was 58 seconds. What
was Ivan's time?   1 minute, 10 seconds

3. The whole rectangle is divided
(80) into 5 equal parts. Each part is
what percent of the rectangle?
(*Hint*: Divide 100 by 5.)   20%

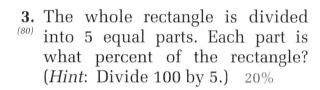

4. How many 6-inch-long sticks can be cut from a 72-
(62) inch-long stick of sugar cane?   12 six-inch-long sticks

5. One fifth of the leaves had fallen. What fraction of the
(71) leaves had not fallen? $\frac{4}{5}$

6. Which of these arrows could be pointing to 5263?   A
(13)

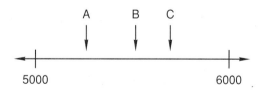

7. What fraction of the year is made up of months that
(84) have 31 days? $\frac{7}{12}$

8. The prefix *kilo-* means what number?   1000
(88)

9. Estimate the sum of 393, 589, and 241 by rounding
(70) each number to the nearest hundred before adding.
1200

10. The sides of this triangle are equal
(79) in length. How many millimeters
is the perimeter of the triangle?
60 mm

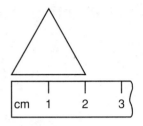

11. Three liters equals how many
(83) milliliters?   3000 mL

12. Wilma could run 5 miles in 1 hour. How long would it
(70) take her to run 40 miles?   8 hours

13.   103,279
(61) + 97,814
        ————
         201,093

14. $36.14
(28) + $27.95
        ————
        $64.09

15.   3615
(61)   294
              18
             378
         + 4290
         ————
           8595

16.   39,420
(62) − 29,516
        ————
          9904

17. $60.50
(20) −   N $17.30
        ————
        $43.20

18.   604
(68) ×   9
        ————
        5436

19.   87
(77) ×   60
        ————
        5220

20. $6.75
(68) ×   4
        ————
        $27.00

21. 3)618   206
(90)

22. 5)$21.50 $4.30
(90)

23.   N   992
(30) + 1467
        ————
        2459

24. $\dfrac{600}{4}$ 150
(90)

25. 543 ÷ 6
(81)   90 r 3

26. 472 ÷ 8   59
(75)

27. 9 × W = 9² + (9 × 2)
(69) 11

28.   4
(2)   2
              3
              N   9
              7
         + 2
         ————
           27

29.   5
(2)   2
              3
              1
              4
         + N   12
         ————
           27

30. N × 2 = 150   75
(50)

LESSON 91

Rounding to the Nearest Thousand

a. 27
b. 17
c. 43
d. 33
e. 49
f. 39

Facts Practice: 90 Division Facts (Test I in Test Masters)

Mental Math: Counting by 5's from 1, 2, 3, 4, or 5, we find five different final digit patterns: 1 and 6, 2 and 7, 3 and 8, 4 and 9, and 5 and 0. When a number ending in 5 is added to or subtracted from another number, the final digit of that number and of the answer will fit one of these five patterns.

| **a.** 22
 + 5 | **b.** 22
 − 5 | **c.** 38
 + 5 | **d.** 38
 − 5 | **e.** 44
 + 5 | **f.** 44
 − 5 |

When we round a number to the nearest ten, we get a multiple of 10. The multiples of 10 are the numbers we get when we count by tens. **The multiples of 10 have a zero as the last digit.**

$$10, 20, 30, 40, 50, 60, \ldots$$

When we round a number to the nearest hundred, we get a multiple of 100. The multiples of 100 are the numbers we get when we count by hundreds. **The multiples of 100 have zeros as the last two digits.**

$$100, 200, 300, 400, 500, 600, \ldots$$

When we round a number to the nearest thousand, we get a multiple of 1000. The multiples of 1000 are the numbers we get when we count by thousands. **The multiples of 1000 have zeros as the last three digits.**

$$1000, 2000, 3000, 4000, 5000, 6000, \ldots$$

We will use a number line to help us understand rounding to the nearest thousand.

Example Round 2781 to the nearest thousand.

Solution The number 2781 is between the thousand numbers 2000 and 3000. Halfway between 2000 and 3000 is 2500. As we see on the number line below, 2781 is nearer 3000 than 2000.

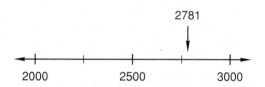

2000   2500   3000

Rounding 2781 to the nearest thousand gives us **3000.**

Practice   Round each number to the nearest thousand:

a. 5263   **b.** 4986   **c.** 7814   **d.** 8176
5000   5000   8000   8000

Problem set   **1.** Cecilia skated 27 times around the rink forward and
91   (12)   33 times around the rink backward. In all, how many
times did she skate around the rink?   60 times

2. Nectarines cost 68¢ per pound. What is the price for 3
(59)   pounds of nectarines? $2.04

3. In bowling, the sum of Amber's score and Beth's score
(82)   was equal to Sarah's score. If Sarah's score was 113
and Beth's score was 55, what was Amber's score?   58

4. One third of the 84 students were
(80)   assigned to each room. How many
students were assigned to each
room?   28 students

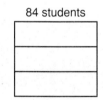
84 students

5. Round 2250 to the nearest thousand.   2000
(91)

6. What fraction of the letters in ARIZONA are not A's? $\frac{5}{7}$
(84)

7. The African elephant weighed 7 tons. How many
(87)   pounds is that?   14,000 lb

8. The tip of this shoelace is how many millimeters long?
(79)   15 mm

mm 10   20   30   40   50

9. Pick the more reasonable measure:
(88,83)
   (a) Box of cereal: 400 g or 400 kg   400 g

   (b) Pail of water: 10 mL or 10 L   10 L

10. According to this calendar, what
(64) is the date of the last Tuesday in
February, 2019?   February 26, 2019

FEBRUARY 2019						
S	M	T	W	T	F	S
					1	2
3	4	5	6	7	8	9
10	11	12	13	14	15	16
17	18	19	20	21	22	23
24	25	26	27	28		

11. Forty-two thousand, seven hundred is how much
(38) greater than thirty-four thousand, nine hundred?
7800

12. Find the perimeter and area of this rectangle.
(76) 30 units; 50 square units

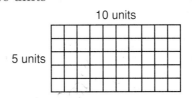

10 units

5 units

13. Michelle could pack 75 packages in 3 hours. How
(70) many packages could she pack in 1 hour?   25 packages

14. 6743 − (507 × 6)   **15.** $70.00 − $63.17
(55) 3701   *(51)* $6.83

16. 3 × 7 × 0   0   **17.** $8.15 × 6 $48.90
(72)   *(68)*

18. 67¢ × 10 $6.70   **19.** 43,162 + 5,917   49,079
(77)   *(61)*

20. 2)1216   608   **21.** 6)4321   720 r 1   **22.** 8)4537   567 r 1
(90)   *(90)*   *(86)*

23. 963 ÷ √9   **24.** 5^3 ÷ 5   **25.** $6.57 ÷ 9
(86) 321   *(75)* 25   *(86)* $0.73

26. 200 = 4 × B   50   **27.** D × 7 = 105   15
(50)   *(50)*

28.   473   **29.**   1   **30.**   2
(30)   286   *(21)*   12   *(21)*   33
    + N   184   3   4
      943   14   25
                 5   6
               + 26   + 27
                 61   97

LESSON
92

Line Graphs

a. 51
b. 72
c. 63
d. 16,000
e. $7.25
f. 33
Problem Solving:
 About 40% of the
 circle is shaded.

Facts Practice: 90 Division Facts (Test I in Test Masters)

Mental Math: Use the 5's patterns as you add.

  a. 36 + 15   **b.** 47 + 25   **c.** 28 + 35

Review:

  d. 40 × 40 × 10   **e.** $10.00 − $2.75   **f.** 72 − 39

Problem Solving: Estimate what percent of this circle is shaded.

Line graphs are often used to show how something has changed over a period of time.

Example Sean kept a record of his test scores on a line graph. According to his line graph, how many correct answers did he have on Test 3?

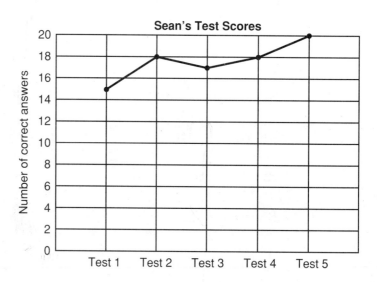

Solution This line graph shows at a glance whether Sean's scores are going up or going down. To read this graph, we compare the level of a point with the scale on the left. The dot above Test 3 is halfway between 16 and 18 on the scale. This means that Sean's score on Test 3 was **17 correct answers.**

Practice Use the graph of Sean's test scores from the example to answer questions a–d:

a. From Test 1 to Test 2, Sean's score improved by how many answers? 3 answers

b. There were 20 questions on each test. How many questions did Sean miss on Test 4? 2 questions

c. On which test did Sean have a perfect score? Test 5

d. Copy and finish this table using information from the line graph.

Sean's Test Scores

TEST	NUMBER OF CORRECT ANSWERS
1	15
2	18
3	17
4	18
5	20

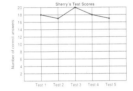

e. On Sherry's first five tests her scores were 18, 17, 20, 18, and 17. Draw a line graph that shows this information.

Problem set 92

1. There were 35 students in the class but only 28 math
   (38) books. How many more math books did the class need? 7 math books

2. Each of the 7 children slid down the water slide 11
   (59) times. How many times did they slide in all? 77 times

3. A bowling lane is 60 feet long. How many yards is
   (49) that? 20 yd

4. Justin carried the baton four hundred forty yards. Eric
   (12) carried it eight hundred eighty yards. Joe carried it one thousand, three hundred twenty yards, and Braulio carried it one thousand, seven hundred sixty yards. In all, how many yards was the baton carried? 4400 yd

5. One third of the members voted no. What fraction of
$^{(71)}$ the members did not vote no? $\frac{2}{3}$

6. Round 6821 and 4963 to the nearest thousand. Then
$^{(91,70)}$ add the rounded numbers. 7000; 5000; 12,000

7. What fraction of the days of the week start with the
$^{(84)}$ letter S? $\frac{2}{7}$

8. Together, Bob's shoes weigh about 1 kilogram. Each
$^{(88)}$ shoe weighs about how many grams? 500 g

Use the information in this line graph to answer
questions 9–11:

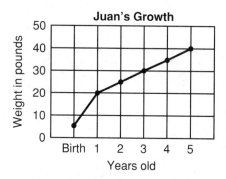

9. About how many pounds did Juan weigh on his
$^{(92)}$ second birthday? 25 lb

10. About how many pounds did Juan gain between his
$^{(92)}$ third and fifth birthdays? 10 lb

11. Copy and complete this table
$^{(92,89)}$ using information from the line
graph.

Juan's Growth

AGE	WEIGHT
At birth	6 pounds
1 year	20 pounds
2 years	25 pounds
3 years	30 pounds
4 years	35 pounds
5 years	40 pounds

12. If 65% of the lights are on, then
$^{(65)}$ what percent of the lights are off?
35%

13. $\$60.75$
(28) $+\ \$95.75$
$\$156.50$

14. $\$16.00$
(51) $-\ \$15.43$
$\$0.57$

15. $\$63.14$
(28) 2.75
39.81
4.62
$+\ \ 0.87$
$\$111.19$

16. 320
(77) $\times\ \ 30$
9600

17. 465
(68) $\times\ \ \ 7$
3255

18. $\$0.98$
(68) $\times\ \ \ \ 6$
$\$5.88$

19. $425 \div 6$ $70\text{ r }5$
(81)

20. $\$6.00 \div 8$ $\$0.75$
(75)

21. $625 \div 5$ 125
(86)

22. $3 \times R = 150$ 50
(50)

23. $10^2 + T = 150$ 50
$(72,30)$

24. $1 + 7 + 2 + 6 + 9 + 4 + N = 37$ 8
(2)

25. If the 3-inch square is covered
(76) with 1-inch squares, how many of
the 1-inch squares are needed?
9 one-inch squares

LESSON 93

Sales Tax • Change Back

a. 26
b. 47
c. 39
d. 750
e. $9.53
f. 28
Patterns:
First sequence:
25 and 36
Second sequence:
28 and 36

Facts Practice: 64 Multiplication Facts (Test G in Test Masters)

Mental Math: Use the 5's patterns as you subtract.
a. $41 - 15$ **b.** $72 - 25$ **c.** $84 - 45$
Review:
d. 25×30 **e.** $\$6.54 + \$2.99$ **f.** $56 - 28$

Patterns: Find the next two numbers in each sequence.
$1, 4, 9, 16, \_\_, \_\_, \ldots$
$1, 3, 6, 10, 15, 21, \_\_, \_\_, \ldots$

Sales tax Sales tax is an extra amount of money that must be paid when items are purchased. The amount of tax depends upon the amount purchased. The sales tax rate varies from state to state and sometimes from county to county.

Example 1   Sam bought six bolts for 89¢ each. The sales tax was 32¢. How much did Sam spend in all?

Solution   First we find the price of the six bolts. Then we add the sales tax.

$$
\begin{array}{r}
^{5} \\
89¢ \\
\times\ \ 6 \\
\hline
534¢ = \$5.34
\end{array}
$$

The six bolts cost $5.34. To this we add the sales tax.

$$
\begin{array}{ll}
\$5.34 & \text{price of bolts} \\
+\ \$0.32 & \text{sales tax} \\
\hline
\$5.66 & \text{total price}
\end{array}
$$

The total price, including tax, was **$5.66.**

Change back   If we do not have the exact amount of money we need to buy something at a store, we pay more than the price and then we get money back. To find how much we should get in change, we subtract the total price from how much we paid.

Example 2   Midge bought a pair of pants for $23.99. The tax was $1.56. She paid the clerk $40.00. How much money should she get back?

Solution   First we figure out the total price.

$$
\begin{array}{ll}
\$23.99 & \text{price of pants} \\
+\ \$\ 1.56 & \text{sales tax} \\
\hline
\$25.55 & \text{total price}
\end{array}
$$

Now we subtract the total price from how much she paid.

$$
\begin{array}{ll}
\$40.00 & \text{how much she paid} \\
-\ \$25.55 & \text{total price} \\
\hline
\$14.45 & \text{change back}
\end{array}
$$

Midge should get **$14.45** back from the clerk.

Practice **a.** Sarah bought three pairs of socks for $2.24 each pair. The sales tax was 34¢. What was the total price?
$7.06

b. Mark paid $10.00 for a tape that cost $6.95. The sales tax was 49¢. How much money should Mark get back in change? $2.56

Problem set **1.** Ali Baba brought home 30 bags. Each bag contained
93 (59) 320 gold coins. How many coins were there in all?
9600 coins

2. The movie was 3 hours long. If it started at 11:10 a.m.,
(33) at what time did it end?   2:10 p.m.

3. Tony is reading a 212-page book. If he has finished
(31) page 135, how many pages does he still have to read?
77 pages

4. Brad, Jan, and Jordan each scored
(80) one third of the team's 42 points. They each scored how many points?   14 points

42 points

5. Round 4286 to the nearest thousand.   4000
(91)

6. The shirt cost $16.98. The tax was $1.02. Sam paid
(93) $20. How much money should Sam get back? $2.00

7. What fraction of the letters in the following word is
(84) made up of I's? $\frac{7}{34}$

SUPERCALIFRAGILISTICEXPIALIDOCIOUS

Use the information given to answer questions 8–10:

In the first 8 games of this season, the Rio Hondo football team won 6 games and lost 2 games. They won their next game by a score of 24 to 20. The team plays 12 games in all.

8. In the first 9 games of the season, how many games
(82) did Rio Hondo win?   7 games

9. Rio Hondo won its ninth game by how many points?
(82)   4 points

10. What is the greatest number of games Rio Hondo could win this season?   10 games
(82)

11. Compare: $3 \times 4 \times 5 \textcircled{=} 5 \times 4 \times 3$
(72,15)

12.
(20)
$$\begin{array}{r} M \\ -\ 13{,}728 \\ \hline 25{,}723 \end{array}$$ 39,451

13.
(30)
$$\begin{array}{r} N \\ +\ 95{,}486 \\ \hline 568{,}372 \end{array}$$ 472,886

14.
(28)
$$\begin{array}{r} \$\ 8.53 \\ 12.47 \\ 5.25 \\ 0.67 \\ +\ 14.37 \\ \hline \$41.29 \end{array}$$

15.
(77)
$$\begin{array}{r} 638 \\ \times\ \ \ 50 \\ \hline 31{,}900 \end{array}$$

16.
(68)
$$\begin{array}{r} 472 \\ \times\ \ \ 9 \\ \hline 4248 \end{array}$$

17.
(68)
$$\begin{array}{r} \$6.09 \\ \times\ \ \ \ 6 \\ \hline \$36.54 \end{array}$$

18. $3\overline{)921}$ 307
(90)

19. $5\overline{)678}$ 135 r 3
(86)

20. $4\overline{)2400}$ 600
(90)

21. $12.60 ÷ 5 $2.52
(86)

22. $14.34 ÷ 6 $2.39
(86)

23. $46.00 ÷ 8 $5.75
(86)

24. $9^2 = 9 \times N$ 9
(69)

25. $5 \times W = 5 \times 10^2$ 100
(69)

26.
(2)
$$\begin{array}{r} 5 \\ 4 \\ 3 \\ A\ \ 19 \\ 4 \\ 7 \\ 6 \\ 5 \\ +\ 9 \\ \hline 62 \end{array}$$

27. One fourth of the months start with the letter J. What percent of the months start with the letter J?   25%
(65)

LESSON 94

Area, Part 2

a. 68
b. 64
c. 91
d. 3000
e. $0.62
f. 93

Problem Solving:
 AB = $1\frac{1}{4}$ inch;
 BC = $1\frac{1}{2}$ inch;
 Segment *BC* is $\frac{1}{4}$ inch longer than segment *AB*.

Facts Practice: 64 Multiplication Facts (Test G in Test Masters)

Mental Math: Use the 5's patterns as you subtract.
 a. 83 − 15   **b.** 29 + 35   **c.** 76 + 15

Review:
 d. 100 × 30   **e.** $5.00 − $4.38   **f.** 67 + 26

Problem Solving: How long is segment *AB*? How long is segment *BC*? Segment *BC* is how much longer than segment *AB*?

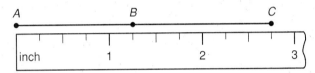

We can find the area of a figure by counting the number of squares of a certain size needed to cover the figure. We might use square centimeters, square meters, square inches, or square feet to measure an area. We even use square miles to measure large areas of land. We often use the letters "sq." as an abbreviation for the word *square*.

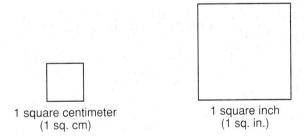

1 square centimeter
(1 sq. cm)

1 square inch
(1 sq. in.)

Large squares like square meters, square feet, and square miles are too large to fit on a page in this book, so we use scale drawings that are smaller than actual size. Here we show a scale drawing of a 4-feet-by-2-feet tabletop.

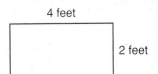

4 feet

2 feet

To find the area of this tabletop, we calculate the number of 1-foot-by-1-foot squares needed to cover it. The length of the sides of the tabletop show us that we could fit 2 rows of 4 squares on the table.

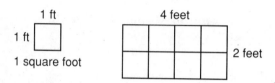

We find that the area is 8 square feet.

Example   Morton Ranch is 4 miles long and 3 miles wide. What is the area of Morton Ranch?

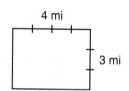

Solution   The area of the ranch is the number of square miles of land it occupies. Mile marks have been made on the illustration. By extending these marks across the drawing, we find that the area of the ranch is **12 square miles.**

Practice   Find the area of each rectangle:

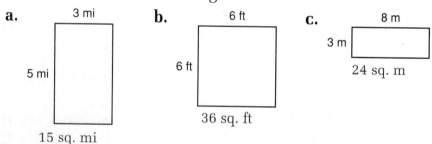

Problem set 94

1. If it is not a leap year, what is the total number of days
   (64) in January, February, and March?   90 days

2. The shoemaker's wife made each of the 12 elves a pair
   (59) of pants and 2 shirts. How many pieces of clothing did she make?   36 pieces of clothing

3. John did seven more chin-ups than Larry did. If John
   (38) did eighteen chin-ups, how many chin-ups did Larry do?   11 chin-ups

4. Jan drove 200 miles on 8 gallons of gas. Her car
(70) averaged how many miles on each gallon of gas?
25 miles

5. Melinda paid $20.00 for a book that cost $8.95. The
(93) tax was 54¢. How much money should she get back?
$10.51

6. The tally for 8 is 卌 |||. What is the tally for 9?
(85) 卌 ||||

7. If each side of an octagon is 1 centimeter, what is its
(79) perimeter in millimeters?   80 mm

8. $\sqrt{36} + N = 7 \times 8$ 50
(69)

18 marbles

6 marbles	$\left.\begin{matrix} \end{matrix}\right\}$ $\frac{1}{3}$ cat's-eyes
6 marbles	
6 marbles	$\left.\begin{matrix} \end{matrix}\right\}$ $\frac{2}{3}$ not
6 marbles	cat's-eyes

9. Illustrate this fraction-of-a-group problem: One third
(80) of the 18 marbles were cat's-eyes. How many of the
marbles were cat's-eyes?   6 marbles

10. Robert picked 46 peaches in 1 day. At that rate, how
(67) many peaches could he pick in 6 days?   276 peaches

11. Mary picked 3640 peaches in 7 days. She picked an
(70) average of how many peaches each day?   520 peaches

12.
(30)
$$\begin{array}{r} F \\ +\ 27{,}415 \\ \hline 271{,}052 \end{array}$$ 243,637

13.
(28)
$$\begin{array}{r} \$96.47 \\ +\ \$5.85 \\ \hline \$102.32 \end{array}$$

14.
(21)
$$\begin{array}{r} 35 \\ 45 \\ 25 \\ 65 \\ 115 \\ 20 \\ +\ 25 \\ \hline 330 \end{array}$$

15. $3 \times 6 \times 3^2$
(72)   162

16. $462 \times \sqrt{9}$
(68)   1386

17.
(77)
$$\begin{array}{r} 36 \\ \times\ 50 \\ \hline 1800 \end{array}$$

18.
(68)
$$\begin{array}{r} 476 \\ \times\ 7 \\ \hline 3332 \end{array}$$

19. $\dfrac{524}{4}$ 131
(86)

20. $6\overline{)4216}$ 702 r 4
(90)

21. $5\overline{)\$26.30}$ $5.26
(86)

22. $\$3.70 \div 2$
(86) $1.85

23. $786 \div 3$
(86)   262

24. $4902 \div 7$
(90)   700 r 2

25.
(2)
$$
\begin{array}{r}
4 \\
3 \\
2 \\
7 \\
6 \\
8 \\
+\ N \quad 17 \\
\hline
47
\end{array}
$$

26. Find the perimeter and area of this square.   12 yd; 9 sq. yd
(94,60)

3 yards

3 yards

LESSON 95

Multiplying by Tens, Hundreds, and Thousands

a. $2.50
b. 8000
c. 93
d. 2500
e. $9.63
f. 47

Problem Solving:

Sandra received 3 quarters and 2 dimes or 1 half dollar, 1 quarter, 1 dime, and 2 nickels in change.

Facts Practice: 64 Multiplication Facts (Test G in Test Masters)

Mental Math: Review.

a. $10.00 - $7.50   b. 400×20 c. $58 + 35$
d. 250×10 e. $7.68 + $1.95   f. $85 - 38$

Problem Solving: Sandra bought a CD for $12.95. Sales tax was $1.10. She paid for her purchase with a $10 bill and a $5 bill. Sandra got back five coins. What were the coins Sandra received in change?

When we multiply a whole number by 10, the answer has the same digits as the number that was multiplied, and the answer has an additional zero at the end.

$$
\begin{array}{r}
123 \\
\times \quad 10 \\
\hline
1230
\end{array}
$$

When we multiply a whole number by 100, there are two additional zeros at the end.

$$
\begin{array}{r}
123 \\
\times \quad 100 \\
\hline
12{,}300
\end{array}
$$

When we multiply a whole number by 1000, there are three additional zeros at the end.

$$
\begin{array}{r}
123 \\
\times \quad 1{,}000 \\
\hline
123{,}000
\end{array}
$$

When we multiply dollars and cents, we remember to place the decimal point two places from the right-hand side of the product.

Example Multiply mentally:

(a) 37 × 10   (b) $6.12 × 100   (c) 45¢ × 1000

Solution (a) We write "37" with one zero at the end: **370.**

(b) We write "612" with two zeros at the end, and then place the decimal point and dollar sign: **$612.00.**

(c) We write "45" with three zeros at the end. This makes 45000¢, which is **$450.00.**

Practice Multiply mentally:

    a. 365 × 10   **b.** 52 × 100   **c.** 7 × 1000
       3650   5200   7000

    d. $3.60 × 10   **e.** 420 × 100   **f.** $2.50 × 1000
       $36.00   42,000 $2500.00

Problem set 95 Use the information in the graph to answer questions 1–3:

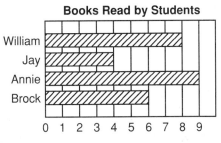

Books Read by Students

1. Which student has read exactly twice as many books
(85) as Jay?   William

2. Brock's goal is to read 10 books. How many more
(85) books does he need to read to reach his goal?   4 books

3. If the books Annie has read have an average of 160
(85) pages each, how many pages has she read?   1440 pages

4. Jim saw some pentagons. The pentagons had a total of
(73) 100 sides. How many pentagons did Jim see?
20 pentagons

5. Tom bought a rectangular piece of land that was 3
(94) miles long and 2 miles wide. Fifty percent of the land
could be farmed. How many square miles could be
farmed?   3 square miles

6. Max bought 10 pencils for 24¢ each. The tax was 14¢.
(93) What was the total price? $2.54

7. A pitcher of orange juice is about: B. 2 liters
(83)
A. 2 ounces   B. 2 liters   C. 2 gallons

8. Draw a triangle so that two sides are perpendicular.
(29) answer varies

48 gems
| 12 gems | } ¼ rubies |
| 12 gems |
| 12 gems | } ¾ not rubies |
| 12 gems |

9. Illustrate this fraction-of-a-group problem: One fourth
(80) of the 48 gems were rubies. How many of the gems
were rubies?   12 gems

10. What percent of the gems in problem 9 were not
(65) rubies?   75%

11.   463,271
(61) + 175,349
        ‾‾‾‾‾‾‾‾
         638,620

12.   728
(30)   +   C   477
        ‾‾‾‾‾‾
         1205

13.   68,418
(62) − 47,615
        ‾‾‾‾‾‾
         20,803

14. $30.00
(51) − $14.75
        ‾‾‾‾‾‾
         $15.25

15. 36 × 10
(95) 360

16. 100 × 42
(95) 4200

17. $2.75 × 1000
(95) $2750.00

18.   317
(68) ×   4
        ‾‾‾‾‾
         1268

19.   206
(68) ×   5
        ‾‾‾‾‾
         1030

20.   37
(77) × 40
        ‾‾‾‾‾
         1480

21. 3$\overline{)492}$
$\overset{164}{}$
(86)

22. 5$\overline{)860}$
$\overset{172}{}$
(86)

23. 6$\overline{)\$9.30}$
$\overset{\$1.55}{}$
(86)

24. 168 ÷ 2³
(75)   21

25. \$20.00 ÷ 8
(90)   \$2.50

26. 2315 ÷ √16
(86)   578 r 3

27. Find the perimeter and area of
(94,60) this rectangle.   32 ft; 60 sq. ft

10 ft

6 ft

LESSON
96

a. 250
b. 2500
c. 25,000
d. \$3.25
e. 93
f. 18
Problem Solving:
  About 80% of the
  circle is shaded.

Multiplying Round Numbers Mentally

Facts Practice: 64 Multiplication Facts (Test G in Test Masters)

Mental Math: Multiply by tens, hundreds, and thousands.

  a. 25 × 10   **b.** 25 × 100   **c.** 25 × 1000

Review:

  d. \$10.00 − \$6.75   **e.** 58 + 35   **f.** 37 − 19

Problem Solving: Estimate what percent of this circle is shaded.

If we have memorized the multiplication facts, we can multiply round numbers "in our head." To do this, we multiply the first digits and count zeros. Study the multiplication below.

40 ⌐ two zeros
× 30 ⌐
─────
1200

4 × 3 ⌐   └─ two zeros

We can find the product of 40 and 30 by multiplying 4 and 3 and then attaching two zeros.

Example 1   Multiply mentally: 60 × 80

Solution   We multiply six times eight and get 48. There is one zero in 60 and one zero in 80. We attach two zeros to 48 and get 4800.

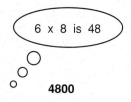

6 x 8 is 48

4800

Example 2   Multiply mentally: 30 × $7.00

Solution   We multiply three times seven and get 21. There are three zeros in the problem. We attach three zeros to 21 and get 21,000. Since we multiplied dollars and cents, we place the decimal point two places from the right and write a dollar sign.

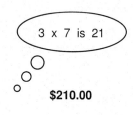

3 x 7 is 21

$210.00

Example 3   Multiply mentally: 400 × 700

Solution   Four times seven is 28. We attach four zeros and get 280,000.

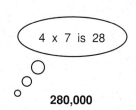

4 x 7 is 28

280,000

Practice   Multiply mentally:

a. 70 × 80   5600   **b.** 40 × 50   2000

c. 40 × $6.00 $240.00   **d.** 30 × 800   24,000

Problem set 96

1. It takes Jennifer 20 minutes to walk to school. At what time should she start for school if she wants to arrive at 8:10 a.m.?   7:50 a.m.
(33)

2. Before her haircut Rapunzel weighed 125 pounds. After her haircut she weighed 118 pounds. What was the weight of the hair that was cut?   7 lb
(31)

3. Lucy bought a hamburger for $2.89, fries for $0.89, and a drink for 79¢. The tax was 28¢. She paid with a $5 bill. How much money should Lucy get back?   15¢
(93)

4. $5^2 + 5^2 + N = 10^2$ 50
(69)

5. According to this calendar, Octo-
(64) ber 30, 1902, was what day of the
week?   Sunday

OCTOBER 1902						
S	M	T	W	T	F	S
						1
2	3	4	5	6	7	8
9	10	11	12	13	14	15
16	17	18	19	20	21	22
23	24	25	26	27	28	29
30	31					

6. The tally for 16 is ⊞ ⊞ ⊞ I. What
(85) is the tally for 17?
⊞ ⊞ ⊞ II

7. Round three thousand, seven hundred eighty-two to
(91) the nearest thousand.   4000

8. The limousine weighed 2 tons. How many pounds is 2
(87) tons?   4000 lb

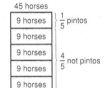

9. Illustrate this fraction-of-a-group problem: One fifth
(80) of the 45 horses were pintos. How many of the horses
were pintos?   9 horses

10. What percent of the horses in
(80) problem 9 were pintos? (*Hint*:
Find $\frac{1}{5}$ of 100%.)   20%

11. Debby could run 90 laps in 3
(70) hours. How many laps could she
run in 1 hour?   30 laps

12. Mick could run 30 laps in 1 hour. How many laps
(67) could he run in 5 hours?   150 laps

13.   17,414
(61) + 89,875
‾‾‾‾‾‾‾‾
    107,289

14. $36.47
(28) + $9.68
‾‾‾‾‾‾‾
    $46.15

15.   6
(21)   8
        17
        23
       110
        25
    + 104
‾‾‾‾‾‾
       293

16.   31,425
(62) − 17,633
‾‾‾‾‾‾‾
    13,792

17. $30.00
(51) − $13.45
‾‾‾‾‾‾‾
    $16.55

18.   476
(68) ×   7
‾‾‾‾‾‾
    3332

19.   804
(68) ×   5
‾‾‾‾‾‾
    4020

20. $100 \times 23¢$ **21.** 60×30 **22.** $70 \times \$2.00$
(95) $23.00   (96)   1800   (96) $140.00

23. $3\overline{)\$6.27}$ $2.09   **24.** $7\overline{)820}$ 117 r 1   **25.** $6\overline{)333}$ 55 r 3
(90)   (86)   (78)

26. $625 \div \sqrt{25}$ **27.** $4000 \div 2^3$ **28.** $1370 \div 2$
(86)   125   (90)   500   (86)   685

29. Find the perimeter and area of   10 m
(94,60) this square.   40 m; 100 sq. m

LESSON 97

Multiplying Two Two-Digit Numbers, Part 1

a. 5   b. 20
c. 24   d. 32
e. 43   f. $6.53
g. 112   h. 48
Patterns:

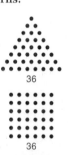

36

36

Facts Practice: 64 Multiplication Facts (Test G in Test Masters)

Mental Math: Find half of each number.

   a. 10   **b.** 40   **c.** 48   **d.** 64   **e.** 86

Review:

   f. $3.54 + $2.99   **g.** 75 + 37   **h.** 86 − 38

Patterns: Fifteen dots can be arranged in a triangle pattern. Sixteen dots can be arranged in a square pattern. Thirty-six dots can be arranged in either a triangle pattern or a square pattern. Make a triangle and a square using 36 dots for each pattern.

15   16

When we multiply by a two-digit number, we take three steps. First we multiply by the ones' digit. Next we multiply by the tens' digit. Then we add the products together. To multiply 34 by 12, we multiply 34 by 2 and multiply 34 by 10. Then we add.

$$\begin{array}{rll} 34 \times 2 = & 68 & \text{product} \\ 34 \times 10 = & 340 & \text{product} \\ \hline 34 \times 12 = & 408 & \text{total} \end{array}$$

It is easier to write the numbers one above the other when we multiply.

$$\begin{array}{r} 34 \\ \times\,12 \\ \hline \end{array}$$

First we multiply 34 by 2 and write the answer with the last digit in the ones' column.

$$\begin{array}{r} 34 \\ \times\,12 \\ \hline 68 \end{array}$$

Next we multiply 34 by 1. **Since this 1 is actually 10, we record the last digit of this multiplication in the tens' column, as we show on the left.** Then we add the results of the two multiplications and get 408.

$$\begin{array}{r} 34 \\ \times\,12 \\ \hline 68 \\ 34 \\ \hline 408 \end{array} \quad \text{or} \quad \begin{array}{r} 34 \\ \times\,12 \\ \hline 68 \\ 340 \\ \hline 408 \end{array}$$

On the right, we show another way. We put the zero after the 34 to show that 10 times 34 is 340. Then we add. We get the same answer both ways.

Example   Multiply:
$$\begin{array}{r} 31 \\ \times\,23 \\ \hline \end{array}$$

Solution   We multiply 31 by 3 and write the last digit of the product in the ones' column.

$$\begin{array}{r} 31 \\ \times\,23 \\ \hline 93 \end{array}$$

Now we multiply 31 by 2. Since this 2 is actually 20, we write the last digit of the product in the tens' column. Then we add to get **713**.

$$\begin{array}{r} 31 \\ \times\,23 \\ \hline 93 \\ 62 \\ \hline 713 \end{array} \quad \text{or} \quad \begin{array}{r} 31 \\ \times\,23 \\ \hline 93 \\ 620 \\ \hline 713 \end{array}$$

Practice

a. 32 ×23 ───── 736	**b.** 24 ×32 ───── 768	**c.** 43 ×12 ───── 516	**d.** 34 ×21 ───── 714
e. 32 ×32 ───── 1024	**f.** 23 ×14 ───── 322	**g.** 13 ×32 ───── 416	**h.** 33 ×33 ───── 1089

Problem set 97

Use this information to answer questions 1–3:

Freeman rode his bike 2 miles from his house to Daniel's house. Together, they rode 4 miles to the lake. Daniel caught 8 fish. At 3:30 p.m., they rode back to Daniel's house. Then Freeman rode home.

1. Altogether, how far did Freeman ride his bike?   12 mi
(82)

2. It took Freeman an hour and a half to get home from the lake. At what time did he get home?   5:00 p.m.
(82)

3. Daniel caught twice as many fish as Freeman. How many fish did Freeman catch?   4 fish
(82)

4. Shep bought some feed for $12.97. Tax was 91¢. He paid $20.00. How much money should he get back?
(93)
$6.12

5. Estimate the sum of 4876 and 3149. Round each number to the nearest thousand before adding.   8000
(91)

6. This is the tally for what number?   ɪɪɪɪ ɪɪɪɪ ɪɪɪɪ   14
(85)

7. What is the perimeter of a pentagon if each side is 20 centimeters long?   100 cm
(73,60)

8. Find the length of this segment to the nearest quarter inch. $3\frac{1}{2}$ in.
(48)

| inch | 1 | 2 | 3 | 4 |

9. Illustrate this fraction-of-a-group problem: One half of the 18 players were on the field. How many players were on the field?   9 players
(80)

18 players
9 players } $\frac{1}{2}$ on the field
9 players } $\frac{1}{2}$ off the field

10. A dime is $\frac{1}{10}$ of a dollar. What fraction of a dollar is a penny? $\frac{1}{100}$
(28)

11. A dime is what percent of a dollar? (*Hint:* Find $\frac{1}{10}$ of
(80) 100%.) 10%

12. 21,316 − 14,141 7175 **13.** $20 − 20¢ $19.80
(62)   *(53)*

14. 31   **15.** 32   **16.** 14
(97) × 21   *(97)* × 31   *(97)* × 32
      ‾‾‾‾   ‾‾‾‾   ‾‾‾‾
       651   992   448

17. 11   **18.** 12   **19.** 30 × 800
(97) × 11   *(97)* × 14   *(96)* 24,000
      ‾‾‾‾   ‾‾‾‾
       121   168

            142 r 6   159   507
20. 7)‾1000   **21.** 3)‾477   **22.** 5)‾2535
(86)   *(86)*   *(90)*

23. $64.80 ÷ 9   **24.** 716 ÷ 4   **25.** 352 ÷ 8
(90) $7.20   *(86)* 179   *(75)* 44

26. Find the perimeter and area of   20 in.
(94,60) this rectangle. 60 in.; 200 sq. in.

| | 10 in. |

LESSON
98

Division Word Problems
with Remainders

a. 10
b. 12
c. 25
d. 23
e. 60
f. $1.33
g. 91
h. 17
Problem Solving:
  Ten 100-lb bags of
  cement

Facts Practice: 90 Division Facts (Test I in Test Masters)

Mental Math: Find half of each number.
  a. 20   **b.** 24   **c.** 50   **d.** 46   **e.** 120
Review:
  f. $5.00 − $3.67   **g.** 52 + 39   **h.** 42 − 25

Problem Solving: A half-ton pickup truck can carry a load
                     weighing half of a ton. How many 100-pound
                     sacks of cement can a half-ton pickup truck
                     carry?

We have been practicing division word problems in which
there are no remainders. In this lesson we will begin
practicing division word problems in which there are
remainders. These problems should be read with special
care so that we know exactly what the question is.

Example The packer placed 100 bottles into boxes that held 6 bottles each.

(a) How many boxes were **filled?**

(b) How many bottles were **left over?**

(c) How many boxes were needed to hold **all the bottles?**

Solution These three questions have three different answers. To answer all three questions, we begin by dividing 100 by 6.

$$
\begin{array}{r}
16 \text{ r } 4 \\
6\overline{)100} \\
\underline{6} \\
40 \\
\underline{36} \\
4
\end{array}
$$

This means that the 100 bottles can be separated into 16 groups of 6. Then there will be 4 extra bottles.

(a) The result 16 r 4 means that **16 boxes can be filled,** but there are still 4 more bottles.

(b) The result 16 r 4 means that after filling 16 boxes, there are still **4 bottles left over.**

(c) The result 16 r 4 means that after filling 16 boxes, there are still 4 more bottles. These 4 bottles will not fill another box, but another box is needed to hold them. Thus, in order to hold all the bottles, **17 boxes are needed.**

Practice Tomorrow 32 students are going on a field trip. Each car can carry 5 students.

a. How many cars can be filled?   6 cars

b. How many cars will be needed?   7 cars

Rafik found 31 quarters in his bank. He made stacks of 4 quarters each.

c. How many stacks of 4 quarters did he make?   7 stacks

d. How many extra quarters did he have?   3 quarters

e. If he made a "short stack" with the extra quarters, how many stacks were there in all?   8 stacks

Problem set 98

1. Peter packed 6 ping-pong balls in each package. There
(98) were 100 ping-pong balls to pack.

(a) How many packages could he fill?   16 packages

(b) How many ping-pong balls were left over?
        4 ping-pong balls

2. One hundred twenty-three is how much less than
(38) three hundred twenty-one?   198

3. Four giant pretzels are 59¢ each. Sales tax is 16¢. What
(93) is the total price? $2.52

4. Twenty-four inches is how many feet?   2 ft
(49)

5. What is the length of segment *YZ* in millimeters? In
(79,50) centimeters?   40 mm; 4 cm

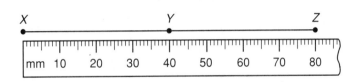

6. $7 + 7 + N = 7^2$ 35
(69)

7. It is morning. What time will it be
(33) 5 hours and 20 minutes from
now?   12:23 p.m.

8. Write the number 7,528 in
(42) expanded form. Then use words
to write the number.
7000 + 500 + 20 + 8; seven thousand, five hundred twenty-eight

9. Illustrate this fraction-of-a-group problem: One fifth
(80) of the 25 band members missed the note. How many
band members missed the note?   5 band members

10. What percent of the band members in problem 9
(80) missed the note?   20%

11. $6.35 + $14.25 + $0.97 + $5 $26.57
(53)

12. 16,456 − 7638   8818
(62)

13. $10.00 − (46¢ + $1.30)
(55) $8.24

14. 28 × 1000
(95)   28,000

15.   13
(97)   × 13
         169

16.   12
(97)   × 11
         132

17. $8.67
(68)   ×   9
       $78.03

18.   31
(97)   × 31
        961

19.   16
(97)   × 31
        496

20.   506
(90)   7)3542

21. $5.50
(90)   6)$33.00

22.   620 r 5
(90)   8)4965

23. 482 ÷ 5
(78)   96 r 2

24. 2700 ÷ 9
(90)   300

25. 2700 ÷ $\sqrt{9}$
(90)   900

26. 3 × N = 6^2 12
(69)

27.   4
(2)   2
             3
             5
             N 14
             8
             6
           + 3
            45

28. The classroom was 40 feet long
(94) and 30 feet wide. How many 1-
      foot floor tiles were needed to
      cover the floor?
      1200 one-foot floor tiles

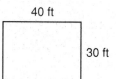
40 ft
30 ft

LESSON
99

Mixed Numbers and Improper Fractions

a. 40
b. 70
c. 130
d. 210
e. 1400
f. $9.33
g. 463
h. 36
Patterns:
$1.50, $1.75, $2.00,
$2.25, $2.50, $2.75,
$3.00

Facts Practice: 90 Division Facts (Test I in Test Masters)

Mental Math: Find half of each number.

  a. 80   **b.** 140   **c.** 260   **d.** 420   **e.** 2800

Review:

  f. $2.95 + $6.38   **g.** 428 + 35   **h.** 75 − 39

Patterns: In this sequence, 25¢ is added to each term to make the next term. Copy this sequence and continue it to $3.00.

$$\$0.25, \$0.50, \$0.75, \$1.00, \$1.25, \ldots$$

Here we show a picture of $1\frac{1}{2}$ shaded circles. Each whole circle has been divided into two half circles. We see that $1\frac{1}{2}$ is the same as **three halves,** which is written $\frac{3}{2}$.

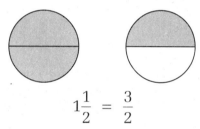

$$1\frac{1}{2} = \frac{3}{2}$$

The mixed number $1\frac{1}{2}$ equals the fraction $\frac{3}{2}$. The fraction $\frac{3}{2}$ is greater than 1. Fractions that are greater than or equal to 1 are called **improper fractions.** In this lesson we will draw pictures to show which mixed numbers and improper fractions are equal to each other.

Example Draw circles to show that $2\frac{3}{4}$ equals $\frac{11}{4}$.

Solution We begin by drawing 3 circles and shading $2\frac{3}{4}$.

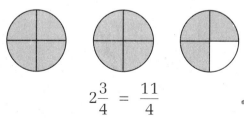

$$2\frac{3}{4} = \frac{11}{4}$$

We see that the fraction part of $2\frac{3}{4}$ is **fourths. So we divide all the circles into fourths.** We count 11 shaded fourths. This shows that $2\frac{3}{4}$ equals $\frac{11}{4}$.

Practice   **a.** Draw circles to show that $1\frac{3}{4} = \frac{7}{4}$.

b. Draw circles to show that $2\frac{1}{2} = \frac{5}{2}$.

c. Draw circles to show that $1\frac{1}{3} = \frac{4}{3}$.

Problem set 99

1. The coach divided 33 players as equally as possible
$_{(98)}$ into 4 teams.

(a) How many teams had exactly 8 players?   3 teams

(b) How many teams had 9 players?   1 team

2. On the package there were two 25-cent stamps, two
$_{(53)}$ 20-cent stamps, and one 15-cent stamp. Altogether,
how much did the stamps that were on the package
cost? $1.05

3. Don read 20 pages each day. How many pages did he
$_{(59)}$ read in 2 weeks?   280 pages

4. The Frog Prince leapt 27 feet to get out of the well.
$_{(49)}$ How many yards did he leap?   9 yd

5. What is the perimeter of this tri-
$_{(79,60)}$ angle in centimeters?   7 cm

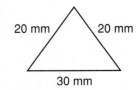

6. This is the tally for what number?
$_{(85)}$ 18

7. This dropperful of water is about:
$_{(83)}$

A. 2 milliliters   A

B. 2 liters

C. 2 pints

8. $87 + 0 = 87 \times N$ 1
$_{(69)}$

24 students

8 students	} $\frac{1}{3}$ finished early
8 students	} $\frac{2}{3}$ did not
8 students	finish early

9. Illustrate this fraction-of-a-group problem: One third of the 24 students finished early. How many students finished early?   8 students

(80)

10. What percent of a dollar is a quarter?   25%

(65)

11. $478.63
(28)   + $32.47
_____
          $511.10

12.   137,140
(62)   − 129,536
_____
            7604

13. $60.00
(51)   − $24.38
_____
          $35.62

14. 70 × 90
(96) 6300

15.   11
(97) × 13
_____
        143

16.   12
(97) × 12
_____
        144

17. $4.76
(68) ×   8
_____
       $38.08

18.   21
(97) × 13
_____
        273

19.   17
(97) × 21
_____
        357

20. 4)3000 (750)
(90)

21. 5)635 (127)
(86)

22. 7)426 (60 r 6)
(81)

23. 8)3614 (451 r 6)
(86)

24. $\frac{2736}{6}$ 456
(86)

25. How much is one fourth of $10.00? $2.50

(80)

26. Draw and shade circles to show that $1\frac{1}{2}$ equals $\frac{3}{2}$.

(99)

5 cm

4 cm

27. Use a pencil and a ruler to sketch a rectangle that is 5 cm long and 4 cm wide.

(25)

28. What is the perimeter and area of the rectangle in problem 27?   18 cm; 20 sq. cm

(94,60)

LESSON
100

a. 60
b. 120
c. 2400
d. $2.50
e. 295
f. 219
Problem Solving:
   32 cups

> **Facts Practice:** 90 Division Facts (Test I in Test Masters)
>
> **Mental Math:** Find half of each product.
>   **a.** Half of 10 × 12   **b.** Half of 10 × 24   **c.** Half of 10 × 480
> **Review:**
>   **d.** $20.00 − $17.50 **e.** 56 + 239   **f.** 284 − 65
>
> **Problem Solving:** There were two gallons of punch for the class party. The punch was served in 8-ounce cups. Two gallons of punch was enough to fill how many cups? (Remember that 16 ounces is a pint, two pints is a quart, two quarts is a half gallon, and two half gallons is a gallon.)

We remember that three steps are required to multiply by a two-digit number:

1. Multiply by the ones' digit. Record the last digit of this product in the ones' column.

2. Multiply by the tens' digit. **Record the last digit of this product in the tens' column.**

3. Add to find the total.

In this lesson we will do multiplications that require carrying.

Example 1   Multiply: 46
                            × 27

Solution   First we multiply 46 by 7. This product is 322.

$$
\begin{array}{r}
4 \\
46 \\
\times\ 27 \\
\hline
322
\end{array}
$$

Now we multiply 46 by the 2 of 27. First we multiply 6 by 2 and get 12. Since we are actually multiplying by 20, **we record the 2 in the tens' column** and write the 1 above the 4.

$$
\begin{array}{r}
1 \\
4 \\
46 \\
\times\ 27 \\
\hline
322 \\
2
\end{array}
$$

Then we multiply the 4 by 2 and add 1 to get 9. Then we add the products and get **1242**.

$$
\begin{array}{r}
1 \\
4 \\
46 \\
\times\ 27 \\
\hline
322 \\
92 \\
\hline
1242
\end{array}
\quad \text{or} \quad
\begin{array}{r}
1 \\
4 \\
46 \\
\times\ 27 \\
\hline
322 \\
920 \\
\hline
1242
\end{array}
$$

Example 2   Multiply:

$$
\begin{array}{r}
46 \\
\times\ 72 \\
\hline
\end{array}
$$

Solution   First we multiply 46 by 2 and get 92.

$$
\begin{array}{r}
1 \\
46 \\
\times\ 72 \\
\hline
92
\end{array}
$$

Next we multiply 46 by 7 and add the products to get **3312**.

$$
\begin{array}{r}
4 \\
1 \\
46 \\
\times\ 72 \\
\hline
92 \\
322 \\
\hline
3312
\end{array}
\quad \text{or} \quad
\begin{array}{r}
4 \\
1 \\
46 \\
\times\ 72 \\
\hline
92 \\
3220 \\
\hline
3312
\end{array}
$$

Practice

a.   38
    × 26
    ─────
     988

b.   49
    × 82
    ─────
    4018

c.   84
    × 67
    ─────
    5628

d.   65
    × 48
    ─────
    3120

Problem set 100

Use the information in the graph to answer questions 1–3:

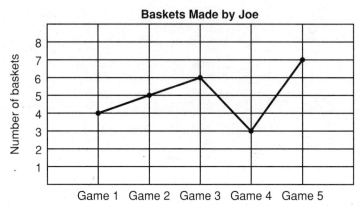

Baskets Made by Joe

Number of baskets

Game 1   Game 2   Game 3   Game 4   Game 5

1. How many baskets did Joe make in the first game?
(92) 4 baskets

2. Each basket is worth 2 points. How many points did
(92) Joe score in Game 5?   14 points

3. How many more points did Joe score in Game 5 than
(92) in Game 3?   2 points

4. The 3-pound melon cost $1.44. What was the cost per
(62) pound? $0.48

5. What is the product of the fourth multiple of 5 and the
(65) tenth multiple of 7?   1400

6. Sammy bought a pair of shoes for $47.99. The sales tax
(93) was $2.88. Sammy gave the clerk $60.00. How much
money should he get back? $9.13

7. If the perimeter of a square is 1 foot, how many inches
(60) long is each side?   3 in.

8. A dollar bill weighs about 1 gram. How many dollar
(88) bills would it take to weigh 1 kilogram?
1000 dollar bills

64 clowns	
16 clowns	$\frac{1}{4}$ had red noses
16 clowns	
16 clowns	$\frac{3}{4}$ did not have red noses
16 clowns	

9. Illustrate this fraction-of-a-group problem: One fourth
(80) of the 64 clowns had red noses. How many clowns
had red noses?   16 clowns

10. What percent of the clowns in problem 9 did not have
(65) red noses?   75%

11. Kerry knew that her trip would take about 7 hours. If
(33) she left at half past nine in the morning, at what time
would she plan to arrive?   4:30 p.m.

12. Jill's boat would hold 42 containers. Each container
(59) would hold 8 big fish. How many big fish could Jill
put in her 42 containers?   336 big fish

13. Eighty-eight horseshoes are enough to shoe how many
(62) horses?   22 horses

14. $\begin{array}{r} 37{,}134 \\ + 52{,}891 \\ \hline 90{,}025 \end{array}$
(61)

15. $\begin{array}{r} \$85.00 \\ - \$68.65 \\ \hline \$16.35 \end{array}$
(51)

16. $\begin{array}{r} 26 \\ 32 \\ 54 \\ 213 \\ 60 \\ 143 \\ + \quad 8 \\ \hline 536 \end{array}$
(21)

17. 47 × 100
(95)   4700

18. 60 × 700
(96)   42,000

19. $\begin{array}{r} 328 \\ \times \quad 4 \\ \hline 1312 \end{array}$
(68)

20. $\begin{array}{r} 43 \\ \times \ 32 \\ \hline 1376 \end{array}$
(97)

21. $\begin{array}{r} 25 \\ \times \ 35 \\ \hline 875 \end{array}$
(100)

22. $\begin{array}{r} 863 \text{ r } 2 \\ 5\overline{)4317} \end{array}$
(86)

23. $\begin{array}{r} \$5.50 \\ 8\overline{)\$44.00} \end{array}$
(90)

24. $\begin{array}{r} 660 \text{ r } 3 \\ 6\overline{)3963} \end{array}$
(90)

25. 426 ÷ 3   142
(86)

26. 2524 ÷ 4   631
(86)

27. Draw and shade circles to show that $2\frac{1}{2}$ equals $\frac{5}{2}$.
(99)

28. 4 + 3 + 27 + 35 + 8 + N = 112   35
(2)

LESSON
101

Decimal Place: Tenths

a. 90
b. 220
c. 1300
d. $16.54
e. 19
f. 403
Patterns:
    16, 32, 64

Facts Practice: 90 Division Facts (Test I in Test Masters)

Mental Math: Find half of each product.
   a. Half of 10 × 18   **b.** Half of 10 × 44   **c.** Half of 10 × 260

Review:
   d. $14.56 + $1.98   **e.** 37 − 18   **f.** 248 + 155

Patterns: Each number in this sequence is doubled to make the next number in the sequence. Find the next three numbers.

1, 2, 4, 8, __, __, __, ...

Part of this square is shaded. We show three ways to write how much of the square is shaded.

One tenth is shaded.

$\frac{1}{10}$ is shaded.

0.1 is shaded.

One tenth can be written with words.

One tenth can be written as a fraction: $\frac{1}{10}$

One tenth can be written as a decimal number: 0.1

We use **place value** to write "tenths" as a decimal number. We remember that the dot is called a **decimal point.** The digit just to the right of the decimal point is in the tenths' place. The digit in the tenths' place tells how many tenths. When we use a decimal point to help us write a number, we call the number a **decimal number** or just a **decimal.**

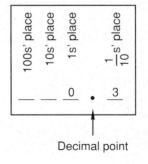

Decimal point

The digit in the tenths' place in 0.3 is 3. We read this number as "three tenths." We say the digit in the tenths' place and then say the word *tenths*. We usually write a zero in front of the decimal point.

.3 and 0.3 and $\frac{3}{10}$ are read as "three tenths"

.1 and 0.1 and $\frac{1}{10}$ are read as "one tenth"

.5 and 0.5 and $\frac{5}{10}$ are read as "five tenths"

Example 1   Write the shaded part of this square as a fraction and as a decimal number.

Solution   The square is divided into 10 parts. Three of these parts are shaded. Three tenths of the square is shaded.

$\frac{3}{10}$ is the fraction   **0.3** is the decimal number

Example 2   Which of these fractions equals 0.7?

A. $\frac{1}{7}$ B. $\frac{7}{8}$ C. $\frac{7}{10}$

Solution   The decimal number 0.7 is seven tenths. The correct choice is **C** because

$$0.7 = \frac{7}{10}$$

Practice   **a.** What fraction names the shaded part of this square? $\frac{1}{10}$

b. What decimal number names the shaded part of the square?   0.1

c. What fraction names the part that is not shaded? $\frac{9}{10}$

d. What decimal number names the part that is not shaded?   0.9

e. Write a fraction equal to 0.6. $\frac{6}{10}$

f. Write a decimal number equal to $\frac{4}{10}$.   0.4

g. Write seven tenths as a fraction and as a decimal number. $\frac{7}{10}$; 0.7

**Problem set
101**

1. Three quarters, four dimes, two nickels, and seven
(45) pennies is how much money? $1.32

2. Trudy separated the 37 math books as equally as
(98) possible into 4 stacks.

(a) How many stacks had exactly 9 books?   3 stacks

(b) How many stacks had 10 books?   1 stack

3. Martin paid $1 for a folder and received 52¢ back in
(93) change. If the tax was 3¢, how much did the folder
cost?   45¢

4. Frank wrote each of his 12 spelling words five times.
(59) In all, how many words did he write?   60 words

5. Round 5456 to the nearest thousand. Round 2872 to
(91) the nearest thousand. Find the sum of the two
rounded numbers.   5000; 3000; 8000

6. What is the tally for 10?   ⊬⊬⊬ ⊬⊬⊬
(85)

7. Part of this square is shaded.
(101)
(a) Use a fraction to write the
shaded part. $\frac{7}{10}$
(b) Use a decimal number to write
the shaded part.   0.7

8. Illustrate this fraction-of-a-group problem: One sixth
(80) of the 48 crayons are broken. How many crayons are
broken?   8 crayons

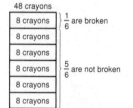

9. Segment *AB* is 32 mm long. Segment *BC* is 26 mm
(50) long. Segment *AD* is 91 mm long. How many
millimeters long is segment *CD*?   33 mm

A   B   C   D

10. 39,279 − 9,816   29,463   **11.** $63.75 + $184.75
(62)   (28) $248.50

12. $60.00 − ($49.38 + 75¢) $9.87
(55)

13. $6.08   **14.**   47   **15.**   36
(68)   ×   8   (100)   × 24   (100)   × 62
       ─────────   ──────   ──────
        $48.64   1128   2232

16. 53 × 30   1590   **17.** 63 × 37   2331
(100)   (100)   864

18. 100 × 32   3200   **19.** 4)3456
(95)   864   (86) $7.20

20. 8)6912   **21.** 7)$50.40
(86)   (90)

22. Draw and shade circles to show that $1\frac{1}{4}$ equals $\frac{5}{4}$.
(99)

23. $5^2 + \sqrt{25} + N = 30$ 0
(72,2)

24. Draw a square with sides 4 cm long.   4 cm
(25)

25. Shade 50% of the square in problem 24. How many
(94,65) square centimeters did you shade?   8 sq. cm

LESSON
102

a. 80
b. 120
c. 140
d. 320
Problem Solving:
About 10% of the
circle is shaded.
About 90% of the
circle is not
shaded.

Naming Hundredths with Decimal Numbers

Facts Practice: 90 Division Facts (Test I in Test Masters)

Mental Math: Five is half of 10. To multiply by 5 we may multiply by half of 10. For example, 5 × 12 equals half of 10 × 12. Find each product by multiplying by "half of 10."

   a. 5 × 16   **b.** 5 × 24   **c.** 5 × 28   **d.** 5 × 64

Problem Solving: About what percent of the circle is shaded? About what percent of the circle is not shaded?

The first place to the right of the decimal point is the tenths' place. If a 1 is written in the tenths' place, it has a value of one tenth.

$$0.1 \quad \text{means} \quad \frac{1}{10}$$

If a 3 is written in the tenths' place, it has a value of three tenths.

$$0.3 \quad \text{means} \quad \frac{3}{10}$$

The second place to the right of the decimal point is the **hundredths' place.** If a 1 is written in the hundredths' place, it has a value of one hundredth.

$$0.01 \quad \text{means} \quad \frac{1}{100}$$

If a 3 is written in the hundredths' place, it has a value of three hundredths.

$$0.03 \quad \text{means} \quad \frac{3}{100}$$

If we write "34" to the right of the decimal point, we mean thirty-four hundredths.

$$0.34 \quad \text{means} \quad \frac{34}{100}$$

When we write the fraction $\frac{34}{100}$, we **show** that the denominator is 100. When we write the decimal number 0.34, we **understand** that the denominator is 100. It is customary, but not necessary, to write a zero in front of the decimal point. The values of .34 and 0.34 are equal.

$$.34 = 0.34$$

Example 1   Part of this square is shaded.

(a) Use a fraction to write the shaded part.

(b) Use a decimal number to write the shaded part.

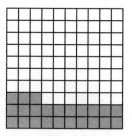

Solution   The square is divided into hundredths. Twenty-three hundredths are shaded.

(a) Twenty-three hundredths as a fraction is $\frac{23}{100}$.

(b) Twenty-three hundredths as a decimal number is **0.23.**

Example 2   (a) Write a fraction that equals 0.37.

(b) Write a decimal number that equals $\frac{29}{100}$.

Solution (a) The decimal number 0.37 is written with two places to the right of the decimal point. That means the denominator is 100. Thus, 0.37 equals $\frac{37}{100}$.

(b) A fraction with a denominator of 100 can be written as a decimal with two places to the right of the decimal point. So $\frac{29}{100}$ equals **0.29**.

Practice Write a fraction for each decimal number:

a. 0.37 $\frac{37}{100}$ **b.** 0.07 $\frac{7}{100}$ **c.** 0.99 $\frac{99}{100}$ **d.** 0.03 $\frac{3}{100}$

Write a decimal number for each fraction:

e. $\frac{61}{100}$ 0.61 **f.** $\frac{9}{100}$ 0.09 **g.** $\frac{25}{100}$ 0.25 **h.** $\frac{4}{100}$ 0.04

i. What decimal number names the shaded part of this square? 0.03

j. What decimal number names the part that is not shaded? 0.97

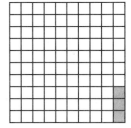

Problem set 102 Use the information given to answer questions 1–3:

Mary invited 14 friends for lunch. She plans to make 12 tuna sandwiches, 10 bologna sandwiches, and 8 roast beef sandwiches.

1. How many sandwiches will she make in all?
(82) 30 sandwiches

2. Including Mary, each person can have how many sandwiches? 2 sandwiches
(82)

3. If she cuts each tuna sandwich in half, how many halves will there be? 24 halves
(82)

4. Five pounds of grapes cost $2.95. What was the cost per pound? $0.59
(62)

5. If each side of a hexagon is 4 inches long, what is the perimeter of the hexagon in feet? 2 ft
(73)

6. Nine hundred forty-seven thousand is how much
(38) greater than two hundred seventy-five thousand?
672,000

7. Part of this square is shaded.
(101)
(a) Use a fraction to write the
shaded part. $\frac{7}{100}$

(b) Use a decimal number to write
the shaded part.   0.07

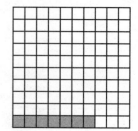

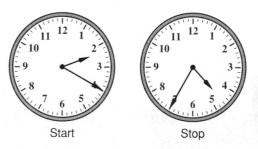

8. Use words to write $7572\frac{1}{8}$.
(44) seven thousand, five hundred seventy-two and one eighth

9. Illustrate this fraction-of-a-group problem: One fifth
(80) of the 80 chariots lost wheels in the chase. How many
of the chariots lost wheels?   16 chariots

10. What percent of the chariots in problem 9 lost wheels?
(80,65) 20%

11. Franca began the trip when it was still dark. She
(33) finished the trip a couple of hours later. How long did
the trip take?   2 hours, 15 minutes

Start   Stop

12. James traveled 301 miles in 7 hours. He traveled an
(70) average of how many miles each hour?
43 miles each hour

13. Marvin bought 3 folders for $1.99 each. Sales tax was
(93) 33¢. He paid with a $20.00 bill. How much money
should he get back? $13.70

14. $25 + $2.75 + $15.44 + 27¢ $43.46
(53)

15. 21,631 − 5,716 15,915   **16.** $100.00 − $89.85 $10.15
(62)   (51)

17. 60 × 900   **18.** 42 × 30 1260   **19.** 21 × 17 357
(96) 54,000   (77)   (97)

20.
$$\begin{array}{r} 36 \\ \times\, 74 \\ \hline 2664 \end{array}$$
(100)

21.
$$\begin{array}{r} 48 \\ \times\, 25 \\ \hline 1200 \end{array}$$
(100)

22.
$$\begin{array}{r} \$4.79 \\ \times\qquad 6 \\ \hline \$28.74 \end{array}$$
(68)

23. $9\overline{)2718}$ $\;302$
(90)

24. $5\overline{)4815}$ $\;963$
(86)

25. $6\overline{)4829}$ $\;804\text{ r }5$
(90)

26. $50.00 ÷ 8
(86) $6.25

27. 2121 ÷ 7
(90) 303

28.
$$\begin{array}{r} 7 \\ 8 \\ 5 \\ N \quad 16 \\ 6 \\ 2 \\ +\; 3 \\ \hline 47 \end{array}$$
(2)

29. $\dfrac{2412}{3}$ $\;804$
(90)

30. Draw and shade rectangles to
(99) show that $1\frac{2}{3}$ equals $\frac{5}{3}$. ▮▮ ▮▯

LESSON
103

a. 230
b. 310
c. 1200
d. $26.82
e. 38
f. 114
Patterns:
$\;\;4, 2, 1, \frac{1}{2}, \frac{1}{4}$

Estimating Two-Digit Multiplication Answers

Facts Practice: 100 Multiplication Facts (Test H in Test Masters)

Mental Math: Find each product by multiplying by "half of 10."

  a. 5 × 46   **b.** 5 × 62   **c.** 5 × 240

Review:

  d. $24.87 + $1.95   **e.** 73 − 35   **f.** 76 + 38

Patterns: Each number in this sequence is one half of the preceding number. Find the next five numbers in this sequence.

       ..., 64, 32, 16, 8, __, __, __, __, __, ...

Estimation can help prevent mistakes. If we estimate the answer before we multiply, we can tell if our answer is reasonable.

Example 1 Jim multiplied 43 by 29 and got 203. Could this answer be correct?

Solution Let's estimate the product by multiplying the rounded numbers 40 and 30.

$$40 \times 30 = 1200$$

Jim's answer of 203 and our estimate of 1200 are very different, **so Jim's answer of 203 is probably not correct.** He should check his multiplication.

Example 2 Estimate the product of 38 and 53. Then find an exact answer.

Solution First we multiply the rounded numbers.

$$40 \times 50 = 2000$$

Now we will get an exact answer.

$$\begin{array}{r} 38 \\ \times 53 \\ \hline 114 \\ 190 \\ \hline 2014 \end{array}$$

Our estimate of the product was **2000,** so our answer of **2014** is reasonable.

Practice Estimate the product of each multiplication. Then find the exact answer.

a. 58 × 23
1200; 1334

b. 49 × 51
2500; 2499

c. 61 × 38
2400; 2318

Problem set 103

1. Ninety-one students are divided as equally as possible
(98) among 3 classrooms.

   (a) How many classrooms have exactly 30 students?

   (b) How many classrooms have 31 students?
   (a) 2 classrooms (b) 1 classroom

2. In 1970 it cost 6¢ to mail a letter. How much did it
(59) cost to mail 20 letters in 1970? $1.20

3. What number is seven hundred ninety more than two
(38) hundred ten? 1000

4. George Washington was born in 1732 and died in
(64) 1799. How many years did he live?   67 years

5. A $1 bill weighs about 1 gram. How much would a $5
(88) bill weigh?   1 gram

6. This is the tally for what number?   ЖТ ЖТ ЖТ IIII
(85) 19

7. Part of this square is shaded.
(101)
(a) Use a fraction to write the
    shaded part. $\frac{9}{10}$

(b) Use a decimal number to write
    the shaded part.   0.9

8. Estimate the product of 49 and 62.   3000
(103)

9. Illustrate this fraction-of-a-group problem: One half of
(80) the 32 chess pieces were still on the board. How many
chess pieces were still on the board?   16 chess pieces

```
32 chess pieces
┌─────────────────┐
│ 16 chess pieces │  } 1/2 on the
│                 │      board
│ 16 chess pieces │  } 1/2 not on
└─────────────────┘      2 the board
```

10. Mary left home at 10:30 a.m. She traveled for 7 hours.
(33) What time was it when she arrived?   5:30 p.m.

11. Mark traveled 42 miles in 1 hour. If he kept going at
(67) the same speed, how far would he travel in 20 hours?
840 mi

12. Violet paid $40 for a toaster that cost $29.99 plus
(93) $1.80 in tax. How much money should she get back?
$8.21

13. 3714 + 238 + 46 + 7   **14.** $15.27 + $85.75
(61) 4005   *(28)* $101.02

15. $18.00 − $15.63   **16.** 10,141 − (363 + 99)
(51) $2.37   *(55)* 9679

17. $2^3 \times \sqrt{25}$ **18.** 30 × 90   **19.** $7.50 × 8
(72,40) 40   *(96)* 2700   *(68)* $60.00

20.   49   **21.**   54   **22.**   74
(100) × 62   *(100)* × 23   *(77)* × 40
       ────   ────   ────
       3038   1242   2960

              $1.59   160   307 r 3
23. 4)$6.36   **24.** 5)800   **25.** 6)1845
(86)   *(90)*   *(90)*

26. $4735 \div 8$
(86)   591 r 7

27. $1800 \div 3$
(90)   600

28.
(2)

```
   3
   5
   1
   4
   7
   N    18
   8
   2
   3
   5
+  2
  58
```

29. Draw and shade circles to show
(99) that $2\frac{1}{4}$ equals $\frac{9}{4}$.

30. Find the perimeter and area of
(94,60) this rectangle.   140 ft; 1000 sq. ft

50 ft

20 ft

LESSON 104

Two-Step Word Problems

a. 600
b. 1200
c. 2400
d. $5.11
e. 124
f. 600
Problem Solving:
The total fine will be $1.05.

Facts Practice: 100 Multiplication Facts (Test H in Test Masters)

Mental Math: Find half of each product.
  a. Half of 100×12 **b.** Half of 100×24 **c.** Half of 100×48

Review:
  d. $10.00 - $4.89   **e.** $151 - 27$ **f.** $340 + 60 + 200$

Problem Solving: On February 4, Edgar remembered that his two library books were due on January 28. The fine for late books is 15¢ per day. If he returns the books on February 4, what will be the total fine?

We have practiced two-step problems by finding total prices and change back. Starting with this lesson, we will practice other kinds of two-step problems. Many math problems require more than one step to solve. Writing down the information that is given or drawing a picture is often helpful in solving these problems.

Example 1   Jim is 5 years older than Tad. Tad is 2 years younger than Blanca. Blanca is 9 years old. How old is Jim?

Solution   We will write down the information we have and see if that helps.

$$\text{Blanca} = 9 \text{ years old}$$

$$\text{Tad} = 2 \text{ years younger than Blanca}$$

$$\text{Jim} = 5 \text{ years older than Tad}$$

We see that Blanca is 9. Tad is 2 years younger than Blanca, so Tad is 7. Jim is 5 years older than Tad, so **Jim is 12 years old.**

Example 2   Jim paid for 5 pounds of apples with a $10 bill. He got back $6. What was the cost of 1 pound of apples?

Solution   We begin by finding how much all 5 pounds of apples cost. If Jim paid for the apples with a $10 bill and got $6 back, then all 5 pounds must have cost $4.

$$
\begin{array}{rl}
\$10 & \text{amount paid} \\
-\ \$\ 6 & \text{change back} \\
\hline
\$\ 4 & \text{cost of 5 pounds of apples}
\end{array}
$$

To find the cost of 1 pound of apples, we divide $4 by 5.

$$
\begin{array}{r}
\$0.80 \\
5\overline{)\$4.00} \\
\underline{4\ 0} \\
00 \\
\underline{0} \\
0
\end{array}
$$

Each pound of apples cost **$0.80.**

Practice   Nancy paid for 4 pounds of peaches with a $5 bill. She got back $3. What was the cost of 1 pound of peaches? (First find the cost of 4 pounds of peaches.) $0.50

Problem set 104

1. Gabriel gave a $5 bill to pay for a half gallon of milk
(93) that cost $1.06 and a box of cereal that cost $2.39. How much money should he get back? $1.55

2. Eighty-one animals crossed the bridge. One third of
(104,80) them were billy goats. The rest were bears. How many bears crossed the bridge? (First find how many billy goats crossed the bridge.)   54 bears

3. Johnny planted 8 rows of apple trees. There were 15
(59) trees in each row. How many trees did he plant?
120 trees

4. Four pounds of bananas cost the Fairy Queen one
(104) hundred fifty-six trinkets. Each pound of bananas cost how many trinkets?   39 trinkets

5. The scale shows a weight of how
(22) many grams?   550 g

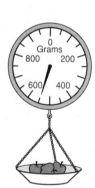

6. Write the tally for 16.   JHT JHT JHT I
(85)

7. Part of this square is shaded.
(102)
(a) Use a fraction to write the shaded part. $\frac{11}{100}$

(b) Use a decimal number to write the shaded part.   0.11

8. Estimate the product of 32 and 48.
(103) Then find the exact product.   1500; 1536

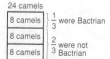

9. Illustrate this fraction-of-a-group problem: One third
(80) of the 24 camels were Bactrian. How many camels were Bactrian?   8 camels

10. A quart is a quarter of a gallon. A quart is what percent
(65) of a gallon?   25%

11. Five hundred seventy people sat in the bleachers.
(31) Then some went home. Only twenty-seven were left.
How many went home?   543 people

12. Matthew could travel 496 miles in 8 hours. How far
(70) could he travel in 1 hour?   62 mi

13.
(30)
$$\begin{array}{r} N \\ +\quad 731 \\ \hline 398,548 \end{array}$$ 397,817

14.
(28)
$$\begin{array}{r} \$46.39 \\ +\ \$54.60 \\ \hline \$100.99 \end{array}$$

15.
(21)
$$\begin{array}{r} 37 \\ 81 \\ 45 \\ 139 \\ 7 \\ 15 \\ +\quad 60 \\ \hline 384 \end{array}$$

16.
(62)
$$\begin{array}{r} 96,410 \\ -\quad 9,641 \\ \hline 86,769 \end{array}$$

17.
(19)
$$\begin{array}{r} \$37.81 \\ -\ \$16.79 \\ \hline \$21.02 \end{array}$$

18. 63 × 1000
(95)   63,000

19. 80 × 50¢
(96) $40.00

20.
(100)
$$\begin{array}{r} 52 \\ \times\ 15 \\ \hline 780 \end{array}$$

21.
(100)
$$\begin{array}{r} 36 \\ \times\ 27 \\ \hline 972 \end{array}$$

22.
(100)
$$\begin{array}{r} 59 \\ \times\ 32 \\ \hline 1888 \end{array}$$

23.
(86)
$$2\overline{)714}\quad ^{357}$$

24.
(86)
$$6\overline{)789}\quad ^{131\ r\ 3}$$

25.
(90)
$$4\overline{)2363}\quad ^{590\ r\ 3}$$

26. 2835 ÷ 7
(90)   405

27. $29.00 ÷ 5
(90) $5.80

28.
(2)
$$\begin{array}{r} 3 \\ 5 \\ 8 \\ 7 \\ 4 \\ N \quad 20 \\ +\ 6 \\ \hline 53 \end{array}$$

29. Draw and shade rectangles to
(99) show that $1\frac{2}{5}$ equals $\frac{7}{5}$. ▮▮▮▮ ▮▮▮▮

30. A room is 5 yards long and 4 yards
(94) wide. How many square yards of
carpet are needed to cover the
floor?   20 square yards

LESSON
105

"Fraction-of-a-Group" Problems,
Part 2

a. 800
b. 2200
c. 1300
d. 3400
e. $37.47
f. 67
g. 201
Patterns:
   32, 64, 128, 256,
   512

Facts Practice: 100 Multiplication Facts (Test H in Test Masters)

Mental Math: Fifty is half of 100. Find each product by multiplying by half of 100.

 a. 50 × 16   **b.** 50 × 44   **c.** 50 × 26   **d.** 50 × 68

Review:

 e. $32.48 + $4.99   **f.** 96 − 29   **g.** 156 + 45

Patterns: Copy this sequence on your paper and continue it until you reach a number greater than 500.

1, 2, 4, 8, 16, ...

The fraction problems in this lesson are two-step problems. First we find the number in one part. Then we can find the number in more than one part.

Example 1 There were 30 leprechauns in the forest. Three fifths of them wore green jackets. How many leprechauns wore green jackets?

Solution The word *fifths* tells us there were 5 equal groups. We need to find the number in each group. Since there were 30 leprechauns in all, we divide 30 by 5.

$$5\overline{)30} = 6$$

There are 6 leprechauns in each group.

$\frac{3}{5}$ wore green jackets

$\frac{2}{5}$ did not wear green jackets

30 leprechauns
6 leprechauns
6 leprechauns
6 leprechauns
6 leprechauns
6 leprechauns

Three fifths wore green jackets. In three groups, there are 3 times 6 leprechauns. That is, **18 leprechauns wore green jackets.** We also see that two groups did not wear green jackets, so 12 leprechauns did not wear green jackets.

Example 2 Two thirds of the 24 elves worked in the toy factory. How many elves worked in the toy factory?

Solution First we divide 24 by 3 and find that the number of elves in **one** third is 8.

Practice Answers

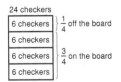

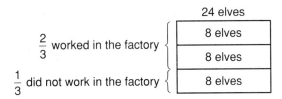

Then we multiply 8 by 2 and find that the number of elves in **two** thirds is 16. We have found that **16 elves** worked in the toy factory.

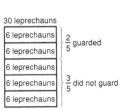

Practice Solve and illustrate each problem:

a. Three fourths of the 24 checkers were still on the board. How many checkers were still on the board?
18 checkers

b. Two fifths of the 30 leprechauns guarded the treasure. How many leprechauns guarded the treasure?
12 leprechauns

40 students

| 5 students |
| 5 students | $\frac{3}{8}$ perfect |
| 5 students |
| 5 students |
| 5 students |
| 5 students | $\frac{5}{8}$ not perfect |
| 5 students |
| 5 students |

c. Three eighths of the 40 students had perfect scores. How many students had perfect scores?   15 students

Problem set 105 Use the information in this tally sheet to answer questions 1–3:

Results of Class Election

Irma	ЖШ II
Brad	ЖШ I
Thanh	ЖШ III
Marisol	ЖШ ЖШ II

1. Who was second in the election?   Thanh
(85)

2. Who received twice as many votes as Brad?   Marisol
(85)

3. Altogether, how many votes were cast?   33 votes
(85)

20 balloons

4 balloons		
4 balloons	$\frac{2}{5}$ yellow
4 balloons	
4 balloons	$\frac{3}{5}$ not yellow
4 balloons	

4. Two fifths of the 20 balloons were yellow. How many
(105) balloons were yellow? Illustrate the problem.
8 balloons

5. Tim is 5 years younger than Brad. Brad is 2 years older
(104) than Linda. Linda is 11 years old. How old is Tim?
8 years old

6. Part of this group is shaded.
(101)
   (a) Write the shaded part as a
      fraction. $\frac{3}{10}$

   (b) Write the shaded part as a
      decimal.   0.3

7. The fraction $\frac{1}{10}$ equals 10%. What percent of the group
(65) in problem 6 is shaded?   30%

8. Estimate the product of 88 and 59. Then find the exact
(103) product.   5400; 5192

9. Sue's birthday is May 2. Her birth-
(64) day will be on what day of the
week in the year 2047?   Tuesday

MAY 2047						
S	M	T	W	T	F	S
		1	2	3	4	5	6
7	8	9	10	11	12	13
14	15	16	17	18	19	20
21	22	23	24	25	26	27
28	29	30	31			

10. Segment *AB* is 17 mm long. Segment *CD* is 36 mm
(50) long. Segment *AD* is 89 mm long. How long is
segment *BC*?   36 mm

```
    A       B           C           D
    •───────•───────────•───────────•
```

11. $32.63 + $42 + $7.56
(53) $82.19

12. $86.45 − ($74.50 + $5)
(55) $6.95

13. 83 × 40
(77)   3320

14. 1000 × 53
(95)   53,000

15. 9^3
(72)   729

16.
(100)
$$\begin{array}{r} 32 \\ \times\ 16 \\ \hline 512 \end{array}$$

17.
(100)
$$\begin{array}{r} 67 \\ \times\ 32 \\ \hline 2144 \end{array}$$

18.
(68)
$$\begin{array}{r} \$8.95 \\ \times\quad\ 4 \\ \hline \$35.80 \end{array}$$

$$\overset{208\text{ r }1}{3)\overline{625}}$$

19.
(90)

$$\overset{178\text{ r }2}{4)\overline{714}}$$

20.
(86)

$$\overset{230\text{ r }5}{6)\overline{1385}}$$

21.
(90)

22. $\dfrac{900}{5}$ 180
(90)

23. 3748 ÷ 9
(86)   416 r 4

24. $28.56 ÷ 8
(86) $3.57

25. This circle shows that $\frac{2}{2}$ equals 1.
(99) Draw a circle that shows that $\frac{3}{3}$
equals 1.

26. (1)	**27.** (1)
1	4
2	4
3	4
4	4
5	4
4	4
3	4
2	4
1	4
6	4
+ 7	+ 4
38	44

28. Find the perimeter and area of
(94,60) this rectangle.   180 mi; 2000 sq. mi

50 mi

40 mi

LESSON
106

Average

a. 6
b. 8
c. 30
d. 100
e. 50
f. $0.58
g. 255
h. 18
Problem Solving:
  Wednesday

Facts Practice: 100 Multiplication Facts (Test H in Test Masters)

Mental Math: Double each number.

  a. 3   **b.** 4   **c.** 15   **d.** 50   **e.** 25

Review:

  f. $1.00 − 42¢   **g.** 199 + 56   **h.** 43 − 25

Problem Solving: There are 365 days in a common year, which is about 52 weeks. However, since 52 weeks is 364 days, the following year does not start on the same day of the week as the preceding year started. If a common year starts on a Tuesday, on what day of the week will the following year begin?

Here we show three stacks of pancakes.

8   3   4

There are 15 pancakes in all. If we rearrange the pancakes to have an equal number in each stack, we get 5 in each stack.

5   5   5

We say that the **average** number of pancakes in each stack is 5. Finding an average is a two-step "equal groups" problem. First we find how many there are altogether. Then we find how many there would be in each group if the groups were equal.

Example Four vans carried the team to the soccer field. There were 5 players in the first van, 4 players in the second van, 3 players in the third van, and 8 players in the fourth van. What was the average number of players in each van?

Solution The average number of players in each van is the number there would be if there were the same number of players in each van. Imagine starting over and reloading the vans equally. First we need to find the total number of players. We find the total by adding the number in each van.

$$\begin{array}{r} 5 \text{ players} \\ 4 \text{ players} \\ 3 \text{ players} \\ + 8 \text{ players} \\ \hline 20 \text{ players} \end{array}$$

Since there are 4 vans, we divide the 20 players into 4 equal groups.

$$\frac{20 \text{ players}}{4 \text{ vans}} = 5 \text{ players in each van}$$

If the vans were loaded equally, there would be 5 players in each van. Even though the vans were not loaded equally, **the average number in each van was 5 players.**

Practice In three classrooms there were 24, 26, and 28 children, respectively. What was the average number of children in each classroom? 26 children

Problem set **1.** Freddie is 2 years older than Ivan. Ivan is twice as old
106 _(104)_ as Becky. Becky is 6 years old. How old is Freddie?
    14 years old

  2. What is the total number of days in the first three
  _(64)_ months of a leap year? 91 days

  3. It cost $1.39 to mail the package. Marty put three 25-
  _(104)_ cent stamps on the package. How much more postage does it need? $0.64

4. Thirty-two desks were arranged as equally as possible
(98) in 6 rows.

(a) How many rows had exactly 5 desks?   4 rows

(b) How many rows had 6 desks?   2 rows

21 riders

| 7 riders |
| 7 riders |
| 7 riders |

$\frac{2}{3}$ rode bareback

$\frac{1}{3}$ did not ride bareback

5. Two thirds of the 21 riders rode bareback. How many
(105) riders rode bareback? Illustrate the problem.   14 riders

6. (a) What decimal number names
(102)   the shaded part of this square?

(b) What decimal number names
the part that is not shaded?

(a) 0.05   (b) 0.95

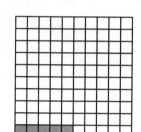

7. Each small square in problem 6 is
(65) 1% of the large square. What percent of the large square is shaded?
5%

8. Round 3874 to the nearest thousand.   4000
(91)

9. Beth opened a liter of milk and poured half of it into a
(83,65) pitcher. How many milliliters of milk did she pour
into the pitcher? What percent of the milk was still in
the container?   500 mL; 50%

10. The sun was up when Mark started. It was dark when
(33) he stopped. How much time had gone by?
9 hours, 10 minutes

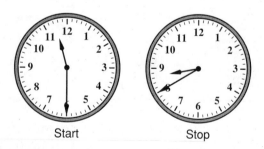

Start   Stop

11. For five days Jan recorded the high temperature. The
(106) temperatures were 79°F, 82°F, 84°F, 81°F, and 74°F,
respectively. What was the average high temperature
for those five days?   80°F

12. Mickey drove 368 miles in 8 hours. If she drove the
(70) same number of miles each hour, how far did she
drive each hour?   46 miles each hour

13.   496,325
(61)   +   3,680
          ─────────
             500,005

14. $36.00
(51) − $30.78
        ────────
          $5.22

15. $12.45
(28)   1.30
             2.00
             0.25
             0.04
             0.32
        +   1.29
        ────────
          $17.65

16. $8.56 × 7
(68) $59.92

17. 60 × 300
(96) 18,000

18. $\frac{432}{6}$ 72
(75)

19.   26
(100)   × 24
          ─────
           624

20.   25
(100)   × 25
          ─────
           625

21. $\overset{120\ r\ 5}{7\overline{)845}}$
(90)

22. $\overset{111\ r\ 1}{9\overline{)1000}}$
(86)

23. $16.40 ÷ 8
(90) $2.05

24. Draw and shade a circle that shows that $\frac{4}{4}$ equals 1.
(99)

25. The wall was 8 feet high and 12 feet wide. How many
(94) square feet of wallpaper were needed to cover the
wall?   96 sq. ft

LESSON 107

Writing Mixed Numbers as Decimals

a. 42
b. 64
c. 110
d. 1200

Facts Practice: 100 Multiplication Facts (Test H in Test Masters)

Mental Math: If we multiply the double of one factor by the half of the other factor, we can find the product.

$$4 \times 18$$
$$\text{double} \downarrow \quad \downarrow \text{half}$$
$$8 \times 9 = 72$$

Find each product by the double and half method.

a. 3×14 **b.** 4×16 **c.** 5×22 **d.** 50×24

The figure below has three squares. Two and three tenths of the squares are shaded. We can describe the shaded parts by using either a mixed number or a decimal number. Both the mixed number and the decimal number are read "two and three tenths."

$2\frac{3}{10}$ is shaded   or   2.3 is shaded

In the decimal number, the whole number part is to the left of the decimal point and the fraction part is to the right of the decimal point.

In the next figure, one and thirty-three hundredths squares are shaded. We can name one and thirty-three hundredths as a mixed number or as a decimal (number).

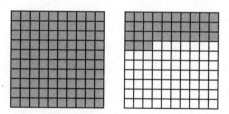

$1\frac{33}{100}$ is shaded   or   1.33 is shaded

Both are read "one and thirty-three hundredths."

Example 1   Write each mixed number as a decimal number:

(a) $3\frac{7}{10}$ (b) $16\frac{17}{100}$ (c) $8\frac{9}{100}$

Solution   We write the whole number to the left of the decimal point and write the fraction to the right of the decimal point. Tenths are written one place to the right of the decimal point. Hundredths are written two places to the right of the decimal point.

(a) **3.7** (b) **16.17** (c) **8.09**

Example 2   Write each decimal number as a mixed number:

(a) 24.9 (b) 5.23 (c) 4.03

Solution   (a) $\mathbf{24\frac{9}{10}}$ (b) $\mathbf{5\frac{23}{100}}$ (c) $\mathbf{4\frac{3}{100}}$

Practice   **a.** Write the number of shaded squares as a mixed number. $1\frac{1}{10}$

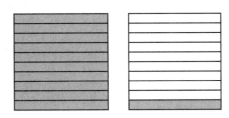

b. Write the number of shaded squares as a decimal number.   1.1

Write each mixed number as a decimal number:

c. $9\frac{99}{100}$ 9.99 **d.** $12\frac{3}{10}$ 12.3 **e.** $10\frac{1}{100}$ 10.01

Write each decimal number as a mixed number:

f. 60.3 $60\frac{3}{10}$ **g.** 6.03 $6\frac{3}{100}$ **h.** 5.67 $5\frac{67}{100}$

Problem set   Use this chart to answer questions 1–4:
107

Mileage Chart

	Atlanta	Boston	Chicago	Kansas City	Los Angeles	New York City	Wash., D.C.
Chicago	730	975		499	2095	840	712
Dallas	805	1819	936	499	1403	1607	1372
Denver	1401	1989	1016	604	1134	1851	1696
Los Angeles	2197	3052	2095	1596		2915	2644
New York City	855	216	840	1319	2915		229
St. Louis	558	1178	288	253	1848	966	801

1. The distance from Los Angeles to Boston is how much
(89)   greater than the distance from Los Angeles to
New York City?   137 mi

2. (a) Which two cities are the same distance from
(89)   Kansas City?   Chicago and Dallas

   (b) How far apart are the two cities in the answer
       to (a)?   936 mi

3. Rebecca is planning a trip from Chicago to Dallas to
(89)   Los Angeles to Chicago. How many miles will her
trip be?   4434 mi

4. There are 3 empty boxes in the chart. What number
(89)   should go in these boxes?   0

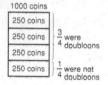

5. Three fourths of the one thousand gold coins were
(105)   doubloons. How many doubloons were there?
Illustrate the problem.   750 doubloons

6. What percent of the gold coins in problem 5 were
(65)   doubloons?   75%

7. Write each mixed number as a decimal:
(107)
   (a) $3\frac{5}{10}$ 3.5   (b) $14\frac{21}{100}$ 14.21   (c) $9\frac{4}{100}$ 9.04

8. Estimate the product of 39 and 406. Then find the
(103) exact product.   16,000; 15,834

9. What is the perimeter of this rect-
(60) angle in millimeters?   80 mm

30 mm

10 mm

10. Use your answer to problem 9 to
(79) find the perimeter of the rectangle
in centimeters.   8 cm

11. Find the area of the rectangle in problem 9.
(94)
300 sq. mm

12. James knew that his trip would take seven and a half
(33) hours. He left at 7 a.m. At what time will he arrive?
2:30 p.m.

13. What is the average number of days per month in the
(106) first three months of a common year?   30 days

14. $2.74 + $0.27 + $6 + 49¢ $9.50
(53)

15. $15.75 − ($2.47 + $10) $3.28
(55)

16. 25 × 40 1000   **17.** 98¢ × 7 $6.86   **18.** $\sqrt{36} \times \sqrt{4}$ 12
(77)   (58)   (40)

19. $\dfrac{3^3}{3}$ 9   **20.**   36   **21.**   35   **22.**   4
(72)   (100) × 34   (100) × 35   (2)   2
                          ‾‾‾‾   ‾‾‾‾   1
                          1224   1225   3

                    $8.75   205 r 4   4
23. 8)$70.00   **24.** 6)1234   7
(86)   (90)   2

                                                           2
25. 800 ÷ 7   **26.** 487 ÷ 3   3
(86)   114 r 2   (86)   162 r 1   4

                                                        + X   10
                                                           ‾‾‾‾
27. Draw and shade circles to show   42
(99) that $2\frac{1}{3}$ equals $\frac{7}{3}$.

LESSON 108

Naming Place Value • Naming Decimal Numbers

a. 54
b. 900
c. 2400
d. $3.25
e. 424
f. 28
Problem Solving:
  8 minutes

Facts Practice: 90 Division Facts (Test J in Test Masters)

Mental Math: Find each product by the double and half method.
  a. 3 × 18   **b.** 15 × 60   **c.** 50 × 48
Review:
  d. $5.00 − $1.75   **e.** 299 + 125   **f.** 76 − 48

Problem Solving: Robert can walk twice as fast as he can swim. He can run twice as fast as he can walk. He can ride a bike twice as fast as he can run. If Robert can ride his bike a quarter mile in one minute, how long would it take him to swim a quarter mile?

In this lesson we will identify decimal place values and write the names of the decimal numbers.

Naming place value

The chart below shows place values from hundreds to hundredths. From the decimal point we find the value of each place. To the left of the decimal point is the ones' place, then the tens' place, and then the hundreds' place. To the right of the decimal point is the tenths' ($\frac{1}{10}$) place, and then the hundredths' ($\frac{1}{100}$) place.

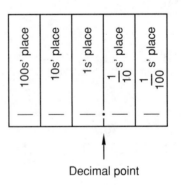

Decimal point

Example 1   Name the place value of the 3 in each number:

  (a) 23.4   (b) 2.34   (c) 32.4   (d) 4.23

Solution   (a) **Ones'**   (b) **Tenths'**

  (c) **Tens'**   (d) **Hundredths'**

Example 2   Which digit in 23.47 is in the same place as the 5 in 8.5?

Solution   In 8.5, the 5 is in the tenths' place. The digit in 23.47 that is in the tenths' place is **4.**

Naming decimal numbers   To name a decimal number, we first name the whole number part. Then we name the decimal part.

To read the decimal number 562.35, we say the whole number part first.

Five hundred sixty-two

Next, we read the decimal point by saying "and."

Five hundred sixty-two **and**

Then we read the number to the right of the decimal point.

Five hundred sixty-two **and** thirty-five

Finally, we name the place value of the last digit.

Five hundred sixty-two **and** thirty-five **hundredths**

Example 3   Use words to name each number:

(a) 12.34   (b) 1.3   (c) 6.07

Solution   (a) **Twelve and thirty-four hundredths**

(b) **One and three tenths**

(c) **Six and seven hundredths**

Practice   Name the place value of the 7 in these numbers:

a. 17.26   ones'   **b.** 61.72   tenths'

c. 26.17   hundredths'   **d.** 72.61   tens'

Which digit is in the tenths' place in these numbers?

e. 43.85   8   **f.** 438.5   5   **g.** 4.38   3   **h.** 1385.4   4

Use words to name each decimal number:

i. 4.38   four and thirty-eight hundredths   **j.** 43.8   forty-three and eight tenths

k. 10.6   ten and six tenths   **l.** 1.06   one and six hundredths

Problem set 108

Use the facts given to answer questions 1–3:

In the Jones family there are 3 children. John is 10 years old. James is 2 years younger than Jill. James is 4 years older than John.

1. How old is James?   14 years old
(104)

2. How old is Jill?   16 years old
(104)

3. When James is 16, how old will Jill be?   18 years old
(104)

4. Denise bought 6 pounds of carrots and an artichoke for
(104) $2.76. If the artichoke cost 84¢, how much was 1 pound of carrots? (First find the cost of all the carrots.)
32¢

5. Write each of these mixed numbers as a decimal
(107) number:

(a) $5\frac{31}{100}$ 5.31   (b) $16\frac{7}{10}$ 16.7   (c) $5\frac{7}{100}$ 5.07

6. Three fifths of the team's 40 points were scored in the
(105) first half. How many points did the team score in the first half? Illustrate the problem.   24 points

7. One fifth is 20%. What percent is three fifths?   60%
(65)

8. Use words to write 7.68.   seven and sixty-eight hundredths
(108)

9. Use words to write 76.8.   seventy-six and eight tenths
(108)

10. Estimate the product of 78 and 91.   7200
(103)

11. Name the number of shaded squares:
(107)
(a) as a mixed number. $1\frac{3}{10}$

(b) as a decimal.   1.3

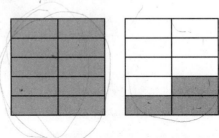

12. There were 24 people in one line and 16 people in the
(106) other line. What was the average number of people in
each line?   20 people

13. In the beginning it was dark. What
(33)   time was it 5 hours and 20 minutes later?   3:00 a.m.

Beginning

14. Mr. Toto could bake 27 pizzas in 3
(70)   hours. How many could he bake
in 1 hour? How many could he
bake in 5 hours? (Multiply the
first answer by 5.) 9 pizzas; 45 pizzas

15. $15 + $6.15 + $13.85   **16.** $13.70 − $6.85 $6.85
(53) $35.00   (53)

17. 26 × 100   **18.** 9 × 87¢   **19.** 14 × 16   224
(95) 2600   (58) $7.83   (100)

20.   15   **21.** $\frac{456}{6}$ 76 ·   **22.**   47
(100) × 15   (75)   (77)   × 60
      225   2820

            708   163 $9.80
23. 6)4248   **24.** 1)163   **25.** 5)$49.00
(90)   (86)   (90)

26. 1 + 3 + 5 + P + 7 + 3 + 2 + 3 = 44   20
(2)

27. How many square foot floor tiles are needed to cover
(94)   the floor of a room that is 15 feet long and 10 feet
wide?   150 square foot floor tiles

28. A penny is what fraction of a dollar? $\frac{1}{100}$
(84)

LESSON 109

Decimal Numbers and Money

a. 56
b. 2000
c. 3200
d. $1.84
e. $7.63
f. 27
Problem Solving:
   Percent left-
   handed:
      10%
   Percent not left-
   handed:
      90%

Facts Practice: 90 Division Facts (Test J in Test Masters)

Mental Math: Find each product by the double and half method.

   a. 4×14 **b.** 25×80 **c.** 50×64

Review:

   d. $10.00 - $8.16   **e.** $4.68 + $2.95   **f.** $62 - 35$

Problem Solving: Three of the 30 students in Marshall's class are left-handed. What percent of the students are left-handed? What percent are not left-handed?

We remember that there are two forms for writing money. In one form the unit is *cents*. For writing cents, we use a cent sign (¢) and no decimal point. When we write

25¢

we mean 25 **whole cents** (or 25 pennies). In the other form of money the unit is *dollars*. For writing dollars, we use a dollar sign ($). We also use a decimal point to show fractions of a dollar. When we write

$0.25

we mean twenty-five hundredths of a dollar (a fraction of a dollar).

A penny is 1 cent.

A penny is also $\frac{1}{100}$ of a dollar.

1¢ = $0.01

Sometimes we see notations for money written incorrectly.

Example   Something is wrong with this sign. What should be changed so that the sign is correct?

Solution   The notation .50¢ is incorrect. We can use the ¢ sign and a whole number to tell how many cents. Or we can use a dollar sign and a decimal point to write the fractional part of a dollar.

50¢ is correct   **$0.50 is also correct**

Practice   At a vegetable stand Martin saw this incorrect sign. Draw two different signs to show ways to correct this error.

Corn
10¢
each
ear

Corn
$0.10
each
ear

Corn
0.10¢
each
ear

**Problem set
109**

1. Robin divided his 53 merry men into groups of 6.
   (98)

   (a) How many groups of 6 could he make?   8 groups

   (b) How many merry men were left over?   5 merry men

   (c) If the remaining merry men formed a group, how many groups were there in all?   9 groups

2. Abraham Lincoln was born in 1809 and died in 1865.
   (64) How long did he live?   56 years

3. The parking lot charges $1.25 for the first hour. It
   (12) charges 50¢ for each additional hour. How much does it cost to park a car in the lot for 3 hours? $2.25

45 points

15 points } $\frac{2}{3}$ scored in
15 points }   second half
15 points } $\frac{1}{3}$ not scored in
             second half

4. Two thirds of the team's 45 points were scored in the
   (105) second half. How many points did the team score in the second half? Draw a diagram to illustrate the problem.   30 points

5. Something is wrong with this
(109) sign. Draw two different signs to
show ways to correct this error.

6. What is the value of 3 ten-dollar
(45) bills, 4 one-dollar bills, 5 dimes,
and 2 pennies? $34.52

7. Use words to write 6412.5. six thousand, four hundred
(108) twelve and five tenths

8. Round 5139 to the nearest thousand. Round 6902 to
(91) the nearest thousand. Then add the rounded numbers.
5000; 7000; 12,000

9. James opened a gallon bottle of milk and poured out 1
(83) quart. How many quarts of milk were left in the bottle?
3 quarts

10. What percent of the milk in problem 9 was left in the
(65) bottle? 75%

11. Estimate the product of 39 and 41. Then find the exact
(103) product.   1600; 1599

12. Thirteen little people came to the party every hour.
(67) After 11 hours, how many little people were at the
party?   143 little people

13. Five full buses held 240 students. What was the
(106) average number of students on each bus?   48 students

14. $68.57   **15.** $100.00   **16.**   15
(28)   + $36.49   (51)   − $5.43   (21)   24
      ⎯⎯⎯⎯⎯   ⎯⎯⎯⎯⎯   36
       $105.06 $94.57   75

17.   12   **18.** $5.08   21
(97)   × 12   (68)   ×   7   8
      ⎯⎯⎯⎯   ⎯⎯⎯⎯⎯   36
        144                  $35.56   + 420
                                                   ⎯⎯⎯⎯⎯
                                                     635

19.
(2)
```
    1
    2
    3
    4
 P  16
    6
    7
    8
 + 9
 ──
   56
```

20.
(1)
```
    1
    2
    4
    6
    8
    6
    4
    3
 + 3
 ──
   37
```

21. 50^2
(72)   2500

22. 49 × 51
(100)   2499

23. 33 × 25
(100)   825

24. $\dfrac{848}{8}$ 106
(90)

25. $9\overline{)6300}$ with quotient 700
(90)

26. $\sqrt{144}$ 12
(40)

27. $5.72 ÷ 4 $1.43
(86)

28. Draw and shade circles to show that $2\frac{2}{3}$ equals $\frac{8}{3}$.
(99)

3 in. ‾ 1 in. rectangle

29. Draw a rectangle that is three inches long and one inch
(25) wide.

30. What is the perimeter and area of the rectangle in
(94,60) problem 29?   8 in.; 3 sq. in.

LESSON 110

Circles: Radius and Diameter

a. 48
b. 24,000
c. 1075
d. $13.75
e. 564
f. 14

Problem Solving:
The book will be
due on May 13. If
renewed on May
13, the final due
date will be June 3.

Facts Practice: 90 Division Facts (Test I in Test Masters)

Mental Math: Review.

  a. 3×16 **b.** 600×40 **c.** $850 + 200 + 25$

  d. $\$20.00 - \$6.25$ **e.** $399 + 165$ **f.** $71 - 57$

Problem Solving: The library loans books for three weeks and
will renew books once for three more weeks.
If Salina borrows a book on April 22, when
will the book be due? If she renews the book
on the due date, what will be the final due date?

Many of the words we use in mathematics are based on
Latin or Greek words. The Latin word for "ring" is *circus*.
The Latin word for the spoke of a wheel is *radius*. The
Latin word for "through-measure" is *diametron*.

   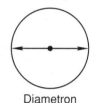

     Circus   Radius   Diametron

From these Latin words we get the English words **circle,
radius,** and **diameter.** The distance from the center to the
circle is the *radius*. The distance across a circle through
the center is the *diameter*.

     Circle   Radius   Diameter

**A diameter is twice as long as a radius. A radius is half as
long as a diameter.**

Example The diameter of this circle is 4 cm. What is its radius?

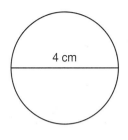

4 cm

Solution The radius is the distance from the center to the circle. The radius is half the diameter. Since half of 4 cm is 2 cm, the radius is **2 cm.**

Practice **a.** What is the name for the distance across the center of a circle? diameter

b. What is the name for the distance from the center to the circle? radius

c. If the radius of a circle is 4 cm, what is its diameter?
8 cm

Problem set **1.** One hundred fifty feet equals how many yards? 50 yd
110 *(49)*

2. Tammy gave the clerk $6 to pay for a record. She
(93) received 64¢ in change. Tax was 38¢. What was the price of the record? $4.98

3. Sergio is 2 years older than Rebecca. Rebecca is twice
(104) as old as Dina. Sergio is 12 years old. How old is Dina? (First find Rebecca's age.) 5 years old

4. Write these decimal numbers as mixed numbers:
(107) (a) 3.29 $3\frac{29}{100}$ (b) 32.9 $32\frac{9}{10}$ (c) 3.09 $3\frac{9}{100}$

84 contestants

21 contestants	
21 contestants	$\frac{3}{4}$ guessed wrong
21 contestants	
21 contestants	$\frac{1}{4}$ did not guess wrong

5. Three fourths of the 84 contestants guessed wrong.
(105) How many contestants guessed wrong? Draw a diagram to illustrate the problem. 63 contestants

6. What percent of the contestants in problem 5 guessed
(65) wrong? 75%

7. (a) What is the diameter of this circle? 1 in.
(110) (b) What is the radius of this circle? $\frac{1}{2}$ in.

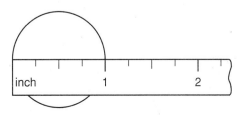

8. Use words to write 8.75. eight and seventy-five hundredths
(108)

9. Estimate the product of 47 and 62. Then find the
(103) actual product. 3000; 2914

10. The radius of a circle is 2 cm. How many centimeters
(110) is its diameter? 4 cm

11. The first five odd numbers are 1, 3, 5, 7, and 9. What is
(106) the average of these five numbers? 5

12. $43.62 + $3.60 + 56¢   **13.** $16.25 − ($6 − 50¢)
(53) $47.78   (55) $10.75

14. 5 × 7 × 9   **15.** $7.83 × 6   **16.** 54 × 1000
(72) 315   (68) $46.98   (95) 54,000

17.   45   **18.**   32   **19.**   46
(100) × 45   (77) × 40   (100) × 44
      ‾‾‾‾‾   ‾‾‾‾‾   ‾‾‾‾‾
      2025   1280   2024

20. 6)3625   604 r 1   **21.** 5)3000   600   **22.** 7)987   141
(90)   (90)   (86)

23. $\dfrac{10^3}{\sqrt{25}}$ 200   **24.** $13.76 ÷ 8   **25.** $\dfrac{234}{4}$ 58 r 2
(90,72)   (86) $1.72   (78)

 26. Draw and shade a circle to show that $\frac{8}{8}$ equals 1.
(99)

27. The perimeter of this square is 12
(60) inches. How long is each side of
the square? 3 in.

28. What is the area of the square in
(94) problem 27? 9 sq. in.

LESSON
111

Circle Graphs

a. 525
b. 175
c. $3.00
d. 3300
e. $8.05
f. 18

Problem Solving:

A common year ends on the same day of the week as it starts. A leap year ends one day of the week later than it starts.

Facts Practice: 90 Division Facts (Test J in Test Masters)

Mental Math: Thinking of quarters can make adding and subtracting numbers ending in 25, 50, and 75 easier to do mentally.

  a. 350 + 175   **b.** 325 − 150   **c.** $1.75 + $1.25

Review:

  d. 50 × 66   **e.** $10.00 − $1.95   **f.** 36 − 18

Problem Solving: Recall that 52 weeks is 364 days, that a common year is 365 days, and that a leap year is 366 days. If we know the day of the week on which a year begins, what rule will tell us the day of the week the year will end?

We have studied pictographs, bar graphs, and line graphs. Another kind of graph is the **circle graph.** This is often called a **pie graph** because the circle is divided into sections that look like slices of a pie.

Example Use the information in this circle graph to answer these questions:

Activities of 100 Children at the Park

(a) How many children were there altogether?

(b) Which activity were most children doing?

(c) How many children were not catching polliwogs?

Solution (a) The title of the graph states that there were **100 children.**

(b) The numbers inside each "slice of pie" show how many children were doing each activity. The largest number of children were **flying kites.**

(c) Only 19 of the 100 children were catching polliwogs. The rest were not. We subtract 19 from 100 and find that **81 children** were not catching polliwogs.

Practice Use the information from the graph on the preceding page to answer these questions:

a. How many children were either hiking or skating?
27 children

b. How many more children were flying kites than were catching polliwogs?   1 child

c. What number should be in the section named "other"?
1

Problem set 111 Use the information in the circle graph to answer questions 1–3:

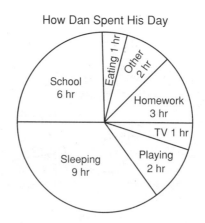

How Dan Spent His Day

1. What is the total number of hours shown in the graph?
(111) 24 hours

2. What fraction of Dan's day was spent watching TV? $\frac{1}{24}$
(111)

3. If Dan's school starts at 8:30 a.m., at what time does
(111) it end?   2:30 p.m.

288 marchers

48 marchers
48 marchers
48 marchers
48 marchers
48 marchers
48 marchers

$\frac{5}{6}$ were out of step

$\frac{1}{6}$ were not out of step

4. Five sixths of the 288 marchers were out of step. How
(105) many marchers were out of step? Illustrate the
problem.   240 marchers

5. Something is wrong with this
(109) sign. Draw two different signs that
show ways to correct this error.

6. (a) What is the radius of this
(110)   circle?   1 cm

   (b) What is the diameter of this
       circle?   2 cm

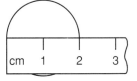

7. The chance of rain is 60%. Is it more likely that it will
(65) rain or that it will not rain?   that it will rain

8. Estimate the product of 88 and 22. Then find the
(103) actual product.   1800; 1936

9. Apples were priced at 53¢ per pound. What was the
(59) cost of 5 pounds of apples? $2.65

10. Write the number 3,708 in expanded form. Then use
(42) words to write this number.
   3000 + 700 + 8; three thousand, seven hundred eight

11. Find the sum of two hundred ninety-three thousand
(61) and seven thousand.   300,000

12. Four pounds of pears cost $1.20. What did 1 pound of
(104) pears cost? What did 6 pounds of pears cost?
   $0.30; $1.80

13. Mike drove his car 150 miles in 3 hours. What was his
(106) average speed in miles per hour?   50 miles per hour

14. $46.00
(51)   − $45.56
          $0.44

15.   10,165
(62)   −   856
              9309

16. $0.63
(28)   1.49
           12.24
            0.38
            0.06
            5.00
        +   1.20
          $21.00

17. 70^2 4900
(72)

18. 71 × 69   4899
(100)

19.   37
(77)   × 60
          2220

20.   56
(100)   × 42
          2352

21. $5.97
(68)   ×   8
          $47.76

22. 4)$30.00 $7.50
(90)

23. 3)263   87 r 2
(78)

24. 5)4080   816
(86)

25. $\frac{344}{8}$ 43
(75)

26.   1
(2)   2
           4
           3
           5
           7
           8
           2
        + N   3
          35

27.   9
(2)   8
           4
           A   4
           6
           2
           9
           4
        + 3
          49

28. Draw and shade circles to show that 2 equals $\frac{4}{2}$.
(99)

29. Draw a square with sides 4 cm long.   4 cm
(24)

30. Find the perimeter and the area of the square in
(94,60) problem 29.   16 cm; 16 sq. cm

LESSON
112

Decimal Number Line: Tenths

a. 400
b. 250
c. $5.50
d. 72
e. $5.63
f. 417
Problem Solving:
   Answer varies

Facts Practice: 100 Addition Facts (Test A in Test Masters)

Mental Math: Think of quarters as you add or subtract.
   a. 325 + 75   **b.** 425 − 175   **c.** $3.75 + $1.75

Review:
   d. 4 × 18   **e.** $3.65 + $1.98   **f.** 456 − 39

Problem Solving: Amber said, "An inch is less than 10% of a foot." Write a short paragraph explaining why you agree or disagree with Amber's statement.

The arrow is pointing to three and one tenth on this number line. We may write three and one tenth as a mixed number or as a decimal.

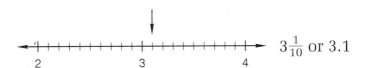

$3\frac{1}{10}$ or 3.1

Centimeter scales are often divided into tenths. Since a millimeter is a tenth of a centimeter, each tenth of a centimeter mark on a centimeter scale also marks a millimeter.

Example 1 Find the length of this segment to the nearest tenth of a centimeter. Write the length as a decimal number.

Solution The length of the segment is 4 centimeters plus a fraction. The fraction is two tenths. The length of the segment is **4.2 cm.**

Example 2   (a) Find the length of the segment below in millimeters.

(b) Find the length of the segment below in centimeters.

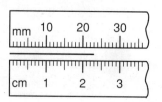

Solution   (a) **23 mm**   (b) **2.3 cm**

Practice   Write the decimal number to which each arrow points:
a. 4.3   **b.** 5.5   **c.** 6.8   **d.** 7.4

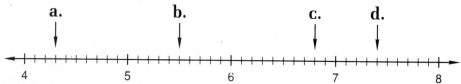

Problem set 112

1. All 110 books must be packed in boxes. Each box will
   (98)   hold 8 books.

   (a) How many boxes can be filled?   13 boxes

   (b) How many boxes are needed to hold all the books?
       14 boxes

2. What number is five more than the product of six and
   (104)   seven?   47

3. Gabriel gave the man $7 to pay for the tape. He got
   (93)   back a quarter and two dimes. Tax was 42¢. What was
   the price of the tape? $6.13

4. Four fifths of the 600 gymnasts did back handsprings.
   (105)   How many gymnasts did back handsprings? Illustrate
   the problem.   480 gymnasts

600 gymnasts
120 gymnasts
120 gymnasts
120 gymnasts
120 gymnasts
120 gymnasts
120 gymnasts

$\frac{4}{5}$ did back handsprings

$\frac{1}{5}$ did not do back handsprings

5. What percent of the gymnasts in problem 4 did not do
   (80)   back handsprings?   20%

6. What is the value of 2 hundred-dollar bills, 5 ten-
   (45)   dollar bills, 4 one-dollar bills, 3 dimes, and 1 penny?
   $254.31

7. (a) Find the length of this line segment in millimeters.
(112)

(b) Find the length of the segment in centimeters. Write the answer as a decimal number.

(a) 35 mm   (b) 3.5 cm

8. Use words to write 12.67.
(108) twelve and sixty-seven hundredths

9. Round 3834 to the nearest thousand.   4000
(91)

10. The diameter of a circle is 1 meter. What is the radius
(110) of the circle in centimeters?   50 cm

11. Find the sum of two hundred eighty-six thousand, five
(61) hundred fourteen and one hundred thirty-seven thousand, two.   423,516

12. Seven whirligigs cost $56. What did 1 whirligig cost?
(104) What would 12 whirligigs cost? $8; $96

13. There were 36 children in one line and 24 children in
(106) the other line. What is the average number of children in each line?   30 children

14. $15 + $8.75 + $0.49   **15.** $10.00 − (37¢ + $6)
(53) $24.24   (55) $3.63

16. 40 × 50   **17.** 41 × 49   **18.** $2^3 \times 5 \times \sqrt{49}$
(96)   2000   (100)   2009   (72)   280

19.   32   **20.**   38
(100)   × 17   (77)   × 40
        544   1520

21. 7 + 4 + 6 + 8 + 5 + 2 + 7 + 3 + K = 47   5
(2)

            452   620 r 2   502 r 2
22. 8$\overline{)3616}$ **23.** 4$\overline{)2482}$ **24.** 7$\overline{)3516}$
(86)   (90)   (90)

25. $4.38 ÷ 6
(75) $0.73

26. 7162 ÷ 9
(86)   795 r 7

27. $\frac{1414}{2}$ 707
(90)

28. Draw and shade circles to show that 2 equals $\frac{8}{4}$.
(99)

29. What percent of a dollar is a dime?   10%
(80,65)

30. How many square yards of carpet are needed to cover
(76)   the floor of a classroom that is 15 yards long and 10
yards wide?   150 square yards

LESSON
113

a. 1000
b. 275
c. $9.25
d. 2100
e. $0.38
f. 418
Problem Solving:
    February 29

Fractions Equal to 1

> **Facts Practice:** 100 Addition Facts (Test A in Test Masters)
>
> **Mental Math:** Think of quarters as you add or subtract.
>   **a.** 750 + 250   **b.** 450 − 175   **c.** $6.75 + $2.50
> **Review:**
>   **d.** 50 × 42   **e.** $1.00 − 62¢   **f.** 463 − 45
>
> **Problem Solving:** Which date occurs only once every four years?

Each of these circles equals 1 whole circle. The fraction
below each circle equals the number 1. If the top number
and the bottom number of a fraction are the same, the
fraction equals 1.

$1 = \frac{2}{2}$ $1 = \frac{3}{3}$ $1 = \frac{4}{4}$ $1 = \frac{5}{5}$

Example 1   Which of these fractions equals 1?

A. $\frac{1}{6}$ B. $\frac{6}{6}$ C. $\frac{7}{6}$

Solution   A fraction equals 1 if its numerator and denominator are
equal. The fraction equal to 1 is **B.** $\frac{6}{6}$.

Example 2   Write a fraction equal to 1 that has a denominator of 7.

Solution   The denominator is the bottom number of the fraction. A fraction equals 1 if its top and bottom numbers are the same. So if the denominator is 7, the numerator must also be 7. We write $\frac{7}{7}$.

Practice   **a.** Write a fraction equal to 1 that has a denominator of 6.
$\frac{6}{6}$

b. Which of these fractions equals 1? $\frac{9}{10}, \frac{10}{10}, \frac{11}{10}$ $\frac{10}{10}$

What fraction name for 1 is shown by each picture?

c. $\frac{6}{6}$ **d.** $\frac{9}{9}$

Problem set   **1.** Find an even number between 79 and 89 that can be
113   *(11)* divided by 6 without a remainder.   84

2. How many minutes are in 3 hours?   180 minutes
(59,23)

3. Bill has $8. Jim has $2 less than Bill. How much
(104) money do they have altogether? $14

4. Write each fraction or mixed number as a decimal
(107) number:

(a) $\frac{3}{10}$ 0.3   (b) $4\frac{99}{100}$ 4.99   (c) $12\frac{1}{100}$ 12.01

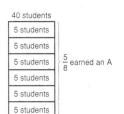

5. Five eighths of the 40 students earned an A on the test.
(105) How many students earned an A on the test? Illustrate the problem.   25 students

6. (a) What is the diameter of this
(110)   circle?   20 mm

(b) What is the radius of this circle?   10 mm

7. The radius of a circle is what percent of the diameter?
(110,65) 50%

8. Estimate the product of 49 and 68. Then find the
(103) actual product.   3500; 3332

9. Jimbo found that 20 blocks would fill 4 containers.
(104) How many blocks could he put in 1 container? How many blocks could he put in 20 containers?
5 blocks; 100 blocks

10. In Row 1 there were 6 students, in Row 2 there were 4
(106) students, in Row 3 there were 6 students, and in Row 4 there were 4 students. What was the average number of students in each row?   5 students

11. Gretchen paid $20 for five bottles of fruit juice. She
(104) received $6.00 in change. What was the price of one bottle of juice? $2.80

12. $37.50
(53)   − $26.35
        $11.15

13. $73.27
(28)   + $56.73
        $130.00

14.   16
(21)   15
       23
       8
       217
       20
       6
    + 317
       622

15. $3.85
(68)   ×   7
        $26.95

16.   48
(100)   × 29
        1392

17. 60² 3600
(72)

18. 59 × 61 3599
(100)

19.   5
(2)   4
      3
      7
      2
      5
      8
      1
      4
   + N   6
      45

20. 400/5 80
(81)

21. 6)5824 970 r 4
(90)

22. 9)$37.53 $4.17
(86)

23. 7)4205 600 r 5
(90)

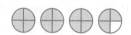

24. Draw and shade circles to show that $3\frac{3}{4}$ equals $\frac{15}{4}$.
(99)

25. The perimeter of this square is 20
(94,60) inches. Find the length of each side. Then find the area.
5 in.; 25 sq. in.

LESSON
114

a. 799
b. 226
c. $6.75
d. 600
e. $7.70
f. 48
Problem Solving:
    48 times

Changing Improper Fractions to Whole or Mixed Numbers

Facts Practice: 100 Addition Facts (Test A in Test Masters)

Mental Math: Think of one cent more or less than quarters.

    a. 425 + 374　　　　**b.** 550 − 324　　　　**c.** $4.49 + $2.26

Review:

    d. 15 × 40　　　　**e.** $4.75 + $2.95　　　　**f.** 83 − 35

Problem Solving: Todd wrapped a piece of tape around his front bicycle wheel. Then he rode his bicycle down his 50-foot driveway and counted eight full turns of the wheel. How many times will his wheel turn if he rides 100 yards?

If the top number of a fraction is as large as or larger than the bottom number, the fraction is an **improper fraction.** All of these fractions are improper fractions.

$$\frac{12}{4} \quad \frac{10}{3} \quad \frac{9}{4} \quad \frac{3}{2} \quad \frac{5}{5}$$

To write an improper fraction as a mixed number, we first need to find out how many wholes the number has. To do this, we divide. The division will tell us how many wholes we have. The remainder is the numerator of the fraction in the mixed number.

Example 1 Write $\frac{13}{5}$ as a mixed number. Draw a picture.

Solution To find the number of wholes, we divide.

$$\begin{array}{r} 2 \\ 5\overline{)13} \\ \underline{10} \\ 3 \end{array} \quad\begin{array}{l} \leftarrow \text{ wholes} \\ \\ \\ \leftarrow \text{ remainder of 3} \end{array}$$

This division tells us that $\frac{13}{5}$ equals two wholes and three fifths left over. We write this as **$2\frac{3}{5}$.** We can see this if we draw a picture.

　　　$$\frac{13}{5} = 2\frac{3}{5}$$

Example 2   Write $\frac{10}{3}$ as a mixed number. Then draw a picture.

Solution   First we divide.

$$3\overline{)10} \quad \begin{array}{r} 3 \\ \hline 9 \\ \hline 1 \end{array}$$

We have three wholes and one third left over. We write **$3\frac{1}{3}$**. The picture shows us that $\frac{10}{3}$ equals $3\frac{1}{3}$.

 $\dfrac{10}{3} = 3\dfrac{1}{3}$

Example 3   Write $\frac{12}{4}$ as a whole number. Then draw a picture.

Solution   First we divide.

$$4\overline{)12} \quad \begin{array}{r} 3 \\ \hline 12 \\ \hline 0 \end{array}$$

We have three wholes and a remainder of zero.

    $\dfrac{12}{4} = 3$

Practice   Change each improper fraction to a whole number or to a mixed number. Then draw a picture.

a. $\frac{7}{2}$ $3\frac{1}{2}$ **b.** $\frac{12}{3}$ 4

c. $\frac{8}{3}$ $2\frac{2}{3}$ **d.** $\frac{15}{5}$ 3

Problem set 114

1. If the perimeter of a square is 280 feet, how long is
(60)   each side of the square?   70 ft

2. There are 365 days in a common year. How many full
(98)   weeks are there in 365 days?   52 full weeks

3. Barbara passed out cookies to her 6 friends. Each of
(104) her friends received 3 cookies. There were 2 cookies
left for Barbara. How many cookies did Barbara have
when she began?   20 cookies

4. Three fifths of the 60 leprechauns were less than 2 feet
(105) tall. How many leprechauns were less than 2 feet tall?
Illustrate the problem.   36 leprechauns

5. (a) Find the length of this line segment in millimeters.
(112) (b) Find the length of the line segment in centimeters.
Write the answer as a decimal number.
(a) 43 mm   (b) 4.3 cm

6. What fraction name for 1 is shown
(113) by this circle? $\frac{8}{8}$

7. Use words to write 432.58.
(108) four hundred thirty-two and fifty-eight hundredths

8. Estimate the product of 87 and 71. Then find the
(103) actual product.   6300; 6177

9. Change the improper fraction $\frac{5}{4}$ to a mixed number.
(114) Draw a picture to show that the fraction and the mixed
number are equal. $1\frac{1}{4}$

10. The chance of winning the game was 10%. What was
(65) the chance of not winning?   90%

11. The cook used about 30 pounds of flour each day to
(59) cook pancakes and bread. How many pounds of flour
did the cook use in 73 days?   2190 lb

12. The cook found that 132 pounds of potatoes would
(106) last 6 days. On average, how many pounds of potatoes
were eaten each day?   22 lb

13. $6.52 + $12 + $1.74 + 26¢ $20.52
(53)

14. 43,217 + 367,490
(61) 410,707

15. $80 − ($63.72 + $2)
(55) $14.28

16. 37,614 − 29,148   8466
(62)

17. 3^4 81
(72)

18. 24 × 1000   24,000
(95)

19. 79¢ × 6 $4.74
(58)

20.
(96)
$$\begin{array}{r} 50 \\ \times\ 50 \\ \hline 2500 \end{array}$$

21.
(100)
$$\begin{array}{r} 51 \\ \times\ 49 \\ \hline 2499 \end{array}$$

22.
(100)
$$\begin{array}{r} 47 \\ \times\ 63 \\ \hline 2961 \end{array}$$

23.
(86)
$$4\overline{)2304}\quad 576$$

24.
(86)
$$5\overline{)4815}\quad 963$$

25.
(2)

26.
(90)
$$6\overline{)3629}\quad 604\ r\ 5$$

27. 1435 ÷ $\sqrt{49}$
(90,40)   205

$$\begin{array}{r} 7 \\ 2 \\ A\quad 25 \\ 6 \\ 5 \\ 7 \\ 3 \\ +\ 2 \\ \hline 57 \end{array}$$

28. $18.56 ÷ 8
(86) $2.32

29. $\dfrac{234}{9}$ 26
(75)

30. The area of this square is 9 square
(94,60) feet. Find the length of each side
and the perimeter.   3 ft; 12 ft

LESSON
115

Dividing by 10

a. 501
b. 426
c. $9.26
d. 3000
e. $3.75
f. 37
Patterns:
   12, 17, 15, 20, 18

Facts Practice: 100 Addition Facts (Test A in Test Masters)

Mental Math: Think of one cent more or less than quarters.
   a. 126 + 375   **b.** 651 − 225   **c.** $6.51 + $2.75
Review:
   d. 50 × 60   **e.** $20.00 − $16.25   **f.** 84 − 47

Patterns: This sequence has an alternating pattern. Copy this
   sequence on your paper and continue the sequence to 18.

   0, 5, 3, 8, 6, 11, 9, 14, ...

We have used a four-step procedure to divide by one-digit
numbers. We will use the same four-step procedure to
divide by two-digit numbers. In this lesson we will learn
how to divide by 10.

Example $10\overline{)432}$

Solution   Ten will not divide into 4 but will divide into 43 four times. In Step 1, we are careful to write the 4 above the 3 in 432.

Step 1. We divide $10\overline{)43}$ and write "4."

Step 2. We multiply 4×10 and write "40."

Step 3. We subtract $43 - 40$ and write "3."

Step 4. We bring down the 2, making 32.

$$\begin{array}{r} \textbf{43 r 2} \\ 10\overline{)432} \\ -\ 40 \\ \hline 32 \\ -\ 30 \\ \hline 2 \end{array}$$

REPEAT:

Step 1. We divide $10\overline{)32}$ and write "3."

Step 2. We multiply 3×10 and write "30."

Step 3. We subtract $32 - 30$ and write "2."

Step 4. There is no number to bring down. The answer is 43 with a remainder of 2.

Practice
a. $\overset{7\ r\ 3}{10\overline{)73}}$

b. $\overset{34\ r\ 2}{10\overline{)342}}$

c. $\overset{24\ r\ 3}{10\overline{)243}}$

d. $\overset{72}{10\overline{)720}}$

e. $\overset{56\ r\ 1}{10\overline{)561}}$

f. $\overset{38}{10\overline{)380}}$

Problem set 115

1. How many 6¢ mints can be bought with 2 quarters?
(98)   8 mints

2. Two quarters is what percent of a dollar?   50%
(65)

3. Jason has $8. David has $2 more than Jason. How
(104)   much money do they have altogether? $18

4. Three eighths of the 32 elves packed toys on the
(105)   sleigh. How many elves packed toys on the sleigh? Illustrate the problem.   12 elves

5. What is the value of 6 hundred-dollar bills, 4 ten-
(45)   dollar bills, 2 one-dollar bills, 1 dime, and 3 pennies?
$642.13

6. Write a fraction equal to one that has a denominator
(113)   of 10. $\frac{10}{10}$

7. Use words to write 8674.3.
(108) eight thousand, six hundred seventy-four and three tenths

8. Estimate the difference when 496 is subtracted
(70) from 604.   100

9. Change each improper fraction to a whole number or a
(114) mixed number:

(a) $\frac{9}{5}$ $1\frac{4}{5}$ (b) $\frac{9}{3}$ 3   (c) $\frac{9}{2}$ $4\frac{1}{2}$

10. Soon after James Marshall discovered gold at John
(104) Sutter's mill in California on January 24, 1848, the
"gold rush" began. If 2400 people came in 10 days,
about how many came each day? About how many
people came in 1 week?   240 people; 1680 people

11. The seasons spring, summer, winter, and fall are each
(98) one fourth of a year. A season lasts about how many
days?   91 days

12. One miner bought 6 bags of flour at $4.20 a bag and 8
(104) pounds of salt at 12¢ per pound. How much money
did the miner spend? $26.16

13. $26.47 + $8.52 $34.99   **14.** 49,249 − 3,755 45,494
(53)   (62)

15. 30 × 30   **16.** 28 × 32   **17.**   5   **18.**   1
(96) 900   (100) 896   (2)   1   (2)   6

19. 54 × 29   1566   6   3
(100)   8   5

       23   4 K 17
20. 10$\overline{)230}$ 3   7
(115)   7   2

      340 r 3   2   1
21. 7$\overline{)2383}$ 4   8
(90)   5   6

      37 r 2 $+ N$ 17 $+ 2$
22. 10$\overline{)372}$ ——————   ——————
(115)   62   58

23. $5.76 ÷ 8 $0.72
(75)

24. 412 ÷ 10   41 r 2
(115)

25.   351,426
(61)   + 449,576
       801,002

26. $50.00
(51)   − $49.49
      $0.51

27.   12
(21)   26
     13
     35
   110
      8
 + 15
    219

28. $12.49
(86)   ×   8
    $99.92

29.   73
(100) × 62
  4526

30. A field is 300 feet long and 200
(60) feet wide. How many feet of fencing would be needed to go around the field?   1000 ft

300 ft
200 ft

LESSON 116

Adding Decimal Numbers

a. 12
b. 8
c. 6
d. 72
e. $8.26
f. 16
Problem Solving:
  cup: $\frac{1}{2}$ lb
  quart: 2 lb
  half gallon: 4 lb
  gallon: 8 lb

Facts Practice: 100 Addition Facts (Test A in Test Masters)

Mental Math: Find each fraction of 24.
  a. $\frac{1}{2}$ of 24   **b.** $\frac{1}{3}$ of 24   **c.** $\frac{1}{4}$ of 24

Review:
  d. 4 × 18   **e.** $3.75 + $4.51   **f.** 54 − 38

Problem Solving: Two cups make a pint. Two pints make a quart. Two quarts make a half gallon, and two half gallons make a gallon. A pint of water weighs about one pound. Find the approximate weight of a cup, a quart, a half gallon, and a gallon of water.

We remember that when we add money, we line up all the decimal points.

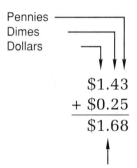

Pennies
Dimes
Dollars

  $1.43
+ $0.25
  $1.68

All decimal points are in line.

We also line up the decimal points when we add other decimal numbers. When we add decimal numbers, we must be careful to line up the decimal points so that we add digits with the same place value.

Example   Add: 3.47
                       0.36
                     + 1.4

Solution   We add decimal numbers with all the decimal points in line. The decimal point in the answer is also in line. We think of empty places as zeros.

$$\begin{array}{r} 3.47 \\ 0.36 \\ + \ 1.4 \\ \hline \mathbf{5.23} \end{array}$$

Practice   Add these decimal numbers. Put the decimal point in each answer in line with the other decimal points.

a.   2.37   b.   1.36   c.   3.65   d.   3.4
      4.6   0.47   12.4   6.75
    + 1.25   + 6.2   + 0.57   + 15.1
    ─────   ─────   ──────   ──────
     8.22   8.03   16.62   25.25

Problem set 116   Use the information given to answer questions 1–3:

Samantha has 6 cats. Each cat eats $\frac{1}{2}$ can of food each day. Cat food costs 47¢ per can.

1. How many cans of cat food are used each day?   3 cans
(104)

2. How much does Samantha spend on cat food per day?
(104) $1.41

3. How much does Samantha spend on cat food in a
(104)   week? $9.87

4. If the perimeter of a square is 240 inches, how long is
(60)   each side?   60 in.

28 students

| 4 students |
| 4 students |
| 4 students | $\frac{5}{7}$ math was the
| 4 students | favorite class
| 4 students |
| 4 students |
| 4 students | $\frac{2}{7}$ math was not
                the favorite
                class

5. Math was the favorite class of five sevenths of the 28
(105)   students. Math was the favorite class of how many students? Illustrate the problem.   20 students

6.
(109) Something is wrong with this sign. Draw two different signs to show two ways to correct this error.

Admission
.75¢
★ each ★

Admission
75¢
★ each ★

Admission
$0.75
★ each ★

7.
(110) (a) What is the radius of this circle? $\frac{1}{2}$ in.

(b) What is the diameter of this circle?   1 in.

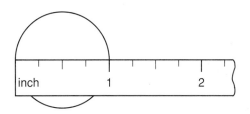

8.
(108) Use words to write 523.43.
five hundred twenty-three and forty-three hundredths

9.
(103) Estimate the product of 61 and 397.   24,000

10.
(114) Change each improper fraction to a whole number or mixed number:

(a) $\frac{10}{10}$ 1   (b) $\frac{10}{5}$ 2   (c) $\frac{10}{3}$ $3\frac{1}{3}$

11.
(53) Jewell went to the fair with $20. She paid $6.85 for a doll and $4.50 for lunch. Then she bought a soft drink for 75¢. How much money did she have left? $7.90

12.
(93) Mary Jane bought 2 dolls for $7.40 each. The tax was 98¢. She paid the clerk with a $20 bill. How much change did she get back? $4.22

13.
(106) The big truck that transported the ferris wheel could go only 140 miles in 5 hours. What was the truck's average speed in miles per hour?   28 miles per hour

14.
(116)
$$\begin{array}{r} 37.49 \\ +\ 6.35 \\ \hline 43.84 \end{array}$$

15.
(116)
$$\begin{array}{r} 5.43 \\ 12.7 \\ +\ 3.2 \\ \hline 21.33 \end{array}$$

16.
(116)
$$\begin{array}{r} 73.48 \\ 5.63 \\ +\ 17.9 \\ \hline 97.01 \end{array}$$

17.
(51)
$$\begin{array}{r} \$65.00 \\ -\ \$29.87 \\ \hline \$35.13 \end{array}$$

18.
(62)
$$\begin{array}{r} 24{,}375 \\ -\ 8{,}416 \\ \hline 15{,}959 \end{array}$$

19.
(68)
$$\begin{array}{r} \$3.68 \\ \times\ \ \ 9 \\ \hline \$33.12 \end{array}$$

20. 90^2 8100   **21.** 89 × 91 8099   **22.**
(72)   (100)   (2)

2
5
7
4
N 8
2

23. $\frac{36}{\sqrt{36}}$ 6   **24.** $3\overline{)763}$ $\;254 \text{ r } 1$
(57,40)   (86)

5
8
1

25. $10\overline{)430}$ $\;43$ **26.** $6\overline{)\$57.24}$ $\;\$9.54$
(115)   (86)

$\underline{+\; 6}$
48

27. 765 ÷ 9 85   **28.** 563 ÷ 10 56 r 3
(75)   (115)

LESSON 117

Subtracting Decimal Numbers

a. 15
b. 10
c. 6
d. 1400
e. $2.25
f. 76

Problem Solving:
The Sunday in spring:
   23 hours long
The Sunday in fall:
   25 hours long

Facts Practice: 100 Subtraction Facts (Test B in Test Masters)

Mental Math: Find each fraction of 30.
   a. $\frac{1}{2}$ of 30   **b.** $\frac{1}{3}$ of 30   **c.** $\frac{1}{5}$ of 30

Review:
   d. 50 × 28   **e.** $5.00 − $2.75   **f.** 47 + 29

Problem Solving: In parts of the country where "daylight savings time" is observed, we follow the rule, "Spring forward and fall back." This rule means we turn the clock forward one hour in the spring and back one hour in the fall. Officially, clocks are reset at 2 a.m. on Sunday. How many hours long are those particular Sundays?

When we subtract money, we put all the decimal points in line.

$6.57
$\underline{-\;\$1.30}$
$5.27

Pennies
Dimes
Dollars

When we subtract other decimal numbers, we are careful to put all the decimal points in line. This way we subtract digits with the same place value. The decimal point in the answer is below the other decimal points.

Example Subtract: 6.57
                          − 1.3

Solution All the decimal points are in line. We think of empty places as zeros. The decimal point in the answer is directly below the other decimal points.

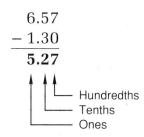

$$\begin{array}{r} 6.57 \\ -1.30 \\ \hline \mathbf{5.27} \end{array}$$

Hundredths
Tenths
Ones

Practice Subtract:

a. $\begin{array}{r}26.45\\-12.14\\\hline14.31\end{array}$	**b.** $\begin{array}{r}5.46\\-2.3\\\hline3.16\end{array}$	**c.** $\begin{array}{r}42.7\\-6.4\\\hline36.3\end{array}$	**d.** $\begin{array}{r}15.31\\-8.5\\\hline6.81\end{array}$

Problem set 117

1. Wendy bought 5 tickets for $2.75 each. She paid for them with a $20 bill. How much money did she get back? $6.25
(93)

2. If fifty cents is divided equally among 3 friends, there will be some cents left. How many cents will be left?   2 cents
(98)

3. What is the result we get when four hundred nine is subtracted from nine hundred four?   495
(37)

45 stamps

5 stamps
5 stamps } $\frac{2}{9}$ were from Brazil
5 stamps
5 stamps
5 stamps
5 stamps } $\frac{7}{9}$ were not from Brazil
5 stamps
5 stamps
5 stamps

4. Two ninths of the 45 stamps were from Brazil. How many of the stamps were from Brazil? Illustrate the problem.   10 stamps
(105)

5. (a) Find the length of this line segment in millimeters.   27 mm
(112)

   (b) Find the length of the segment in centimeters.   2.7 cm

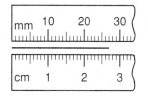

6. The pizza was cut into 10 equal
(113) slices. The entire sliced pizza
shows what fraction name for 1?
$\frac{10}{10}$

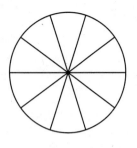

7. One slice of the pizza in problem
(65) 6 is what percent of the whole
pizza?   10%

8. Use words to write 3722.91.   three thousand, seven
(108) hundred twenty-two and ninety-one hundredths

9. Round 5167 to the nearest thousand.   5000
(91)

10. Change the improper fraction $\frac{9}{4}$ to a mixed number.
(114) $2\frac{1}{4}$

11. Which of these fractions is **not** equal to 1?   C. $\frac{11}{10}$
(113)
   A. $\frac{12}{12}$ B. $\frac{11}{11}$ C. $\frac{11}{10}$ D. $\frac{10}{10}$

12. In the summer of 1926, there were only 17 stores in
(82) the town. Today there are 8 times as many stores in
the town. How many stores are there in the town
today?   136 stores

13. The wagon train took 9 days to make the 243-mile
(106) journey. What was the average number of miles
traveled per day?   27 miles

14.   36.27
(116)   + 14.7
     ‾‾‾‾‾‾
     50.97

15.   3.62
(116)   12.8
  + 17.42
     ‾‾‾‾‾‾
     33.84

16.   26.14
(116)   8.9
  + 13.7
     ‾‾‾‾‾‾
     48.74

17.   36.31
(117)   − 7.4
     ‾‾‾‾‾‾
     28.91

18.   8.41
(117)   − 3.26
     ‾‾‾‾‾‾
     5.15

19.   23.73
(117)   − 9.8
     ‾‾‾‾‾‾
     13.93

20. 27 × 32   864   **21.** 62 × 15   930   **22.** $7^2 \times \sqrt{49}$ 343
(100)   (100)   (72,40)

$$\overset{46}{10\overline{)460}}$$
23. 10)460
(115)

$$\overset{\$3.04}{9\overline{)\$27.36}}$$
24. 9)$27.36
(90)

25. 9
(2)
8
7
2
4

$$\overset{386}{6\overline{)2316}}$$
26. 6)2316
(86)

27. 1543 ÷ 7 220 r 3
(90)

6
5
4
3

28. 532 ÷ 10
(115) 53 r 2

29. $\frac{256}{8}$ 32
(75)

$\begin{array}{r} + N \\ \hline 55 \end{array}$ 7

30. How many square feet of shingles
(94) are needed to cover a roof that is
40 feet wide and 60 feet long?
2400 square feet of shingles

LESSON
118

a. 18
b. 12
c. 9
d. 3600
e. $12.25
f. 15
Patterns:
   13, 21, 34, 55

Setting Up Decimal
Addition Problems

Facts Practice: 100 Subtraction Facts (Test B in Test Masters)

Mental Math: Find each fraction of 36.
   a. $\frac{1}{2}$ of 36   **b.** $\frac{1}{3}$ of 36   **c.** $\frac{1}{4}$ of 36
Review:
   d. 36 × 100   **e.** $8.50 + $3.75   **f.** 83 − 68

Patterns: In this sequence, each term is the sum of the two
   preceding terms. Copy this sequence and find the next
   four terms.

   1, 1, 2, 3, 5, 8, __, __, __, __, ...

When we add numbers, we add digits that have the same
place values. To be sure we add digits with the same place
values when we add decimal numbers, we line up the
decimal points.

Example   Add: 36.4 + 4.26 + 3.1

Solution   We begin by writing the numbers in a column with the decimal points in line. This lines up digits with the same place values. Next, we put the decimal point of the answer in line with the other decimal points. Then we add.

$$
\begin{array}{r}
36.4 \\
4.26 \\
+\ 3.1 \\
\hline
 .
\end{array}
$$
← decimal point

$$
\begin{array}{r}
36.4 \\
4.26 \\
+\ 3.1 \\
\hline
\mathbf{43.76}
\end{array}
$$

Practice   Add these decimal numbers:

a. 4.6 + 12.57   17.17   b. 2.36 + 42.8   45.16

c. 3.6 + 0.27 + 1.29   5.16   d. 14.6 + 36.4 + 16.35
                                      67.35

Problem set   **1.** Nelson bought 8 pounds of oranges. He gave the
118   (104) storekeeper a $5 bill and received $1.96 back in change. What did 1 pound of oranges cost? (First find how much *all* the oranges cost.) $0.38

2. Mark had a dozen cookies. He ate two cookies and
(104) then gave half of the rest to a friend. How many cookies did he have left?   5 cookies

3. What number is six less than the product of five and
(104) four?   14

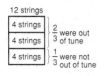

4. Two thirds of the 12 guitar strings were out of tune.
(105) How many of the guitar strings were out of tune? Illustrate the problem.   8 guitar strings

5. What is the value of 7 ten-dollar bills, 4 one-dollar
(45) bills, 3 dimes, and 2 pennies? $74.32

6. Write a fraction equal to 1 that has a denominator of 5.
(113) $\frac{5}{5}$

7. Use words to write $397\frac{3}{4}$.
(44) three hundred ninety-seven and three fourths

8. Estimate the sum of 4178 and 6899.   11,000
(70)

9. Change these improper fractions to whole numbers or
(114) mixed numbers:

(a) $\frac{7}{3}$ $2\frac{1}{3}$ (b) $\frac{8}{4}$ 2   (c) $\frac{9}{5}$ $1\frac{4}{5}$

10. The hiking club went on hikes of 8 miles, 15 miles, 11
(106) miles, and 18 miles, respectively. What was the
average length of the four hikes?   13 miles

11. For the first 3 hours the hikers hiked at 3 miles per
(104,67) hour. For the next 2 hours they hiked at 4 miles per
hour. If the total trip was 25 miles, how far did they
still have to go?   8 miles

12. What percent of a quart is a pint?   50%
(83,65)

13. 41.6 + 13.17 + 9.2   **14.** 45.32 + 4.39 + 16.2
(118) 63.97   *(118)*   65.91

15. 23.4 + 17.8 + 3.27   **16.** 43.17 + 2.86 + 17.4
(118) 44.47   *(118)*   63.43

17. $0.35   **18.**   54   **19.**   67
(58) $\times$ 8   *(100)* $\times$ 12   *(77)* $\times$ 30
        $2.80   648   2010

20. 80 × 80 6400   **21.** 78 × 82 6396   **22.** $\sqrt{25}$ × $\sqrt{25}$ 25
(96) $1.59   *(100)*   52   *(40,34)*

23. 4$\overline{)\$6.36}$ **24.** 10$\overline{)520}$ **25.**   6
(86)   620 r 5   *(115)*   *(2)*   2
26. 7$\overline{)4345}$ **27.** 24 ÷ 1   24   5
(90)   *(74)*   9

28. 5448 ÷ 6   **29.** $\frac{175}{5}$ 35   3
(90) 908   *(75)*   7

30. What is the perimeter and area of   8
(94,60) this square?   40 m; 100 sq. m   2
                                                     3
                                                     4
                        10 m   + N   8
                                                    57

LESSON
119

a. 20
b. 10
c. 4
d. 2400
e. $8.05
f. 210
Problem Solving:
   Tuesday

> **Facts Practice:** 100 Subtraction Facts (Test B in Test Masters)
>
> **Mental Math:** Find each fraction of 40.
>   **a.** $\frac{1}{2}$ of 40   **b.** $\frac{1}{4}$ of 40   **c.** $\frac{1}{10}$ of 40
> **Review:**
>   **d.** 120×20 **e.** $10.00 − $1.95   **f.** $145 + 65$
>
> **Problem Solving:** Jimmy was born on a Monday in April of 1990. On what day of the week was his first birthday?

When we subtract numbers, we subtract digits that have the same place values. To be sure we subtract digits with the same place values, we line up the decimal points.

Example 1   Subtract: $36.45 - 4.2$

Solution   We write the first number on top. We write the second number underneath **so that the decimal points are lined up. Then we write the decimal point in the answer so that this decimal point is lined up with the other two decimal points.** Then we subtract. We think of empty places as zeros.

$$\begin{array}{r} 36.45 \\ -\ 4.2 \\ \hline . \end{array}$$ ← decimal point

$$\begin{array}{r} 36.45 \\ -\ 4.2 \\ \hline \mathbf{32.25} \end{array}$$

Example 2   Subtract: $\begin{array}{r} 4.5 \\ -\ 3.27 \end{array}$

Solution   We subtract the bottom digits from the top digits. We see that we need a digit above the 7, so we write a zero in the empty place. Then we subtract.

$$\begin{array}{r} 4.\overset{4}{\cancel{5}}\overset{1}{0} \\ -\ 3.27 \\ \hline \mathbf{1.23} \end{array}$$ ← We write a zero here.

Practice Subtract:

a.	b.	c.	d.
3.63	26.2	8.7	1.9
− 1.4	− 12.56	− 6.54	− 0.19
2.23	13.64	2.16	1.71

e. 3.45 − 2.1   **f.** 36.47 − 3.6   **g.** 34.6 − 3.46

1.35   32.87   31.14

Problem set 119 Use the information given to answer questions 1 and 2:

Mark kept a tally of the number of vehicles that drove by his house during 1 hour.

Number of Vehicles

Cars	JHT JHT JHT JHT IIII
Trucks	JHT JHT
Motorcycles	II
Bicycles	JHT II

1. How many more cars than trucks drove by Mark's
(85) house?   14 more cars

2. Altogether, how many vehicles drove by Mark's
(85) house?   43 vehicles

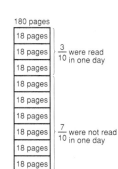

3. What number is six less than the sum of seven and
(104) eight?   9

4. Beth read three tenths of 180 pages in one day. How
(105) many pages did she read in one day? Illustrate the
problem.   54 pages

5. What percent of the pages in problem 4 did Beth read
(80,65) in one day?   30%

6. (a) What is the diameter of the
(110)   dime?   18 mm

(b) What is the radius of the
dime?   9 mm

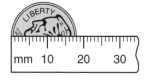

7. The candy bar was broken into 4 equal pieces. The
(113) broken candy bar is what fraction name for 1? $\frac{4}{4}$

8. Estimate the product of 78 and 32. Then find the
(103) actual product.   2400; 2496

9. Change the improper fraction $\frac{5}{2}$ to a mixed number.
(114) Draw a picture that shows that the fraction and the
mixed number are equal. $2\frac{1}{2}$;

Use the information in this story to answer questions 10
and 11:

*The camel walked 12 miles the first day. Each of
the next 4 days it walked 2 more miles than it
walked the day before.*

10. How far did the camel walk in 5 days?   80 miles
(104)

11. What was the average number of miles the camel
(106) walked in each of the 5 days?   16 miles

12. Solve this problem by guessing and then checking
(119) your guess: There were red checkers and black
checkers on the checkerboard. There were 8 more red
checkers than black checkers. Altogether, there were
20 checkers. How many were red and how many were
black?[†]   14 red and 6 black

13. 86.34 + 7.96 + 3.1   **14.** 29.15 + 4.6 + 16.2
(118)   97.4   (118)   49.95

[†]*Guess and check* (also called *trial and error*) is a strategy for solving some
kinds of problems. In this problem there are two conditions that need to be
met:

  1. The total number of checkers needs to be 20 checkers.
  2. There needs to be 8 more red checkers than black checkers.

We begin by guessing an answer like 15 red checkers and 5 black checkers.
This guess meets the condition of totaling 20 checkers. However, the guess is
wrong because there are not 8 more red checkers than black checkers. So we
use what we have learned from our first guess and guess again.

15. $24.34 - 8.5$ 15.84
(119)

16. $26.4 - 15.18$ 11.22
(119)

17. $4 \times 3 \times 2 \times 1$ 24
(72)

18. 26×30 780
(77)

19. 46×12 552
(100)

20. 20×20 400
(96)

21. 18×22 396
(100)

22. $\sqrt{36} \times \sqrt{64}$ 48
(40,34)

23. $8\overline{)\$16.48}$ $2.06
(90)

24. $6\overline{)3744}$ 624
(86)

25.
(2)

$$\begin{array}{r} 8 \\ 4 \\ 7 \\ 6 \\ 8 \\ 4 \\ 7 \\ 6 \\ 2 \\ + K \quad 3 \\ \hline 55 \end{array}$$

26. $\dfrac{360}{10}$ 36
(115)

27. $\dfrac{3000}{5}$ 600
(90)

28. $423 \div 10$ 42 r 3
(115)

29. $\dfrac{138}{6}$ 23
(75)

30. How many square feet of paper
(94) are needed to cover a bulletin board that is 3 feet high and 6 feet wide?   18 sq. ft

LESSON 120

Dividing by Multiples of 10, Part 1

a. 50
b. 25
c. 10
d. 230
e. $7.35
f. 18

Problem Solving:
4 pennies,
2 nickels,
1 dime,
1 quarter, and
1 half dollar

Facts Practice: 100 Subtraction Facts (Test B in Test Masters)

Mental Math: Find each fraction of 100.

a. $\frac{1}{2}$ of 100   **b.** $\frac{1}{4}$ of 100   **c.** $\frac{1}{10}$ of 100

Review:

d. 5×46 **e.** $4.37 + 2.98$ **f.** $86 - 68$

Problem Solving: Using at least one of each coin, which nine coins would be needed to make 99¢, but not more than 99¢?

We have practiced dividing by 10. In this lesson we will begin dividing by multiples of 10. Multiples of 10 are 20, 30, 40, 50, 60, and so on. Dividing by multiples of 10 is a little harder than dividing by one-digit numbers because we have not memorized the division facts for two-digit numbers. To help us divide by a two-digit number, we may think of dividing by the first digit only.

To help us divide this, → $20\overline{)72}$

we may think this: → $2\overline{)7}$

We use the answer to the easier division to estimate the answer to the more difficult division. Since there are three 2s in 7, we estimate that there are also three 20s in 72. We write "3" above the 72 and finish by doing the multiplication and subtraction steps.

$$\begin{array}{r} 3 \text{ r } 12 \\ 20\overline{)72} \\ 60 \\ \hline 12 \end{array}$$ ← We write the answer this way.

Since we divided 72 by 20, we put the 3 above the 2 in 72.

$$\begin{array}{r} 3 \\ 20\overline{)72} \end{array}$$

This is not correct!

Do not write the 3 above the 7.

This means there are three 20s in 7, which is not true.

$$\begin{array}{r} 3 \\ 20\overline{)72} \end{array}$$

This is the correct way.

The 3 above the 2 means there are three 20s in 72.

It is important to place the digits in the answer correctly!

Example $30\overline{)127}$

Solution   To help us divide this, we may mentally block out the last digit of each number.

We see $30\overline{)127}$, but we think $3\overline{)12}$.

Since there are four 3s in 12, we estimate that there are also four 30s in 127. We write "4" above the 7 of 127. Next, we multiply 4 × 30 and write "120." Then we subtract 120 from 127 and write "7." This is the remainder. The answer is **4 r 7.**

$$
\begin{array}{r}
4\ r\ 7 \\
30\overline{)127} \\
120 \\
\hline
7
\end{array}
$$

Practice

a. $30\overline{)72}$ 2 r 12

b. $20\overline{)87}$ 4 r 7

c. $40\overline{)95}$ 2 r 15

d. $20\overline{)127}$ 6 r 7

e. $40\overline{)127}$ 3 r 7

f. $30\overline{)217}$ 7 r 7

Problem set 120

1. *(98)* Eighty students were divided among three classrooms as equally as possible. For your answer, write three numbers to show how many students were in each classroom. 26; 27; 27

2. *(104)* If the sum of three and four is subtracted from the product of three and four, what is the difference? 5

3. *(104)* Irma is twice as old as her sister and three years younger than her brother. Irma's sister is six years old. How old is Irma's brother? (First find Irma's age.) 15 years old

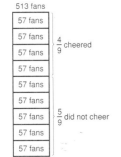

4. *(105)* Four ninths of 513 fans cheered when the touchdown was scored. How many fans cheered? Draw a diagram to illustrate the problem. 228 fans

5. *(109)* Something is wrong with this sign. Draw two different signs to show ways to correct this error.

Cash for cans .85¢ per pound

6. *(113)* This circle shows what fraction name for 1? $\frac{12}{12}$

7. *(65)* The chance of winning the jackpot is 1%. Which is more likely, winning or not winning? not winning

8. Estimate the sum of 589 and 398.   1000
(70)

9. Change the improper fraction $\frac{5}{2}$ to a mixed number.
(114) $2\frac{1}{2}$

10. Jim ran 7 miles in 42 minutes. What was the average
(106) number of minutes it took Jim to run one mile?
6 minutes

11. Salamona bought 3 scarves for $2.75 each. Tax was
(93) 58¢. She paid with a $10 bill. How much change did
she receive? $1.17

12. Two tickets for the play cost $26. How much would
(104) twenty tickets cost? $260.00

13. 7.43 + 6.25 + 12.7   **14.** 13.24 + 12.5 + 1.37
(118)   26.38   *(118)*   27.11

15. 14.36 − 7.5   6.86   **16.** 28.6 − 2.86   25.74
(119)   *(119)*

17. 90 × 800   72,000   **18.** 8 × 73¢ $5.84
(96)   *(58)*

19. 7 × 6 × 5 × 0   0   **20.** 24 × 30   720
(72)   *(77)*

21. 60 × 25   1500   **22.** $\sqrt{49}$ × $\sqrt{49}$ 49
(77)   *(40,34)*

                 $7.43
23. 5$\overline{)\$37.15}$ **24.** 423 ÷ 7   **25.**   1
(86)   *(81)*   60 r 3   *(2)*   2
                                                                5
                                                                3
            1240   4   6
26. $\frac{1240}{10}$ 124   **27.** 60$\overline{)240}$ 5
(115)   *(120)*   4
                                                                7
            3 r 5   2 r 8   9
28. 30$\overline{)95}$ **29.** 40$\overline{)88}$ 2
(120)   *(120)*   + N   4
                                                              ─────
                                                                48

30. This square has a perimeter of
(94,60) 8 cm. Find the length of each side
and the area.   2 cm; 4 sq. cm

LESSON
121

Adding Fractions with Like Denominators

a. 5
b. 10
c. 15
d. 1800
e. $12.50
f. 95
Problem Solving:
  Nathan moved 7 books.
  The tall stack had 22 books.

Facts Practice: 100 Subtraction Facts (Test B in Test Masters)

Mental Math: Find each fraction of 20.
  a. $\frac{1}{4}$ of 20   **b.** $\frac{2}{4}$ of 20   **c.** $\frac{3}{4}$ of 20

Review:
  d. 60×30 **e.** $20.00 - $7.50   **f.** $48 + 47$

Problem Solving: There was a tall stack and a short stack of books on the shelf. There were 8 books in the short stack. Nathan moved some books from the tall stack to the short stack so that both stacks had 15 books. How many books did Nathan move? How many books were in the tall stack before Nathan began moving the books?

Adding fractions is something like adding apples.

1 apple + 1 apple = 2 apples

1 third + 1 third = 2 thirds

$$\frac{1}{3} + \frac{1}{3} = \frac{2}{3}$$

When we add fractions, we add the top numbers (numerators). We do not add the bottom numbers (denominators).

Example Add: $\frac{3}{5} + \frac{1}{5}$

Solution Three fifths plus one fifth is four fifths. **We add the top numbers only.** $\dfrac{3}{5} + \dfrac{1}{5} = \dfrac{4}{5}$

Practice Add these fractions:

a. $\dfrac{1}{3} + \dfrac{1}{3}$ $\frac{2}{3}$ **b.** $\dfrac{1}{4} + \dfrac{2}{4}$ $\frac{3}{4}$ **c.** $\dfrac{1}{5} + \dfrac{2}{5}$ $\frac{3}{5}$

d. $\dfrac{3}{10} + \dfrac{4}{10}$ $\frac{7}{10}$ **e.** $\dfrac{5}{12} + \dfrac{6}{12}$ $\frac{11}{12}$ **f.** $\dfrac{8}{25} + \dfrac{9}{25}$ $\frac{17}{25}$

g. How much is three eighths plus four eighths? $\frac{7}{8}$

Problem set 121 The table below shows how much is charged to ship a package to different parts of the country. Use the information given to answer questions 1–3:

WEIGHT	SHIPPING CHARGES		
	ZONE 1	ZONE 2	ZONE 3
Up to 4 pounds	$1.75	$1.93	$2.36
4 pounds, 1 ounce to 7 pounds	$1.91	$2.15	$2.68
7 pounds, 1 ounce to 10 pounds	$2.07	$2.38	$3.02
Over 10 pounds	$2.48	$2.71	$3.38

1. How much does it cost to ship an 8-pound package to Zone 2? $2.38
(89)

2. How much more does it cost to ship a 12-pound package to Zone 3 than to Zone 2? $0.67
(89)

3. What is the total cost to ship two 5-pound packages to Zone 1 and five 2-pound packages to Zone 3? $15.62
(89)

4. If 2 apples cost 30¢, how much will 4 apples cost? 60¢
(104)

70 polliwogs

14 polliwogs	
14 polliwogs	$\frac{2}{5}$ had back legs
14 polliwogs	
14 polliwogs	
14 polliwogs	$\frac{3}{5}$ did not have back legs
14 polliwogs	

5. Two fifths of the 70 polliwogs already had back legs.
(105) How many of the polliwogs had back legs?

28 polliwogs

6. What percent of the polliwogs already had back legs?
(80,65) 40%

7. (a) Find the length of this line segment in millimeters.
(112) (b) Find the length of this segment in centimeters.

(a) 39 mm   (b) 3.9 cm

```
mm   10    20    30    40    50
     ‖‖‖‖‖‖‖‖‖‖‖‖‖‖‖‖‖‖‖‖‖‖‖‖‖

     ‖‖‖‖‖‖‖‖‖‖‖‖‖‖‖‖‖‖‖‖‖‖‖‖‖
cm    1     2     3     4     5
```

8. The apple was cut into 8 equal slices. The sliced apple
(113) is what fraction name for 1? $\frac{8}{8}$

9. One third of the students earned an A. One third of the
(121) students earned a B. What fraction of the students
earned an A or a B? $\frac{2}{3}$

10. Change each improper fraction to a whole number or a
(114) mixed number:

(a) $\frac{11}{2}$ $5\frac{1}{2}$ (b) $\frac{11}{3}$ $3\frac{2}{3}$ (c) $\frac{11}{4}$ $2\frac{3}{4}$

11. Michelle took 6 strokes on the first hole, 7 strokes on
(106) the second hole, and 5 strokes on the third hole. What
was the average number of strokes Michelle took on
each of the first three holes?   6 strokes

12. Solve this problem by guessing and checking your
(119) guess: Mike and Carl played the first hole on the golf
course. Together, they hit the ball a total of 13 times.
Carl hit the ball 3 more times than Mike did. How
many times did Carl hit the ball?   8 times

13. 9.7 + 14.6 + 0.83   **14.** 8.79 + 16.4 + 7.3
(118)   25.13   *(118)*   32.49

15. 86.34 − 19.2   67.14   **16.** 13.6 − 4.21   9.39
(119)   *(119)*

17.
(121)
$\dfrac{5}{9} + \dfrac{2}{9}$ $\frac{7}{9}$

18.
(121)
$\dfrac{2}{10} + \dfrac{3}{10}$ $\frac{5}{10}$

19. One fifth plus two fifths equals what fraction? $\frac{3}{5}$
(121)

20. 27 × 60   1620
(77)

21. 36 × 35   1260
(100)

22. 30 × 200   6000
(96)

23. $1\overline{)54}$ $\overset{54}{}$
(74)

24. $23.80 ÷ 10 $2.38
(115)

25. $8^2 ÷ \sqrt{16}$ 16
(72,40)

26. $30\overline{)153}$ 5 r 3
(120)

27. $20\overline{)84}$ 4 r 4
(120)

28. $40\overline{)367}$ 9 r 7
(120)

8 cm
3 cm

29. Draw a rectangle that is 8 cm long and 3 cm wide.
(24)

30. Find the perimeter and area of the rectangle in
(94,60) problem 29.   22 cm; 24 sq. cm

LESSON 122

Subtracting Fractions with Like Denominators

a. 6
b. 12
c. 18
d. 480
e. $11.24
f. 38

Problem Solving:

426
− 139
287

Facts Practice: 64 Multiplication Facts (Test G in Test Masters)

Mental Math: Find each fraction of 30.

  a. $\frac{1}{5}$ of 30   **b.** $\frac{2}{5}$ of 30   **c.** $\frac{3}{5}$ of 30

Review:

  d. 4 × 120   **e.** $7.50 + $3.74   **f.** 93 − 55

Problem Solving: Copy this subtraction problem on your paper and fill in the missing digits.

4_6
− 13_
_87

We remember that when we add fractions, we add only the top numbers (numerators). We do not add the bottom numbers (denominators).

$$\dfrac{3}{7} + \dfrac{2}{7} = \dfrac{5}{7}$$

When we subtract fractions, we subtract only the top numbers. The bottom number does not change. Five sevenths minus two sevenths is three sevenths.

$$\frac{5}{7} - \frac{2}{7} = \frac{3}{7}$$

Example 1   Subtract: $\dfrac{3}{5} - \dfrac{1}{5}$

Solution   **We subtract only the numerators.** Three fifths minus one fifth is two fifths. $\dfrac{3}{5} - \dfrac{1}{5} = \dfrac{2}{5}$

Example 2   Subtract: $\dfrac{8}{23} - \dfrac{5}{23}$

Solution   When we subtract fractions, we subtract the top numbers (numerators). We do not change the bottom numbers. $\dfrac{8}{23} - \dfrac{5}{23} = \dfrac{3}{23}$

Practice   Subtract these fractions:

a. $\dfrac{2}{3} - \dfrac{1}{3}$ $\frac{1}{3}$

b. $\dfrac{3}{4} - \dfrac{2}{4}$ $\frac{1}{4}$

c. $\dfrac{4}{5} - \dfrac{2}{5}$ $\frac{2}{5}$

d. $\dfrac{9}{10} - \dfrac{6}{10}$ $\frac{3}{10}$

e. $\dfrac{8}{12} - \dfrac{3}{12}$ $\frac{5}{12}$

f. $\dfrac{5}{6} - \dfrac{5}{6}$ 0

Problem set   Use the information given in the graph to answer
122   questions 1–3:

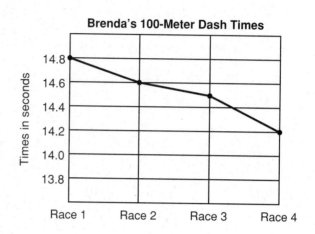

Brenda's 100-Meter Dash Times

1. What was Brenda's time for the 100-meter dash in
(92) Race 3?   14.5 seconds

2. Are Brenda's times getting faster or slower?   faster
(92)

3. Tania ran one second slower in Race 3 than Brenda.
(92) What was Tania's time in Race 3?   15.5 seconds

4. Johnny planted two thousand apple seeds. Five
(17) hundred twenty grew to be trees. How many seeds did
not grow to be trees?   1480 seeds

5. Write each decimal number as a mixed number:
(107)
   (a) 12.41 $12\frac{41}{100}$ (b) 24.1 $24\frac{1}{10}$ (c) 2.03 $2\frac{3}{100}$

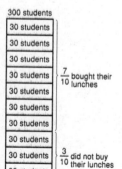

6. Seven tenths of the 300 students bought their lunch.
(105) How many of the students bought their lunch? Draw a
diagram to illustrate the problem.   210 students

7. What percent of the students in problem 6 bought
(65) their lunch?   70%

8. Estimate the product of 41 and 39. Then find the
(103) actual product.   1600; 1599

9. Change the improper fraction $\frac{8}{3}$ to a mixed number.
(114) $2\frac{2}{3}$

10. In Greek mythology, Jason sailed the ship *Argo* in
(106,67) search of the Golden Fleece. His shipmates were called *Argonauts*. They sailed 33 miles in 3 days.

(a) What was the average number of miles they sailed each day?   11 mi

(b) At the same rate, how far could they sail in 7 days?
77 mi

11. Jason found five eighths of a pie in the refrigerator. He
(122) ate two eighths of the pie. What fraction of the pie was left? $\frac{3}{8}$

12. Solve this problem by guessing and checking your
(119) guess: For dessert they had ambrosia. Altogether, Jason and Castor ate 33 spoonfuls of ambrosia. Jason ate 5 more spoonfuls than Castor did. How many spoonfuls did each man eat?
Jason, 19 spoonfuls; Castor, 14 spoonfuls

13. 3.6 + 4.25 + 16.7   **14.** 5.34 + 1.9 + 16.18
(118)   24.55   *(118)*   23.42

15. 43.27 − 12.6   30.67   **16.** 16.4 − 1.64   14.76
(119)   *(119)*

17. $\frac{4}{10} + \frac{5}{10}$ $\frac{9}{10}$ **18.** $\frac{5}{11} + \frac{3}{11}$ $\frac{8}{11}$
(121)   *(121)*

19. $\frac{3}{5} + \frac{2}{5}$ 1   **20.** $\frac{8}{9} - \frac{4}{9}$ $\frac{4}{9}$ **21.** $\frac{5}{7} - \frac{4}{7}$ $\frac{1}{7}$
(121)   *(122)*   *(122)*

22.   3   **23.**   54   **24.** $\frac{1}{3} - \frac{1}{3}$ 0
(2)   7   *(21)*   17   *(122)*
           6   14
           4   68
        $+ N$ 10 $+ 20$
        ‾‾‾‾‾   ‾‾‾‾‾
          30   173

25. $4.39   **26.**   49   **27.** $\frac{120}{40}$ 3
(68) $\times$ 8   *(100)* $\times 73$ *(120)*
       ‾‾‾‾‾‾‾‾   ‾‾‾‾‾‾
        $35.12   3577

$$
\begin{array}{r} 8 \\ \textbf{28.} \ 60\overline{)480} \end{array}
$$
(120)

$$
\begin{array}{r} 9 \text{ r } 1 \\ \textbf{29.} \ 30\overline{)271} \end{array}
$$
(120)

30. How many square feet of sod are
(94) needed to cover a yard that is 60
feet long and 40 feet wide?
2400 sq. ft

60 ft

40 ft

LESSON
123

Equivalent Fractions

a. 5
b. 15
c. 25
d. 280
e. $3.02
f. 501
Patterns:
  1.4, 1.6, 1.8, 2.0,
  2.2

Facts Practice: 64 Multiplication Facts (Test G in Test Masters)

Mental Math: Find each fraction of 40.

  a. $\frac{1}{8}$ of 40   **b.** $\frac{3}{8}$ of 40   **c.** $\frac{5}{8}$ of 40

Review:

  d. 20 × 14   **e.** $5.00 − $1.98   **f.** 126 + 375

Patterns: Find the next five numbers in this sequence.

    0.2, 0.4, 0.6, 0.8, 1.0, 1.2, __, __, __, __, __, ...

The same fraction of each circle below has been shaded.
We see that different fractions are used to name the
shaded parts.

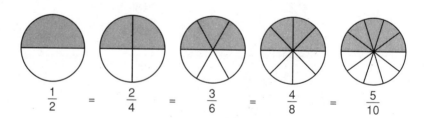

$$\frac{1}{2} = \frac{2}{4} = \frac{3}{6} = \frac{4}{8} = \frac{5}{10}$$

These fractions all name the same amount. Different
fractions that name the same amount are called **equivalent
fractions.**

Example 1 The rectangle on the left has three equal parts. We see that two parts are shaded. Two thirds of the figure is shaded.

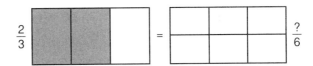

The rectangle on the right has six equal parts. How many parts must be shaded so that the same fraction of this rectangle is shaded?

Solution We see that **four** of the six parts must be shaded. Two thirds is the same as four sixths.

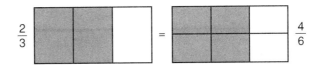

$$\frac{2}{3} \text{ and } \frac{4}{6} \text{ are equivalent fractions}$$

Example 2 What equivalent fractions are shown?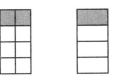

Solution The same fraction of each rectangle is shaded. The rectangles show that

$$\frac{2}{8} = \frac{1}{4}$$

Practice Name the equivalent fractions shown:

a. 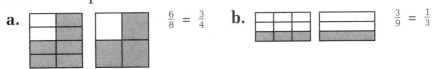 $\frac{6}{8} = \frac{3}{4}$ b. $\frac{3}{9} = \frac{1}{3}$

Draw pictures to show that the following pairs of fractions are equivalent:

c. $\frac{2}{4} = \frac{1}{2}$ d. $\frac{4}{6} = \frac{2}{3}$ e. $\frac{2}{8} = \frac{1}{4}$

Problem set
123

1. A pie was cut into 8 equal slices. Half the pie was
(123) eaten. What fraction of the pie was left? Write two
equivalent fractions for the answer. $\frac{4}{8} = \frac{1}{2}$

2. A can of soup serves 3 people. How many cans of soup
(98) are needed to serve 14 people?   5 cans

3. Mark was 9 years old when his brother was 12. How
(82) old will Mark be when his brother is 21 years old?
18 years old

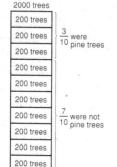

4. Three tenths of the 2000 trees in the forest were pine
(105) trees. How many pine trees were in the forest?
Illustrate the problem.   600 pine trees

5. What percent of the trees in problem 4 were pine
(65) trees?   30%

6. Change each improper fraction to a mixed number:
(114)
   (a) $\frac{19}{3}$ $6\frac{1}{3}$ (b) $\frac{19}{4}$ $4\frac{3}{4}$ (c) $\frac{19}{5}$ $3\frac{4}{5}$

7. Use words to write 4.56.   four and fifty-six hundredths
(108)

8. What equivalent fractions are
(123) shown? $\frac{3}{4} = \frac{6}{8}$

9. Draw a picture to show that $\frac{2}{4}$ and
(123) $\frac{1}{2}$ are equivalent fractions.

10. Jamie drove 135 miles in 3 hours. What was her
(106,67) average speed in miles per hour? At the same rate,
how far could she drive in 9 hours?
45 miles per hour; 405 miles

11. There were 30 seats in each room. There were 15
(59) rooms. How many students could sit in all the rooms?
450 students

12. $16.24 - 5.7$
(119) 10.54

13. $32.4 - 1.26$
(119) 31.14

14.
(116)
$$3.4$$
$$2.7$$
$$1.52$$
$$3.6$$
$$+ 1.47$$
$$\overline{12.69}$$

15. $\dfrac{7}{10} + \dfrac{2}{10}$ $\frac{9}{10}$
(121)

16. $\dfrac{1}{4} + \dfrac{1}{4} + \dfrac{1}{4}$ $\frac{3}{4}$
(121)

17. $\dfrac{3}{7} - \dfrac{1}{7}$ $\frac{2}{7}$
(122)

18. $\dfrac{5}{12} - \dfrac{4}{12}$ $\frac{1}{12}$
(122)

19. $\dfrac{3}{4} - \dfrac{3}{4}$ 0
(122)

20.
(68)
$$\$4.53$$
$$\times \quad 7$$
$$\overline{\$31.71}$$

21.
(100)
$$78$$
$$\times 36$$
$$\overline{2808}$$

22.
(77)
$$64$$
$$\times 80$$
$$\overline{5120}$$

23. $\$56.40 \div 6$ $\$9.40$
(90)

24. $27 \div 1$ 27
(74)

25.
(21)
$$24$$
$$36$$
$$25$$
$$43$$
$$19$$
$$7$$
$$66$$
$$43$$
$$50$$
$$+ 93$$
$$\overline{406}$$

26. $9\overline{)545}$ $\dfrac{60\text{ r }5}{}$
(81)

27. $260 \div 10$ 26
(115)

28. $275 \div 30$ 9 r 5
(120)

29. $350 \div 50$ 7
(120)

30. A sheet of plywood is 8 feet long
(94) and 4 feet wide. What is the area of one side of a sheet of plywood?
32 sq. ft

LESSON
124

Estimating Area

a. 20
b. 40
c. 60
d. 2300
e. $9.54
f. 37
Problem Solving:
  In order:
    100, 95, 95, 95,
    90, 90, 85, 80, 75
  Middle score:
    90
  Most number of
  times:
    95

Facts Practice: 64 Multiplication Facts (Test G in Test Masters)

Mental Math: Find each fraction of 60.

  a. $\frac{1}{3}$ of 60   **b.** $\frac{2}{3}$ of 60   **c.** $\frac{3}{3}$ of 60

Review:

  d. 50 × 46   **e.** $6.59 + $2.95   **f.** 62 − 25

Problem Solving: On Gabriella's first nine tests she earned these scores:

  90, 95, 80, 85, 100, 95, 75, 95, 90

List these scores in order from highest to lowest. Which score is the middle score in the ordered list? Which score did Gabriella earn the most number of times?

Remember that a square unit is a square with a side of a certain length. Here we show a **square centimeter** and a **square inch** in actual size.

1 square centimeter   1 square inch

To measure the areas of shapes that are not rectangles, we may use a grid to estimate the area. Here we show a triangle drawn on grid paper. What is the area of this triangle? We will describe two strategies that can be used to estimate its area.

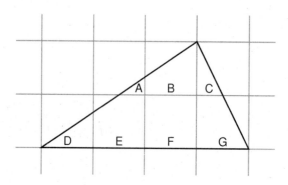

First strategy:

Look within the outline of the figure. Count all of the entire squares. Then estimate the number of entire squares that could be formed with the remaining partial squares.

Using this strategy, we see that F is an entire square. C and G could be fit together like a puzzle to make another square. D and B could make a third square. A and E would make a fourth square. Using this strategy, we estimate that the area of the triangle is about four square units.

Second strategy:

Look within the outline of the figure. Count all the entire squares as in the first strategy. Then count all the squares that seem to have at least half their area within the outline of the figure. Do not count the squares that have less than half their area within the figure.

Using this strategy, we again count F as an entire square. Then we count E, B, and G because at least half the area of each square is within the outline of the triangle. We do not count A, C, or D. Using this strategy, we again estimate the area of the triangle is about four square units.

Both strategies help us to estimate areas. An estimate is an approximation. Estimates may differ slightly from person to person. The purpose is to make each estimate carefully.

Activity   Materials needed:

- a sheet of square-inch grid paper for each student[†]
- Optionally, a square-inch grid transparency may be used as an overlay to measure areas of figures, much as a ruler is used to measure lengths.

Have each student outline a shoe or a hand on the grid paper. Then use the strategies described to estimate the area of the shoe print or handprint.

[†]Master available in *Math 54 Test Masters*.

Practice   Estimate the area of each figure on these grids:

a.
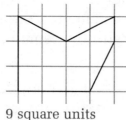

9 square units

b.
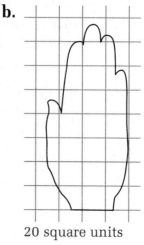

20 square units

c. On the floor of the classroom, mark off 1 square foot, 1 square yard, and 1 square meter. Estimate the number of each kind of square it would take to cover the whole floor.   answer varies

Problem set 124

1. Three hundred seconds is how many minutes? (There are 60 seconds in each minute.)   5 minutes
   (62)

2. David, Ann, and Chad were playing marbles. Ann had twice as many marbles as David had, and Chad had 5 more marbles than Ann had. David had 9 marbles. How many marbles did Chad have? (First find how many marbles Ann had.)   23 marbles
   (104)

3. On each of 5 bookshelves there are 44 books. How many books are on all 5 shelves?   220 books
   (59)

4. Nine tenths of the 30 students remembered their homework. How many students remembered their homework?   27 students
   (105)

5. What percent of the students in problem 5 did not remember their homework?   10%
   (65)

6. What fraction name for 1 has a denominator of 3? $\frac{3}{3}$
   (113)

7. What equivalent fractions are
(123) shown? $\frac{5}{10} = \frac{1}{2}$

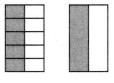

8. Draw a picture to show that $\frac{6}{8}$ and
(123) $\frac{3}{4}$ are equivalent fractions.

9. This is a golf card for 9 holes of golf. What was
(106) Michelle's average score on each hole?   4

Putt 'N' Putt

PLAYER	1	2	3	4	5	6	7	8	9	TOTAL
Michelle	6	7	5	2	4	1	3	5	3	36
Mathea	5	4	4	3	4	3	2	5	3	33

10. Sarah had to hurry. The laboratory had to be cleaned
(33) by 4:20 p.m. It was already 11:00 a.m. How much time
did she have to clean the lab?   5 hours, 20 minutes

11. Sixty minutes is how many seconds?   3600 seconds
(59)

12. 4.3 + 12.6 + 3.75   **13.** 0.24 + 6.7 + 83.49
(118)   20.65   *(118)*   90.43

14. 2126.47 − 183.5   **15.** 364.1 − 16.41   347.69
(119)   1942.97   *(119)*

16. $\frac{5}{8} + \frac{2}{8}$ $\frac{7}{8}$ **17.** $\frac{3}{5} + \frac{1}{5}$ $\frac{4}{5}$ **18.** $\frac{9}{10} - \frac{2}{10}$ $\frac{7}{10}$
(121)   *(121)*   *(122)*

19. 60 × 800   **20.** 73 × 48   **21.** 9 × 78¢
(96)   48,000   *(100)*   3504   *(58)* $7.02

22. 10^3 1000   **23.** $35.00 ÷ 4   **24.** $\frac{4824}{8}$ 603
(72)   *(86)* $8.75   *(90)*

25. $60\overline{)540}$ with quotient 9
(120)

26.   9
(2)   4
           3
           6
           N   4
           2
           5
           7
         + 3
         ———
          43

16 square units

27. Estimate the area of this figure.
(124)

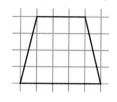

$$\begin{array}{r} 46\ r\ 3 \\ 10\overline{)463} \end{array}$$
28.
(115)

$$\begin{array}{r} 4\ r\ 15 \\ 70\overline{)295} \end{array}$$
29.
(120)

4 cm · 1 cm

30. Draw a rectangle that is 4 cm long and 1 cm wide and
(65) shade 25% of it.

LESSON 125

Reducing Fractions

a. 15
b. 30
c. 45
d. 360
e. $4.37
f. 82
Patterns:

$\frac{5}{10}, \frac{6}{12}, \frac{7}{14}, \frac{8}{16}, \frac{9}{18}$

Facts Practice: 64 Multiplication Facts (Test G in Test Masters)

Mental Math: Find each fraction of 60.

   a. $\frac{1}{4}$ of 60   **b.** $\frac{2}{4}$ of 60   **c.** $\frac{3}{4}$ of 60

Review:

   d. 30×12 **e.** $\$10.00 - \$5.63$ **f.** $37 + 45$

Patterns: Find the next five terms in this sequence.

$$\frac{1}{2}, \frac{2}{4}, \frac{3}{6}, \frac{4}{8}, \text{—}, \text{—}, \text{—}, \text{—}, \text{—}, \cdots$$

When we **reduce** a fraction, we find an equivalent fraction written with **smaller** numbers. The picture below shows $\frac{4}{6}$ reduced to $\frac{2}{3}$.

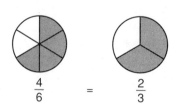

$$\frac{4}{6} = \frac{2}{3}$$

Not all fractions can be reduced. Only a fraction whose top and bottom numbers can be divided by the same number can be reduced. Since the top and bottom numbers of $\frac{4}{6}$ can both be divided by 2, we can reduce the fraction $\frac{4}{6}$.

To reduce a fraction, we divide the fraction by a name for 1. We reduce $\frac{4}{6}$ by dividing 4 by 2 and dividing 6 by 2.

$$\frac{4}{6} \div \mathbf{1}\frac{2}{2} = \frac{2}{3} \quad \begin{matrix}(4 \div 2 = 2)\\(6 \div 2 = 3)\end{matrix}$$

When deciding if a fraction can be reduced, it is helpful to look at three numbers. The three numbers are the numerator, the denominator, and the difference between the numerator and the denominator.

numerator ⟶ ④
denominator ⟶ ⑥ $6 - 4 = ②$ ⟵ difference

The three circled numbers are the numerator, the denominator, and the difference. A reducing name for 1 must be able to divide all three numbers.

Example   Write the reduced form of each fraction:

(a) $\frac{6}{8}$ (b) $\frac{6}{9}$ (c) $\frac{6}{7}$

Solution   (a) The numerator and denominator of $\frac{6}{8}$ are 6 and 8. The difference of 8 and 6 is 2. All three of these numbers can be divided by 2. That means we can reduce the fraction by dividing by $\frac{2}{2}$.

$$\frac{6}{8} \div \mathbf{1}\frac{2}{2} = \frac{3}{4}$$

Illustration:

$$\frac{6}{8} \quad = \quad \frac{3}{4}$$

(b) The numerator and denominator of $\frac{6}{9}$ are 6 and 9. Their difference $(9 - 6)$ is 3. Each of these numbers can be divided by 3. So we reduce $\frac{6}{9}$ by dividing by $\frac{3}{3}$.

$$\frac{6}{9} \div \mathbf{1}\frac{3}{3} = \frac{2}{3}$$

Illustration:

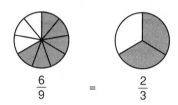

$$\frac{6}{9} \quad = \quad \frac{2}{3}$$

(c) The numerator, denominator, and difference of $\frac{6}{7}$ are 6, 7, and 1 $(7 - 6)$, respectively. The only number that divides all three of these numbers is 1. Dividing a fraction by $\frac{1}{1}$ does not reduce the fraction.

$$\frac{6}{7} \div \mathbf{1}\frac{1}{1} = \frac{6}{7}$$

This fraction cannot be reduced. Any fraction whose numerator and denominator have a difference of 1 cannot be reduced.

Practice Write the reduced form of each fraction:

a. $\frac{2}{4}$ $\frac{1}{2}$ b. $\frac{2}{6}$ $\frac{1}{3}$ c. $\frac{3}{9}$ $\frac{1}{3}$ d. $\frac{3}{8}$ $\frac{3}{8}$

e. $\frac{2}{10}$ $\frac{1}{5}$ f. $\frac{6}{10}$ $\frac{3}{5}$ g. $\frac{9}{12}$ $\frac{3}{4}$ h. $\frac{9}{10}$ $\frac{9}{10}$

Problem set 125

Use the information below to answer questions 1 and 2:

One fence board costs 90¢. It takes 10 boards to build 5 feet of fence.

1. How many boards are needed to build 50 feet of fence?
(104)   100 boards

2. What will the boards in problem 1 cost? $90.00
(104)

3. Find the perimeter and area of
(76)   this rectangle.   16 cm; 15 sq. cm

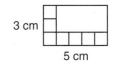
3 cm

5 cm

4. (a) Find the length of this line segment in millimeters.
(112)
(b) Find the length of the segment in centimeters.
(a) 34 mm   (b) 3.4 cm

```
mm   10    20    30    40    50
     |..|..|..|..|..|..|..|..|..|..|..|

     |||||||||||||||||||||||||||||||||
cm    1     2     3     4     5
```

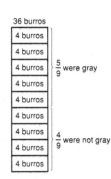

36 burros

4 burros
4 burros
4 burros $\frac{5}{9}$ were gray
4 burros
4 burros
4 burros
4 burros $\frac{4}{9}$ were not gray
4 burros
4 burros

5. Five ninths of the 36 burros were gray. How many of
(105) the burros were gray? Illustrate the problem.   20 burros

6. Change each improper fraction to a whole number or
(114) to a mixed number:

(a) $\frac{15}{2}$ $7\frac{1}{2}$ (b) $\frac{15}{3}$ 5   (c) $\frac{15}{4}$ $3\frac{3}{4}$

7. What equivalent fractions are
(123) shown? $\frac{1}{2} = \frac{6}{12}$

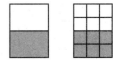

8. What percent of each rectangle in
(65)   problem 7 is shaded?   50%

9. Write the reduced form of each fraction:
(125)
(a) $\frac{3}{6}$ $\frac{1}{2}$ (b) $\frac{4}{6}$ $\frac{2}{3}$ (c) $\frac{5}{6}$ $\frac{5}{6}$

10. In three tries Rodney bounced the ball on his head 23
(106) times, 36 times, and 34 times. What was the average
number of bounces in each try?   31 bounces

11. T-shirts cost $5 each. Mark had $27. He bought 5 T-
(93) shirts. Tax was $1.50. How much money did he have
left? $0.50

12. 25.42 − 24.8   **13.** 36.2 − 4.27   **14.**   37.2
(119) 0.62   (119) 31.93   (116)   135.7
                                                            10.62
                                                             2.47
15. $\frac{3}{9} + \frac{4}{9}$ $\frac{7}{9}$ **16.** $\frac{1}{7} + \frac{2}{7} + \frac{3}{7}$ $\frac{6}{7}$ + 14.0
(121)   (121)   199.99

17. $\frac{5}{8} - \frac{5}{8}$ 0   **18.** $\frac{11}{12} - \frac{10}{12}$ $\frac{1}{12}$ **19.** $\frac{8}{10} - \frac{5}{10}$ $\frac{3}{10}$
(122)   (122)   (122)

20.   48   **21.**   72   **22.** $4.08
(100)   × 36   (100)   × 58   (68)   ×   7
        ────   ────   ──────
        1728   4176 $28.56

                                      364 r 1
23. $\frac{4716}{6}$ 786   **24.** 7)2549   **25.** $19.40 ÷ 5
(86)   (86)   (86) $3.88

26. 490 ÷ 10   **27.** 90 ÷ 20   **28.** 171 ÷ 40
(115) 49   (120) 4 r 10   (120) 4 r 11

29. Estimate the area of this footprint.
(124) Each small square is one square
inch.   25 sq. in.

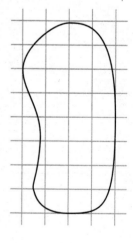

**LESSON
126**

Dividing by Multiples of 10, Part 2

a. 18
b. 26
c. 38
d. 2300
e. $6.61
f. 19
Problem Solving:
   10 books

> **Facts Practice:** 64 Multiplication Facts (Test G in Test Masters)
>
> **Mental Math:** We find half of a number by dividing the number by 2. We can often divide by 2 mentally. Find half of each number.
>
> **a.** $\frac{1}{2}$ of 36   **b.** $\frac{1}{2}$ of 52   **c.** $\frac{1}{2}$ of 76
>
> **Review:**
>
> **d.** 50×46 **e.** $4.63 + $1.98   **f.** $54 - 35$
>
> **Problem Solving:** There were three stacks of books on the shelf. There were six books in the first stack and eleven books in the second stack. Teresa rearranged the books so that there were nine books in each of the three stacks. How many books were in the third stack before the books were rearranged?

When we divide by multiples of 10, we continue to follow the four-step division method. We divide, multiply, subtract, and bring down. We have practiced division problems with one-digit answers. In this lesson, we will practice division problems with two-digit answers.

Example 1 $30\overline{)963}$

Solution   **Step 1.** We begin by breaking the problem into the smaller division problem, $30\overline{)96}$, and write "3."

Step 2. We multiply 3×30 and write "90."

$$
\begin{array}{r}
\mathbf{32}\ \mathbf{r}\ \mathbf{3} \\
30\overline{)963} \\
\underline{90} \\
63 \\
\underline{60} \\
3
\end{array}
$$

Step 3. We subtract $96 - 90$ and write "6."

Step 4. We bring down the 3, making 63.

REPEAT:

Step 1. We divide $30\overline{)63}$ and write "2."

Step 2. We multiply 2 × 30 and write "60."

Step 3. We subtract 63 − 60 and write "3."

Step 4. There are no more numbers to bring down. The answer is 32 with a remainder of 3.

Example 2 40$\overline{)2531}$

Solution **Step 1.** We begin by breaking the problem into a smaller division problem. Since 40$\overline{)25}$ does not give an answer of 1 or more, we start with the division 40$\overline{)253}$ and write "6" above the 3.

$$
\begin{array}{r}
63 \text{ r } 11 \\
40\overline{)2531} \\
240 \\
\hline
131 \\
120 \\
\hline
11 \\
\end{array}
$$

Step 2. We multiply 6 × 40 and write "240."

Step 3. We subtract 253 − 240 and write "13."

Step 4. We bring down the 1, making 131.

REPEAT:

Step 1. We divide 40$\overline{)131}$ and write "3."

Step 2. We multiply 3 × 40 and write "120."

Step 3. We subtract 131 − 120 and write "11."

Step 4. There are no more numbers to bring down. The answer is 63 with a remainder of 11.

Practice Divide:

a. $\overset{43 \text{ r } 2}{20\overline{)862}}$ **b.** $\overset{29}{30\overline{)870}}$ **c.** $\overset{22 \text{ r } 8}{40\overline{)888}}$

d. $\overset{46}{50\overline{)2300}}$ **e.** $\overset{40}{60\overline{)2400}}$ **f.** $\overset{35 \text{ r } 3}{70\overline{)2453}}$

Problem set 126

1. Admission to the zoo was $3.25 for adults and $1.50
$^{(82)}$ for children. Gary bought tickets for 2 adults and 3 children. Altogether, how much did the tickets cost?
$11.00

2. Find the perimeter and area of
(76) this square.   12 ft; 9 sq. ft

3 ft

3 ft

3. Ten quarters is the same as how
(104) many nickels?   50 nickels

4. Something is wrong with this
(109) sign. Draw two different signs to
show ways to correct the error.

5. What fraction of the letters in
(84) AARDVARK are A's? $\frac{3}{8}$

6. What fraction name for 1 has a
(113) denominator of 4? $\frac{4}{4}$

7. Use words to write 7.8.   seven and eight tenths
(108)

8. Draw a picture to show that $\frac{1}{3}$ and $\frac{2}{6}$ are equivalent
(123) fractions.

9. The champion bike rider could ride 58 miles in 2
(104) hours. At the same speed, how far could the champion
ride in 10 hours?   290 mi

10. The bikers bought 11 caps at $5.40 each and 7 straps at
(93) $1.20 each. Tax was $3.55. They paid for the items
with a $100 bill. How much change did they receive?
$28.65

11. There were three piles of books on the shelf. Maria
(106) rearranged the three piles so that there were the same
number of books in each pile. Then how many books
were in each pile?   7 books

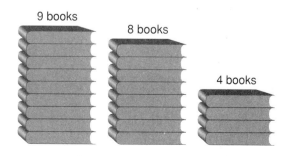

9 books

8 books

4 books

12. 38.42 + 5.71 + 14.3
(118)   58.43

13. $6 + 6¢ + $3.45 $9.51
(53)

14. 43.0 − 7.49   35.51
(119)

15. 125.46 − 24.9   100.56
(119)

16. $\dfrac{1}{9} + \dfrac{1}{9}$ $\frac{2}{9}$
(121)

17. $\dfrac{4}{11} + \dfrac{5}{11}$ $\frac{9}{11}$
(121)

18. $\dfrac{8}{9} - \dfrac{1}{9}$ $\frac{7}{9}$
(122)

19. $\dfrac{8}{12} - \dfrac{1}{12}$ $\frac{7}{12}$
(122)

20. $9^2 \times 10^2$
(72)   8100

21. 8 × $3.75
(68) $30.00

22. 47 × 36
(100)   1692

23. $36.28 ÷ 4
(90) $9.07

26. $9\overline{)4321}$ 480 r 1
(90)

27. $\dfrac{456}{6}$ 76
(75)

28. $30\overline{)480}$ 16
(126)

29. $20\overline{)1240}$ 62
(126)

24.
(2)
```
    4
    3
    8
    5
    2
    7
    9
    9
    4
  + N    22
 ___
   73
```

25.
(21)
```
   17
   22
   33
   42
   17
   85
   21
   37
   46
   13
 + 20
 ____
  353
```

30. Write the reduced form of each fraction:
(125)
    (a) $\frac{8}{10}$ $\frac{4}{5}$
    (b) $\frac{8}{9}$ $\frac{8}{9}$
    (c) $\frac{6}{8}$ $\frac{3}{4}$

LESSON 127

Multiplying a Three-Digit Number by a Two-Digit Number

a. $1\frac{1}{2}$
b. $3\frac{1}{2}$
c. $5\frac{1}{2}$
d. $10\frac{1}{2}$
e. $16\frac{1}{2}$

Patterns:
64, 125, 216

Facts Practice: 90 Division Facts (Test I in Test Masters)

Mental Math: An odd number may be written as an even number plus 1. For example, 9 is 8 + 1. Half of 9 is half of 8 plus half of 1. Since half of 8 is 4 and half of 1 is $\frac{1}{2}$, half of 9 is $4\frac{1}{2}$. Find half of each of these odd numbers.

    a. 3   **b.** 7   **c.** 11   **d.** 21   **e.** 33

Patterns: Notice that $1 \times 1 \times 1 = 1$, $2 \times 2 \times 2 = 8$, and $3 \times 3 \times 3 = 27$. The products 1, 8, and 27 begin this sequence. Find the next three numbers in the sequence.

$$1, 8, 27, \_\_, \_\_, \_\_, \ldots$$

We have learned to multiply a two-digit number by another two-digit number. In this lesson we will learn to multiply a three-digit number by a two-digit number.

Example 1 Multiply: 364 × 24

Solution We write the three-digit number on top. We write the two-digit number underneath so that the last digits are lined up. We multiply 364 by 4. Next we multiply 364 by 2. Since this 2 is actually 20, we write the last digit of this product in the tens' place, which is under the 2 in 24. Then we add and find that the product is **8736.**

$$
\begin{array}{r}
{\scriptstyle 1} \\
{\scriptstyle 2\,1} \\
364 \\
\times\ \ 24 \\
\hline
1456 \\
728\ \ \\
\hline
8736
\end{array}
$$

Example 2 Multiply:
$$
\begin{array}{r}
\$4.07 \\
\times\ \ \ \ 38 \\
\hline
\end{array}
$$

Solution We will ignore the dollar sign and decimal point until we are finished multiplying. First we multiply 407 by 8. Then we multiply 407 by 3, which is actually 30. We write the last digit of this product in the tens' place. We add and find the product is 15466. Now we place the dollar sign and decimal point. The answer is **$154.66.**

$$
\begin{array}{r}
\overset{2}{}\overset{5}{} \\
\$4.07 \\
\times \quad 38 \\
\hline
32\ 56 \\
122\ 1 \\
\hline
\$154.66
\end{array}
$$

Practice   Multiply:

a. 235 × 24   **b.** 14 × 430   **c.** $1.25 × 24

   5640   6020 $30.00

d.   406   **e.** $6.20   **f.**   562

   × 32   ×   31   × 47

   12,992 $192.20   26,414

Problem set   **1.** Carrie's cousin lives 3000 miles away. If Carrie drove

127   *(17)* 638 miles the first day, 456 miles the second day, and 589 miles the third day, how much farther does she need to drive to get to her cousin's house?   1317 mi

2. Find the perimeter and area of
(94,60) this square.   28 in.; 49 sq. in.

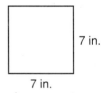

7 in.

7 in.

3. If the perimeter of a square is 2
(27) meters, each side is how many centimeters long?   50 cm

4. Gracie found 35 pinecones. Four sevenths of the
(105) pinecones still had seeds. How many of the pinecones still had seeds? Illustrate the problem.   20 pinecones

5. Round 6843 to the nearest thousand.   7000
(91)

6. Write the reduced form of each fraction:
(125)

(a) $\frac{4}{5}$ $\frac{4}{5}$ (b) $\frac{5}{10}$ $\frac{1}{2}$ (c) $\frac{4}{10}$ $\frac{2}{5}$

7. Use words to write 374.25.
(108) three hundred seventy-four and twenty-five hundredths

8. Draw a picture to show that $\frac{1}{2}$ and $\frac{4}{8}$ are equivalent fractions. 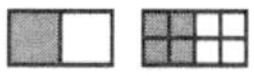
(123)

9. A decade is what percent of a century? 10%
(64)

10. Daniel Boone furnished the settlers with 750 pounds of meat in 5 days. What was the average amount of meat he furnished each day? 150 lb
(106)

11. The explorer Zebulon Pike estimated that the mountain was eight thousand, seven hundred forty-two feet high. His estimate was five thousand, three hundred sixty-eight feet less than the actual height. Today, we call this mountain *Pike's Peak*. How high is Pike's Peak? 14,110 ft
(12)

12. $30.07 - 3.7$ 26.37
(119)

13. $46.0 - 12.46$ 33.54
(119)

14. (116)
$$\begin{array}{r} 37.15 \\ 6.84 \\ 1.29 \\ 29.1 \\ +\ \ 3.6 \\ \hline 77.98 \end{array}$$

15. $\frac{8}{15} + \frac{6}{15}$ $\frac{14}{15}$
(121)

16. $\frac{3}{10} + \frac{3}{10} + \frac{3}{10}$ $\frac{9}{10}$
(121)

17. $\frac{5}{15} - \frac{3}{15}$ $\frac{2}{15}$
(122)

18. $\frac{7}{8} - \frac{7}{8}$ 0
(122)

19. $\frac{5}{6} - \frac{4}{6}$ $\frac{1}{6}$
(122)

20. (127)
$$\begin{array}{r} \$3.20 \\ \times\ \ \ 46 \\ \hline \$147.20 \end{array}$$

21. (2)
$$\begin{array}{r} N \\ 4 \\ 3 \\ 2 \\ 2 \\ +\ 1 \\ \hline 15 \end{array}$$
3

22. (21)
$$\begin{array}{r} 25 \\ 31 \\ 42 \\ 22 \\ +\ 13 \\ \hline 133 \end{array}$$

23. (77)
$$\begin{array}{r} 142 \\ \times\ \ 30 \\ \hline 4260 \end{array}$$

24. (127)
$$\begin{array}{r} 307 \\ \times\ \ 25 \\ \hline 7675 \end{array}$$

25. $6\overline{)4837}$ 806 r 1
(90)

26. $\frac{1372}{\sqrt{16}}$ 343
(86,40)

27. $30.00 ÷ 8
(86) $3.75

$$\begin{array}{r} 24 \\ 40\overline{)960} \end{array}$$
28.
(126)

$$\begin{array}{r} 68 \\ 20\overline{)1360} \end{array}$$
29.
(126)

30. Estimate the area of this triangle.
(124) Each small square is one square
centimeter.   15 sq. cm

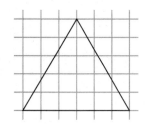

LESSON
128

a. $2\frac{1}{2}$

b. $7\frac{1}{2}$

c. $12\frac{1}{2}$

d. 420

e. $1.75

f. 949

Problem Solving:

$$\begin{array}{ccc} 7 & 8 & 9 \\ \times\,2 & \times\,3 & \times\,6 \\ \hline 14 & 24 & 54 \end{array}$$

Finding Equivalent Fractions by Multiplying

Facts Practice: 90 Division Facts (Test I in Test Masters)

Mental Math: Find $\frac{1}{2}$ of each odd number.

   a. $\frac{1}{2}$ of 5   **b.** $\frac{1}{2}$ of 15   **c.** $\frac{1}{2}$ of 25

Review:

   d. 3 × 140   **e.** $20.00 − $18.25   **f.** 474 + 475

Problem Solving: Find the missing digits in each of these multiplication facts.

$$\begin{array}{ccc} 7 & \underline{} & 9 \\ \times\,\underline{} & \times\,3 & \times\,\underline{} \\ \hline \_4 & \_4 & \_4 \end{array}$$

We remember that when we multiply a number by 1, the answer equals the number we multiplied.

$$2 \times 1 = 2 \qquad 2000 \times 1 = 2000 \qquad \frac{1}{2} \times 1 = \frac{1}{2}$$

We also remember that there are many ways to write "1."

$$1 = \frac{2}{2} = \frac{3}{3} = \frac{4}{4} = \frac{5}{5} = \frac{6}{6} = \ldots$$

We can use these two facts to find equivalent fractions. If we multiply a fraction by a fraction name for 1, the result is an equivalent fraction.

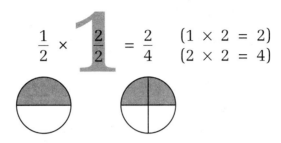

$$\frac{1}{2} \times \mathbf{1}\frac{2}{2} = \frac{2}{4} \quad \begin{matrix} (1 \times 2 = 2) \\ (2 \times 2 = 4) \end{matrix}$$

We found that $\frac{1}{2}$ is equivalent to $\frac{2}{4}$ by multiplying $\frac{1}{2}$ by $\frac{2}{2}$, which is a fraction name for 1. We can find other fractions equivalent to $\frac{1}{2}$ by multiplying by other fraction names for 1.

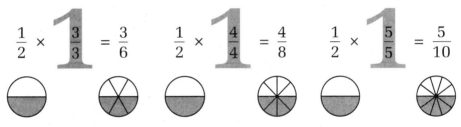

$$\frac{1}{2} \times \mathbf{1}\frac{3}{3} = \frac{3}{6} \qquad \frac{1}{2} \times \mathbf{1}\frac{4}{4} = \frac{4}{8} \qquad \frac{1}{2} \times \mathbf{1}\frac{5}{5} = \frac{5}{10}$$

Example   Find four fractions equivalent to $\frac{1}{3}$ by multiplying $\frac{1}{3}$ by $\frac{2}{2}$, $\frac{3}{3}$, $\frac{4}{4}$, and $\frac{5}{5}$.

Solution

$$\frac{1}{3} \times \frac{2}{2} = \frac{2}{6} \qquad\qquad \frac{1}{3} \times \frac{3}{3} = \frac{3}{9}$$

$$\frac{1}{3} \times \frac{4}{4} = \frac{4}{12} \qquad\qquad \frac{1}{3} \times \frac{5}{5} = \frac{5}{15}$$

We find that four fractions equivalent to $\frac{1}{3}$ are

$$\mathbf{\frac{2}{6}, \frac{3}{9}, \frac{4}{12},} \text{ and } \mathbf{\frac{5}{15}}$$

Practice   Find four equivalent fractions for each of these fractions by multiplying each fraction by $\frac{2}{2}$, $\frac{3}{3}$, $\frac{4}{4}$, and $\frac{5}{5}$:

a. $\dfrac{1}{4}$ $\frac{2}{8}, \frac{3}{12}, \frac{4}{16}, \frac{5}{20}$ **b.** $\dfrac{5}{6}$ $\frac{10}{12}, \frac{15}{18}, \frac{20}{24}, \frac{25}{30}$

c. $\dfrac{2}{5}$ $\frac{4}{10}, \frac{6}{15}, \frac{8}{20}, \frac{10}{25}$ **d.** $\dfrac{1}{10}$ $\frac{2}{20}, \frac{3}{30}, \frac{4}{40}, \frac{5}{50}$

Problem set Use the information in the table to answer questions 1
128 and 2:

Lengths of Rivers

RIVER	MILES	KILOMETERS
Nile	4145	6671
Amazon	3915	6300
Yangtze	3900	6276
Congo	2718	4374
Mississippi	2348	3778

1. The Nile is how many kilometers longer than the
(89) Yangtze?   395 km

2. The Amazon is how many miles longer than the
(89) Congo?   1197 mi

3. How many feet are in 10 yards?   30 ft
(49)

4. The squirrel found 1236 acorns during the summer. It
(105) saved two thirds of the acorns for winter. How many
acorns did the squirrel save for winter?   824 acorns

5. Find the perimeter and area of
(94,60) this rectangle.   10 cm; 6 sq. cm

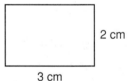

2 cm

3 cm

6. Estimate the sum of 627 and 288.
(70)   900

7. Use words to name $3578\frac{2}{3}$.
(44)   three thousand, five hundred seventy-eight and two thirds

8. Find three fractions equivalent to $\frac{1}{2}$ by multiplying by
(128) $\frac{3}{3}$, $\frac{6}{6}$, and $\frac{10}{10}$. $\frac{3}{6}$; $\frac{6}{12}$; $\frac{10}{20}$

9. Write the reduced form of each fraction:
(125)
(a) $\frac{9}{10}$ $\frac{9}{10}$ (b) $\frac{9}{12}$ $\frac{3}{4}$ (c) $\frac{10}{12}$ $\frac{5}{6}$

10. Solve this problem by guessing and checking your
(119) answer: In one week Balboa saw 77 buffalo and deer.
He saw 13 more buffalo than deer. How many deer did
he see?   32 deer

11. Only 1% of those who enter the contest win. What
(65) percent of those who enter the contest do not win?
99%

12. 4.63 + 26.7 + 0.34   **13.** 8.4 + 23.57 + 16.9
(118) 31.67   (118) 48.87

14. 23.91 − 9.3   14.61   **15.** 60.4 − 0.64   59.76
(119)   (119)

16. $\dfrac{8}{12} + \dfrac{3}{12}$ $\frac{11}{12}$ **17.** $\dfrac{2}{7} + \dfrac{3}{7}$ $\frac{5}{7}$
(121)   (121)

18. $\dfrac{15}{16} - \dfrac{6}{16}$ $\frac{9}{16}$ **19.** $\dfrac{3}{8} - \dfrac{2}{8}$ $\frac{1}{8}$
(122)   (122)

20. 234 × 42   9828   **21.** 36 × 47   1692
(127)   (100)

22.   7   **23.**   42   **24.** 408 × 29
(2)   4   (21)   23   (127) 11,832
             2   35
             1   47   109
             4   74   **25.** 9)‾981‾
             N   29   53   (90)
             2   32
             7   24   **26.** $25.00 ÷ 4
             4   21   (86) $6.25
           + 8   5
          ‾‾‾‾   + 7   **27.** $\dfrac{\sqrt{64}}{\sqrt{4}}$ 4
            68   ‾‾‾‾‾   (56,40)
                                   363

              15   32   28 r 3
28. 50)‾750‾   **29.** 40)‾1280‾   **30.** 30)‾843‾
(126)   (126)   (126)

LESSON 129

Chance and Probability

a. 14
b. 19
c. $4\frac{1}{2}$
d. 880
e. $8.42
f. 54
Patterns:
   Answer varies

Facts Practice: 90 Division Facts (Test I in Test Masters)

Mental Math: The percent form of $\frac{1}{2}$ is 50%. Find 50% of each number.

   a. 50% of 28   **b.** 50% of 38   **c.** 50% of 9

Review:

   d. 20 × 44   **e.** $6.47 + $1.95   **f.** 82 − 28

Patterns: Write five different fractions equal to $\frac{1}{2}$.

When a meteorologist states that the chance of rain is 80%, then the prediction is that it will probably rain. If the chance of rain is 20%, then the meteorologist means that it might rain, but it probably will not rain. Meteorologists use percentages to describe the chance, or the likelihood, of rain.

   We can also use a fraction to describe the likelihood of an event. When we use a fraction, we refer to the likelihood of an event as *probability*. For instance, if a coin is flipped, the probability that it will land "heads up" is $\frac{1}{2}$.

$$\text{There are 2 possibilities:} \longrightarrow \frac{1}{2} \quad \begin{array}{l}\longleftarrow \text{Only 1 of the} \\ \text{2 possibilities} \\ \text{is heads up.}\end{array}$$
heads up and tails up.

Since 50% is equivalent to $\frac{1}{2}$, we may also say that the chance that the coin will land heads up is 50%. Events that are more likely than not to happen have probabilities greater than $\frac{1}{2}$ and chances greater than 50%. Events which are more likely not to happen have probabilities less than $\frac{1}{2}$ and chances less than 50%.

Example   A number cube is rolled. What is the probability that the number rolled will be an even number?

Solution   When we write a probability, the bottom number is the total of all possible outcomes, while the top number is the number of described outcomes.

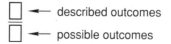
□ ← described outcomes
□ ← possible outcomes

With a number cube there are 6 possible outcomes, so 6 is the bottom number. Three of the 6 numbers on the cube are even, so there are 3 ways to roll an even number.

$$\frac{3}{6}$$ ← described outcomes
← possible outcomes

The probability of rolling an even number is $\frac{3}{6}$. We usually reduce fractions, so the probability is also $\frac{1}{2}$.

Practice

a. What is the probability of a flipped coin landing tails up? $\frac{1}{2}$

b. What is the probability of rolling a square number with one roll of a number cube? $\frac{1}{3}$

c. What is the probability of this spinner stopping on 4? $\frac{1}{4}$

d. The meteorologist said that the chance of rain is 50%. What does that forecast mean? The meteorologist means that it is equally likely to rain as not to rain.

Problem set 129

1. A stagecoach was pulled by a 4-horse team, and a
(82) covered wagon was pulled by a 6-horse team. Altogether, how many horses were needed to pull 3 stagecoaches and 7 covered wagons? 54 horses

2. Find the perimeter and area of
(94,60) this rectangle. 26 cm; 40 sq. cm

8 cm

5 cm

3. Sixteen quarters equals how many
(104) dimes? 40 dimes

60 minutes	
6 minutes	
6 minutes	$\frac{2}{10}$ commercials were on
6 minutes	
6 minutes	
6 minutes	
6 minutes	
6 minutes	$\frac{8}{10}$ commercials were not on
6 minutes	
6 minutes	
6 minutes	

4. Gilbert watched TV for 60 minutes. He found that
(105) commercials were on for two tenths of the time. Commercials were on for how many minutes? Draw a diagram to illustrate the problem.   12 minutes

5. The commercials in problem 4 were on for what
(80,65) percent of the hour the TV was watched?   20%

6. (a) What is the radius of this circle? $\frac{3}{4}$ in.
(110) (b) What is the diameter of the circle? $1\frac{1}{2}$ in.

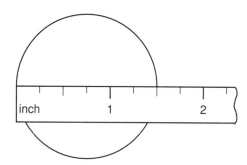

7. Write the reduced form of each fraction:
(125) (a) $\frac{4}{6}$ $\frac{2}{3}$ (b) $\frac{5}{10}$ $\frac{1}{2}$ (c) $\frac{6}{7}$ $\frac{6}{7}$

8. Draw a picture to show that $\frac{4}{6}$ and $\frac{2}{3}$ are equivalent
(123) fractions.   ▦▦ ▰▰▱

9. Find three fractions equivalent to $\frac{2}{3}$ by multiplying by
(128) $\frac{2}{2}$, $\frac{3}{3}$, and $\frac{4}{4}$. $\frac{4}{6}$, $\frac{6}{9}$, $\frac{8}{12}$

10. In three batches of cookies there were 20, 28, and 30
(106) cookies, respectively. What was the average number of cookies in each batch?   26 cookies

11. James bought 15 apples at 23¢ each, 13 oranges at 41¢
(82) each, and 3 cans of juice at 63¢ each. How much money did he spend? $10.67

12. What is the probability that the spinner in practice
(129) problem (c) will stop on an odd number? $\frac{1}{2}$

13. 7.6 − 0.76   6.84   **14.** 26.04 − 25.7   0.34
(119)   *(119)*

15. $\frac{1}{10} + \frac{2}{10}$ $\frac{3}{10}$
(121)

16. $\frac{5}{13} + \frac{4}{13} + \frac{3}{13}$ $\frac{12}{13}$
(121)

17. $\frac{4}{9} - \frac{3}{9}$ $\frac{1}{9}$
(122)

18. $\frac{6}{7} - \frac{3}{7}$ $\frac{3}{7}$
(122)

19. $\frac{4}{33} - \frac{4}{33}$ 0
(122)

20.   502
(127) $\times$ 52
     26,104

21.   327
(127) $\times$ 26
     8502

22.   490
(77) $\times$ 70
     34,300

23. $1000 \div 5$
(90)   200

24. $\$42.72 \div 6$
(86) $\$7.12$

25. $\frac{3627}{3^2}$ 403
(90,72)

26. $60\overline{)1320}$ 22
(126)

27. $30\overline{)2220}$ 74
(126)

28. $40\overline{)963}$ 24 r 3
(126)

Change each improper fraction to a mixed number:

29. $\frac{35}{8}$ $4\frac{3}{8}$
(114)

30. $\frac{35}{9}$ $3\frac{8}{9}$
(114)

Dividing by Two-Digit Numbers, Part 1

a. 17
b. $12\frac{1}{2}$
c. 25
d. 330
e. $0.87
f. 296

Problem Solving:
It will not rain:
   70% chance it
   will not rain
More likely:
   It is more likely
   not to rain.
Chance of rain:
   If it were as
   likely to rain as
   not to rain, the
   chance would be
   50%.

Facts Practice: 90 Division Facts (Test I in Test Masters)

Mental Math: Find the stated percent of each number.
   a. 50% of 34   **b.** 50% of 25   **c.** 100% of 25

Review:
   d. 5×66 **e.** $\$10.00 - \$9.13$ **f.** $67 + 29 + 200$

Problem Solving: The weather forecast stated that the chance of rain was 30%. What was the chance that it would not rain? Was it more likely to rain or not to rain? If it were as likely to rain as not to rain, what would be the chance of rain?

We have divided by two-digit numbers that are multiples of 10. In this lesson we will begin dividing by other two-digit numbers. When we divide by two-digit numbers, sometimes we accidentally choose an answer to a division problem that is too large. If this happens, we start over and try a smaller number for the answer.

Example 1   31$\overline{)95}$

Solution   **Step 1.** To help us divide 31$\overline{)95}$, we think 3$\overline{)9}$ and try that answer. We write "3."

$$\begin{array}{r} 3\ \text{r}\ 2 \\ 31\overline{)95} \\ \underline{93} \\ 2 \end{array}$$

Step 2. We multiply 3 × 31 and write "93."

Step 3. We subtract 93 from 95 and write "2."

Step 4. There are no digits to bring down. The answer is **3 with a remainder of 2.**

Example 2   43$\overline{)246}$

Solution   **Step 1.** To help us divide 43$\overline{)246}$, we may think 4$\overline{)24}$ and try that answer. We write "6."

$$\begin{array}{r} 6 \\ 43\overline{)246} \\ \underline{258} \end{array}$$ ← too large

Step 2. We multiply 6 × 43 and write "258." We see that 258 is greater than 246. We tried 6, but 6 was too large.

START OVER:

Step 1. This time we try 5 as the division answer.

$$\begin{array}{r} 5\ \text{r}\ 31 \\ 43\overline{)246} \\ \underline{215} \\ 31 \end{array}$$

Step 2. We multiply 5 × 43 and write "215."

Step 3. We subtract and write "31."

Step 4. There are no digits to bring down. The answer is **5 with a remainder of 31.**

Practice Divide:

a. $32\overline{)128}$ = 4

b. $21\overline{)90}$ = 4 r 6

c. $25\overline{)68}$ = 2 r 18

d. $42\overline{)250}$ = 5 r 40

e. $46\overline{)164}$ = 3 r 26

f. $31\overline{)225}$ = 7 r 8

Problem set 130

1. There are 60 minutes in 1 hour and 24 hours in 1 day.
   (67) How many minutes are in 1 day?   1440 minutes

2. Davey had 56 baseball cards. He gave half of them to
   (104) Janeen. Janeen gave half of those to Jason. How many
   cards did Jason get?   14 cards

3. How many 1 square foot floor tiles are needed to cover
   (76) the floor of a room that is 12 feet long and 8 feet wide?
   96 square foot floor tiles

4. If 2 apples cost 60¢, how much money would 6 apples
   (104) cost? $1.80

5. (a) What is the diameter of the
   (110)   quarter?   2.4 cm

   (b) What is the radius of the
       quarter?   1.2 cm

6. A number cube is rolled. What is the probability that
   (129) the number rolled will be more than four? $\frac{1}{3}$

7. Write the reduced form of each fraction:
   (125)
   (a) $\frac{3}{6}$ $\frac{1}{2}$

   (b) $\frac{3}{12}$ $\frac{1}{4}$

   (c) $\frac{8}{10}$ $\frac{4}{5}$

8. Find three fractions equivalent to $\frac{3}{4}$ by multiplying $\frac{3}{4}$
   (128) by $\frac{2}{2}$, $\frac{3}{3}$, and $\frac{4}{4}$. $\frac{6}{8}$, $\frac{9}{12}$, $\frac{12}{16}$

9. Guess and check your guess to solve this problem:
   (119) There were 14 rocks and bricks in all. There were 2
   more rocks than bricks. How many rocks were there?
   8 rocks

Use the information in this description to answer questions 10 and 11:

Able, Baker, and Charlie carried weights. Able could carry twice as much as Baker. Baker could carry ten pounds. Charlie could carry one pound more than Able.

10. Together, how many pounds could all three boys carry?   51 lb
(104)

11. What was the average weight each of the three boys could carry?   17 lb
(106)

12. 39.42 + 9.5 + 16.1   **13.** 6.34 + 0.17 + 19.8
(118) 65.02   *(118)* 26.31

14. 37.1 − 9.46   27.64   **15.** 4.91 − 4.91   0
(119)   *(119)*

16. $\dfrac{3}{10} + \dfrac{6}{10}$ $\frac{9}{10}$ **17.** $\dfrac{1}{8} + \dfrac{4}{8}$ $\frac{5}{8}$
(121)   *(121)*

18. $\dfrac{5}{7} - \dfrac{1}{7}$ $\frac{4}{7}$ **19.** $\dfrac{15}{16} - \dfrac{8}{16}$ $\frac{7}{16}$
(122)   *(122)*

20. 476 × 14   **21.** 240 × 68   **22.** 34 × 904
(127) 6664   *(127)* 16,320   *(127)* 30,736

23. $8\overline{)4325}$ 540 r 5   **24.** $47.16 ÷ 9   **25.** $\dfrac{1221}{3}$ 407
(90)   *(86)* $5.24   *(90)*

26. $40\overline{)3210}$ 80 r 10   **27.** $32\overline{)98}$ 3 r 2   **28.** $34\overline{)184}$ 5 r 14
(126)   *(130)*   *(130)*

29. Estimate the area of this fish pond. Each small square is one square foot.   36 sq. ft
(124)

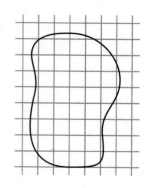

LESSON
131

Adding Mixed Numbers •
Subtracting Mixed Numbers

a. 20
b. 5
c. $2\frac{1}{2}$
d. 100
e. $0.37
f. 910
Problem Solving:
Blocks used:
18 blocks
Blocks needed:
12 more blocks

Facts Practice: 90 Division Facts (Test I in Test Masters)

Mental Math: The percent form of $\frac{1}{4}$ is 25%. Find the stated
percent of each number.

  a. 25% of 80   **b.** 25% of 20   **c.** 50% of 5

Review:

  d. 4×25 **e.** $1.00 - 63¢   **f.** 280 + 630

Problem Solving: Robert used toy blocks to build
these steps. How many blocks
did he use? How many more
blocks would he need to add
another step?

Adding
mixed
numbers

We remember that a mixed number is a number with a
whole number part and a fraction part. To add mixed
numbers, we add the fraction parts together. Then we add
the whole number parts together.

Example 1   Add: $2\frac{3}{5} + 3\frac{1}{5}$

Solution   We may write the numbers one above
the other. We add the fractions and
get $\frac{4}{5}$. We add the whole numbers and
get 5. The sum of the mixed numbers
is $\mathbf{5\frac{4}{5}}$.

$$\begin{array}{r} 2\frac{3}{5} \\ + 3\frac{1}{5} \\ \hline 5\frac{4}{5} \end{array}$$

Example 2   Add: $3 + 1\frac{1}{3}$

Solution   The number 3 is a whole number, not
a mixed number. Therefore, there is
no fraction to add to $\frac{1}{3}$. We add the
whole numbers and get $\mathbf{4\frac{1}{3}}$.

$$\begin{array}{r} 3 \\ + 1\frac{1}{3} \\ \hline 4\frac{1}{3} \end{array}$$

Subtracting mixed numbers

To subtract mixed numbers, we subtract the fractions. Then we subtract the whole numbers.

Example 3 Subtract: $5\frac{2}{3} - 1\frac{1}{3}$

Solution We must subtract the second number from the first number. To do this, it is helpful to write the first number above the second number. Then we subtract the fractions and get $\frac{1}{3}$. Then we subtract the whole numbers and get 4. The difference is **$4\frac{1}{3}$.**

$$\begin{array}{r} 5\frac{2}{3} \\ -\ 1\frac{1}{3} \\ \hline 4\frac{1}{3} \end{array}$$

Practice **a.** $2\frac{1}{4} + 4\frac{2}{4}$ $6\frac{3}{4}$ **b.** $5\frac{3}{8} + 1\frac{2}{8}$ $6\frac{5}{8}$ **c.** $8 + 1\frac{2}{5}$ $9\frac{2}{5}$

d. $4\frac{3}{5} - 1\frac{1}{5}$ $3\frac{2}{5}$ **e.** $9\frac{3}{4} - 4\frac{2}{4}$ $5\frac{1}{4}$ **f.** $12\frac{8}{9} - 3\frac{3}{9}$ $9\frac{5}{9}$

g. $3\frac{1}{3} - 2\frac{1}{3}$ 1 **h.** $6\frac{1}{2} - 3$ $3\frac{1}{2}$ **i.** $2\frac{3}{4} - 2\frac{2}{4}$ $\frac{1}{4}$

Problem set 131

1. If Thorton can do 1 problem in 3 seconds, how many
(104) **minutes** will it take him to do 100 problems? 5 minutes

2. (a) What is the area of this rectangle? 36 sq. in.
(94,60) (b) What is the perimeter of this rectangle? 26 in.

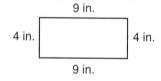

9 in.

4 in.   4 in.

9 in.

3. Gilbert earned $40. He saved $\frac{5}{8}$ of what he earned. How
(105) much money did he save? $25

4. After spending $2.50 on a ticket and $1.25 on
(82) popcorn, Jill still had 75¢. How much money did she start with? $4.50

5. Tim's shoes weigh $2\frac{1}{4}$ pounds. The rest of his clothes
(131) weigh $3\frac{2}{4}$ pounds. What is the total weight of Tim's
shoes and clothes? $5\frac{3}{4}$ lb

6. Draw a circle and shade 75% of it.
(65,32)

7. Write the reduced form of each fraction:
(125)   (a) $\frac{2}{8}$ $\frac{1}{4}$ (b) $\frac{4}{10}$ $\frac{2}{5}$ (c) $\frac{4}{9}$ $\frac{4}{9}$

8. Draw a picture to show that $\frac{5}{10}$ and $\frac{1}{2}$ are equivalent
(123) fractions.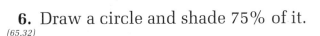

9. The first weight was twice the second weight. The
(82) third weight was three times the second weight. The
second weight was 20 pounds. What was the sum of
the three weights?   120 lb

10. Allison kept track of the number
(106,89) of laps she swam each day on a
table like this. What was the average number of laps she swam on
the days shown?   18 laps

Swimming Chart	
DAY	LAPS
Monday	15
Tuesday	18
Wednesday	16
Thursday	20
Friday	21

11. What is the probability that the
(129) number on a rolled number cube
will be less than six? $\frac{5}{6}$

12. 36.4 + 6.75 + 7.3   **13.** 6.3 − (4.21 − 3.6)   5.69
(118)   50.45   (55)

14. $3 + 1\frac{1}{4}$ $4\frac{1}{4}$ **15.** $3\frac{2}{5} + 1\frac{1}{5}$ $4\frac{3}{5}$
(131)   (131)

16. $12\frac{1}{3} + 1\frac{1}{3}$ $13\frac{2}{3}$ **17.** $5\frac{4}{5} - 3\frac{1}{5}$ $2\frac{3}{5}$
(131)   (131)

18. $3\frac{1}{2} - 1\frac{1}{2}$ 2   **19.** $6\frac{2}{3} - 4$ $2\frac{2}{3}$
(131)   (131)

20.   473   **21.**   590   **22.** $12.57
(127)   ×   62   (127)   ×   37   (68)   ×   6
     29,326   21,830 $75.42

23. $2.92 \div 4$
(75) $0.73

24. (2)
4
7
$N \quad 4$
3
2
1
6
4
$+ \ 2$
___
33

25. (21)
14
21
43
88
77
66
31
25
$+ \ 43$
___
408

26. (90)
$$\overset{509 \text{ r } 2}{7\overline{)3565}}$$

27. (86)
$\dfrac{6876}{9}$ 764

28. (126)
$$\overset{81 \text{ r } 40}{60\overline{)4900}}$$

29. (130)
$$\overset{4 \text{ r } 5}{21\overline{)89}}$$

30. (130)
$$\overset{5 \text{ r } 34}{42\overline{)244}}$$

LESSON 132

Simplifying Fraction Answers

a. 6
b. 12
c. 18
d. 5000
e. $6.66
f. 18

Problem Solving:

$$\overset{89}{3\overline{)267}}$$
$\underline{24}$
27
$\underline{27}$
0

Facts Practice: 100 Multiplication Facts (Test H in Test Masters)

Mental Math: The percent form of $\frac{3}{4}$ is 75%. Find the stated percent of 24.

   a. 25% of 24   **b.** 50% of 24   **c.** 75% of 24

Review:

   d. 20×250 **e.** $3.67 + $2.99   **f.** $56 - 38$

Problem Solving: Copy this division problem on your paper and fill in the missing digits.

$$\begin{array}{r} 8\_ \\ \_\ \overline{)\_\_7} \\ 24 \\ \hline 2\_ \\ == \\ 0 \end{array}$$

It is customary to write math answers in the simplest form possible. If an answer contains a fraction, there are two procedures that we usually follow.

   1. Improper fractions are written as mixed numbers (or whole numbers).

   2. Fractions are reduced when possible.

Example 1 Add: $\dfrac{2}{3} + \dfrac{2}{3}$

Solution We add to get the sum $\frac{4}{3}$. We notice that $\frac{4}{3}$ is an improper fraction. We take an extra step and change $\frac{4}{3}$ to the mixed number $1\frac{1}{3}$.

$$\dfrac{2}{3} + \dfrac{2}{3} = \dfrac{4}{3}$$

$$\dfrac{4}{3} = \mathbf{1\dfrac{1}{3}}$$

Example 2 Subtract: $\dfrac{3}{4} - \dfrac{1}{4}$

Solution We subtract and get the difference $\frac{2}{4}$. We notice that $\frac{2}{4}$ can be reduced. We take an extra step and reduce $\frac{2}{4}$ to $\frac{1}{2}$.

$$\dfrac{3}{4} - \dfrac{1}{4} = \dfrac{2}{4}$$

$$\dfrac{2}{4} = \mathbf{\dfrac{1}{2}}$$

Example 3 Add: $3\dfrac{1}{3} + 4\dfrac{2}{3}$

Solution We add and get the sum $7\frac{3}{3}$. We notice that $\frac{3}{3}$ is an improper fraction that equals 1. So $7\frac{3}{3} = 7 + 1$, which is 8.

$$3\dfrac{1}{3} + 4\dfrac{2}{3} = 7\dfrac{3}{3}$$

$$7\dfrac{3}{3} = \mathbf{8}$$

Example 4 Add: $5\dfrac{3}{5} + 6\dfrac{4}{5}$

Solution We add and get $11\frac{7}{5}$. We notice that $\frac{7}{5}$ is an improper fraction which can be changed to $1\frac{2}{5}$. So $11\frac{7}{5}$ equals $11 + 1\frac{2}{5}$, which is $12\frac{2}{5}$.

$$5\dfrac{3}{5} + 6\dfrac{4}{5} = 11\dfrac{7}{5}$$

$$11\dfrac{7}{5} = \mathbf{12\dfrac{2}{5}}$$

Example 5 Subtract: $6\dfrac{5}{8} - 1\dfrac{3}{8}$

Solution We subtract and get $5\frac{2}{8}$. We notice that $\frac{2}{8}$ can be reduced. We reduce $\frac{2}{8}$ to $\frac{1}{4}$. So $5\frac{2}{8}$ equals $5\frac{1}{4}$.

$$6\dfrac{5}{8} - 1\dfrac{3}{8} = 5\dfrac{2}{8}$$

$$5\dfrac{2}{8} = \mathbf{5\dfrac{1}{4}}$$

Practice   Simplify each answer:

a. $\dfrac{4}{5} + \dfrac{4}{5}$ $1\frac{3}{5}$ b. $\dfrac{5}{6} - \dfrac{1}{6}$ $\frac{2}{3}$ c. $3\dfrac{2}{3} + 1\dfrac{2}{3}$ $5\frac{1}{3}$

d. $5\dfrac{1}{4} + 6\dfrac{3}{4}$ 12 e. $7\dfrac{7}{8} - 1\dfrac{1}{8}$ $6\frac{3}{4}$ f. $5\dfrac{3}{5} + 1\dfrac{3}{5}$ $7\frac{1}{5}$

Problem set 132

1. Sharon made 70 photocopies. If she paid 6¢ per copy
   $^{(93)}$ and the total tax was 25¢, how much change did she
   get back from a $5 bill? $0.55

2. (a) What is the area of this
   $^{(94,60)}$ square?   36 sq. cm
   (b) What is the perimeter of this
   square?   24 cm

6 cm

Use the information in this description to answer
questions 3 and 4:

*Danny has $9. David has twice as much money as
Danny. Chris has $6 more than David.*

3. How much money does Chris have? $24
$^{(104)}$

4. What is the average amount of money each boy has?
$^{(106)}$ $17

5. There are 40 quarters in a roll of quarters. What is the
   $^{(104)}$ value of 2 rolls of quarters? $20

6. Estimate the product of 29 and 312. Then find the
   $^{(103)}$ actual product.   9000; 9048

7. Write the reduced form of each fraction:
   $^{(125)}$ (a) $\frac{2}{12}$ $\frac{1}{6}$ (b) $\frac{6}{8}$ $\frac{3}{4}$ (c) $\frac{3}{9}$ $\frac{1}{3}$

8. Find three fractions equivalent to $\frac{1}{6}$ by multiplying by
   $^{(128)}$ $\frac{2}{2}, \frac{3}{3},$ and $\frac{4}{4}.$ $\frac{2}{12}, \frac{3}{18}, \frac{4}{24}$

9. Draw diagrams to help work this problem: Their
   $^{(82)}$ noses were black, red, and green. Green came just
   before black, and red was not last. Who came first?
   red

10. If an event cannot happen, its probability is 0. If an
(129) event is certain to happen, its probability is 1. What is
the probability of rolling a 7 with one roll of a number
cube?   0

11. Dresses were on sale for 50% off. If the regular price
(80) was $40, what was the sale price? $20

12. 4.62 + 16.7 + 9.8   **13.** 14.62 − (6.3 − 2.37)
(118) 31.12   (55)   10.69

14. $\frac{3}{5} + \frac{4}{5}$ $1\frac{2}{5}$ **15.** $16 + 3\frac{3}{4}$ $19\frac{3}{4}$ **16.** $1\frac{2}{3} + 3\frac{1}{3}$ 5
(132)   (131)   (132)

17. $\frac{2}{5} + \frac{3}{5}$ 1   **18.** $7\frac{4}{5} + 7\frac{1}{5}$ 15 **19.** $6\frac{2}{3} + 3\frac{2}{3}$ $10\frac{1}{3}$
(132)   (132)   (132)

20. 372 × 39   **21.** 47 × 142   **22.** 360 × $\sqrt{36}$
(127) 14,508   (127) 6674   (68,40) 2160

23. Estimate the area of this circle.
(124) Each small square is one square
centimeter.   28 sq. cm

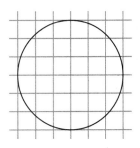

                604 r 2
24. 8$\overline{)4834}$ **25.**   2
(90)   (2)   5

26. $\frac{2840}{2^3}$ 355   1
(86,72)   3

                                       2

27. $36.00 ÷ 5 $7.20   3
(90)
                32 r 3   7
28. 30$\overline{)963}$ 8
(126)
                6 r 4   2
29. 51$\overline{)310}$ + N   15
(130)
                5 r 4   ————
30. 24$\overline{)124}$ 48
(130)

LESSON
133

Renaming Fractions

a. 9
b. 27
c. 36
d. 1000
e. $0.75
f. 185
Patterns:
$1.00, $0.10, $0.01

Facts Practice: 100 Multiplication Facts (Test H in Test Masters)

Mental Math: Find the stated percent of 36.
  a. 25% of 36   **b.** 75% of 36   **c.** 100% of 36
Review:
  d. 4 × 250   **e.** $5.00 − $4.25   **f.** 156 + 29

Patterns: What are the next three terms in this sequence?
$1000.00, $100.00, $10.00, __, __, __, ...

We remember that if we multiply a fraction by a fraction that equals 1, the result is an equivalent fraction. If we multiply $\frac{1}{2}$ by $\frac{2}{2}$, we get $\frac{2}{4}$. The fractions $\frac{1}{2}$ and $\frac{2}{4}$ are equivalent fractions because they have the same value.

$$\frac{1}{2} \times \mathbf{1}\frac{2}{2} = \frac{2}{4}$$

Sometimes we must choose a particular multiplier that is equal to 1.

Example 1 Find the equivalent fraction for $\frac{1}{4}$ whose denominator is 12.

Solution To change 4 to 12, we must multiply by 3. So we multiply $\frac{1}{4}$ by $\frac{3}{3}$.

$$\frac{1}{4} \times \mathbf{1}\frac{3}{3} = \frac{3}{12}$$

The fraction $\frac{1}{4}$ is equivalent to $\frac{3}{12}$.

Example 2 Complete the equivalent fraction: $\frac{2}{3} = \frac{?}{15}$

Solution The bottom number changed from 3 to 15. The bottom number was multiplied by 5. The correct multiplier is $\frac{5}{5}$.

$$\frac{2}{3} \times \frac{5}{5} = \frac{10}{15}$$

The fraction $\frac{2}{3}$ and the fraction $\frac{10}{15}$ are equivalent fractions.

Practice Find the top numbers so the pairs of fractions will be equivalent fractions:

a. $\frac{1}{4} = \frac{?}{12}$ 3   b. $\frac{2}{3} = \frac{?}{12}$ 8   c. $\frac{5}{6} = \frac{?}{12}$ 10

d. $\frac{3}{5} = \frac{?}{10}$ 6   e. $\frac{2}{3} = \frac{?}{9}$ 6   f. $\frac{3}{4} = \frac{?}{8}$ 6

Problem set 133

1. If a can of soup costs $1.50 and serves 3 people, how
(104) much would it cost to serve soup to 12 people? $6.00

2. (a) What is the perimeter of this rectangle?   24 ft
(94,60) (b) What is the area of this rectangle?   35 sq. ft

```
        ┌──────────────┐
  5 ft  │              │  5 ft
        └──────────────┘
             7 ft
```

3. What number is eight less than the product of nine
(104) and ten?   82

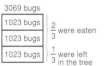

4. The woodpecker found 3069 bugs in the tree and ate $\frac{2}{3}$
(105) of them. How many bugs were left in the tree?
Illustrate the problem.   1023 bugs

5. (a) Find the length of the line segment in centimeters.
(112) (b) Find the length of the segment in millimeters.
    (a) 3.7 cm   (b) 37 mm

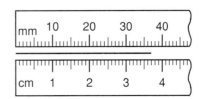

6. Use words to write 356,420.
(42) three hundred fifty-six thousand, four hundred twenty

7. Complete each equivalent fraction:
(133)
(a) $\frac{1}{2} = \frac{?}{6}$ 3 (b) $\frac{1}{3} = \frac{?}{6}$ 2 (c) $\frac{2}{3} = \frac{?}{6}$ 4

8. Write the reduced form of each fraction:
(125)
(a) $\frac{2}{6}$ $\frac{1}{3}$ (b) $\frac{6}{9}$ $\frac{2}{3}$ (c) $\frac{9}{16}$ $\frac{9}{16}$

9. There were 40 workers on the job. Of those workers,
(125) 10 had worked overtime. What fraction of the workers had worked overtime? (Remember to reduce the fraction.) $\frac{1}{4}$

10. What percent of the workers in problem 9 had worked
(65) overtime? 25%

11. Bill received $10 for his tenth birthday. Each year after
(104) that he received $1 more than he did on his previous birthday. He saved all his birthday money. Altogether, how much birthday money did he have on his fifteenth birthday? $75

12. 9.36 − (4.37 + 3.8)   **13.** 24.32 − (8.61 + 12.5)
(55) 1.19   *(55)*   3.21

14. $\frac{4}{5} + \frac{4}{5}$ $1\frac{3}{5}$ **15.** $5\frac{5}{8} + 3\frac{3}{8}$ 9   **16.** $6\frac{3}{10} + \frac{2}{10}$ $6\frac{1}{2}$
(132)   *(132)*   *(132)*

17. $8\frac{2}{3} - 5\frac{1}{3}$ $3\frac{1}{3}$ **18.** $4\frac{3}{4} - 2\frac{1}{4}$ $2\frac{1}{2}$ **19.** $7\frac{1}{2} - 5$ $2\frac{1}{2}$
(131)   *(132)*   *(131)*

20. 60 × 400   **21.** 536 × 3³   **22.** 12 × $1.50
(96) 24,000   *(127,72)* 14,472   *(127)* $18.00

23. $6\overline{)3642}$ 607   **24.** $125 ÷ 5 $25   **25.** 26
(90)   *(75)*   *(21)*   9
                              14
26. $40\overline{)645}$ 16 r 5   **27.** $41\overline{)165}$ 4 r 1   11
(126)   *(130)*   2
                              + 34
28. $\frac{4380}{10}$ 438   96
(115)

29. Estimate the area of this piece of
(124) land. Each small square is one
square mile.   22 sq. mi

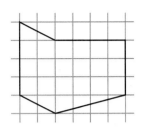

30. What is the probability that the
(129) spinner will stop on a number
greater than 5? $\frac{3}{8}$

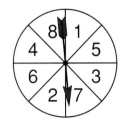

LESSON
134

Naming Geometric Solids

a. 10
b. 30
c. 4
d. 2400
e. $13.25
f. 46
Problem Solving:
 Tails up:
  1 out of 2
 Rolling a 6:
  1 out of 6
 Rolling an even
 number:
  3 out of 6 or
  1 out of 2

Facts Practice: 100 Multiplication Facts (Test H in Test Masters)

Mental Math: The percent form of $\frac{1}{10}$ is 10%. Find the stated
 percent of 40.

  a. 25% of 40   **b.** 75% of 40   **c.** 10% of 40

Review:

  d. 50 × 48   **e.** $8.75 + $4.50   **f.** 71 − 25

Problem Solving: The probability of a flipped coin landing
 heads up is 1 out of 2. The probability of
 rolling a 1 with a number cube is 1 out of 6.
 What is the probability of a coin landing tails
 up? What is the probability of rolling a six
 with one number cube? What is the
 probability of rolling an even number with
 one number cube?

We have practiced naming shapes such as triangles,
rectangles, and circles. These are flat shapes. They do not
take up **space.** Objects that take up space are things like
cars, basketballs, desks, houses, and people.

Geometric shapes that take up space are called **geometric solids.** The chart below shows the names of some geometric solids.

SHAPE	NAME
▢ ▢ ▢ ▢	Cube
▭ ▭ ▬ ▬	Rectangular solid
△ △ ▲ ▲	Pyramid
▢ ▢ ⬤ ⬤	Cylinder
◯ ◯ ● ●	Sphere
△ △ ▲ ▲	Cone

Example 1   Name each shape:

(a)   (b)   (c)

Solution   If we check each shape with the chart, we see that (a) is a **sphere,** (b) is a **cube,** and (c) is a **cone.**

Example 2   What is the shape of a soup can?

Solution   A soup can has the shape of a **cylinder.**

Example 3   This rectangular solid is made of how many small cubes?

Solution   We see that the rectangular solid is made of 2 layers of cubes with 6 cubes on each layer (2 × 6 = 12). The rectangular solid is made of **12 small cubes.**

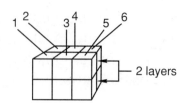

Practice   Name the shape of each object listed:

    a. Basketball   sphere   **b.** Shoebox   rectangular solid

    c. Ice-cream cone   cone

    d. What is the shape of this Egyptian landmark?   pyramid

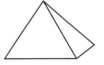

    e. This rectangular solid is made of how many small cubes?
18 small cubes

Problem set 134   Use the information given in the graph to answer questions 1–3:

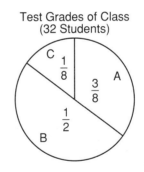

Test Grades of Class
(32 Students)

    1. Of the 32 students in the class, how many earned a C
(111)   on the test?   4 students

    2. How many students earned an A?   12 students
(111)

    3. Altogether, how many students earned an A or a B?
(111)   28 students

    4. If the perimeter of a square is 3 feet, each side is how
(60)   many inches long?   9 in.

    5. This rectangular solid is made of
(134)   how many small cubes?
16 small cubes

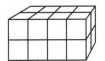

6. Name each shape:
(134)

(a) rectangular solid   (b) pyramid   (c) cylinder

7. Complete each equivalent fraction:
(133)

(a) $\frac{1}{2} = \frac{?}{8}$ 4   (b) $\frac{1}{4} = \frac{?}{8}$ 2   (c) $\frac{3}{4} = \frac{?}{8}$ 6

8. Write the reduced form of each fraction:
(125)

(a) $\frac{9}{10}$ $\frac{9}{10}$ (b) $\frac{10}{15}$ $\frac{2}{3}$ (c) $\frac{4}{8}$ $\frac{1}{2}$

9. Draw diagrams to help solve this problem: Wilbur
(82) was not first. Roger came just before Sarah. Sarah was not last. Who was in the middle?   Sarah

10. The first five square numbers are 1, 4, 9, 16, and 25.
(39) What are the next five square numbers?
36, 49, 64, 81, 100

11. There were 5 containers for 37 items. The items were
(98) divided as evenly as possible between the containers. List the number of items in each container.
3 contain 7 items; 2 contain 8 items

12. $9.43 - (6.43 + 1.7)$ **13.** $16.1 - (1.23 + 12.3)$
(55)   1.3   (55)   2.57

14. $\frac{2}{3} + \frac{2}{3} + \frac{2}{3}$ 2   **15.** $3\frac{1}{2} + 4\frac{1}{2}$ 8
(132)   (132)

16. $5\frac{1}{6} + 1\frac{1}{6}$ $6\frac{1}{3}$ **17.** $3\frac{1}{3} - 1\frac{1}{3}$ 2
(132)   (131)

18. $4\frac{3}{8} - 1\frac{1}{8}$ $3\frac{1}{4}$ **19.** $4\frac{1}{4} - 2$ $2\frac{1}{4}$
(132)   (131)

20. Four is what percent of 4^2?   25%
(65)

21. $25 \times \$6.40$ \$160.00   **22.** 68×47 3196
(127)   (100)

23. $6\overline{)4564}$ 760 r 4   **24.** $\$12.40 \div 10$ \$1.24   **25.** $\frac{4624}{8}$ 578
(90)   (115)   (86)

26. $30\overline{)246}$ 8 r 6   **27.** $41\overline{)246}$ 6   **28.** $32\overline{)246}$ 7 r 22
(120)   (130)   (130)

29. Brad's drawer contains only white socks and blue
(129) socks. There are 12 white socks and 8 blue socks. If
Brad takes one sock from his drawer without looking,
what is the probability that the sock will be blue? $\frac{2}{5}$

**LESSON
135**

Roman Numerals Through 39

a. 25
b. 5
c. 10
d. 24,000
e. $8.05
f. 210
Problem Solving:
  4 pennies, 1 nickel,
  2 dimes, 1 quarter,
  and 1 half dollar or
  4 pennies, 2 nick-
  els, 1 dime, 1 quar-
  ter, and 1 half
  dollar

Facts Practice: 100 Multiplication Facts (Test H in Test Masters)

Mental Math: The percent form of $\frac{2}{10}$ is 20%. Find the stated
percent of 50.
  a. 50% of 50 **b.** 10% of 50 **c.** 20% of 50
Review:
  d. 20 × 30 × 40 **e.** $10.00 − $1.95 **f.** 147 + 63

Problem Solving: There were only 9 coins in the cash register,
but it was enough to make change for any
purchase of less than one dollar. What coins
were in the cash register? (*Hint*: It should be
possible to make any amount of money from
1¢ to 99¢ with the coins.)

Roman numerals are letters used by the ancient Romans to
write numbers. Roman numerals are still used today on
clocks and buildings and are used to number such things
as book chapters and Super Bowl games.

Some Roman numerals and their values are

I   which equals 1

V   which equals 5

X   which equals 10

Roman numerals do not use place value. Instead, the
values of the digits are added or sometimes subtracted.

II   means   2 ones, which is 2, not 11

The Roman numerals for the numbers 1–20 are listed below. Study the patterns.

I = 1	XI = 11
II = 2	XII = 12
III = 3	XIII = 13
IV = 4	XIV = 14
V = 5	XV = 15
VI = 6	XVI = 16
VII = 7	XVII = 17
VIII = 8	XVIII = 18
IX = 9	XIX = 19
X = 10	XX = 20

The multiples of 5 include 5, 10, 15, and 20. The numbers that are one less than these (4, 9, 14, and 19) have Roman numerals that involve subtraction.

$$4 = IV \qquad \text{(one less than five)}$$
$$9 = IX \qquad \text{(one less than ten)}$$
$$14 = XIV \qquad \text{(ten and one less than five)}$$
$$19 = XIX \qquad \text{(ten and one less than ten)}$$

In each of these cases, a smaller Roman numeral (I) precedes a larger Roman numeral (V or X).

Example   (a) Write XXVII in our number system.[†]

(b) Write 34 in Roman numerals.

Solution   (a) We add 2 tens plus 5 ones plus 2 ones and get 27.

$$\text{XX} \quad \text{V} \quad \text{II}$$
$$20 + 5 + 2 = \mathbf{27}$$

[†]The modern world has adopted the Hindu-Arabic number system with the digits 0, 1, 2, 3, 4, 5, 6, 7, 8, 9, and base 10 place value. For simplicity, we refer to the Hindu-Arabic system as "our number system."

(b) We think of 34 as 30 plus 4.

$$30 + 4$$
$$\text{XXX} \quad \text{IV}$$

So 34 is written **XXXIV**.

Practice Write the Roman numerals in order from 1–39.
See Lesson 135

**Problem set
135**

1. Grampa bought meat for $4.70, potatoes for $1.59,
(93) bananas for $1.65, and lettuce for 87¢. He gave the
grocer $10. How much did he get back? $1.19

2. What is the area of this rectangle?   150 sq. mm
(94)

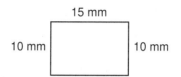

15 mm

10 mm   10 mm

3. Bill can blow up 1 balloon in 1 minute. At that rate,
(104) how many balloons can Bill blow up in ten hours?
600 balloons

4. This rectangular solid is made of
(134) how many small cubes?
24 small cubes

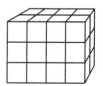

5. The number V is what percent of X?   50%
(135)

6. Draw a diagram to help with this problem: You have
(50) to drive south through Dalton to get to Calhoun from
Chattanooga. It is 21 miles from Chattanooga to
Dalton. It is 39 miles from Chattanooga to Calhoun.
How far is it from Dalton to Calhoun?   18 miles

7. Wilba's lunch cost $4.85. Norton's lunch cost $3.94.
(106) Danielle's lunch was $5.22. What was the average
price of the three lunches? $4.67

8. (a) Write XXIV in our number system. 24
(135)
(b) Write 36 in Roman numerals. XXXVI

9. Name the shape of each object:
(134)
(a) Marble sphere   (b) Cereal box
rectangular solid

10. Complete each equivalent fraction:
(133)
(a) $\frac{1}{2} = \frac{?}{10}$ 5   (b) $\frac{1}{5} = \frac{?}{10}$ 2   (c) $\frac{4}{5} = \frac{?}{10}$ 8

11. Write the reduced form of each fraction:
(125)
(a) $\frac{2}{10}$ $\frac{1}{5}$ (b) $\frac{4}{6}$ $\frac{2}{3}$ (c) $\frac{4}{12}$ $\frac{1}{3}$

12. 4.76 + 12.8 + 6.7   **13.** 24.3 − (12.14 − 3.2)
(118) 24.26   (55) 15.36

14. $\frac{5}{8} + \frac{6}{8}$ $1\frac{3}{8}$ **15.** $4\frac{1}{4} + 2\frac{3}{4}$ 7   **16.** $3 + 4\frac{5}{6}$ $7\frac{5}{6}$
(132)   (132)   (131)

17. $5\frac{3}{5} + 3\frac{1}{5}$ $8\frac{4}{5}$ **18.** $8\frac{1}{4} + 3\frac{1}{4}$ $11\frac{1}{2}$ **19.** $\frac{7}{8} + \frac{1}{8}$ 1
(131)   (132)   (132)

20. What is the probability that the
(129) spinner will stop on a number
less than 7? $\frac{3}{4}$

21. 24 × 15¢ $3.60   **22.**   1
(100)   (2)
6
23. 472 × 60 28,320   3
(77)   N   19
4
24. 54 × 23 1242   8
(100)   9
7
25. $6.72 ÷ 8 $0.84   + 6
(75)   ‾‾‾
73 r 7   63
26. 10)737
(115)

$\frac{4935}{7}$
27.   705
(90)

71 r 10   5 r 5   6 r 24
28. 60)4270   **29.** 41)210   **30.** 31)210
(126)   (130)   (130)

LESSON
136

Common Denominators

a. 6
b. 12
c. 18
d. 200
e. $8.61
f. 39

Problem Solving:
16 tapes with some arrangements or 17 tapes with other arrangements

Facts Practice: 100 Multiplication Facts (Test H in Test Masters)

Mental Math: The percent form of $\frac{3}{10}$ is 30%. Find the stated percent of 60.

a. 10% of 60   **b.** 20% of 60   **c.** 30% of 60

Review:

d. 8×25 **e.** $4.63 + $3.98   **f.** $84 - 45$

Problem Solving: Samantha keeps video tapes in a box that is 16 inches long, 8 inches wide, and 4 inches tall. The tapes are 4 inches long, 1 inch wide, and $7\frac{1}{2}$ inches tall. How many tapes can she fit into the box?

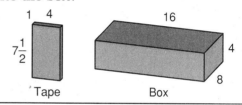

Two fractions have common denominators if the denominators are equal.

$$\frac{3}{8} \qquad \frac{5}{8} \qquad\qquad \frac{3}{8} \qquad \frac{5}{9}$$

These two fractions have common denominators.

These two fractions do **not** have common denominators.

Fractions that do not have common denominators can be renamed so that they do have common denominators.

Example 1 Rename $\frac{2}{3}$ and $\frac{3}{4}$ so that they have a common denominator of twelve.

Solution To rename a fraction, we multiply the fraction by a name for one. To change the denominator of $\frac{2}{3}$ to twelve, we multiply by $\frac{4}{4}$. To change the denominator of $\frac{3}{4}$ to twelve, we multiply by $\frac{3}{3}$.

RENAME $\frac{2}{3}$ RENAME $\frac{3}{4}$

$\frac{2}{3} \times \mathbf{1} \boxed{\frac{4}{4}} = \frac{8}{12}$ $\frac{3}{4} \times \mathbf{1} \boxed{\frac{3}{3}} = \frac{9}{12}$

$\frac{2}{3} = \frac{8}{12}$ $\frac{3}{4} = \frac{9}{12}$

Example 2   Rename $\frac{1}{2}$ and $\frac{1}{3}$ so that they have a common denominator.

Solution   This time we need to figure out a common denominator before we can rename the fractions. The denominators are 2 and 3. We will list some multiples of 2 and of 3 to find multiples they have in common.

> Multiples of 2: 2, 4, ⑥, 8, 10, ⑫, ...
>
> Multiples of 3: 3, ⑥, 9, ⑫, 15, 18, ...

We see that 6 and 12 are both multiples of 2 and 3. Since 6 is less than 12, we will use 6 as the common denominator and multiply by $\frac{3}{3}$ and $\frac{2}{2}$, respectively.

RENAME $\frac{1}{2}$ RENAME $\frac{1}{3}$

$\frac{1}{2} \times \mathbf{1} \boxed{\frac{3}{3}} = \frac{3}{6}$ $\frac{1}{3} \times \mathbf{1} \boxed{\frac{2}{2}} = \frac{2}{6}$

$\frac{1}{2} = \frac{3}{6}$ $\frac{1}{3} = \frac{2}{6}$

Note: If we had used 12 as the common denominator, the fractions would have been $\frac{6}{12}$ and $\frac{4}{12}$. Usually, we try to write fractions with the **lowest** common denominators.

Practice   **a.** Rename $\frac{1}{2}$ and $\frac{1}{5}$ so that they have a common denominator of 10. $\frac{5}{10}; \frac{2}{10}$

b. Rename $\frac{3}{4}$ and $\frac{5}{6}$ so that they have a common denominator of 12. $\frac{9}{12}; \frac{10}{12}$

Rename each pair of fractions so that they have the lowest common denominators:

c. $\frac{1}{2}$ and $\frac{2}{3}$ $\frac{3}{6}; \frac{4}{6}$ **d.** $\frac{1}{3}$ and $\frac{1}{4}$ $\frac{4}{12}; \frac{3}{12}$

e. $\frac{1}{2}$ and $\frac{3}{5}$ $\frac{5}{10}; \frac{6}{10}$ **f.** $\frac{2}{3}$ and $\frac{2}{5}$ $\frac{10}{15}; \frac{6}{15}$

Problem set
136

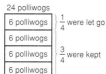

1. Tim caught 24 polliwogs. If he let one fourth of them
(80) go, how many did he keep? Illustrate the problem.
18 polliwogs

2. Rectangular Park was 2 miles long
(60) and 1 mile wide. Gordon ran around the park twice. How many miles did he run?   12 mi

3. If 2 oranges cost 42¢, how much would 8 oranges cost?
(104) $1.68

4. Three fourths of the 64 baseball cards showed players
(105) from the American League. How many of the baseball cards showed American League players? Illustrate the problem.   48 baseball cards

5. What percent of the baseball cards in problem 4
(80,65) showed players from the American League?   75%

6. (a) Write XIX in our number system.   19
(135) (b) Write 28 in Roman numerals.   XXVIII

7. Complete each equivalent fraction:
(133) (a) $\frac{1}{2} = \frac{?}{12}$ 6   (b) $\frac{1}{3} = \frac{?}{12}$ 4   (c) $\frac{1}{4} = \frac{?}{12}$ 3

8. Write the reduced form of each fraction:
(125) (a) $\frac{5}{10}$ $\frac{1}{2}$ (b) $\frac{8}{15}$ $\frac{8}{15}$ (c) $\frac{6}{12}$ $\frac{1}{2}$

9. Randy paid 42¢ for 6 clips and 64¢ for 8 erasers. Find
(104) the cost for 1 clip and for 1 eraser. What would be the
cost of 10 clips and 20 erasers?

7¢ per clip; 8¢ per eraser; $2.30

10. There were 14 volunteers the first year, 16 volunteers
(82) the second year, and 18 volunteers the third year. If
they continued to increase at 2 volunteers per year,
how many volunteers would there be in the tenth
year?   32 volunteers

11. (a) Rename $\frac{1}{4}$ and $\frac{2}{3}$ so that they have a common
(136) denominator of 12. $\frac{3}{12}$; $\frac{8}{12}$

(b) Rename $\frac{1}{3}$ and $\frac{3}{4}$ so that they have the lowest
common denominator. $\frac{4}{12}$; $\frac{9}{12}$

12. A number cube is rolled. What is the probability that
(129) the number rolled will be less than seven?   1

13. 47.14 − (3.63 + 36.3)   **14.** 50.1 + (6.4 − 1.46)
(55) 7.21   *(55)* 55.04

15. $\frac{3}{4} + \frac{3}{4} + \frac{3}{4}$ $2\frac{1}{4}$ **16.** $4\frac{1}{6} + 1\frac{1}{6}$ $5\frac{1}{3}$ **17.** $5\frac{3}{5} + 1\frac{2}{5}$ 7
(132)   *(132)*   *(132)*

18. $\frac{5}{6} + \frac{1}{6}$ 1   **19.** $12\frac{3}{4} + 3\frac{1}{4}$ 16   **20.** $6\frac{1}{5} + 1\frac{1}{5}$ $7\frac{2}{5}$
(132)   *(132)*   *(131)*

21. 340 × 15   **22.** 26 × 307   **23.** 70 × 250
(127) 5100   *(127)* 7982   *(127)* 17,500

24. $\frac{3550}{5}$ 710   **25.** $20.00 ÷ 8   **26.** $9\overline{)5784}$ 642 r 6
(90)   *(90)* $2.50   *(86)*

27. 432 ÷ 30   **28.** 342 ÷ 42   **29.** 243 ÷ 43
(126) 14 r 12   *(130)* 8 r 6   *(130)* 5 r 28

30. Estimate the area of this pentagon.
(124) Each small square is one square
inch.   19 sq. in.

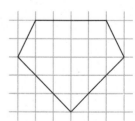

LESSON
137

Naming Numbers Through Hundred Millions

a. 7
b. 14
c. 21
d. 28
e. 42
f. 70
Patterns:

$\frac{4}{16}, \frac{5}{20}, \frac{6}{24}, \frac{7}{28}$

Facts Practice: 90 Division Facts (Test J in Test Masters)

Mental Math: The percent forms of $\frac{4}{10}$, $\frac{5}{10}$, and $\frac{6}{10}$ are 40%, 50%, and 60%, respectively. Find the stated percent of 70.

a. 10% of 70	**b.** 20% of 70	**c.** 30% of 70
d. 40% of 70	**e.** 60% of 70	**f.** 100% of 70

Patterns: These fractions all equal one fourth. Write four more fractions equal to one fourth that continue this sequence.

$$\frac{1}{4}, \frac{2}{8}, \frac{3}{12}, \underline{}, \underline{}, \underline{}, \underline{}, \cdots$$

The table below names the values of the first nine whole number places.

— — — , — — — , — — — .
hundred-millions' ten-millions' millions' comma hundred-thousands' ten-thousands' thousands' comma hundreds' tens' ones' decimal point

Example 1 Which digit is in the ten-millions' place in 156,374,289?

Solution We see that the ten-millions' place is eight places from the right. We count eight places in 156,374,289 and find that the digit in the ten-millions' place is **5**.

Example 2 The 3 is in what place in 23,485,179?

Solution The 3 is seven places from the right. We see that seven places from the right is the **millions' place.**

To read whole numbers of more than six digits, we use two commas. To read the number

496874235

we place the thousands' comma three places from the right-hand end. Then we place the millions' comma three places to the left of the thousands' comma.

496 , 874 , 235

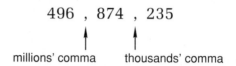

millions' comma   thousands' comma

To write this number in words, we read the number to the left of the millions' comma.

Four hundred ninety-six

Now we read the millions' comma by saying "million," and we put a comma after the word *million*.

Four hundred ninety-six million,

Then we read the rest of the number.

Four hundred ninety-six million,
eight hundred seventy-four thousand,
two hundred thirty-five

We remembered to write a comma after the word *thousand* just as we did after the word *million*.

Example 3 Use words to write the number 374196285.

Solution We use commas to separate the number into three sections, which we read one section at a time. When we get to the first comma, we write "million." When we get to the second comma, we write "thousand."

374   ,   196   ,   285
million   thousand

**Three hundred seventy-four million,
one hundred ninety-six thousand,
two hundred eighty-five**

Practice   Use words to name each of these numbers. Insert commas as necessary.

    a. 27196384   twenty-seven million, one hundred ninety-six thousand, three hundred eighty-four

    b. 176245398   one hundred seventy-six million, two hundred forty-five thousand, three hundred ninety-eight

    c. 3541286   three million, five hundred forty-one thousand, two hundred eighty-six

Problem set 137

1. Robin separated his 45 merry men as equally as possible into 4 groups. How many merry men were in the largest group?   12 merry men
(98)

2. (a) What is the area of this rectangle?   96 sq. cm
(94,60) (b) What is the perimeter of this rectangle?   40 cm

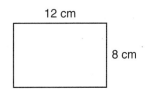

12 cm

8 cm

3. Tom answered $\frac{5}{6}$ of the 90 questions correctly. How many questions did Tom answer correctly? Illustrate the problem.   75 questions
(105)

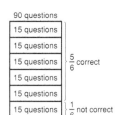

90 questions

15 questions
15 questions
15 questions
15 questions $\Big\}\frac{5}{6}$ correct
15 questions
15 questions
15 questions $\Big\}\frac{1}{6}$ not correct

4. Name the shape of each object:
(134) (a) Roll of paper towels   (b) Baseball   sphere
    cylinder

5. Write the reduced form of each fraction:
(125) (a) $\frac{3}{6}$ $\frac{1}{2}$ (b) $\frac{5}{15}$ $\frac{1}{3}$ (c) $\frac{8}{12}$ $\frac{2}{3}$

6. Rename $\frac{3}{4}$ and $\frac{5}{6}$ so that they have a common denominator. $\frac{9}{12}$; $\frac{10}{12}$
(136)

7. Which digit is in the ten-millions' place in 328,496,175?   2
(137)

8. Draw a picture to help you solve this problem: Winder is on the road from Atlanta to Athens. It is 60 miles from Athens to Atlanta. It is 18 miles from Winder to Athens. How far is it from Winder to Atlanta?   42 mi
(50)

9. The chance of rain is 80%. What is the chance that it
(65) will not rain?   20%

10. A nickel is what percent of a dime?   50%
(65)

11. 4.36 + 12.7 + 10.72   **12.** 8.54 − (4.2 − 2.17)
(118) 27.78   (118) 6.51

13. $\frac{5}{9} + \frac{5}{9}$ $1\frac{1}{9}$ **14.** $3\frac{2}{3} + 1\frac{2}{3}$ $5\frac{1}{3}$ **15.** $4\frac{5}{8} + 1$ $5\frac{5}{8}$
(132)   (132)   (131)

16. $7\frac{2}{3} + 1\frac{2}{3}$ $9\frac{1}{3}$ **17.** $4\frac{4}{9} + 1\frac{1}{9}$ $5\frac{5}{9}$ **18.** $\frac{11}{12} + \frac{1}{12}$ 1
(132)   (131)   (132)

19. 570 × 64   **20.** 382 × 31   **21.** 54 × 18   972
(127) 36,480   (127) 11,842   (100)

22. $\frac{3731}{7}$ 533   **23.** $9\overline{)5432}$ $^{603\ r\ 5}$ **24.** \$20.80 ÷ 8
(86)   (90)   (90) \$2.60

25. $60\overline{)548}$ $^{9\ r\ 8}$ **26.** $13\overline{)50}$ $^{3\ r\ 11}$ **27.** $72\overline{)297}$ $^{4\ r\ 9}$
(120)   (130)   (130)

28. If the perimeter of a square is 6 centimeters, each side
(79,60) is how many millimeters long?   15 mm

29. This cube is made of how many
(134) smaller cubes?   8 smaller cubes

30. Write   the   Roman   numerals
(135) between XX and XXX.
See Lesson 135

LESSON
138

Dividing by Two-Digit Numbers, Part 2

a. 20
b. 60
c. 24
d. 1600
e. $4.26
f. 86

Problem Solving:

$$
\begin{array}{r}
5\ 2 \\
7\overline{)3\ 6\ 5} \\
\underline{3\ 5} \\
1\ 5 \\
\underline{1\ 4} \\
1
\end{array}
$$

Facts Practice: 90 Division Facts (Test J in Test Masters)

Mental Math: Find the stated percent of 80.

   a. 25% of 80   **b.** 75% of 80   **c.** 30% of 80

Review:

   d. 50 × 32   **e.** $5.00 − $0.74   **f.** 47 + 39

Problem Solving: Copy this division problem on your paper and fill in the missing digits.

$$
\begin{array}{r}
5\ \_ \\
\_\overline{)\_\ \_\ \_} \\
\underline{3\ 5} \\
1\ \_ \\
\underline{\quad} \\
1
\end{array}
$$

We have used four steps to do two-digit division problems that have one-digit answers. In this lesson we will practice two-digit division problems that have two-digit answers.

    We will continue to follow the four steps: divide, multiply, subtract, and bring down.

Example $21\overline{)487}$

Solution   **Step 1.** We break the problem into a smaller division problem, $21\overline{)48}$, and write "2."

$$
\begin{array}{r}
2 \\
21\overline{)487} \\
\underline{42} \\
67
\end{array}
$$

         Step 2. We multiply 2 × 21 and write "42."

         Step 3. We subtract 42 from 48 and write "6."

         Step 4. We bring down the 7, making 67.

REPEAT:

Step 1. We divide $21\overline{)67}$ and write "3."

$$\begin{array}{r} 23 \text{ r } 4 \\ 21\overline{)487} \\ 42 \\ \hline 67 \\ 63 \\ \hline 4 \end{array}$$

Step 2. We multiply 3×21 and write "63."

Step 3. We subtract 63 from 67 and write "4."

Step 4. There are no digits to bring down. The answer is **23 with a remainder of 4.**

Practice

a. $\overset{32}{21\overline{)672}}$ **b.** $\overset{32}{12\overline{)384}}$ **c.** $\overset{21 \text{ r } 3}{32\overline{)675}}$

d. $\overset{22 \text{ r } 4}{23\overline{)510}}$ **e.** $\overset{21 \text{ r } 19}{41\overline{)880}}$ **f.** $\overset{50 \text{ r } 5}{11\overline{)555}}$

Problem set 138

Use the information in the graph to answer questions 1–3:

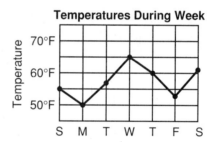

Temperatures During Week

1. On what day was the temperature the highest?
(92)   Wednesday

2. What was the temperature on Tuesday?   57°F
(92)

3. From Monday to Wednesday, the high temperature
(92)   went up how many degrees?   15°F

4. (a) What is the perimeter of this
(94,60)   rectangle?   78 m

(b) What is the area of this
    rectangle?   360 sq. m

15 m

24 m

5. The first five square numbers are 1, 4, 9, 16, and 25,
(106)   and their average is 11. What is the average of the next
    five square numbers?   66

6. What percent of the months of the year begin with the
(84,65) letter J?   25%

7. What is the probability of drawing an ace from a full
(129) deck of cards? (There are 52 cards in a deck, and 4 of
these cards are aces.) $\frac{1}{13}$

8. Name each shape:
(134)
(a)   cylinder   (b)   cone   (c) ![sphere] sphere

9. Write the reduced form of each fraction:
(125)
(a) $\frac{6}{8}$ $\frac{3}{4}$ (b) $\frac{4}{9}$ $\frac{4}{9}$ (c) $\frac{4}{16}$ $\frac{1}{4}$

10. Rename $\frac{2}{3}$ and $\frac{3}{4}$ so that they have common
(136) denominators. $\frac{8}{12}; \frac{9}{12}$

11. Use words to name 27386415.   twenty-seven million,
(137) three hundred eighty-six thousand, four hundred fifteen

12. 4.75 + 16.14 + 10.9   **13.** 18.4 − (4.32 − 2.6)
(118) 31.79   (55)   16.68

14. $4\frac{4}{5} + 3\frac{3}{5}$ $8\frac{2}{5}$ **15.** $5\frac{1}{6} + 1\frac{2}{6}$ $6\frac{1}{2}$ **16.** $7\frac{3}{4} + \frac{1}{4}$ 8
(132)   (132)   (132)

17. $5\frac{3}{8} + 5\frac{1}{8}$ $10\frac{1}{2}$ **18.**   5   **19.**   28
(132)   (2)   2   (21)   47
                                        4   74
20. $4\frac{1}{6} + 2\frac{1}{6}$ $6\frac{1}{3}$ 7   36
(132)   3   91
                                        5   87
21. 720 × 36   25,920   3   21
(127)   6   12
                                        5   + 14
22. 147 × 54   7938   N   11   410
(127)
                    720 r 6   + 4
23. 8)5766   55
(90)

24. $36.30 ÷ 10
(115) $3.63

                                                21
25. $\frac{4735}{5}$ 947   **26.** 21)441
(86)   (138)

$$\begin{array}{r} 30 \\ \textbf{27. } 32\overline{)960} \end{array}$$
(138)

$$\begin{array}{r} 43\text{ r }2 \\ \textbf{28. } 12\overline{)518} \end{array}$$
(138)

29. Estimate the area of this figure.
(124) Each small square is one square inch. 19 sq. in.

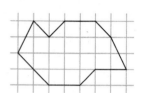

LESSON 139

Adding and Subtracting Fractions with Unlike Denominators

a. 45
b. 9
c. 81
d. 420
e. $6.51
f. 18
Problem Solving:
The wall is about 6 feet tall.

Facts Practice: 90 Division Facts (Test J in Test Masters)

Mental Math: Find the stated percent of 90.
  a. 50% of 90   **b.** 10% of 90   **c.** 90% of 90

Review:
  d. 5 × 84   **e.** $2.75 + $3.76   **f.** 66 − 48

Problem Solving: The wall is four cubits tall. A cubit is about 18 inches. So the wall is about how many feet tall?

We have practiced adding and subtracting fractions that have the same denominators. In this lesson, we will begin adding and subtracting fractions that have different denominators.

SAME DENOMINATORS

$$\frac{1}{5} \longleftrightarrow \frac{3}{5}$$

DIFFERENT DENOMINATORS

$$\frac{1}{2} \longleftrightarrow \frac{3}{4}$$

> **To add or subtract fractions that have different denominators, we must first change the name of the fractions so that they will have the same denominators.**

Recall that we change the name of a fraction by multiplying the fraction by a fraction name for 1.

Example 1 Add: $\dfrac{1}{4} + \dfrac{3}{8}$

Solution The denominators are not the same. We multiply $\frac{1}{4}$ by $\frac{2}{2}$ and get $\frac{2}{8}$. Now we can add.

$$
\begin{array}{r}
\overset{\text{Rename}}{\longrightarrow} \\[4pt]
\dfrac{1}{4} \times \dfrac{2}{2} = \dfrac{2}{8} \\[8pt]
+\ \dfrac{3}{8} \qquad\ = \dfrac{3}{8} \\[4pt]
\hline
\dfrac{5}{8}
\end{array}
\quad \text{Add}
$$

Example 2 Subtract: $\dfrac{5}{6} - \dfrac{1}{2}$

Solution The denominators are not the same. We change $\frac{1}{2}$ to a fraction whose denominator is 6. Then we subtract. We reduce the answer.

$$
\begin{array}{r}
\overset{\text{Rename}}{\longrightarrow} \\[4pt]
\dfrac{5}{6} \qquad\ = \dfrac{5}{6} \\[8pt]
-\ \dfrac{1}{2} \times \dfrac{3}{3} = \dfrac{3}{6} \\[4pt]
\hline
\dfrac{2}{6} = \dfrac{1}{3}
\end{array}
\quad \text{Subtract}
$$

$$\underset{\text{Reduce}}{\longrightarrow}$$

Practice Add or subtract. Reduce when possible.

a. $\dfrac{1}{2} + \dfrac{2}{6}$ $\frac{5}{6}$ **b.** $\dfrac{1}{3} + \dfrac{1}{9}$ $\frac{4}{9}$ **c.** $\dfrac{1}{8} + \dfrac{1}{2}$ $\frac{5}{8}$

d. $\dfrac{3}{8} - \dfrac{1}{4}$ $\frac{1}{8}$ **e.** $\dfrac{2}{3} - \dfrac{2}{9}$ $\frac{4}{9}$ **f.** $\dfrac{7}{8} - \dfrac{1}{2}$ $\frac{3}{8}$

Problem set 139

1. Clotilda laid 1-foot-square floor tiles in a room 15 feet long and 12 feet wide. How many floor tiles did she use?   180 floor tiles
(94)

2. What is the perimeter of this triangle?   5.3 cm
(60)

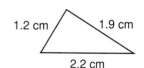

1.2 cm   1.9 cm   2.2 cm

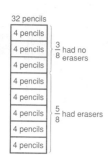

32 pencils

4 pencils
4 pencils } $\frac{3}{8}$ had no erasers
4 pencils
4 pencils
4 pencils
4 pencils } $\frac{5}{8}$ had erasers
4 pencils
4 pencils

3. Tim found that $\frac{3}{8}$ of the 32 pencils in the room had no erasers. How many pencils had no erasers? Illustrate the problem.   12 pencils
(105)

4. Seventy-two eggs is how many dozen eggs?   6 dozen eggs
(50)

5. How many eggs is 50% of one dozen eggs?   6 eggs
(65)

6. This cube is made of how many smaller cubes?   27 smaller cubes
(134)

7. Farmica bought 10 tapes at $4.23 each and 2 compact disks at $10.95 each. The tax was $3.80. What was the total price? $68.00
(93)

8. Roger drove 285 miles in 5 hours. What was his average speed in miles per hour?   57 miles per hour
(106)

9. (a) Write XXIX in our number system.   29
(135)
    (b) Write 24 in Roman numerals.   XXIV

10. Write the reduced form of each fraction:
(125)
    (a) $\frac{8}{10}$ $\frac{4}{5}$ (b) $\frac{6}{15}$ $\frac{2}{5}$ (c) $\frac{8}{16}$ $\frac{1}{2}$

11. Use words to name the number 123415720.   one hundred twenty-three million, four hundred fifteen thousand, seven hundred twenty
(137)

12. 8.3 + 4.72 + 0.6 + 12.1   25.72
(118)

13. 17.42 − (6.7 − 1.23)   11.95
(55)

14. $3\frac{3}{8} + 3\frac{3}{8}$ $6\frac{3}{4}$ **15.** $\frac{1}{4} + \frac{1}{8}$ $\frac{3}{8}$ **16.** $\frac{1}{2} + \frac{1}{6}$ $\frac{2}{3}$
(132)   *(139)*   *(139)*

17. $5\frac{5}{6} - 1\frac{1}{6}$ $4\frac{2}{3}$ **18.** $\frac{1}{4} - \frac{1}{8}$ $\frac{1}{8}$ **19.** $\frac{1}{2} - \frac{1}{6}$ $\frac{1}{3}$
(132)   *(139)*   *(139)*

20. 87×16 **21.** 49×340 **22.** 504×30
(100)   1392   *(127)*   16,660   *(127)*   15,120

23. $\$35.40 \div 6$ **24.** $\dfrac{5784}{4}$ 1446   **25.** $7\overline{)2385}$ 340 r 5
(90) $5.90   *(86)*   *(90)*

26. $30\overline{)450}$ 15   **27.** $32\overline{)450}$ 14 r 2   **28.** $15\overline{)450}$ 30
(126)   *(138)*   *(138)*

29. What is the probability of drawing a heart from a full
(129) deck of cards? (There are 13 hearts in a deck.) $\frac{1}{4}$

30. Draw a rectangle that is 5 cm long and 2 cm wide.
(65) Draw lines to divide the rectangle into square
centimeters. Then shade 30% of the rectangle.

LESSON
140

Writing Numbers Through Hundred Millions

a. 75
b. 70
c. 100
d. 460
e. $7.25
f. 162
Patterns:
  $1\frac{1}{8}$, $1\frac{1}{4}$, $1\frac{3}{8}$, $1\frac{1}{2}$, $1\frac{5}{8}$,
  $1\frac{3}{4}$, $1\frac{7}{8}$, 2

Facts Practice: 90 Division Facts (Test J in Test Masters)

Mental Math: Find the stated percent of 100.
  a. 75% of 100   **b.** 70% of 100   **c.** 100% of 100
Review:
  d. 20×23 **e.** $\$20.00 - \$12.75$ **f.** $127 + 35$

Patterns: Find the next eight numbers in this sequence.
  $\frac{1}{8}$, $\frac{1}{4}$, $\frac{3}{8}$, $\frac{1}{2}$, $\frac{5}{8}$, $\frac{3}{4}$, $\frac{7}{8}$, 1, ___, ___, ___, ___, ___, ___, ___, ___, ...

For a few lessons, we have practiced naming numbers
through hundred millions. In this lesson we will begin
writing these numbers.

Example   Use digits to write forty-six million, eight hundred ninety-five thousand, two hundred seventy.

Solution   It is a good idea to read the entire number before we begin writing it. We see *millions* and *thousands*, so we know the number will have this form:

———, ———, ———

We go back and read "forty-six million" and write "46" and a comma. We read "eight hundred ninety-five thousand" and write "895" and a comma. We read "two hundred seventy" and write "270."

46,895,270

Practice   Use digits to write each number:

a. Nine million, two hundred sixty-three thousand, five hundred twelve   9,263,512

b. Eleven million, one hundred twenty-three thousand, four hundred   11,123,400

c. Nine hundred eighty-seven million, six hundred fifty-four thousand, three hundred twenty-one   987,654,321

d. Sixteen million, five hundred forty-three thousand   16,543,000

e. Ninety-three million   93,000,000

f. Seven hundred fifty-three million, eight hundred seventy-two thousand, one hundred ninety   753,872,190

Problem set 140

1. The Martins drank 11 gallons of milk each week. How
(83)   many quarts of milk did they drink each week?
44 quarts

60 fleas
15 fleas	} ¼ perished
15 fleas	
15 fleas	} ¾ survived
15 fleas	

2. Sixty fleas leaped on Rover as he ran through the field.
(80)   If one fourth of them perished from flea powder, how many survived? Illustrate the problem.   45 fleas

3. (a) What is the area of this
(94,60) square? 100 sq. mm

□ | 10 mm

(b) What is the perimeter of this
square? 40 mm

4. Mark is 8 inches taller than Jim. Jim is 5 inches taller
(104) than Jan. Mark is 61 inches tall. How many inches tall
is Jan? 48 in.

5. What is the average height of the three children in
(106) problem 4? 54 in.

6. Mayville is on the road from Altoona to Watson. It is
(50) 47 miles from Mayville to Altoona. It is 24 miles from
Mayville to Watson. How far is it from Altoona to
Watson? 71 mi

7. What is the probability of this
(129) spinner stopping on a number
greater than 4? $\frac{1}{3}$

8. (a) Write XXXIII in our number system. 33
(135) (b) Write 39 in Roman numerals. XXXIX

9. Name each shape:
(134)
(a) pyramid (b)   (c) cone

rectangular solid

10. Write the reduced form of each fraction:
(125)
(a) $\frac{9}{15}$ $\frac{3}{5}$ (b) $\frac{10}{12}$ $\frac{5}{6}$ (c) $\frac{12}{16}$ $\frac{3}{4}$

11. Use digits to write one hundred nineteen million, two
(140) hundred forty-seven thousand, nine hundred eighty-
four. 119,247,984

12. 14.94 − (3.6 + 4.7)   **13.** 6.8 − (1.37 + 2.2) 3.23
(55) 6.64   (55)

14. $3\dfrac{2}{5} + 1\dfrac{4}{5}$ $5\frac{1}{5}$ **15.** $\dfrac{5}{8} + \dfrac{1}{4}$ $\frac{7}{8}$ **16.** $\dfrac{1}{3} + \dfrac{1}{6}$ $\frac{1}{2}$
(132)   *(139)*   *(139)*

17. $5\dfrac{9}{10} - 1\dfrac{1}{10}$ $4\frac{4}{5}$ **18.** $\dfrac{5}{8} - \dfrac{1}{4}$ $\frac{3}{8}$ **19.** $\dfrac{1}{3} - \dfrac{1}{6}$ $\frac{1}{6}$
(132)   *(139)*   *(139)*

20. 38×217 **21.** 173×60 **22.** 90×500
(127)   8246   *(127)*   10,380   *(96)*   45,000

23. $\dfrac{6752}{4}$ 1688   **24.**
(86)   *(2)*

26. $7\overline{)2942}$ 420 r 2
(90)

27. $\$80.01 \div 9$ $\$8.89$
(86)

28. $10\overline{)453}$ 45 r 3
(115)

29. $11\overline{)453}$ 41 r 2
(138)

30. $22\overline{)453}$ 20 r 13
(138)

24.
```
   7
   5
   8
   6
   9
N  15
   8
   7
   6
 + 4
 ────
  75
```

25.
```
   27
   99
   77
   86
   68
   54
   45
   74
   85
 + 27
 ────
  642
```
(21)

LESSON
141

Reading Roman Numerals Through Thousands

a. 150
b. 140
c. 200
d. 480
e. $12.25
f. 161
Patterns:
$\frac{5}{8}$, $\frac{3}{4}$, $\frac{7}{8}$, 1, $1\frac{1}{8}$, $1\frac{1}{4}$, $1\frac{3}{8}$, $1\frac{1}{2}$

Facts Practice: 90 Division Facts (Test J in Test Masters)

Mental Math: Find the stated percent of 200.

   a. 75% of 200   **b.** 70% of 200   **c.** 100% of 200

Review:

   d. 20×24 **e.** $\$20.00 - \$7.75$ **f.** $136 + 25$

Patterns: Find the next eight numbers in this sequence.

$$\frac{1}{8}, \frac{1}{4}, \frac{3}{8}, \frac{1}{2}, \underline{}, \underline{}, \underline{}, \underline{}, \underline{}, \underline{}, \underline{}, \underline{}, \dots$$

We have practiced using these Roman numerals.

I   V   X

In this lesson, we will practice using more Roman numerals. These are listed in the table.

NUMERAL	VALUE
I	1
V	5
X	10
L	50
C	100
D	500
M	1000

Example   Write each Roman numeral in our number system.

(a) LXX   (b) DCCL   (c) XLIV   (d) MMI

Solution   (a) LXX is 50 + 10 + 10, which is **70.**

(b) DCCL is 500 + 100 + 100 + 50, which is **750.**

(c) XLIV is 10 less than 50 and 1 less than 5. That is, 40 + 4 = **44.**

(d) MMI is 1000 + 1000 + 1, which is **2001.**

Practice   Write each Roman numeral in our number system:

a. CCCLXII   **b.** CCLXXXV   **c.** CD
362   285   400

d. XLVII   **e.** MMMCCLVI   **f.** MCMXCIX
47   3256   1999

Problem set 141

1. Beth is reading a 210-page book. If she has read one third of the book, how many pages does she still have to read? Illustrate the problem.   140 pages
(80)

210 pages

70 pages	} $\frac{1}{3}$ has been read
70 pages	} $\frac{2}{3}$ still has to
70 pages	be read

2. Iceland covers an area of 39,768 square miles. The area of Virginia is 40,767 square miles. How much greater is the area of Virginia than the area of Iceland?   999 sq. mi
(38)

3. Molly Pitcher carried 21 buckets of water to the thirsty troops. If each bucket held 3 gallons, how many **quarts** of water did she deliver?   252 quarts
(104)

4. What is the perimeter of this
(132) triangle? $2\frac{1}{4}$ in.

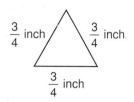

$\frac{3}{4}$ inch $\frac{3}{4}$ inch

$\frac{3}{4}$ inch

5. Write each Roman numeral in our number system:
(140) (a) MDCLXVI   (b) CCXXIV 224 (c) XCIX 99
1666

6. Write the reduced form of each fraction:
(125) (a) $\frac{9}{12}$ $\frac{3}{4}$ (b) $\frac{12}{15}$ $\frac{4}{5}$ (c) $\frac{10}{20}$ $\frac{1}{2}$

7. This cube is made of how many
(134) smaller cubes?   64 smaller cubes

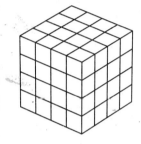

8. Use digits to write ninety-three
(140) million, one hundred seventy-five
thousand, two hundred twelve.
93,175,212

9. Rita flipped a coin 21 times. It came up heads 17
(84) times. What fraction tells the number of times it did
not come up heads? $\frac{4}{21}$

10. Five red shirts cost $100. Six green jackets cost $480.
(104) What did each red shirt and each green jacket cost?
What would be the cost of 6 red shirts and 5 green
jackets? $20 per shirt; $80 per jacket; $520

11. The number C is what percent of the number M? 10%
(65)

12. 59.34 − (12.6 + 7.5)   **13.** 47.6 − (3.7 + 12.23)
(55) 39.24   (55) 31.67

14. $8\frac{1}{4} + 1\frac{3}{4}$ 10 **15.** $\frac{1}{2} + \frac{3}{10}$ $\frac{4}{5}$ **16.** $\frac{2}{3} + \frac{1}{6}$ $\frac{5}{6}$
(132)   (139)   (139)

17. $7\frac{3}{8} - 1\frac{1}{8}$ $6\frac{1}{4}$ **18.** $\frac{1}{2} - \frac{3}{10}$ $\frac{1}{5}$ **19.** $\frac{2}{3} - \frac{1}{6}$ $\frac{1}{2}$
(132)   (139)   (139)

20. 47×31 1457   **21.**
(100)   (2)

23. 430×26 11,180
(127)

24. 48×250 12,000
(127)

$$\begin{array}{r} 803 \\ \textbf{25. } 9\overline{)7227} \end{array}$$
(90)

26. $\$37.00 \div 4$ $9.25
(86)

$$\textbf{27. } \frac{810}{6} \quad 135$$
(86)

$$\begin{array}{r} 92 \\ \textbf{28. } 70\overline{)6440} \end{array}$$
(126)

21.
$$\begin{array}{r} 4 \\ 7 \\ 3 \\ 2 \\ 5 \\ 8 \\ 6 \\ N \quad 14 \\ +\ 5 \\ \hline 54 \end{array}$$

22.
(21)
$$\begin{array}{r} 27 \\ 32 \\ 11 \\ 22 \\ 33 \\ 41 \\ 14 \\ 26 \\ +\ 48 \\ \hline 254 \end{array}$$

29. The front cover of this book has an area of about how
(94,48) many square inches? (Measure each side to the nearest inch.) 80 sq. in.

30. If there is one correct answer, and the choices are A, B,
(129) C, and D, then what is the probability of guessing the correct answer? $\frac{1}{4}$

Appendix A

Multiplication by 10's, 11's, and 12's

We know that when we multiply by 10 the answer has a zero at the end.

1 × 10 = 10	5 × 10 = 50	9 × 10 = 90
2 × 10 = 20	6 × 10 = 60	10 × 10 = 100
3 × 10 = 30	7 × 10 = 70	11 × 10 = 110
4 × 10 = 40	8 × 10 = 80	12 × 10 = 120

Multiplying by 11 is easy also because every answer listed below except the last three has double digits that are the same.

1 × 11 = 11	5 × 11 = 55	9 × 11 = 99
2 × 11 = 22	6 × 11 = 66	10 × 11 = 110
3 × 11 = 33	7 × 11 = 77	11 × 11 = 121
4 × 11 = 44	8 × 11 = 88	12 × 11 = 132

Multiplying by 12 is important because many items are sold in sets of 12. A set of 12 things is called a **dozen.** Memorizing the 12's table requires practice in saying the table aloud.

1 × 12 = 12	5 × 12 = 60	9 × 12 = 108
2 × 12 = 24	6 × 12 = 72	10 × 12 = 120
3 × 12 = 36	7 × 12 = 84	11 × 12 = 132
4 × 12 = 48	8 × 12 = 96	12 × 12 = 144

Appendix B

Supplemental Practice Problems for Selected Lessons

This appendix contains additional practice problems for concepts presented in selected lessons. It is very important that no problems in the regular problem sets be omitted to make room for these problems. This book is designed to produce long-term retention of concepts, and long-term practice of all the concepts is necessary. The practice problems in the problem sets provide enough initial exposure to concepts for most students. If a student continues to have difficulty with certain concepts, some of these problems can be assigned as remedial exercises.

Supplemental Practice for Lesson 19

1.	42 − 23 19	**2.**	30 − 16 14	**3.**	24 − 17 7	**4.**	54 − 27 27

5.   31
− 24
7   **6.**   60
− 36
24   **7.**   23
− B 17
6   **8.** D 40
− 19
21

9.   57
− F 28
29   **10.** H 70
− 36
34   **11.**   42
− J 37
5   **12.** L 74
− 47
27

13. $36 - 18$ 18   **14.** $24 - 17$ 7   **15.** $40 - 23$ 17

16. $60 - R = 33$ 27   **17.** $P - 39 = 18$ 57   **18.** $72 - 64$ 8

19. $T - 46 = 28$ 74   **20.** $35 - W = 7$ 28

Supplemental Practice for Lesson 21

1.	12 8 15 + 7 42	**2.**	36 8 24 + 16 84	**3.**	12 23 24 + 20 79	**4.**	16 36 54 + 32 138
5.	74 37 60 + 46 217	**6.**	57 24 38 + 83 202	**7.**	95 9 78 + 35 217	**8.**	47 58 62 + 55 222
9.	34 27 8 + 27 96	**10.**	67 15 436 + 25 543	**11.**	314 28 116 + 42 500	**12.**	9 32 154 + 97 292
13.	374 257 38 + 146 815	**14.**	66 207 84 + 259 616	**15.**	360 45 179 + 78 662	**16.**	40 95 379 + 86 600

17. 36	**18.** 436	**19.** 363	**20.** 273
275	39	247	54
175	147	152	106
+ 384	+ 88	+ 148	+ 50
870	710	910	483

Supplemental Practice for Lesson 37

1. 263	**2.** 432	**3.** 520	**4.** 287
− 147	− 141	− 336	− 179
116	291	184	108

5. 196	**6.** 479	**7.** 360	**8.** 424
− 57	− 286	− 134	− 254
139	193	226	170

9. 316	**10.** 260	**11.** 415
− 79	− 146	− 387
237	114	28

12. 247 − 79 168 **13.** 163 − 127 36 **14.** 459 − 367 92

15. 770 − 287 483 **16.** 612 − 78 534 **17.** 340 − 149 191

18. 210 − 86 124 **19.** 436 − 156 280 **20.** 520 − 417 103

Supplemental Practice for Lesson 43

Use words to write each of these numbers:

1. 363   three hundred sixty-three

2. 1,246   one thousand, two hundred forty-six

3. 12,280   twelve thousand, two hundred eighty

4. 25,362   twenty-five thousand, three hundred sixty-two

5. 123,570
one hundred twenty-three thousand, five hundred seventy

6. 253,500   two hundred fifty-three thousand, five hundred

7. 112,060   one hundred twelve thousand, sixty

8. 220,405   two hundred twenty thousand, four hundred five

9. 204,050   two hundred four thousand, fifty

10. 546,325
five hundred forty-six thousand, three hundred twenty-five

Use digits to write each of these numbers:

11. One thousand, two hundred seventy-eight   1,278

12. Eleven thousand, five hundred forty-four   11,544

13. Twenty-two thousand, four hundred thirty   22,430

14. Fifty-seven thousand, nine hundred   57,900

15. One hundred seventy-one thousand, two hundred thirty   171,230

16. Two hundred ten thousand, nine hundred   210,900

17. Five hundred sixty-three thousand, fifty-eight
563,058

18. Nine hundred eighty-seven thousand, six hundred fifty-four   987,654

19. One hundred five thousand, seventy   105,070

20. Six hundred fifty thousand, four hundred three
650,403

Supplemental Practice for Lesson 46   Use a fraction or mixed number to name every point marked with an arrow on these number lines:

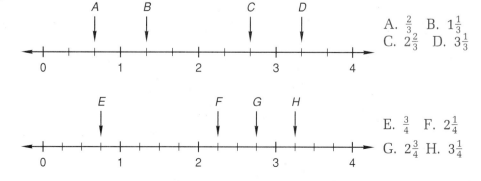

A. $\frac{2}{3}$ B. $1\frac{1}{3}$
C. $2\frac{2}{3}$ D. $3\frac{1}{3}$

E. $\frac{3}{4}$ F. $2\frac{1}{4}$
G. $2\frac{3}{4}$ H. $3\frac{1}{4}$

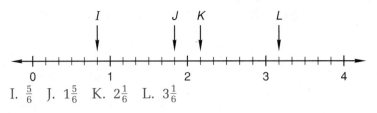

I. $\frac{5}{6}$ J. $1\frac{5}{6}$ K. $2\frac{1}{6}$ L. $3\frac{1}{6}$

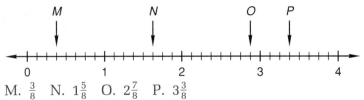

M. $\frac{3}{8}$ N. $1\frac{5}{8}$ O. $2\frac{7}{8}$ P. $3\frac{3}{8}$

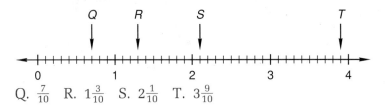

Q. $\frac{7}{10}$ R. $1\frac{3}{10}$ S. $2\frac{1}{10}$ T. $3\frac{9}{10}$

Supplemental Practice for Lesson 51

1. 300
  $-\ 136$
  ‾‾‾‾‾
  164

2. 403
  $-\ 257$
  ‾‾‾‾‾
  146

3. 200
  $-\ 143$
  ‾‾‾‾‾
  57

4. 306
  $-\ 157$
  ‾‾‾‾‾
  149

5. 600
  $-\ 249$
  ‾‾‾‾‾
  351

6. 201
  $-\ 165$
  ‾‾‾‾‾
  36

7. 100
  $-\ \ 36$
  ‾‾‾‾‾
  64

8. 405
  $-\ 229$
  ‾‾‾‾‾
  176

9. 400
  $-\ 349$
  ‾‾‾‾‾
  51

10. 101
  $-\ \ 94$
  ‾‾‾‾‾
  7

11. 700
  $-\ 436$
  ‾‾‾‾‾
  264

12. 501
  $-\ 127$
  ‾‾‾‾‾
  374

13. 100
  $-\ \ 79$
  ‾‾‾‾‾
  21

14. 907
  $-\ \ 65$
  ‾‾‾‾‾
  842

15. 500
  $-\ 249$
  ‾‾‾‾‾
  251

16. 804
  $-\ 756$
  ‾‾‾‾‾
  48

17. 800
  $-\ \ 48$
  ‾‾‾‾‾
  752

18. 602
  $-\ 575$
  ‾‾‾‾‾
  27

19. 900
  $-\ 617$
  ‾‾‾‾‾
  283

20. 107
  $-\ \ 28$
  ‾‾‾‾‾
  79

Supplemental Practice for Lesson 53

1. $6.35 + $4 $10.35

2. $4.84 − $3 $1.84

3. 48¢ + 67¢ $1.15

4. $0.49 − 15¢   34¢

5. $0.36 + 85¢ $1.21

6. $1.25 − 8¢ $1.17

7. $2.45 + 6¢ $2.51

8. 75¢ − $0.67 8¢

9. 98¢ + $12 $12.98

10. $1.00 − 95¢ 5¢

11. $3.46 + $2 + 49¢ $5.95

12. 50¢ − $0.07 43¢

13. 36¢ + $0.12 + $2.14 $2.62

14. $2 − $1.37 $0.63

15. $15 + $1.50 + 15¢ $16.65

16. $1 − 37¢ $0.63

17. 36¢ + 24¢ + 78¢ $1.38

18. $5 − $4.63 $0.37

19. $5 + $0.36 + 9¢ $5.45

20. 87¢ − 78¢ 9¢

Supplemental Practice for Lesson 58

1. 36 × 2 = 72

2. 43 × 5 = 215

3. 57 × 3 = 171

4. 24 × 6 = 144

5. 38 × 4 = 152

6. 52 × 7 = 364

7. 27 × 5 = 135

8. 19 × 8 = 152

9. 28 × 6 168

10. 9 × 56 504

11. 47 × 7 329

12. 4 × 89 356

13. 64 × 8 512

14. 5 × 75 375

15. 63 × 9 567

16. 4 × 76 304

17. 97 × 6 582

18. 2 × 68 136

19. 54 × 7 378

20. 3 × 45 135

Supplemental Practice for Lesson 62

1. 3486 − 1687 = 1799

2. 2175 − 1346 = 829

3. 3747 − 1654 = 2093

4. 4403 − 1475 = 2928

5. 6300 − 3149 = 3151

6. 2048 − 1951 = 97

7. 3000 − 1346 = 1654

8. 4005 − 2418 = 1587

9. 3040 − 1535 = 1505

10. 6000 − 2164 3836	**11.** 8010 − 7825 185	**12.** 5007 − 1838 3169
13. 36,247 − 1,456 34,791	**14.** 30,148 − 23,109 7,039	**15.** 40,015 − 16,438 23,577
16. 30,000 − 256 29,744	**17.** 30,604 − 1,915 28,689	**18.** 90,040 − 37,478 52,562

19. 376,142
− 36,174
339,968

20. 403,700
− 394,672
9028

Supplemental Practice for Lesson 63

1. $2\overline{)15}$ 7 r 1   **2.** $5\overline{)23}$ 4 r 3   **3.** $3\overline{)25}$ 8 r 1   **4.** 26 ÷ 6 4 r 2

5. 31 ÷ 4 7 r 3   **6.** 50 ÷ 7 7 r 1   **7.** $5\overline{)37}$ 7 r 2   **8.** $8\overline{)35}$ 4 r 3

9. $6\overline{)43}$ 7 r 1   **10.** 30 ÷ 9 3 r 3   **11.** 45 ÷ 7 6 r 3   **12.** 17 ÷ 2 8 r 1

13. $8\overline{)49}$ 6 r 1   **14.** $3\overline{)25}$ 8 r 1   **15.** $9\overline{)60}$ 6 r 6   **16.** 27 ÷ 4 6 r 3

17. 15 ÷ 8 1 r 7   **18.** 32 ÷ 5 6 r 2   **19.** $3\overline{)20}$ 6 r 2   **20.** $6\overline{)34}$ 5 r 4

Supplemental Practice for Lesson 68

1. 136
× 2
272   **2.** 235
× 5
1175   **3.** 430
× 3
1290

4. 216 × 6 1296   **5.** 450 × 4 1800   **6.** 7 × 642 4494

7. 307
× 5
1535   **8.** 458
× 8
3664   **9.** 740
× 6
4440

10. 368 × 7 2576   **11.** 9 × 403 3627   **12.** 490 × 8 3920

13. 609
× 2
1218   **14.** 470
× 9
4230   **15.** 518
× 3
1554

16. 2 × 296 592   **17.** 708 × 4 2832   **18.** 3 × 430 1290

19. 275 × 5 1375   **20.** 4 × 308 1232

Supplemental Practice for Lesson 74

1. $3\overline{)48}$ → 16
2. $2\overline{)56}$ → 28
3. $4\overline{)72}$ → 18
4. $7\overline{)98}$ → 14
5. $5\overline{)80}$ → 16
6. $8\overline{)96}$ → 12
7. $6\overline{)90}$ → 15
8. $3\overline{)81}$ → 27
9. $7\overline{)91}$ → 13
10. $4\overline{)68}$ → 17
11. $2\overline{)76}$ → 38
12. $5\overline{)90}$ → 18
13. $3\overline{)54}$ → 18
14. $6\overline{)84}$ → 14
15. $3\overline{)78}$ → 26
16. $7\overline{)84}$ → 12
17. $4\overline{)84}$ → 21
18. $5\overline{)85}$ → 17
19. $6\overline{)72}$ → 12
20. $5\overline{)65}$ → 13

Supplemental Practice for Lesson 75

1. $2\overline{)110}$ → 55
2. $9\overline{)126}$ → 14
3. $3\overline{)222}$ → 74
4. $8\overline{)432}$ → 54
5. $4\overline{)256}$ → 64
6. $7\overline{)455}$ → 65
7. $5\overline{)320}$ → 64
8. $2\overline{)192}$ → 96
9. $6\overline{)342}$ → 57
10. $3\overline{)204}$ → 68
11. $7\overline{)266}$ → 38
12. $4\overline{)100}$ → 25
13. $8\overline{)456}$ → 57
14. $5\overline{)365}$ → 73
15. $9\overline{)468}$ → 52
16. $6\overline{)162}$ → 27
17. $4\overline{)252}$ → 63
18. $7\overline{)665}$ → 95
19. $8\overline{)600}$ → 75
20. $5\overline{)245}$ → 49

Supplemental Practice for Lesson 76

1. $4\overline{)93}$ → 23 r 1
2. $2\overline{)115}$ → 57 r 1
3. $5\overline{)182}$ → 36 r 2
4. $3\overline{)173}$ → 57 r 2
5. $6\overline{)289}$ → 48 r 1
6. $4\overline{)181}$ → 45 r 1
7. $7\overline{)164}$ → 23 r 3
8. $5\overline{)319}$ → 63 r 4
9. $8\overline{)218}$ → 27 r 2
10. $6\overline{)235}$ → 39 r 1
11. $9\overline{)220}$ → 24 r 4
12. $7\overline{)442}$ → 63 r 1
13. $2\overline{)189}$ → 94 r 1
14. $8\overline{)595}$ → 74 r 3
15. $3\overline{)109}$ → 36 r 1
16. $9\overline{)892}$ → 99 r 1
17. $4\overline{)218}$ → 54 r 2
18. $2\overline{)55}$ → 27 r 1
19. $5\overline{)232}$ → 46 r 2
20. $3\overline{)220}$ → 73 r 1

Supplemental Practice for Lesson 77

1.
$$\begin{array}{r} 32 \\ \times\ 20 \\ \hline 640 \end{array}$$

2.
$$\begin{array}{r} 43¢ \\ \times\ 30 \\ \hline \$12.90 \end{array}$$

3.
$$\begin{array}{r} 56 \\ \times\ 40 \\ \hline 2240 \end{array}$$

4.
$$\begin{array}{r} \$0.68 \\ \times\ 20 \\ \hline \$13.60 \end{array}$$

5.
$$\begin{array}{r} 47 \\ \times\ 60 \\ \hline 2820 \end{array}$$

6.
$$\begin{array}{r} \$1.68 \\ \times\ 20 \\ \hline \$33.60 \end{array}$$

7. 20×75 1500
8. $30 \times 49¢$ $14.70
9. 40×87 3480
10. $\$0.97 \times 50$ $48.50
11. $70 \times \$1.49$ $104.30
12. 60×38 2280

13. 80 × 76 6080   **14.** 48¢ × 90   **15.** 20 × 89 1780
                                    $43.20

16. $2.25 × 50   **17.** $0.39 × 60   **18.** 30 × 78 2340
      $112.50 $23.40

19. 40 × 67¢ $26.80   **20.** 84 × 70   5880

Supplemental Practice for Lesson 86

$$\begin{array}{c}233\ r\ 1\\3\overline{)700}\end{array}$$

1. 3)700 233 r 1   **2.** 6)738 123   **3.** 4)892 223   **4.** 7)868 124

5. 5)1606 321 r 1   **6.** 8)915 114 r 3   **7.** 6)1275 212 r 3   **8.** 9)1926 214

9. 7)2415 345   **10.** 3)1603 534 r 1   **11.** 8)1161 145 r 1   **12.** 4)1111 277 r 3

13. 9)3000 333 r 3   **14.** 5)625 125   **15.** 3)1333 444 r 1   **16.** 6)1518 253

17. 4)2250 562 r 2   **18.** 7)1162 166   **19.** 8)1000 125   **20.** 5)3743 748 r 3

Supplemental Practice for Lesson 90

1. 4)960 240   **2.** 5)1600 320   **3.** 3)1206 402   **4.** 9)936 104

5. 4)2082 520 r 2   **6.** 6)1820 303 r 2   **7.** 7)2801 400 r 1   **8.** 2)1819 909 r 1

9. 5)3404 680 r 4   **10.** 3)2712 904   **11.** 6)3000 500   **12.** 4)2681 670 r 1

13. 7)5650 807 r 1   **14.** 8)3275 409 r 3   **15.** 3)450 150   **16.** 5)2001 400 r 1

17. 2)381 190 r 1   **18.** 8)6080 760   **19.** 9)3686 409 r 5   **20.** 6)4202 700 r 2

Supplemental Practice for Lesson 100

1. 12 × 36   432   **2.** 46 × 15   690   **3.** 31 × 27   837

4.   74   **5.**   36   **6.**   35
     × 16   × 63   × 35
     ─────   ─────   ─────
      1184   2268   1225

7. 14 × 63   882   **8.** 78 × 22   1716   **9.** 25 × 37   925

10.   74   **11.**   63   **12.**   18
      × 58   × 49   × 65
      ─────   ─────   ─────
       4292   3087   1170

13. 96 × 32 3072   **14.** 51 × 76 3876   **15.** 38 × 24 912

16.   38   **17.**   49   **18.**   29
      × 47   × 86   × 31
      ─────   ─────   ─────
       1786   4214   899

19. 33 × 79   2607   **20.** 57 × 42   2394

Supplemental Practice for Lesson 114

Change each improper fraction to a mixed number or a whole number:

1. $\dfrac{3}{2}$ $1\frac{1}{2}$ 2. $\dfrac{9}{3}$ 3 3. $\dfrac{4}{3}$ $1\frac{1}{3}$ 4. $\dfrac{7}{4}$ $1\frac{3}{4}$

5. $\dfrac{12}{5}$ $2\frac{2}{5}$ 6. $\dfrac{4}{2}$ 2 7. $\dfrac{5}{4}$ $1\frac{1}{4}$ 8. $\dfrac{7}{5}$ $1\frac{2}{5}$

9. $\dfrac{3}{3}$ 1 10. $\dfrac{9}{5}$ $1\frac{4}{5}$ 11. $\dfrac{5}{2}$ $2\frac{1}{2}$ 12. $\dfrac{8}{4}$ 2

13. $\dfrac{15}{15}$ 1 14. $\dfrac{5}{3}$ $1\frac{2}{3}$ 15. $\dfrac{9}{4}$ $2\frac{1}{4}$ 16. $\dfrac{6}{2}$ 3

17. $\dfrac{6}{3}$ 2 18. $\dfrac{10}{3}$ $3\frac{1}{3}$ 19. $\dfrac{7}{2}$ $3\frac{1}{2}$ 20. $\dfrac{7}{3}$ $2\frac{1}{3}$

Supplemental Practice for Lesson 118

1. $3.6 + 2.17$ 5.77

2. $5.28 + 12.4$ 17.68

3. $15.4 + 23.56$ 38.96

4. $6.7 + 15.8$ 22.5

5. $16.36 + 14.7$ 31.06

6. $45.3 + 2.91$ 48.21

7. $0.4 + 45.91$ 46.31

8. $3.71 + 6.3$ 10.01

9. $103.7 + 7.41$ 111.11

10. $9.09 + 90.9$ 99.99

11. $1.3 + 4.26 + 2.7$ 8.26

12. $12.4 + 1.5 + 3.3$ 17.2

13. $2.1 + 1.91 + 12.12$ 16.13

14. $6.58 + 3.7 + 0.4$ 10.68

15. $29.6 + 2.96 + 29.62$ 62.18

16. $3.4 + 4.56 + 1.41$ 9.37

17. $36.4 + 6.4 + 0.64$ 43.44

18. $1.2 + 0.21 + 12.1 + 10.21$ 23.72

19. $3.5 + 0.35 + 5.03 + 35.53 + 35.0$ 79.41

20. $2.4 + 4.12 + 20.4 + 42.21 + 1.2$ 70.33

Supplemental Practice for Lesson 119

1. $3.45 - 1.2$ 2.25   **2.** $23.1 - 2.2$ 20.9

3. $14.25 - 1.6$ 12.65   **4.** $15.3 - 4.4$ 10.9

5. $7.59 - 1.8$ 5.79   **6.** $25.34 - 1.21$ 24.13

7. $16.25 - 1.9$ 14.35   **8.** $8.19 - 0.4$ 7.79

9. $13.26 - 12.2$ 1.06

10.
$$\begin{array}{r} 3.4 \\ -\,1.26 \\ \hline 2.14 \end{array}$$

11.
$$\begin{array}{r} 4.0 \\ -\,2.14 \\ \hline 1.86 \end{array}$$

12.
$$\begin{array}{r} 12.4 \\ -\,1.24 \\ \hline 11.16 \end{array}$$

13. $7.4 - 1.22$ 6.18   **14.** $3.68 - 1.7$ 1.98

15. $12.1 - 1.21$ 10.89   **16.** $30.1 - 3.01$ 27.09

17. $34.05 - 6.4$ 27.65   **18.** $58.0 - 2.14$ 55.86

19. $3.09 - 1.8$ 1.29   **20.** $20.1 - 3.19$ 16.91

Supplemental Practice for Lesson 126

1. $20\overline{)460}$ 23   **2.** $30\overline{)630}$ 21   **3.** $40\overline{)520}$ 13

4. $50\overline{)1600}$ (32)   **5.** $60\overline{)720}$ (12)   **6.** $70\overline{)1470}$ (21)

7. $80\overline{)1700}$ (21 r 20)   **8.** $90\overline{)1200}$ (13 r 30)   **9.** $20\overline{)680}$ (34)

10. $40\overline{)1325}$ (33 r 5)   **11.** $60\overline{)1450}$ (24 r 10)   **12.** $70\overline{)2177}$ (31 r 7)

13. $80\overline{)2001}$ (25 r 1)   **14.** $90\overline{)1359}$ (15 r 9)   **15.** $20\overline{)920}$ (46)

16. $40\overline{)2088}$ (52 r 8)   **17.** $60\overline{)2640}$ (44)   **18.** $70\overline{)1624}$ (23 r 14)

19. $30\overline{)1680}$ (56)   **20.** $50\overline{)2710}$ (54 r 10)

Supplemental Practice for Lesson 127

1. 320 × 12 3840   2. 132 × 21 2772   3. 143 × 23 3289

4.   150
   × 32
   ————
   4800

5.   304
   × 13
   ————
   3952

6.   315
   × 24
   ————
   7560

7. 42 × 163 6846   8. 230 × 15 3450   9. 25 × 402
                                            10,050

10.   357
    × 34
    ————
    12,138

11.   780
    × 56
    ————
    43,680

12.   406
    × 17
    ————
    6902

13. 28 × 196
    5488

14. 460 × 39
    17,940

15. 43 × 179 7697

16.   108
    × 39
    ————
    4212

17.   349
    × 74
    ————
    25,826

18.   470
    × 68
    ————
    31,960

19. 29 × 357   10,353   20. 186 × 37   6882

Supplemental Practice for Lesson 129

Reduce each fraction:

1. $\frac{5}{10}$ $\frac{1}{2}$ 2. $\frac{2}{4}$ $\frac{1}{2}$ 3. $\frac{6}{8}$ $\frac{3}{4}$ 4. $\frac{2}{6}$ $\frac{1}{3}$

5. $\frac{3}{9}$ $\frac{1}{3}$ 6. $\frac{4}{10}$ $\frac{2}{5}$ 7. $\frac{3}{6}$ $\frac{1}{2}$ 8. $\frac{2}{12}$ $\frac{1}{6}$

9. $\frac{9}{12}$ $\frac{3}{4}$ 10. $\frac{4}{6}$ $\frac{2}{3}$ 11. $\frac{6}{9}$ $\frac{2}{3}$ 12. $\frac{8}{10}$ $\frac{4}{5}$

13. $\frac{2}{8}$ $\frac{1}{4}$ 14. $\frac{3}{12}$ $\frac{1}{4}$ 15. $\frac{2}{10}$ $\frac{1}{5}$ 16. $\frac{4}{8}$ $\frac{1}{2}$

17. $\frac{8}{12}$ $\frac{2}{3}$ 18. $\frac{6}{10}$ $\frac{3}{5}$ 19. $\frac{4}{12}$ $\frac{1}{3}$ 20. $\frac{6}{12}$ $\frac{1}{2}$

Supplemental Practice for Lesson 130

1. $12\overline{)72}$ 6   2. $31\overline{)124}$ 4   3. $11\overline{)100}$ 9 r 1   4. $41\overline{)125}$ 3 r 2

5. $13\overline{)91}$ 7   6. $21\overline{)107}$ 5 r 2   7. $52\overline{)212}$ 4 r 4   8. $25\overline{)130}$ 5 r 5

9. $32\overline{)130}$ 4 r 2   10. $22\overline{)135}$ 6 r 3   11. $51\overline{)310}$ 6 r 4   12. $14\overline{)80}$ 5 r 10

$$\overset{4\ r\ 12}{13.\ 42\overline{)180}} \quad \overset{7}{14.\ 23\overline{)161}} \quad \overset{5\ r\ 5}{15.\ 34\overline{)175}} \quad \overset{7}{16.\ 15\overline{)105}}$$

$$\overset{3\ r\ 21}{17.\ 43\overline{)150}} \quad \overset{8\ r\ 8}{18.\ 24\overline{)200}} \quad \overset{9\ r\ 3}{19.\ 33\overline{)300}} \quad \overset{5\ r\ 5}{20.\ 19\overline{)100}}$$

Supplemental Practice for Lesson 131

1. $3\frac{1}{2} + 1$ $4\frac{1}{2}$

2. $3\frac{1}{3} + 1\frac{1}{3}$ $4\frac{2}{3}$

3. $1\frac{1}{5} + \frac{3}{5}$ $1\frac{4}{5}$

4. $4 + \frac{1}{2}$ $4\frac{1}{2}$

5. $6\frac{3}{5} + 1\frac{1}{5}$ $7\frac{4}{5}$

6. $5\frac{5}{8} + 6$ $11\frac{5}{8}$

7. $3\frac{3}{7} + 2\frac{2}{7}$ $5\frac{5}{7}$

8. $6 + 7\frac{1}{2}$ $13\frac{1}{2}$

9. $\frac{5}{9} + 3\frac{2}{9}$ $3\frac{7}{9}$

10. $3\frac{3}{10} + 6\frac{6}{10}$ $9\frac{9}{10}$

11. $5\frac{2}{3} - 1\frac{1}{3}$ $4\frac{1}{3}$

12. $3\frac{3}{4} - 2$ $1\frac{3}{4}$

13. $6\frac{1}{2} - \frac{1}{2}$ 6

14. $8\frac{3}{4} - 1\frac{3}{4}$ 7

15. $2\frac{5}{8} - 2\frac{2}{8}$ $\frac{3}{8}$

16. $4\frac{4}{5} - \frac{1}{5}$ $4\frac{3}{5}$

17. $4\frac{4}{9} - 3$ $1\frac{4}{9}$

18. $1\frac{4}{5} - \frac{4}{5}$ 1

19. $3\frac{1}{2} - 1\frac{1}{2}$ 2

20. $4\frac{5}{7} - 1\frac{3}{7}$ $3\frac{2}{7}$

Supplemental Practice for Lesson 132

Simplify each fraction answer:

1. $\frac{1}{2} + \frac{1}{2}$ 1

2. $\frac{1}{3} - \frac{1}{3}$ 0

3. $\frac{1}{4} + \frac{1}{4}$ $\frac{1}{2}$

4. $\frac{3}{8} - \frac{1}{8}$ $\frac{1}{4}$

5. $\frac{1}{6} + \frac{2}{6}$ $\frac{1}{2}$

6. $\frac{5}{6} - \frac{1}{6}$ $\frac{2}{3}$

7. $\frac{2}{3} + \frac{2}{3}$ $1\frac{1}{3}$

8. $\frac{7}{8} - \frac{1}{8}$ $\frac{3}{4}$

9. $\frac{4}{5} + \frac{3}{5}$ $1\frac{2}{5}$

10. $3\frac{1}{2} - 1\frac{1}{2}$ 2

11. $2\frac{2}{3} + 1\frac{1}{3}$ 4

12. $3\frac{3}{4} - 1\frac{1}{4}$ $2\frac{1}{2}$

13. $4\frac{2}{3} + 5\frac{2}{3}$ $10\frac{1}{3}$

14. $3\frac{4}{9} - 1\frac{1}{9}$ $2\frac{1}{3}$

15. $1\frac{1}{6} + 1\frac{1}{6}$ $2\frac{1}{3}$

16. $6\frac{7}{10} - 4\frac{1}{10}$ $2\frac{3}{5}$

17. $4\frac{5}{12} - 1\frac{1}{12}$ $3\frac{1}{3}$

18. $5\frac{3}{4} + 4\frac{1}{4}$ 10

19. $7\frac{4}{5} + 4\frac{4}{5}$ $12\frac{3}{5}$

20. $7\frac{7}{8} - 3\frac{3}{8}$ $4\frac{1}{2}$

Supplemental Practice for Lesson 133

In problems 1–8, find the fraction name for 1 used to make the equivalent fraction:

1. $\frac{1}{2} \times M = \frac{3}{6}$ $\frac{3}{3}$

2. $\frac{1}{2} \times Z = \frac{5}{10}$ $\frac{5}{5}$

3. $\frac{1}{2} \times R = \frac{6}{12}$ $\frac{6}{6}$

4. $\frac{1}{3} \times Q = \frac{3}{9}$ $\frac{3}{3}$

5. $\frac{1}{6} \times G = \frac{2}{12}$ $\frac{2}{2}$

6. $\frac{3}{4} \times B = \frac{9}{12}$ $\frac{3}{3}$

7. $\frac{2}{5} \times P = \frac{4}{10}$ $\frac{2}{2}$

8. $\frac{2}{3} \times K = \frac{8}{12}$ $\frac{4}{4}$

In problems 9–20, complete the equivalent fraction:

9. $\dfrac{1}{4} = \dfrac{?}{8}$ 2

10. $\dfrac{1}{3} = \dfrac{?}{6}$ 2

11. $\dfrac{1}{2} = \dfrac{?}{4}$ 2

12. $\dfrac{1}{2} = \dfrac{?}{8}$ 4

13. $\dfrac{3}{4} = \dfrac{?}{8}$ 6

14. $\dfrac{2}{3} = \dfrac{?}{9}$ 6

15. $\dfrac{2}{5} = \dfrac{?}{10}$ 4

16. $\dfrac{1}{2} = \dfrac{?}{12}$ 6

17. $\dfrac{5}{6} = \dfrac{?}{12}$ 10

18. $\dfrac{1}{2} = \dfrac{?}{4}$ 2

19. $\dfrac{3}{4} = \dfrac{?}{12}$ 9

20. $\dfrac{2}{3} = \dfrac{?}{12}$ 8

Supplemental Practice for Lesson 138

1. $11\overline{)253}$ ^23 2. $21\overline{)672}$ ^32 3. $31\overline{)682}$ ^22 4. $12\overline{)504}$ ^42

5. $32\overline{)992}$ ^31 6. $21\overline{)483}$ ^23 7. $11\overline{)165}$ ^15 8. $22\overline{)924}$ ^42

9. $12\overline{)181}$ ^15 r 1 10. $31\overline{)963}$ ^31 r 2 11. $23\overline{)760}$ ^33 r 1 12. $41\overline{)945}$ ^23 r 2

13. $15\overline{)375}$ ^25 14. $25\overline{)555}$ ^22 r 5 15. $11\overline{)375}$ ^34 r 1 16. $21\overline{)924}$ ^44

17. $22\overline{)489}$ ^22 r 5 18. $12\overline{)600}$ ^50 19. $33\overline{)1000}$ ^30 r 10 20. $25\overline{)800}$ ^32

Supplemental Practice for Lesson 139

1. $\dfrac{1}{4} + \dfrac{1}{2}$ $\frac{3}{4}$ 2. $\dfrac{1}{4} + \dfrac{1}{8}$ $\frac{3}{8}$ 3. $\dfrac{1}{2} + \dfrac{1}{8}$ $\frac{5}{8}$

4. $\dfrac{1}{4} - \dfrac{1}{8}$ $\frac{1}{8}$ 5. $\dfrac{1}{2} - \dfrac{1}{8}$ $\frac{3}{8}$ 6. $\dfrac{1}{3} - \dfrac{1}{6}$ $\frac{1}{6}$

7. $\dfrac{2}{3} + \dfrac{1}{6}$ $\frac{5}{6}$ 8. $\dfrac{3}{4} + \dfrac{1}{8}$ $\frac{7}{8}$ 9. $\dfrac{1}{3} + \dfrac{2}{9}$ $\frac{5}{9}$

10. $\dfrac{5}{6} - \dfrac{2}{3}$ $\frac{1}{6}$ 11. $\dfrac{7}{8} - \dfrac{3}{4}$ $\frac{1}{8}$ 12. $\dfrac{9}{10} - \dfrac{4}{5}$ $\frac{1}{10}$

13. $\dfrac{5}{6} + \dfrac{1}{12}$ $\frac{11}{12}$ **14.** $\dfrac{3}{10} + \dfrac{2}{5}$ $\frac{7}{10}$ **15.** $\dfrac{1}{3} + \dfrac{1}{12}$ $\frac{5}{12}$

16. $\dfrac{4}{5} - \dfrac{1}{10}$ $\frac{7}{10}$ **17.** $\dfrac{8}{9} - \dfrac{2}{3}$ $\frac{2}{9}$ **18.** $\dfrac{7}{8} - \dfrac{1}{4}$ $\frac{5}{8}$

19. $\dfrac{3}{5} + \dfrac{3}{10}$ $\frac{9}{10}$ **20.** $\dfrac{2}{3} - \dfrac{7}{12}$ $\frac{1}{12}$

Glossary

addend   A number that is added in an addition problem.

angle   A corner formed by two intersecting lines or segments.

area   The number of squares of a certain size that it takes to cover a given surface.

average   The number that would be in each group if the items were rearranged so that each group had the same number of items.

bar graph   A graph that uses bars to show the information.

century   One hundred years.

chance   The likelihood that something will happen. This is written as a percentage.

circle graph   *See* pie graph.

circumference   The distance around a circle.

common denominators   Two fractions have common denominators if the denominators are equal.

common years   The years with 365 days.

congruent   Figures with the same shape and size.

counting numbers   The numbers in this sequence: 1, 2, 3, 4, 5, 6, 7, ...

decade   Ten years.

decimal point   A dot used to separate the whole part of a decimal number from the fractional part of the decimal number.

denominator   The bottom number of a fraction. This number tells the number of parts in the whole.

diameter   The distance across a circle through the center.

difference   The answer to a subtraction problem.

digit   Any of the following symbols: 0, 1, 2, 3, 4, 5, 6, 7, 8, 9.

division bar   A line segment that indicates that the number above the bar is divided by the number below the bar. The bar that separates the numerator of a fraction from the denominator of the fraction. Also called the *fraction bar.*

equal to   Has the same value as.

equivalent fractions   Two or more fractions that have the same value.

estimate   To mentally determine an approximate measure or calculation.

even numbers   Numbers that can be divided by 2 without a remainder. The digit in the ones' place of an even number is 2, 4, 6, 8, or 0.

expanded form   A way of representing a number which uses the sum of the products of each digit and the place value of each digit.

exponent   A number that shows how many times another number is to be used as a factor.

fact family   A group of three numbers that may be arranged to form four facts.

factor   A number that is multiplied in a multiplication problem.

fraction   A number used to designate a part of a whole.

fraction bar   *See* division bar.

geometric solid   A geometric shape that takes up space.

graph   A picture that shows number information about a certain topic.

greater than   Has a larger value than.

hexagon   A six-sided polygon.

improper fraction   A fraction in which the numerator is greater than or equal to the denominator.

intersecting lines   Lines that cross one another.

leap years   The years with 366 days.

less than   Has a smaller value than.

line graph   A graph that displays information by lines that connect data points.

line segment   A part of a line.

mixed number   A whole number followed by a fraction.

multiple   A number found by multiplying a given number by a whole number greater than zero. For example, the multiples of 5 are 5, 10, 15, 20, …

number line   A line with evenly spaced marks on which a number is associated with each mark.

number sentence   A complete sentence that uses numbers and symbols instead of words.

numerator   The top number of a fraction. This number tells the number of parts being described.

octagon   An eight-sided polygon.

odd numbers   Numbers that have a remainder of 1 when divided by 2. The digit in the ones' place of an odd number is 1, 3, 5, 7, or 9.

ordinal numbers   Numbers that indicate position or order.

parallel lines   Lines that stay the same distance apart.

pentagon   A five-sided polygon.

perimeter   The distance around a closed, flat shape.

perpendicular lines   Intersecting lines that form right angles.

pictograph   A graph that uses pictures of items to show information.

pie graph   A graph that represents information using a circle divided into sections that look like slices of pie.

polygon   A closed, flat shape whose sides are straight lines.

probability   The likelihood that something will happen. Often written as a fraction.

product   The answer to a multiplication problem.

quadrilateral   A four-sided polygon.

radius   The distance from the center of a circle to a point on the circle.

reduced fraction   An equivalent fraction written with smaller numbers.

regular polygon   A polygon with all sides the same length and all angles the same measure.

right angle   A square corner.

Roman numerals Letters used by the ancient Romans to write numbers.

scale A type of number line often used for measuring.

segment Line segment.

sequence An orderly arrangement of numbers determined by following a certain rule.

square unit A square with sides of designated length.

sum The answer to an addition problem.

table A way of presenting information in rows and columns.

tally marks Short, straight marks used for keeping track of the number of times that something occurs.

tally The total of a group of tally marks.

triangle A three-sided polygon.

whole numbers The numbers in this sequence: 0, 1, 2, 3, 4, 5, 6, 7, ...

Index

Abbreviations

U.S. CUSTOMARY		METRIC	
UNIT	ABBREVIATION	UNIT	ABBREVIATION
inch	in.	meter	m
foot	ft	centimeter	cm
yard	yd	millimeter	mm
mile	mi	kilometer	km
ounce	oz	gram	g
pound	lb	kilogram	kg
degree Fahrenheit	°F	degree Celsius	°C
pint	pt	liter	L
quart, gallon	qt, gal	milliliter	mL

OTHER ABBREVIATIONS	
square	sq.
square mile	sq. mi
square centimeter	sq. cm

Equivalence Table for Units

LENGTH	
U.S. CUSTOMARY	METRIC
12 in. = 1 ft	10 mm = 1 cm
3 ft = 1 yd	1000 mm = 1 m
5280 ft = 1 mi	100 cm = 1 m
1760 yd = 1 mi	1000 m = 1 km

WEIGHT	MASS
U.S. CUSTOMARY	METRIC
16 oz = 1 lb	1000 g = 1 kg
2000 lb = 1 ton	

LIQUID MEASURE	
U.S. CUSTOMARY	METRIC
16 oz = 1 pt	1000 mL = 1 L
2 pt = 1 qt	
4 qt = 1 gal	

Time

60 seconds = 1 minute
60 minutes = 1 hour
24 hours = 1 day
7 days = 1 week
365 days = 1 common year
366 days = 1 leap year
10 years = 1 decade
100 years = 1 century

Place Value Chart

hundred millions	ten millions	millions	,	hundred thousands	ten thousands	thousands	,	hundreds	tens	ones	.	tenths	hundredths	thousandths

Geometric Solids

SHAPE	NAME
	Cube
	Rectangular solid
	Pyramid
	Cylinder
	Sphere
	Cone

Common Polygons

SHAPE	NUMBER OF SIDES	NAME
	3	Triangle
	4	Quadrilateral
	5	Pentagon
	6	Hexagon
	8	Octagon

Measures of a Circle

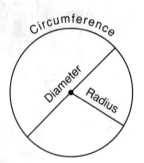

Roman Numerals

NUMERAL	VALUE
I	1
V	5
X	10
L	50
C	100
D	500
M	1000